I0259771

FOOLISHNESS

Don't Learn Lessons the Hard Way

FOOLISHNESS

IS NOT A WORD
Is a Person
Don't Become One

Ancient Wisdom
For Modern Decision-Making

Willie Yeboah

© Copyright 2024 Willie Yeboah
All rights reserved

Guillaume Publishers

First Edition October 2024

Printed in the United States of America

No portion of this publication may be reproduced or transmitted in any form without the written permission of the publisher.

ISBN-13: 979-8-218-52409-8

Scripture Quotations

Scripture quotations are taken from the King James (KJ), New King James (NKJ), Berean Standard Bible (BSB), New Living Translation (NLT), New International Version - UK (NIVUK), Easy to-Read (ER), English Standard (ES), Christian Standard Bible (CSB), The Message (MSG) versions

Other References

For all other mentions, check last pages of the book

Other Books By Willie Yeboah

Living Words Volume 1
Copyright © 2001

33 Principles to Have Good Relations With People
Copyright © 2007

Leading A Successful Life
Copyright © 2009

Courage
Copyright © 2011

God, The Man of God, and The People of God
Copyright © 2013

Honorary

I dedicate this book to my dad, whose random thought-sharing and advice have contributed to and provoked in me a lifelong quest for understanding and things that matter in life.

Acknowledgment

My appreciation to the origin of wisdom, who is divinely Wisdom Himself — God Almighty, the Creator of the universe and all it contains.

TABLE OF CONTENTS

Preface xix

Introduction xxv

Prologue: xxxxi
Team Quatro: Information, Knowledge, Intelligence, and Wisdom

Chapter 1: The Madness of Genesis 49
Don't Glory and Stay In Your Madness 51
What Is Wisdom 58
The Power of Wisdom 62
The Power of Communication 64
The Quest For Knowledge and Wisdom 65
Wisdom Makes the Difference 68

Chapter 2: Rashness Clearance 97
The Power of Your Counsel 99
The Prayer of Solomon 112
The Prayer of David 119

Intelligence Voided of Wisdom ....…... 129
Why Bad Decisions Are Made …….......................…..... 141
Godly Wisdom …….....................................……........... 166
Increasing In Wisdom ………... 174
Power or Wisdom ……..…... 176

Chapter 3: Captain of Your Vessel ….....…....... 181
The Sense and Importance of Direction …....…..…....... 184
Ancient Navigation Tips …….............................…....... 186
The Land: Your Defense, Thriving Place, and Position .. 192
Odors or Scents: Your Alerts or Warnings ……..........…. 195
The Clouds: Observe them, But Do Not Trust Them ….. 199
The Sooner or Later Effects …….............................…... 209
Knowing Your Position In Time During Decisions ….... 214
The Birds: Follow Your God-given Signal ……..........…. 222
The Currents and Prevailing Winds …….................….. 227
Values Determine Validations ……..........................….. 229
The Titanic: Bad Decisions On The Mighty Oceans ….... 236
The Miracle On the Hudson River …….....................…. 248
Life's Panics ……...…...…. 250

Chapter 4: General of Your Army …….....…..... 253
Joshua: Tricks and Regrets …….............................….... 253
Alexander The Great: Potent Will, Adaptable Mind ….. 265
Richard the Lionheart and Philip II: Two Generals with
Ulterior Motives ……...…....... 270
Dangerous and Trappy Transactions ……...........…....... 279
Hannibal: The Path Finder and Defeats Survivor …...... 288

The Toughest Yet, Sure Route 291
Stopping The Hannibalists or the Art of Confusion 292
Catching a Surprise Before It Becomes One 308
The Fear Factor 311

Chapter 5: King of Your Kingdom 323
Titles Without Merit 329
A Divine Royal Bloodline 330
There Is a King or Queen In You 331
The King's Wisdom 331
The King's Council 333
The King's Throne 335
The King's Crown 337
The King's Scepter 341
The King's Dress 347
A King Who Knows the King of Kings 362

Chapter 6: Keeping the Balance 367
Balance and Extremism 370
Balance Is Power 371
Keep Breathing or Die 376
The Balanced God Created a Balanced Universe 380
The Difficult Stop and Return Point 385
Mind the Existing Truths and Principles 386
The Abraham Trap and Extending Grace 393
Tipping Back to Equilibrium 399
It Takes Balance to Keep the Balance 401
The Wrong People at the Right Places 447

Chapter 7: Measuring Against Time 477
Perfection Versus Value 479
Quality or Newness 481
Trying Versus Faking 485
The Power of Time 488
Everything Is Mutable In Humanity 490
Power Without Respect 491
Divine Warnings 497

Chapter 8: Thought Drills 501
Fundamental Thoughts 504
The Power of Thought Drills 505
Adam's Weakness 507
Thinking Up Before Going Up 509
Correcting Your Statements or Words 516
Enforcing Your Decision-Making Golden Rules 517
Personal Thought Drills 518

Preface

I COULD NOT HAVE ENOUGH OF IT. I could not wait for the weekends and school breaks so we could gather for the dance competitions when the cheers and applause of friends and spectators would rise in support. The music was all the motivation and energy I needed to start moving like a robot and dance-talking while watchers interpreted what I was saying with my moves or dance. As kids then, it was a great moment we did not want to miss, and without those activities, something was missing – it was life. It was fun. It was all we wanted.

The song was Pop Rock but electric to feel. If you like music, especially Pop, it is a song you cannot resist moving on. It was taking the world by storm, and even there, in Africa, thousands of miles away from the United States. I remember wanting so badly to own a custom-tailored jacket that was the signature of the album and song, which one of our classmates had, and it was the envy of the class and the whole school when he wore it.

The year was nineteen eighty-two (1982). The person behind the voice was one of the greatest singers, dancers, and entertainers the world has ever known – Michael Jackson. The song's title was "Beat It" from his sixth studio album "Thriller". The funny truth is, as children in that part of the world, in West Africa, where French is the official language, even though some surrounding countries are English-speaking countries, we have little understanding of the English language and words. So, nonetheless, we were singing and dancing to this "hit" song with all our might, but we could not properly sing the lyrics. Instead of singing, "Just beat it", we were singing, "Jazz peere! Jazz peere! Jazz peere."

There is no doubt that Michael Jackson was one of the greatest singers and dancers the world has ever known, and the song was for entertainment. However, when I started maturing, I thought, "Hmm, maybe before I beat anything, I should think twice about what will happen after I 'beat it."

Similarly, I like motivation, and the script of one of the most popular t-shirts that have been around for quite some time reads, "Just Do It." And I thought it was great! Of course, it is to motivate people to stop sleeping on their dreams. But at the same time, I thought, "Hmm, maybe before I do anything, I should think first."

May I suggest to you that before you "Beat It" or you "Do It" think twice?

For a long time, just like any of the books I have written and will write, I carried this book in my heart, wondering what the title could be. It wasn't until when I was about to decide on something crucial that the title hit my mind while I was talking to myself, "Foolishness is not just a word; it's a person – don't become one again." Then, I wrote it down. Later, I thought this could be the title of the book that had been missing for years. "It sounds odd." I reasoned with myself but decided to keep it as such. I knew the "Grammar and Vocabulary People" would come for me about the title and others in the book, but that was less concerning to me. What I care about in writing this book is to note some realities to whomever they may concern as a reminder about the journey through this world.

Planet Earth, or this world, may be illuminated by the sun, moon, or stars, and man-created lights, but in it, unfortunately, are many human beings with dark hearts and minds with-out consideration for morals, values, or love for God and other human beings, but for themselves.

The biggest problem mankind has had since the beginning is Foolishness — Adam and Eve experienced a faulty judgment, and we are dealing with its consequences one way or the other till now. (Genesis 3:1-22). If you think about it honestly, you will realize that many of the troubles in our world today originate from idiocy. The wars, hatred, racism, poverty, greed, selfishness, cheating, and sicknesses — all mainly originate from misunderstanding or bad judgment. One wrong decision established on a faulty understanding or judgment can cause numerous problems everywhere in a relationship, marriage, family, workplace, company, government, region, country, and the whole world.

The ability to choose is one of the most powerful capabilities God has endowed humankind with. However, this free will comes with a noble and considerable moral responsibility. The power to execute or use your judgment to judge whatever you touch, see, hear, smell, taste, and then think, say, or do is not to be taken lightly because it is the key to your goodness, blessings, misery, or curses.

God granted you intelligence and wisdom to protect

yourself, but not to take advantage of, oppress, or manipulate others.

When the devil wants to destroy you, one of the first things he does is attack your understanding or judgment, which is a property of wisdom. When your understanding is polluted or distorted, you will make the wrong decisions that will eventually destroy you directly or indirectly, instantly or progressively.

Figuratively, life is all about transactions — it's Mathematics (What we give and receive), Calculus or changes (What gives us that), Geometry or shapes (What we can perceive or see), and Algebra or operations to solve and get equations (What we identify, associate, and connect ourselves to, and something bigger, or more significant that we yearn for, or need). Evidently, each one of the decisions we make in this world during our lifetime either brings us closer or farther from these inner quests and fulfillment.

Introduction

UNDERSTANDING IS THE FORCE behind decisions, and it's more than the meaning of what people say and do, including you. It's more than people agreeing or disagreeing with you on a matter or subject. It's also not a compromise, or you must agree with people on everything. Understanding is a virtue or attribute of wisdom that you need to make the right decisions or choices, navigate life, and obtain peace, health, stability, security, and prosperity.

People's beliefs are based on their understanding, and their understanding determines their decisions, and their decisions determine the type or quality of relationship you may have with them.

Someone's understanding of God, the universe, humanity, money, materials, success, and overall life in this world determines the type of individual they are, and eventually is the force supporting their wants or desires, lifestyle, and choices or decisions. Furthermore, understanding either creates or influences a character. And the character of someone is what you experience in any kind of relationship or deal with them.

Wisdom might not necessarily be in age or the amount of knowledge or information you have, although age can make a difference. But, whatever you do, ensure that you do not become a disgraceful young man or lady with vigor or a dishonorable old man or lady with gray hair.

Decisions, and unfortunately, even some that other people make, can determine what happens to you, from when you were born here, in this world, to the time you leave, and even in the afterlife. Decisions create your wins and losses, pains and happiness, peace and troubles, safety and dangers, success and failures, liberty and restrictions, health and sickness, and even, in many cases, longevity and premature death. However, at some point in your life, you will be presented with opportunities and have the responsibility to change even what happens to you because of other people's decisions.

Your decisions or choices lead, control, and create your present and future life conditions, and to change them, you have to start making the right decisions or choices.

Life will try to play you, but you must use the decision-making ability and capacity that God trusted you with as the Captain of your vessel or craft, the General of your army, and the King or Queen of your kingdom to make the right decisions to attain goodness, health, peace, happiness, stability, security, prosperity, and eternal life.

Trust is not given; it is earned. You do not trust people because of your relationship with them or because the person is related to you, your family member, friend, husband, wife, co-worker, employer, employee, assistant, business partner, pastor, or leader. But, individuals have to prove to you in your dealings with them that they can be trusted. Do not think or imagine that they can be trusted, but their character and actions should be the measure of the trust you can bestow them.

Sadly, only God knows the heart of men, except He reveals it to you. Believe it or not, not everyone will mean well to you. The Bible says, ***"The Lord saw how great the wickedness of the human race had become on the earth, and that every inclination of the thoughts of the human heart was only evil all the time."*** (Genesis 6: 5, NIV). This is true even now in our world, so you need wisdom to make it through life and minimize the hurt humanity can inflict on you.

Man was not created by God to be evil. Human beings are good creatures. But the ones who let the devil, the evil one, and his demons take hold of them become evil because the devil will operate through them knowingly or unknowingly.

Safety is not only protecting yourself against violence, guns, theft, or even accidents; it's also seriously protecting yourself against any destructive or dangerous activities instigated by bad people with ungodly characters. And if you don't, God will not be blamed for it. And these people are everywhere, including communities, workplaces, schools, hospitals, churches, and families.

Yes, love people. Strive to fulfill the commandments of God. (Exodus 20:1-17). However, be vigilant to protect yourself and yours. And when it's confirmed that someone is bad one way or the other, believe it and graciously classify it as such. You do not have to hate them, but take them seriously and handle things cautiously with them; otherwise, you will regret it sooner or later.

A few years ago, I was flipping through TV channels and came across a documentary program known to me now as "Forensic Files." It was the first time I was watching this type of program, and I was on the edge of my seat, quite struck by the unfolding events. One thing that was clear to me throughout the program is that everyone who was hurt or killed knew or foreseen that it could happen but did not take the necessary actions to prevent it, maybe out of naivety, love, or some kind of feeling or relationship they had with their murder.

I believe wisdom is a divine gift, a usage of your God-given senses (sensors), and may also grow out of your experiences in both natural and spiritual life. You cannot separate wisdom from your five senses and the Spirit of God, who created the human spirit. I will explain more later in this book. Spiritually, and even if you are physically disabled, your five senses are attached to your spirit-man, and your spirit is attached to wisdom.

The five senses (sensors), which you consider natural, also take part in your decision-making process and can help you make the right or wrong decisions.

Life as God designed it in this world and perhaps beyond is governed by choices, actions, and results. These elements derive from understanding and wisdom. You may synonymize or equate understanding to many other essences, but at its core, it stands alone as a primary vital force of life. It's where everything about life in this world and other realms starts and flows from. The ability to understand things; discernment (the ability to judge well); interpretation (the act and art of explaining the meaning of things); knowledge (the discovered and accumulated facts, information, and skills you can possess); mastery (the deep capacity or ability you have to do, control, create and run something) all depend on your understanding. It also determines your range of knowledge or insight about circumstances, and sensitivity (the ability to detect and respond to signs, signals, or influences).

Experience can build your character and understanding, but only if you let it. So many things God allows you to experience or deal with in life are meant to develop your character for the better, but if you still don't get it, you are guilty of not using your experiences efficiently.

After God, your character overshadows everything in your life, especially your relationship with people. Whoever you are and whatever you have, if your character is not genuine, exemplary, or good, it undermines you.

Steadily, everything in our world is becoming a game, even the sacred things, including relationships, marriage, family, work, business, church, and ministry. At this alarming pace, the wickedness of the heart of humanity is propagating at a high speed, and the Godly, righteous, honest, and kind people may be caught up in a crossfire of malice.

There is an old saying, "Life is not a game." I agree. There is a big contrast between life and games. But there are many similar principles in many games we play in life itself. In any game, the winner wins based on little decisions: Moves, runs, stops, dribbles, strikes, and passes the ball to a better-positioned teammate to score. No matter the person or team who dominates the game, the winner is the one or team who scores more than the other.

There is nothing like a small decision; even the decision you think is insignificant will amount to crucial or weighty results or consequences. And there is nothing like a personal decision in a real context; even when it looks like one, all your good or bad choices affect other people directly or indirectly, instantly, or progressively, sooner or later, this includes yourself, immediate family, relatives, your children or descendants, friends, the community, and the world at large. And the domino effect of your decisions is perpetual.

Each decision you make has either physical or spiritual results or consequences.

In this book, the concept of wisdom might not be the definitions or interpretations you have learned. I must say that this book is not from a natural, psychological, or philosophical understanding or perspective, but rather, Biblical and spiritual. Nevertheless, I may figuratively use them to help you understand the realities surrounding your decision-making. I will metaphorically or symbolically use people, events, and things to assist in understanding the lessons of God, life, and time taught many people before us and even now.

You cannot take your decision-making seriously until you understand your importance, I meant your purpose and destiny, and the present and future value of your decisions. You are a puzzle in the big picture of the life of the world, your family, and your descendants. Without your input or wrong input, the big picture is not completed. No matter who you are, what your name is, how you came into this world, and your current situation, you are so important; so are your decisions. And if your choices could bear a price tag, they are priceless.

How much do you love yourself? Or should I start by asking, how much do you love God? Or how much do you love your fellow? If you love yourself, you will surely love God and your fellow. Whether you believe it or not, your decisions are not always based on love; either for yourself, your fellow or humanity, and God. Sometimes your choices just come from your emotions or feelings.

People can be selfish about anything, not only money or material things. Individuals can be self-centered about feelings and other experiences. That's why you wonder why people don't want to feel pain, but want it for someone else. They don't want to be sick, but they want it for someone else. They don't want to die, but they want someone else to die. They are careless as long as it can be someone else.

I have realized that you cannot love God and your fellow or neighbor without loving yourself. If you understand this, I will say, every person and everything you like or love is for you, including God. Why would you love God and your fellow human beings? Because you do not want to experience the consequences of violating God's commandments, right? In other words, you don't want to be punished for it here, in this world, or in the afterlife.

If we love ourselves, we will do our best to get our decisions right in every area of our lives, spiritually and physically. These include honestly educating ourselves about the truths of life, lifestyle, health, relationships, finances, business, ministry, others, and the world. Some occurrences or events that are consequences of our bad decisions in life firmly show that we do not love ourselves, even though we think so. The murderer thinks he loves himself, and that's why he kills to avenge and appease his anger or rob someone to take what does not belong to him. The jealous thinks he loves himself; that's why he's jealous about the progress his fellow has made or what he possesses. The cheater thinks he loves himself, and that's why he wants to gratify himself by cheating. The greedy thinks he loves himself, and that is the cause for him to outsmart or dupe the other person for money or materials. But in all truthfulness, if you really love yourself, you will think otherwise. Understand that any hurt and immorality inflicted on another person surely comes back to you directly or indirectly, spiritually, physically, and emotionally.

The Bible says, **"Taste and see that the LORD is good; blessed is the one who takes refuge in him."** (Psalm 34:8, NIV). The reason you love God is because of his GOODNESS (What He does for you, and to you through His Spirit or presence, physically, spiritually, emotionally -- the comfort, joy, peace, and assurance he gives you about the present and eternal life.) The reason you love your neighbor or fellow like yourself is because you want to obey the commandment of God that says, "-- Love your neighbor as yourself." (Mark 12: 30-31). Indirectly, you are obligated to love others unconditionally because you do not want to be retributed by God for not loving them. So, at the end of it all, you have to love your neighbor or fellow as well for your own benefit or God's blessings or rewards for loving others.

The ultimatum for our relationship or experience with peace, happiness, comfort, security, stability, and prosperity or the contrary thereof, which are unhappiness, irritation, agitation, distress, conflict, and war could be summed up in one declaration, **"Now listen! Today I am giving you a choice [Decision to make] between life and death, between prosperity and disaster."** (Deuteronomy 30:15, NLT). But a loving Father, God has suggested or advised, **"Now choose life, so that you and your descendants may live."** (Deuteronomy 30:19, NKJV).

Living does not only mean having the breath of life that God breathed into man in the beginning. (Genesis 2:7). It also means well-being. And having this essential benefit in life requires good decision-making. If we can all make the right decisions, life will be better, and the world will be a better place for all of us.

Making good decisions starts from the love for yourself (not selfishness), the love for your neighbor or fellow, and above all, the love for God.

Decisions lead to actions and results. But it all starts with a thought. Our thoughts are born out of what we are feeding our minds and hearts. So, our thoughts can be transformed into good or bad, solutions or problems.

Bad decisions are usually made because of a lack of wisdom or the lack of application, which we will talk about a little further in this book. Besides, a lack of information, knowledge, and understanding will not help you to put the end results in perspective so you can decide effectively. Purpose, or the "Why" presses, intrigues or obligates you to ask questions that can lead to hidden information, revelations, or what cannot come to your mind immediately, which mostly can only be apparent or obvious with time. If wisdom is the understanding and application of knowledge/information, how can you understand and apply something that you do not know or are informed of; and consider whether it should be overlooked or taken into consideration?

Who or what you follow, fellowship, or commune with, and listen to in person, online, on TV, radio, or read in books — influences your decisions directly or indirectly. Therefore, choosing who will lead you (your leader) and your fellows wisely is very important.

Our world is full of wrongs, failures, broken hearts, breakdowns, traumas, ungodliness, and immorality to the extent that bad decisions are no longer a concern to many. Because they think after all, making the right decisions does not matter that much — everybody is confused and in shambles anyway. Or, even if I do not get it right, it will be forgotten. People will move on with life and get over it. Or it will only cost me a few years in prison, and maybe the worst is death. But when we understand that our decisions are more than just the physical consequences that we can see sooner or later, our attitude will change. We will make every decision like our breath depends on it, especially important decisions. Keep in mind that little decisions lead to big decisions, and little results lead to big results.

Irrespective, decisions are usually made by one person or individually but can affect more than just you. Your loved ones, your parents, brothers and sisters, cousins, and the entire family. Additionally, your decisions affect more than just your immediate family, and many other people who are not even connected to you directly.

The Creator, God, in the beginning, gave the free will to choose or make decisions to mankind. Adam and Eve had to make a choice to live forever, healthy, and peacefully, with nothing missing and lacking in their lives. But they chose the opposite by a bad decision — They ate the fruit that God had forbidden them to eat. (Genesis 3:1-24).

I will not lie to you. You might not get all your decisions right at all times – mistakes can happen. You might mistakenly make the wrong decisions, but the extent, impact, or consequences of these mistakes will depend on other decisions you can make thereafter.

Life is like an exam or test in which you might not get all the tests right, but a minimum score is required to pass. Generally, and mostly in exams, a certain score is required to pass or be accepted. As a student, you may aim for the maximum and higher scores in your subjects' tests. However, your prayer may be that if you don't get them all, at least you will get the minimum required to pass or be accepted. When your scores fall short, you will fail and repeat that class and test, or you will be denied the expected reward.

There are some words you really fight in school not to see on your test or exam papers because you know what they mean. Every serious or good student is never satisfied with "Mediocre, Passable, Admissible" scores. Even though these scores, notes, or marks can get you to the next class, it is a sign that you have not really done well and may struggle in the next class or grade.

This book is to challenge you to raise your decision-making standards and scores. Anything that may be accepted or allowed to pass without serious objection, adequate, acceptable, tolerable, admissible, moderate, or mediocre, should not be enough for you. You must do your best to get better each time as you progress in life, from the least to the most important things.

You may regret some of your decisions. But, ultimately, thank God that you are still alive to make many other decisions, and hopefully, you will get them right by His grace.
The truths and factors relating to your decision-making are so many and vast to the extent that we cannot exhaust them, but God willing, this book will serve as a reinforcement of things you may already know and help you to not forget the things that really matter after all.

If there is anything history teaches us, one of them is that your decisions or choices are written, even if not in the books of history, they are written in the minds and hearts of people. So make wise decisions.

Sometimes, you already have, or you are surrounded by what you need to fulfill your dreams, vision, purpose, and destiny and change your life's negative circumstances. But bad decisions will keep you going in circles till it's too late to know. What you really need might not necessarily be money or materials, but a good decision or choice — That will change your life.

As the saying goes, "Not all heroes wear the military uniform." That is correct, some heroes are just people like you who use their intelligence, knowledge, and precisely wisdom to dodge or deliver themselves, loved ones, and others from dangers of life that could have destroyed their purpose and destiny, peace, health, joy, progress, success, stability, security, and longevity. When was the last time you honestly and Godly advised yourself and got better? When was the last time you honestly and Godly advised someone and changed their lives positively? Life is more than the biggest things you can imagine — It's the little things, like the little decisions we make daily, that lead to the biggest things as a result.

This book is a reminder because I believe that if you are an adult or a mature person, you would have known or experienced many of the understanding that I will share with you. One of the reasons we continuously make the wrong decisions or choices even when we know better is that we do not have reminders and enforcers. Let this book be a reminder to you.

Don't learn lessons the hard way. Discover how those who lived before you did it and figuratively use it in your decision or choice process to minimize the risk of making the wrong decisions. Prepare yourself to easily know when to say "Yes" or "No" to yourself and others.

I'm not a psychologist, nor am I a communication and character specialist, but by the grace of God, I have observed so many things and people in this world and have learned some personal lessons as an individual, minister, and entrepreneur who deals with people in ministry and business daily. I would not lie to you, I haven't gotten it right all the time. However, I have compiled my decision-making process into a few simple steps to reduce the risk of my mistakes.

This book may sound like a decision-making technique or management you may be taught in school, but my approach to this subject is more than that – it's spiritual and beyond your human capabilities. It's to remind you to double-check beyond your average human senses especially when making crucial decisions.

When it comes to human relations, you must look at things more deeply than what they appear to be, except God directly and specifically tells you differently in many ways. Even if you choose to live according to God's commandments, which you should, you must take the necessary measures to protect yourself and others.

I ask myself these simple questions: Is it a necessary decision, an emergency decision, or a comfort decision? What's the big picture? What's the risk? What are the long and short-term results or consequences? Is there a better way to handle this? Is there a genuine shortcut or a short way to handle this? What does the word of God say about it? Is this to please men, God, or both? Can I wait? Have I made a similar decision in the past? What happened then? How do they connect? What effect will it have on my relationship with God, people, and family? What will this do to my integrity and legacy? How will history remember me for this decision?

Many people you may know who have become heavy drinkers, smokers, and sexually perverted are just trying to forget or ignore the consequences of the bad decisions they have made in the past; which have been converted into emotions, sleepless nights, and irritated consciousness that are continuously leading them into making more wrong choices. Don't let your past wrong decisions push you to continue making wrong decisions. Promise yourself that you will do better, and let your present and future decisions be better than the former ones.

God is wise, and He wants you to be wise. My prayer is that you can wisely, intelligently, and courageously navigate life like an ancient sailor or pilot, lead your life to victory as an army general, and rule yourself and life as a real King or Queen so that, at the end of it all, you can proudly say, *"I have fought the good fight, I have finished the race, I have kept the faith. Now there is in store for me the crown of righteousness, which the Lord, the righteous Judge, will award to me on that day—and not only to me, but also to all who have longed for his appearing."* (2 Timothy 4:7-8, NIV).

I haven't written this book because I'm perfect. Although I'm a Godly and morally mindful individual, I did make some mistakes here and there in my personal life, ministry, and business. But thank God, I have learned and am still growing and maturing everyday. If I had to go back in time, there are past decisions I would have made differently. But now, is the time for you and I to focus on getting the maximum score in our decision-making. Let's do the best we can with the help of God.

Prologue
Team Quatro
Information, Knowledge, Intelligence, and Wisdom

———

"**HELLO, EVERYONE**! I'm Information. May I introduce Knowledge, Intelligence, Wisdom, and I to you?" Said Information.

"Thank you, Information. That's very nice of you." Knowledge responded by joining the conversation.

"Why didn't you mention my nickname to the people? You know I like going by Smarty. Don't you?" Intelligence said.

"There you go again – always thinking you're better than us. Your nickname didn't matter. All I wanted was to communicate to the people about our team and how vital they need the four working for them, not one of us." Information replied.

"Oh, hi, friends! It has been a while since we worked together. How are you doing?" Wisdom riposted.

"Hold on, you people don't care what I'm reminding you?" Ranted Intelligence.

"What are you trying to say? I already know what you are trying to do. You want the people to believe you're the best." Retorted Knowledge.

"My nickname – tell the people my nickname." Affirmatively said Intelligence.

"Alright, friends, enough of who is the best. We were given the assignment to work together to help humanity. Let's work together. Let all four of us form a team to save the world." Said Wisdom while making a heart with his hand.

"People, Wisdom is just afraid of being and working alone. He has monophobia. He always wants company or someone to be with him. And guess what? I can be the only one who helps everybody in the world."

"By the way, what will be the name of our team, and who will be the leader? Let's call it Smarty & Brothers or Smarty & Co." Said Intelligence while patting himself on the chest and taking two steps back.

"No, we may call the group Team Quatro. It will consist of the four of us working together to help humanity make the right decisions. People think they only need one of us but need all four to make the right decision." Wisdom suggested.

"Look, Dumby might show up in a moment. He's always roaming around, causing people to make the wrong decisions. We have to finish our discussions and plans quickly. We must agree on a strategy and method to beat him and save the world. Oh no, he's already here." Said Information with a surprised face.

"I heard that – you said you were planning something. Listen, I'm the world's pain and responsible for all its troubles. I trick people into problems by pressing them to make the wrong decisions. I wander, looking for people I can fool into making the wrong decisions, and when they do, I like seeing them stressed, have sleepless nights, feel ashamed, and have guilt and regrets, and I like those sweet tears they cry after making the wrong decisions. I like it when they say, 'I mess up again.'" Whispered Dumby.

"Hey, Dumby! What's new?" Said Smarty.

"Just trying to live, brother, just to live." Cheerfully said Dumby.

"Sounds to me that you're just all over the place looking to be happy?" Said Smarty while shaking his head.

"Of course! Are you missing anything? Or have I omitted anything in my answer? Have I not just said, 'I'm trying to live?'" Sharply said Dumby.

"I heard you – this is not a fight. I'm just confirming what you have just said, " Smarty said calmly.

"Don't start again. You know I hate energy, motivation, and party-stoppers. Let me have fun. I'm here on earth for a 'short time for a good time.' 'You only have one life, so live it to the fullest.' And make sure 'You live each day with no regrets.' Next time you see me, mind your own business. By the way, we aren't friends any longer." Dumby angrily said.

"Sounds like the same old lines – Have fun, brother. But just ensure your choices don't lead you to the village of regrets, where nobody is guaranteed a second opportunity to get it right. See you!" Smarty said.

"I'm out here trying to have fun, be happy, get rich, and be powerful – nothing wrong with that." Said Dumby while taking a circle-like steps.

"Of course, there is nothing wrong with having pleasure, getting rich, or trying to fulfill your dreams, live a good or better life, but it's not everything in life – and not worth sacrificing everything else for." Said Smarty.

"What do you mean by 'Everything else?" Asked Dumby hesitantly.

"I mean your peace, happiness, sanity, health, morals, respect, honor, and legacy." Said Smarty while laying his right hand on Dumby's left shoulder and looking into his eyes.

"Look, I will think about those later. Now is the time to have fun – have all I want, anyway, and anytime. Have a good day, bye!" Said Dumby while looking down at the ground.

"Hold on, we haven't finished." Said Smarty, trying to hold Dumby's hand.

"Let me ask you, Smarty, what are the days and times you come around here?" Asked Dumby impatiently.

"Why do you want to know?" Smarty queried with a deep breath.

"Because I want to avoid you. I don't want to see you anymore." Replied Dumby while scratching the back of his head.

"Ok. See you tomorrow." A smiling Smarty said.

"I don't want to see you again." Annoyingly said Dumby.

"Alright, have a good one." Said Smarty, shaking Dumby's hand.

The next day, the friends meet again during their regular routine of working with humanity.

"Hello, friend! Can you tell me more about what you

were saying yesterday?" Dumby said expectantly.

"Oh, are we friends again?" Said Smarty while smiling.

"Come on! You don't know me anymore? We have been friends for ages. Remember, we are inseparable. Even if you try moving away from me, 'bad' and 'wrong' will be around the corner waiting for you — and guess what? You will miss the mark again." Said Dumby in a defensive mood.

"That's fine. I know it's difficult to get all together and right – my decisions, but I will keep trying to do my best and get the maximum I can right." Said Smarty in a confident manner.

"Ok. So, now you understand we are inseparable friends?" Said Dumby with a winning smile.

"Oh, yes and no. We are not inseparable friends. You are a separate entity with your mind and heart, and allow fear, pleasure, feelings, greed, and selfishness to blur your understanding of matters. My best friends are Information, Knowledge, and Wisdom." Said Smarty with a rejected face.

"Smarty, I know you're doing your best, but you have already made so many wrong decisions, so why do you want to make good ones now? It's too late." Dumby replied with a pleading attitude.

"Because the good decisions that I can make now have the power to correct the old bad ones, even if they don't, it's better to make good ones now to prevent the results of the bad ones from getting worse." Said Smarty in response.

"Let me remind you again, Smarty, that you can never get all of them right." Said Dumby pitifully.

"Actually, this is the only truth you and I can agree on. Yes, I cannot get all my decisions right because perfection is only found in God, but I can do my best to get the maximum right." Said Smarty, in agreement with Dumby.

"Alright, Smarty, I'm changing my name to Sneaky to make it closer to yours." Added Dumby.

"Dumby, I think you're joking now. Please listen to me: We still have the opportunity to make the right decisions or choices while we are alive." Said Smarty while shaking his head.

"There you go again; you mentioned I'm not trying to get anything right. Now I'm trying to make things right, and you are doubting me?" Said Dumby while interrupting Smarty.

"You can't be serious by changing your name from Dumby to Sneaky. Are you? If you're sincere about getting it right from now on, just mean it. By the way, being smart is not helping me either. Being intelligent without wisdom is not serving me well. We both need help from Wisdom." Said a desperate Smarty.

"Look, I'm tired of instigating people to make the wrong decisions because one bad decision always leads them to multiple wrong decisions to cover up the first one, just like you said. So, I meant it. Can I join your team?" Dumby tells Smarty.

"No. Our team's membership list is closed to only the four of us. You just changed your name from Dumby to Sneaky and want to join our team? Please, you're not invited and welcome. I, Intelligence, aka Smarty, Information, Knowledge, and Wisdom, are the only members of this team to help humanity. That's why we call the squad Team Quatro. By working together, we hope to help humanity make the right decisions.

"However, I don't mind introducing you to my partners,

especially Wisdom." Smarty eagerly elaborated.

"Hello, nice meeting you. By the way, first things first. Let's start by changing your name. Who named you with that name?" Wisdom gently said to Dumby.

"Nice meeting you, Mr. Wisdom. It's a long story." Replied Dumby.

"I don't want to call you Dumby. You are not dumb; your mind has only become a battleground for good and bad." Continued Wisdom.

"Thank you, Mr. Wisdom." Said Dumby.

"Some people think I'm an old man with gray hair and beard, a Greek philosopher who lived in the past, or the Magi from the East, but I'm more than that. I'm not also just a gift or talent; I'm a Spirit. And I'm confident that together with my teammates, Information, Knowledge, and Intelligence, we can help humanity make the right decisions."

"Team Quatro, let's get to work now!" Wisdom defiantly proclaimed.

Chapter 1
The Madness of Genesis

"When I was a child, I talked like a child, I thought like a child, I reasoned like a child. When I became a man, I put the ways of childhood behind me."
I Corinthians 13:11

TRULY, YOUNG AGE OR THE BEGINNING of anything may come with its madness. But thank God for His grace, mercy, favor, and ultimately, His guidance.

Are you growing in any area of your life? You are born to grow in every realm of your life. The formation of maturity can be a beautiful and painful experience at the same time. The process from childhood to adulthood can be fetching yet brutal. It's when you can simultaneously be so conceited, danger-blind, innocent, or naïve as if the world is just full of roses, sugar, honey, wishes, and sweet dreams. Figuratively, you believe night and darkness do not exist; it is always sunshine until the world and life start throwing you some bitter surprise parties here and there. And even then, naivety would tell you a big lie, "It's only this time or this person, and it will never happen again." And you believe it until it happens again, or another person does it to you again. Naiveness is the enemy of wisdom and good judgment.

When we are younger, the essence or image of humanity and things in our minds is untrue. But as we grow in stature and hopefully in wisdom, we start discovering the truth about humanity, people, and things we deal with daily.

> *"When we are younger, the essence or image of humanity and things in our minds is untrue."*

There are unattainable preferences and wishes, and there are things you cannot change, even if you alter them or cover them up. Soon and very soon, your appearance, beauty, attractiveness, and physical energy will change. Your skin will dry, your hair will gray out, your teeth will start falling out or not be the same, and many other things can change.

Lack of understanding, judgment, or wisdom, knowledge, and experience is related to youthfulness but not limited to it. The behavior or appearance characteristic of a young person is not only found in young people or children, but also in adults who refuse to grow.

Insanity, as we know it, has been a friend of everybody one way or the other at some time and in some circumstances in life. Madness doesn't only hold captive the one having a severe mental illness but also the one who easily lets the door of his mind, heart, and emotion open to it. Then, it leads you to make the wrong decisions or choices.

Don't Glory and Stay In Your Madness

A friend shared an incident with us some time ago: Two madmen often visited his hometown's marketplace. One day, both madmen met at the marketplace as usual. And for some reason, one of them was highly agitated, as people with severe mental illness do. Then, the other one was looking at him, called his name, and said, "Oh, oh, oh, you know, we both are madmen, but your madness is beyond mine." And at this, the whole small marketplace erupted in laughter and wondering, "How was he able to recognize that the other man's mental illness was worse than his?" In other words, how can a madman recognize his fellow madman and even differentiate between the status of their mental illness?

Growth and positive change are beautiful things to the beholders or people who knew you to be a certain person in the past. Don't glory and stay in your madness; I mean your wrong decisions. It's always a good thing to grow or mature. You may still have the opportunity to make other decisions and get them right, and perhaps correct the wrong ones you have already made in the past, even though some bad decisions may be irreversible.

> *"Don't glory and stay in your madness."*

No matter how filled and in touch you are with the Holy Spirit or God, there are things God would always leave to age or time to teach you. That is why sometimes people's ages also can influence their wisdom or judgment. You may argue Joseph, Daniel, and many other Wisemen in the Bible were wise even in their younger ages. Yes, they were, but they probably did not have as much life experience generally as they did about spiritual things. Life in this world has its stages of maturity that you may not attain until you live long enough here on earth. Among many other reasons, including the Levitical custom of Jewish priests starting their service at age thirty (30) (Numbers 4:3, 23, 30, and 35), the Lord Jesus did not begin his ministry until he was thirty (30) years old. (Luke 3:23). Perhaps one of the reasons is that by thirty, he has had enough human experiences in this world to better handle or deal with humans even as God in the flesh. (John 1:1-3, 14).

At some point, life has its lessons; it teaches individuals. Or may I say God uses life, age, or time to teach you some things you would never learn and be convinced otherwise? You may have heard of this African proverb, "The youth may walk faster, but the elders know the road." This is to say how experience and knowledge can be acquired over the years or in a lifetime. In other words, there are things only the expedition of life can teach and convince you of. However, as a youngster, you have to take advantage of the storage of wisdom that the elders or experienced older people have around you, far and near. Do not let the madness of young age steal away your well-being, freedom, comfort, peace, and real happiness. Any little mistake can forever take away your dignity and destroy your life.

The future is now, and all your visions and dreams for life start now that you are young. With your present decisions and actions, you choose what life will be like for you sooner or later. You decide what will happen even now.

A Child Forever

Be careful, and do not be a child forever. Sometimes, certain life conditions can negatively influence your growth as an adult and trap you to remain a child; and these are not any medical conditions, but bad upbringings, money, and sometimes early success in life. Additionally, be careful of people who try to keep you as a child forever; it will not serve you well in any way. There is a reason for growth.
The Bible teaches us that we must be like children when it comes to the Kingdom of God. (Matthew 18:2-5). But that passage is self-explanatory. The Lord was advising his disciples about faith and humility. He was not encouraging them to remain children, nor was He encouraging infantilization, or treating a person in a way that's not appropriate for his age or abilities.

"There is a reason for growth."

As you grow, you must remind yourself that you are not a child anymore and behave accordingly. If you are an adult and want to cling to childlike behaviors and struggle to take responsibility and accountability, it will lead you to make the wrong decisions regarding serious or essential life choices. You should also be careful of people who want to intentionally keep you as a child in order to abuse you.

As a child, you must also not try to outgrow your normal or reasonable childhood. Being precocious, or developing certain abilities (proclivities) at an earlier age than usual is a blessing, but do not rush and let it fool you into making the wrong choices. The Bible says, *"To have a fool for a* child brings grief; there is no joy for the parent of a godless fool."* (Proverbs 17:21, NIV).

Ancient Wisdom Is Not Dead

Time and History do not do anyone a favor. From the greatest and famous to the unknown and uncelebrated, young and old, Royals (Kings, Queens, Princes, Princesses), Nobles, Political Leaders, Religious Leaders, Business Leaders, and Military Leaders -- they all became history, but history never forgets the foolishness of the fool, and the wisdom of the wise, the humility of the humble, the arrogance of the arrogant, the envy of the envious, the jealousy of the jealous, the selfishness of the selfish, the greed of the greedy, the immorality of the immoral, the wickedness of the wicked, and the kindness of the kind. Where do you want time and history to classify you? Or should I say, what would your name be, if you were to be identified and called by your decisions or choices?

> *"Time and History do not do anyone a favor... history never forgets the foolishness of the fool."*

The memory of the wise is always celebrated and honored, but that of the fool is dishonored.

Do not let your status or sense of belonging fool you into thinking you are invincible. Throughout history, great people, kings, kingdoms, empires, organizations, armies, and generals have fallen, died, or passed away. From the beginning of the world, every man-made glory falls sooner or later. No matter how powerful, intelligent, and wise some men have been throughout history, records show they all passed away, and while they may have a lot to remember and talk about them, their lives can be summed up in one thing: Decisions.

I wish "Wisdoms" were accepted usage in English. But unfortunately, grammar will not let us say "wisdoms" because "wisdom" is not a countable noun. But that is alright. We can work with its pluralized context – Just know I mean many "wisdoms." So, may I say between us, "Ancient Wisdoms Are Not Dead?"

"This is what the LORD says: *"Stand at the crossroads and look; ask for the ancient paths, ask where the good way is, and walk in it, and you will find rest for your souls. But you said, 'We will not walk in it."* (Jeremiah 6:16, NIV) If there is anything old and has not changed, it is wisdom — It is value in humanity remains the same. But note the Bible says, *"knowledge shall increase."* (Daniel 12:4, KJV). Could it be that while knowledge will increase on earth, wisdom will lack? I would expect wisdom to increase as knowledge also increases. But the word of God only says, "Knowledge shall increase—." Knowledge can be obtained through information or communication, and otherwise divinely or supernaturally. And if wisdom is the understanding and application of that knowledge that comes from information, and insight is the recognition of the principal core of truth, then we need the wisdom to increase as knowledge increases so we can know how to properly use the increased knowledge. The current problem of the world is that we are only aspiring to increase our knowledge or information, but we neglect understanding, good judgment, or wisdom, which can help us effectively apply the latter.

> *"The current problem of the world is that we are only aspiring to increase our knowledge... but we neglect understanding, good judgment."*

We also need an understanding of the knowledge or information we are receiving. Only the understanding of the revelation of the knowledge we are acquiring can help us utilize it correctly. Additionally, we need a system of reminders, which can enforce wisdom and can help us make the right decisions. The Bible says, **"Understanding is a fountain of life to its possessor."** (Proverb 16:22, BSB).

Information is vital. However, you must ensure that the information you have is accurate, valid, and not outdated; otherwise, it's useless and even dangerous. For instance, you may have a whole bag of bad apples, and if someone asks, "Do you have apples?" Your answer could be yes. In reality, you cannot eat bad apples, so you do not have apples — the apples you have are bad. Therefore, it equals nothing — no apples. The same analogy applies to information. When you have the wrong, bad, or outdated information, it's not good for anything. It becomes even more dangerous when you make decisions in consideration of that.

Statistics in marketing have shown that when a customer or prospect wants to use a service or buy a product, the probability of him contacting or doing business with the company which stays in contact with the latter via emails, postcards/mails, text messages, and perhaps phone calls is higher than the companies who do not stay in contact. Why? Because that is how our mind and heart work — We tend to quickly and firstly remember what we are constantly hearing, watching/seeing, reading, or being notified about – what we are connected to.

No matter how much knowledge or information you have acquired, you can still make wrong decisions if the elements of that good knowledge or information are not strong enough in your heart and mind to generate the power to counterattack the impulse or that sudden strong and unreflective urge or desire to do this or the other, which are surely the wrong ones.

It is important to note that keeping our hearts and minds loaded with good morals, proverbs, parables, and above all, the Good News, or the Word of God can only do such a thing to our minds and hearts; and help us make better decisions, which will give us the peace, happiness, comfort, stability, security, prosperity we all long for as human beings.

> *"No matter how much knowledge or information you have acquired, you can still make wrong decisions."*

One thing is to have a tool, and another is to know how to use it. Having a wealth of knowledge or information does not necessarily make one a wise person, and a good decision-maker. You can gain a lifetime of knowledge yet miss the point of good decision-making every time.

The main elements of wisdom are not only understanding and discernment, but also courage, the courage to say yes or no, and to disciple and refrain from what is not good.

> *"One thing is to have a tool, and*

another is to know how to use it."

What Is Wisdom

After all, what is wisdom? There are several definitions for the word "wisdom" depending on people's understanding of what it really means to them. Biblical Scholars believe there are three types of wisdom, and Philosophers believe there are two types of wisdom. The word "wisdom" is from the Greek word Sophia's. And according to some Biblical scholars, wisdom is knowing "Epignosis", or having knowledge of the best course of action to take. Therefore, we may say, Sophia or wisdom, is a result of having the ability to properly judge and choose the best direction or decide based on the knowledge and understanding that we have acquired or granted by the Spirit of God.

"The main elements of wisdom are not only understanding and discernment, but also courage, the courage to say yes or no — discipline."

Philosophers assumed that there are two kinds of wisdom: Theoretical wisdom, which is Sophia or Sophia's, and practical wisdom, which is phronesis. Some people also argue that the difference between theoretical and practical wisdom is not very clear because a practically wise individual must be morally virtuous or cannot be wicked.

Biblical scholars believe there are three types of wisdom revealed in the Bible: Godly wisdom, or neocortical spirit wisdom; earthly wisdom, or worldly reptilian body wisdom; and satanic wisdom, or demonic mammalian soul wisdom.

Neocortical is related to reasoning, the part of the cerebral cortex concerned with sight and hearing in mammals. Reptilian is also internal reasoning, that is part of the human nervous system, which is also called the limbic or reptilian brain. Demonic mammalian is an internal reasoning as well, and ungodly reasoning that demons want humans to have. This type of wisdom is fully demonic because it does not serve any good or Godly purpose.

As I stated in my preface, my focus in this book is not philosophical and psychological; even though I may sound like that at some point. Rather, my focus is Biblical and spiritual. So, I will discuss about Godly wisdom a little further.

The dictionary defines wisdom as "the quality of having experience, knowledge, and good judgment; the quality of being wise." Psychology defines wisdom as "the understanding of the right relations between things, which calls for more distant and removed perspectives, and maybe also the ability or willingness to shift between perspectives;" "The understanding and application of knowledge/information;" "The virtue of good judgment."

The dictionary also defines "Virtue" as "a moral excellence. A virtue is a trait or quality that is deemed to be morally good and thus is valued as a foundation of principle and a good moral being. In other words, it is a behavior that shows high moral standards, doing what is right and avoiding what is wrong." Another related word for virtue in the dictionary is "potency" when it comes to topics like strength and effectiveness.

As you can notice, like me, at this point, we have observed that the quest to understand the concept of wisdom and define it in various domains of life and subjects has been a long journey for humanity, from philosophers, psychologists, spiritual leaders, writers, to life coaches and motivational speakers.

Evidently, to me, wisdom is the ability to discern the revelation of truth, the courage to choose and exercise right over wrong, and knowing the right thing to say and do, when and where. And I perceived this truth from the very first demonstration of wisdom of the man about whom God said, he would give him, including wisdom and knowledge such as no king who was before him ever had and none after him will have — Solomon. (2 Chronicles 1:11-12).

> *"To me, wisdom is the ability to discern the revelation of truth, the courage to choose and exercise right over wrong, and knowing the right thing to say and do, when and where."*

When the two women came to the young King Solomon, both narrated their stories or made their defenses. He listened to them as his court also did. But up to that time he listened to them during the judgment, King Solomon did not know or at least was not sure whose baby the child was. Then Solomon used his wisdom, the ability to get the revelation or discernment he needed to make the right decision. With that ability, he was able to figure out what to do or to say in order to get the revelation or discernment he needed to find the truth, which would lead to his good or right decision. So, he commanded the child to be cut in half and shared between the two women. That command and action quickly led to one of the women immediately renouncing her claim and deciding that she would rather give the child to the other woman instead of having him killed. Solomon's ability to push for the truth, or using that ability to get revelation or discernment, eventually revealed the truth — the woman who decided to give up the child instead of having him killed was the mother of the baby.

Knowing what, or the right thing to say and do, when, and where is a property of wisdom. Note, without not saying and doing the right thing, King Solomon would not have known who the child belonged to and would have made the wrong decision or judgment. Knowing what or the right thing to say and do, when, and where is very important not only for a king, but for you as well. Knowing the right thing to say and do, when and where, can mean death or life, loss or win, failure or success, peace, or trouble.

> *"Knowing the right thing to say and do, when and where, can mean death or life, loss or win, failure or success, peace, or trouble."*

The simplest way to understand wisdom, is to understand what foolishness is. Foolishness is defined by the Oxford English Dictionary as the "lack of good sense or judgment; or stupidity." The American Heritage Dictionary of the English Language defines "Foolishness" as "Lacking or exhibiting a lack of good sense or judgment; silly, absurd or ridiculous." However, stubbornness, impulsivity, influences, and gullibility can determine someone's ability to make reasonable decisions. People do not always make the wrong decisions because they do not know the right from the wrong – sometimes it is just a pure stubbornness.

The Power of Wisdom

King David, the father of Solomon, was a mighty man of war. (1 Chronicles 28:3). And the Bible also describes the men who were in the armed force of David as mighty men. They were powerful, strong, and brave. In fact, some of their exploits make you believe they were even more powerful in war than David himself. They were armed men who knew how to handle their weapons of war, and nothing stood in their way to win battles. The Bible states, *"These were the men who came to David at Ziklag, while he was banished from the presence of Saul son of Kish (they were among the warriors who helped him in battles; they were armed with bows and were able to shoot arrows or to sling stones right-handed or left-handed--"* (1 Chronicles 12:1-2, NIV). Yet, when it was announced to David that Ahithophel, the Gilonite, his royal counselor, had joined his rebellious son Absalom in his royal coup, David was afraid. (2 Samuel 15:12; 31). Why was David, the man who killed the lions, the bears, and Goliath afraid of one man's wisdom, a man who was not even a warrior? Because David knew the power of wisdom.

May I say to you, that knowledge is power, but wisdom is more powerful than knowledge, positions, weapons, armies, and riches. Without it, great generals, armies, kings, queens, kingdoms, empires, riches, positions, and dispositions are powerless and useless. So is your life; without wisdom, you will be powerless and useless. Knowledge without wisdom is powerless. And a property of wisdom is staying away from bad decisions.

> *"Knowledge is power, but wisdom is more powerful than knowledge, positions, weapons, armies, and riches."*

One of my favorite subjects is history for several reasons. And history, is not only "the study of past events, particularly in human affairs," as the Oxford Languages Dictionary defines it. Nevertheless, history provides us with lessons we can learn without suffering what others experienced to discover the consequences of their good and bad decisions. History indirectly prepares us for life – better decision-making – but only if we properly examine our own lives and others'. Not dead people only have a past or history we can learn from, but we have to start from our own history, past decisions, and events.

Wisemen Did Not Die with Their Wisdom

Wise people do not die with their wisdom; they leave it to the world, beginning from people close to them, and who speak their languages.

Communication, is the way to enforce wisdom, even to yourself. People usually become what they have been hearing, reading, or watching.

The Power of Communication

The failure of communication and misunderstanding can cause stress, disagreement, and sometimes war. There is a difference between poor communication and tricky communication. Lack of communication can cause problems, just as miscommunication, or communicating something the wrong way can also result in unpleasant effects. The truth is, people may have good intentions, but may communicate poorly. But sometimes, malicious people may also play into your mind and mislead you by communication. For example, when someone says, "I will give you money." What you heard is he will give you money, but what will the money be for, and what will you have to do to get the money is not clear. So, it is up to you to think ahead and understand or ask the person what the money will be for and how you will get it. People play tricks with communication. So it's also your responsibility to make an effort to properly understand what people mean because it may save your life. So before you agree or disagree, make sure you understand what the person is saying.

> *"The failure of communication and misunderstanding can cause stress, disagreement, and sometimes war."*

Communication is so vital to humanity to the extent that without modern information technology, ancient people tried to find even difficult or brutal ways to communicate values, instructions, announcements, and even save and share information and knowledge, which can help others make the right decisions in various circumstances. Ancient people used several ways to pass on information. And these include oral or mouth to ear method or through word of mouth, writing or designing on stone tablets, paper, parchment (prepared skin of an animal), papyrus, books, scraps, inscribing on keepsakes, item or object placements, landmarks, symbols, poetries, rhyme sounds, limericks, stories, secret codes, games, rituals, moon and stars observation, songs, and music (drumming, whistling, crying), naming… Etc. The point is not how they communicated and transmitted information or knowledge, but how important it was for them. They understood that their goodness or fortune depends on knowledge and wisdom, and for them, the way to utilize knowledge, is to get understanding and wisdom. If having wisdom was essential to them, it must be important to us as well because you cannot succeed and live a peaceful, stable, secure, prosperous, and Godly life without wisdom.

> *"People play tricks with communication."*

The Quest For Knowledge and Wisdom

I will not try to date creation because it will take some time, especially from a Biblical truth and perspective. However, let us fetch a little information, which may help us understand how much wealth of wisdom we have on earth with the help of God. Whether you believe in science that says the earth, the third planet from the sun and the only astronomical object known to harbor life (Even though other planets are being tested for life as I'm writing this book), is about 4.5 billion years, and a universe about 14 billion years old (Known as the secular age of the earth), or in the Biblical genesis of the earth and humanity (Known as the Biblical age of the earth and universe), which is about 6,000 years, you and I, at least can agree on the fact that the world has been in existence for a very long time. And many people endowed by God with wisdom have walked the earth.

The Ambition of Building Repositories of Information and Knowledge

Fast-forward, it is interesting how history conveys to us how the ancient world thirsted for knowledge, which eventually led to the formation of several ancient libraries. Ancient kings or rulers were really interested in gathering information or knowledge, which could among many reasons, dispense realistic help in the affairs of ruling and governing their kingdoms. Ancient leaders had a powerful interest in accumulating and compiling information from various bright areas and minds, especially from the Greeks and ancient kingdoms of the Middle East.

As famous as it was, and it is presently in our hearings in the educational and theological realm, the Library of Alexandria in Egypt was not the only a Library of its kind that existed, and though the timing of its existence is not precisely known, scholars suggest its construction began sometime around 300-200 B.C. The ancient tradition of building and maintaining Libraries in Greece and the Middle East to record and archive written materials suggestively reveals that it originated from the ancient Sumerian city/state, located in the southern region of Sumer (modern day Warka, Iraq) around 3400 BC.

The ancient Hittites (Part of today's Turkey, Lebanon, Cyprus, and Assyria) had large archives accommodating records written in many different languages. Also, history tells us that the most famous library of the ancient Middle East was the Library of Ashurbanipal in Nineveh, founded in the seventh century BC by the Assyrian king Ashurbanipal, who ruled 668–627 B.C. We may also note that in Greece, the Athenian tyrant Peisistratos was said to have founded the first major public library in the sixth century BC.

According to history, a large library also existed in Babylon during the reign of Nebuchadnezzar. This is worth evoking our curiosity. We will get back to it later. We must pay some attention to it.

So, why did these ancient kings or rulers have the ambition of collecting books? The answer is simple: They believed they needed information or knowledge to help them make the best judgment and decisions in matters of ruling, expansion, and governance in their kingdoms — they wanted to be successful, so they went to considerable extents to produce a repository of all knowledge or information.

Kings and rulers not only went to great lengths to gather and build an enormous wealth of knowledge or information, but they also surrounded themselves with people full of knowledge and wisdom as advisers on pertinent matters in their kingdoms, and even conquest wars. They understood that the success and longevity of their rules and kingdoms depended not only on military powers, but also on the significance of their knowledge, information, and wisdom.

Undoubtedly, after examining several facts, you and I may agree that knowledge, and especially wisdom, in the ancient world was regarded as power and a must-have characteristic or virtue to live by and be successful. In other words, an excellence, quality, or power by which individuals and kingdoms build peace, health, wealth or prosperity, longevity, stability, and security.

Wisdom Makes the Difference

Apart from Biblical accounts, history reveals that there have been several young and old, celebrated and uncelebrated Kings, Queens, and Emperors. Each one of them left lessons behind, and their life records show us how much good difference wisdom can make, and how bad decisions can lead to destruction in one's life – Truly, foolishness can make a mockery of even dignitary. Their lives teach us that wisdom is conformity to a standard of morality, a particular moral excellence, and a beneficial quality or power that can either build, destroy, dignify, or ridicule someone.

> *"Truly, foolishness can make a mockery of even dignitary."*

Jehoash or Joash, King of Judah: Saved by Grace, Ruined by Foolishness

Do you remember the proverb or idiom that says, "The apple does not fall far from the tree, or like father, like son, or like mother, like daughter?"

> *"Do better than your predecessors, avoiding, and correcting the mistakes they have made in life."*

As a youngster, you may be no different from your roots, parents, or family. This can be normalized throughout your life because you may grow up witnessing events of life through the mirror of your family. But the truth is, you can become better and do better than the people you came from with all due respect and honor. That should be your aim, even if you come from a good family. Your goal should always be to do better and more than the good things the people who came before you have achieved. This is also not to set higher standards for yourself and feel guilty when you are not able to meet them, but at least it should be your motivation.

Believe it or not, there are some particular traits, characteristics, or behaviors attached to your roots (parents, family, race, or people) that tend to influence your decision-making or choices. And making the wrong decisions, or choices can easily ruin your good start in life as a young person. Therefore, Keeping your roots in mind as a young person should do two things to your life: Fighting to do better than your predecessors, avoiding, and correcting the mistakes they have made in life.

Do not act moral, but be moral. One of the problems of a young age is acting morally sound or doing the right things under the influence of your parents, guardians, or someone you respect until you lose their influence when you reach adulthood, or they die. Then, your acting ceases, and your real moral character appears. Believe it or not, such foolishness will catch up with you and ruin you sooner or later. Compromising moral values and ethics does not make you a better person, neither does it make the world a better place. Throughout history, the only civilizations, persons, and families who survived the test of time or durability were the ones who kept morality.

The history of Joash dates back to his roots or family. His great-grandparents were Ahab and Jezebel, and names familiar to even people who are not Bible students and scholars. (1 Kings 16: 29-33). His grandmother, Athaliah, was the daughter of King Ahab and his wife Jezebel (Some scholars believe Athaliah was an orphan adopted by King Ahab and Jezebel, or at least she lived at the King's house). As the only evil-minded woman who reigned as a monarch in Israel, Judah, Queen Athaliah, after her son Ahaziah's brief rule, killed the remaining members of the dynasty to reign and reigned for six years before she was dethroned.

King Jehoram of Judah reigned for eight years. His father, Jehoshaphat and grandfather Asa were faithful kings who served and worshiped God and kept his commandments. However, Jehoram, their son, chose not to follow their example and rejected God; consequently, his Kingdom was not stable. An attack by the Philistines, Arabs, and Ethiopians destroyed the king's house and took away all of his family except his youngest son, Ahaziah.

After Jehoram's death, Ahaziah, his youngest son, became king of Judah, and Athaliah, his mother, became the Queen Mother. About a year after ascending to the throne, King Ahaziah and Joram of Israel were killed by Jehu, a military commander or General of Joram, king of Israel. Supported by the Prophet Elisha, Jehu led a revolution that killed Ahaziah and Joram in Jezreel and soon after killed Jezebel as well. (2 Kings 9:14-37).

When the news of Ahaziah's death reached Athaliah, his mother, she seized the throne of Judah and killed all possible successors of his son Ahaziah, relatives, including her own grandchildren who should ascend to the throne. (2 Kings 11:1). This woman was evil. It's unbelievable that a woman would kill so many people, including her own grandchildren just to become a Queen.

However, during the massacre of Athaliah, the Bible notes, "But Jehosheba, the daughter of King Jehoram and sister of Ahaziah, took Joash son of Ahaziah and stole him away from among the royal princes, who were about to be murdered. She put him and his nurse in a bedroom to hide him from Athaliah; so he was not killed." (2 Kings 11:2).

Clearly, Joash was saved by grace, not because he was better than his siblings, relatives, or the other royal family members. It was by God's grace and the wisdom of the people who risked their own lives to steal him away and hide him.

Joash remained hidden for six years while his wicked grandmother ruled as Queen. We read, *"He remained hidden with them at the temple of God for six years while Athaliah ruled the land."* (2 Chronicles 22:12).

I have observed that many successful, or at least people who have achieved a level of success in life, even though they may deny or not recognize it, somehow and sometime in the past or history of their families had individuals who faithfully served God and prayerfully asked God to bless their children and descendants. However, these children and their descendants who are enjoying the blessings or fruits of the prayers of their predecessors or ancestors care less about the God who made the wishes of the people who came before them possible.

In short, Joash finally became King, and the people celebrated. (2 Kings 11:13-14). Athaliah had been slain with the sword at the palace. (2 Kings 11:20). We read, *"Joash was seven years old when he became king, and he reigned in Jerusalem for forty years. His mother's name was Zibiah; she was from Beersheba. Joash did what was right in the eyes of the LORD all the years of Jehoiada, the priest."* (2 Chronicles 24:1-2).

Note, "Joash did what was right in the eyes of the LORD all the years of Jehoiada the priest." So, after the death of Jehoiada, the priest, Joash was not making the right decisions or choices and doing the right things anymore.

During the lifetime of Jehoiada, the priest, he listened to him and took advice from him. One of his major achievements was the repair of the temple of God. One would ask, "What happened to Joash the God-fearing young King?" The answer is simple: He may have done all the above under the influence of Jehoiada, the priest, to please him and was acting as a morally sound person, but not a righteous man. Or, he was sincerely serving God, but when his adviser died, he did not value the need to continue living and holding the same moral character. Do not let your moral character die with your parents, guardians, advisors, pastors, or spiritual leaders. You must continue to live a morally sound life in a corrupt world to perpetuate moral character in an untrustworthy or deceitful world. Additionally, keeping moral values is beneficial to your whole human life as well. It keeps your mind, soul, and body healthy and peaceful without fear, regrets, and guilt.

One of the evil acts of Joash is the killing of Zechariah, the very son of Jehoiada, the priest who helped him maintain a good moral character and stabilize his Kingdom. The Bible says, **"King Joash did not remember the kindness Zechariah's father Jehoiada had shown him but killed his son, who said as he lay dying, "May the LORD see this and** *call you to account." At the turn of the year, the army of Aram marched against Joash; it invaded Judah and Jerusalem and killed all the leaders of the people."* (2 Chronicles 24: 22-23).

King Joash, who became King just at seven years of age, observed moral laws but later deviated away from them and was wounded in the battle with the Aramemans. His officials conspired against him for murdering Zechariah, the son of Jehoiada, the priest, and they killed him in his bed. So he died and was buried in the City of David, but not in the tombs of the kings.

Getting away from moral values is a mistake that can cause you dearly and many times will bring you dishonor, shame, regrets, and guilt. And this hidden guilt can lead you to make many more wrong decisions or choices that will sooner or later ruin your life.

> "Getting away from moral values is a mistake that can cause you dearly and many times will bring you dishonor, shame, regrets, and guilt."

Ptolemy XIII: Young, Inexperienced, and Envious

"Experience is the best teacher." You have probably heard this several times. Having little knowledge or experience of a particular thing can be dangerous. Lack of experience, knowledge, or skill can destroy your life in many ways. But do you have to experience it before learning from it? I do not think so. You can learn from the experiences of others and avoid experiencing the pain and loss they endured before learning the lessons and the how. It all comes down to humility and a learning spirit.

> *"Lack of experience, knowledge, or skill can destroy your life in many ways."*

Ptolemy XIII was the 13th ruler of Egypt's Ptolemaic dynasty. He was a young Pharaoh who was crowned in 51 B.C. at the age of eleven or twelve. His kingdom was marked by several unwise decisions and defeats.

According to historians, as a political arrangement commonly known and done in ancient Egypt for siblings to marry in order to maintain the integrity of the royal bloodline, he was married to his sister Cleopatra. First, think about this, it's very confusing how humans try to be conservative in one thing, but pollute the other. The whole idea of having siblings marry each other at the time, especially in royal families was to keep the ruling family's bloodline in power. But they were doing it to the detriment of God's other moral laws, which would surely destroy the family morally and spiritually.

But soon after, when the sister was recognized more than him, he manipulated people and things around, which forced her to run away to Syria, but she soon formed an army of her own, and a civil war broke out in Egypt.

When the Roman general Pompey the Great ran to Egypt to seek for asylum after being defeated by Julius Caesar, the young ruler Ptolemy XIII pretended like he was offering him protection according to his request. But when he arrived, he set up his assassination, got him killed, and decapitated his head, which he later presented to Julius Caesar as the head of his enemy. He honestly believed he was trying to be clever by killing someone to please another person. However, according to sources, instead of being pleased, Julius Caesar was indignant and ordered a search for the body of his war enemy or rival Pompey for a proper Roman funeral.

One of the lessons you have to learn here, and even in the Bible (The story of Abner, the Army General of King Saul, and Joab, the Army General of King David), and many throughout history, is that army Generals tend to respect each other regardless of the outcome of their wars. But yes, there are exceptions, even though generally they respect each other. If you remember, Abner did not want to kill Asahel, Joab's brother because of the respect he has for Joab, the army general of King David. (2 Samuel 2:18-32). Yet, Joab lacked that respect for his counterpart Abner, and would later kill him because of the death of his brother, which resulted from his stubbornness, and who chose to pursue Abner despite the multiple warnings he gave him. (2 Samuel 2:18-32 and 2 Samuel 3:27).

Be a morally sound human being. Do not let misunderstandings lead you to kill someone. But do not also think that what you cannot do to someone because of your moral standards, he also cannot do it to you because he might not have the same moral standards as you. Be vigilant, knowing that not everybody thinks the way you do or fears God the way you do and will not harm you. Stay away from, and love from away people who have revealed themselves to you as your enemies one way or the other, and the ones you are yet to find out that they are. Many who have ignored this have been poisoned, shot, or killed in many unexpected ways by the very people they thought could have never done that.

"Be a morally sound human being."

Ptolemy XIII still in his younger mind, came up with other plans and armies, and with the help of his other sister, Queen Arsinoe IV, he set to fight Julius Caesar's army and his sister and former wife Cleopatra. But he lost the battle.

The young king is believed to have drowned in the Nile River as he tried to flee capture by the Roman army led by Caesar. It is also fascinating to note that the famous Library of Alexandria was burned sometime during those battles.

Do not make a fool of yourself when someone is visible or recognized in any domain more than you. Recognize people's status or popularity, be happy for them, and let it be. Support them if need be. Sometimes we make things look more than what they are when they are about someone else. Not everything that seems to be a threat to our ego, status, and dominance really is. Even though many can advise you otherwise, people respect and honor you more when you are in a position of power, but you can also recognize other people's gifts, talents, and even fame, and respect them as well. The young Pharaoh considered her sister's fame as a threat and wanted to crush that. You may even see this in our societies today, some men can become so jealous of their own wives because they seem to be popular or make more money than them. Unfortunately, this foolishness did not work out in the young Pharaoh's favor.

> *"Do not make a fool of yourself when someone is visible or recognized in any domain more than you."*

Also, learn not to mingle with other families, countries, or tribes' affairs more than necessary because if you are not careful, you will be the one who will be blamed and lose in the end. There is a proverb in the Ewe Language (A language spoken in Togo and Southeastern Ghana, in West Africa) that says, "A brotherhood rod or walking stick does not break, it only bends", meaning no matter what happens between brothers or a people from the same place, it might not break their brotherhood, it can only bend it. Be careful when you are dealing with people from the same family or place when they are fighting. Your misguided action or intervention can cause the other side or both to join and fight you back, and it might not end well for you. The young Pharoah thought assassinating and presenting the head of the Roman General Pompey to Julius Caesar, who was also a Roman General could have pleased him and considered him as an ally and supporter. But no, Julius Caesar's anger was kindled when he learned that his war enemy, rival, but countryman, or who was also a Roman was assassinated and decapitated by another person to please him.

One bad decision can lead you to many other bad decisions. Be careful when you are desperately looking for a solution or a way out of a situation you find yourself in life. Many wrong decisions are made when you are engulfed in despair or hopeless situations. Distress can pressure you to make stupid decisions, and say or do things that you will only regret later.

"One bad decision can lead you to many other bad decisions."

When you are faced with a problem that you probably already caused or not, whatever you do, watch out and never create other problems to solve a problem. This can only worsen or complicate your situation sooner or later. There is a proverb that says, "Don't sell a thief to buy a witch." It can only get worse.

Ivan IV: Childhood Trauma, Anger, and Malice

Do not let your childhood trauma become the source of your anger, and your anger a justification for your wrong decisions and actions or doings. Otherwise, you are giving your abusers the power to control your life forever.
Ivan IV of Russia was the grand prince of Moscow and the rightful heir to the throne after his father died in 1533 when he was only three (3) years old. After succeeding his father at such a young age, a few years later, his mother also died. These events left the boy Emperor with none of his parents and eventually facilitated the control of Moscow by a group of aristocrats or highest-ranking nobles also known as the boyars.

While some scholars disputed the validity or authenticity of the following claims, according to the said letters of the young emperor, he was starved, lacked clothes, neglected, or mistreated by the highest-ranking nobles at the time. These actions perhaps left him isolated and angry. Some scholars also attributed his anger, mental problems, and troubled personality to the untimely death of his first wife, which is believed to be poisoning, and a series of treasons, and disloyalty of his entourage.

Among many of the terrible things he did after becoming an emperor, he invited the highest-ranking nobles believed to have caused him trouble, to a meeting, and cast one of them into a herd of Russian hunting dogs, which are known for their anger, rage, and persistence in hunting even bears, moose, and boars. Maybe or seemingly an act of justice for the way they treated him. I can imagine what happened to that man at the mercy of the Russian hunting dogs.

It is also known that Ivan IV formed a special police unit that publicly executed citizens who were not loyal to him. The emperor's officers roamed around with horses along with dogs literally looking for disloyal citizens to punish.
One of the accounts of his anger also was that he assaulted his pregnant daughter-in-law and murdered his eldest son, who was the heir by striking his head with a scepter.

Some scholars also describe the emperor as smart and God-fearing, but likely suffered from paranoia (a mental condition characterized by delusions of persecution, unwarranted jealousy, or exaggerated self-importance), which triggered his rage, and irregular explosion of mental problems that increased as he aged. We must also note that this presumably unexpected death of his oldest son paved the way for his younger son to become the next emperor, who was recorded by historians as ineffective or unsuccessful. The young emperor Ivan IV grew old and died from a heart attack.

Some historians argued that the mistreatment described by others is not exact, since other scholars dispute the authenticity of a letter believed to have been written by the emperor about his basic needs when he was younger. One could however notice evidence of anger and rage in the life of the emperor. Regardless of the facts surrounding his mistreatments, and if he was ever abused by the older nobles before ascending to the throne, there is no excuse for his anger, rage, and violence; especially towards his own son whom he stroked his head with a scepter.

Do not let your abusers control your life forever. Instead of responding and living the rest of your life in anger, rage, bitterness, and violence, turn the memories into beauty and the mistreatments into treats for yourself and others, and watch happiness overflow your life. When you let your past bad experiences, especially your brutal and abusive childhood encounters with what life can be, rule your life, you are giving your abusers the permission to indirectly control you for the rest of your life and accepting their supremacy over your being as a human.

> *"Do not let your abusers control your life forever — turn the memories into beauty and the mistreatments into treats for yourself and others."*

Wisdom does not equate to malice. There are many people in our world now who think and believe they are intelligent because of their malice. Wrongful intentions do not make anyone wise; they lead you into sin and breaking laws, even the commandments of God, to which there are severe consequences sooner or later. Even if you never face law enforcement or the judiciary, you may live the rest of your life under a heavy cloud of guilt that will often kill your real happiness.

Mary, Queen of Scots: Blind Love, Unreasonable Wish and Expectations

"Follow your heart," and "Love is bling." You have heard this before. And many young people do believe in this, and sometimes adults as well. But when "Blind love" is at work in your life or heart, it becomes destructive. It may lead to dangerous paths, and create unreasonable wishes and expectations as well. Marriages or relationships do not necessarily resolve your problems.

Mary, Queen of Scots, became queen when she was just six days old. She ascended to the throne of Scotland after her father died only six days after her birth. In 1543, King Henry VIII of England wanted to unite Scotland and England, so he proposed a future marriage between the young girl Queen Mary and his son Edward. However, the Scottish parliament denied the proposal and arrangement. King Henry VIII out of an attempt to force the marriage invaded Scotland.

> *"Blind love" — becomes destructive."*

After hiding Queen Mary for a while throughout Scotland, her protectors escaped with her to France at the age of five (5), where she spent most of her childhood while Scotland was governed by regents. She ended up marrying the heir to the throne of France, Francis. After the accession of her husband to the throne and his death, Mary became a Widowed and returned to Scotland. Four years later, she married her half-cousin Henry Stuart, Lord Darnley, and had a son called James.

It is recorded that in February 1567, Queen Mary's husband, Darnley's residence was destroyed by an explosion, and he was found killed in the garden. There was a nobleman named James Hepburn, who was the first (1st) Duke of Orkney and 4th Earl of Bothwell, popularly known as Lord Bothwell, who many suspected was the planner of Queen Mary's husband's death. But he was acquitted of the charge against him in April 1567. Ironically, the following month, Mary Queen of Scots married this man.

How can a woman marry a man suspected of murdering her husband? A question any reasonable person would have asked? This action surely led to an uprising against her and the man. Eventually, she was imprisoned, and on July 24th, 1567, forced to abdicate the Scottish throne and flee to England seeking the protection of her first cousin, Queen Elizabeth I. But things did not work out in her favor over there either. She was arrested and imprisoned on charges of contributing to a plot to overthrow Queen Elizabeth I, her cousin. Almost nineteen (19) years later, she was executed.

One would be left with a reasonable question, "How can someone so intelligent make these horrible mistakes?" While the life of the princess and later Queen was marked by one scandal after another, it is to be noted that she was an intelligent person. Among her intellectual capacity indications, in addition to the Scots dialect of the Lowlands, she was fluent in French and was proficient in Italian, Spanish, and Greek.

Why do intelligent people make stupid mistakes? Because intelligence is not wisdom. Some brilliant people ignore this reality until it becomes evident to them through the consequences of their bad decisions followed by unrestrictive actions.

> *"Why do intelligent people make stupid mistakes? Because intelligence is not wisdom."*

One thing any analytical person would notice about Mary, Queen of Scots, if the events revealed to us through history are true, is that she tends to take pleasure in terminating people's lives or well-being to gain her heart desires. Do not let your heart desires lead you to unrealistic expectations, wrong decisions, and actions.

You have heard many people say, "Follow your heart." The truth is, your heart alone is never enough for you to make the right decisions. The human heart or spirit is generally corrupted as the Bible makes it clear, ***"The Lord saw how great the wickedness of the human race had become on the earth, and that every inclination of the thoughts of the human heart was only evil all the time."*** (Genesis 6:5, NIV). Your heart's desires are not always right. Your desires mostly are selfishness, greed, and wickedness. So you need a rule to control them. And that rule is the word or moral commandments of God. (Exodus 20:1-17). Whenever your heart wants something, check it against moral values and conduct.

Following your heart is different from tuning into the Spirit of God in you. Some people call it intuition, but truthfully, it's the spirit of God working in the spirit of man. I will elaborate on this later in the book.

Some historians believe that the accusations of Mary plotting to kill her cousin, Queen Elizabeth I of England were just allegations and might not be true. But if they were true, that was just a revelation of a character already demonstrated and seen in Scotland, which led to the uprising against her and forced her to abdicate the throne in favor of her son. Remember Queen Mary's husband, Darnley's residence was destroyed by an explosion, and he was found murdered in the garden. There was a nobleman named James Hepburn, popularly known as Lord Bothwell who many suspected was the orchestrator of the murderer, but he was acquitted of the charge and the following month Mary, Queen of Scots married this man.

The Scottish would have been out of touch if they did not question the whole incident leading to the murder of the Queen's husband. Any intelligent person would have questions and want explanations. At the end of it all, she would marry the man suspected to have killed her husband. "How intelligent was this?" You would ask. It looked intelligent, but it was not wise.

Many times, I wonder how in the world someone would plan such a crime and believe people are so stupid and would never know what really happened. They trust their intelligence to the extent that it makes them become stupid. One thing you must keep in mind is that you are not the only intelligent person on earth, you are probably just one among many, who may even be smarter than you. And you cannot get away with crimes, no matter who you are. It may be hidden for a while, a few years, but it will come out one way or the other.

The Queen escaped to England when she was in trouble in Scotland following her mistakes over there. England at the time, was under the governance of her cousin Queen Elizabeth I. It was also recorded that Queen Elizabeth I, was the Godmother of Queen Mary's son, James VI, and I. Now, if you were in trouble somewhere, and you escaped to a place for refuge where your cousin is the Queen, why would you even think of plotting a coup to gain the throne over there? A wise person would have just been humble and lived peacefully there, and perhaps her cousin would have honored her with a better position in her kingdom. But if not, then she should have accepted her loss and just lived peacefully and honorably for the rest of her life. There are some mistakes you cannot correct or change in life and would have to live with them for the rest of your life. She lost her throne in Scotland due to her bad decisions, so why continue making the wrong decisions? The only way for you to change the bad decisions you have already made and the unpleasant circumstances you are in is to make good decisions after that.

The Dangers of the Sense of Entitlement

Be careful of your sense of entitlement because it can lead you to do things you are not supposed to do. The fact of having a right to something does not necessarily mean you have to have it, get it earlier, before your turn, or the appointed time, even if it's to take or destroy someone's life, career, or well-being. A corrupt sense of entitlement becomes selfishness and greed.

"Be careful of your sense of entitlement because it can lead you to do things you are not supposed to do."

Human beings are not disposable. Do not take someone's life because you feel like you do not love the person anymore or you want to get access to their position, property, business, life insurance, and other benefits that might be allocated to you sooner. Believe it or not, you will pay for it even after years. No innocent bloodshed has gone unpunished physically or spiritually. Just do not do it! The word of God says, *"These six things the Lord hates, yes, seven are an abomination to Him: A proud look, a lying tongue, and hands that shed innocent blood."* (Proverbs 6:16-17, NKJV).

You are not entitled to people's things or possessions without their good-will permission, regardless of your relationship with them. And once you start living as everybody owes you something, you will start using people's things in the wrong way, and not only that, you will also not be able to do or work to be who God wants you to be and do the things He wants you to do.

There is a proverb in French that says, "By wanting to win too much, you end up losing." When you are selfish and greedy, you end up losing the little that you already have sooner or later.

Refuse to be used by the devil or his demons in any way, including exciting you against people. One of the ways to know that the enemy wants to use or is already using you against people is when you realize that someone who did absolutely nothing wrong to you has become the center of your anger, resentment, and evil expectations. When all of a sudden you are feeling resentment towards your husband, wife, children, co-worker, manager, or friend for no reason, you have to immediately start resisting that spirit – it is the devil. Most of the time, this spirit will target people who are actually the good people in your life or God has placed in your life for good reasons. And you may not know until the devil pushes them out of your life through you.

Sometimes, people wake up and just hate someone for no reason or for very minor issues, and if you ask them, "What did he or she did wrong?" They cannot tell you anything meaningful the latter has done wrong. When you are feeling resentment towards people for nothing wrong or minor that they got wrong, you must check your heart or spirit – it may be just the spirit of resentment operating through you at that moment, and you may not know it until you decide and do the worst before you realize it.

And, if you are someone who usually finds yourself experiencing resentment from people you did nothing wrong to, you have to understand that you are a target for the devil and he will usually make people resent you one way or the other to cause problems, attacking, delaying, and destroying the good things that God has planned to do in your life. Therefore, instead of fighting back the people hating you for no reason, you have to pray for them to be released by the spirit of resentment.

Fulin, Shunzhi Emperor: Open-minded, Curious, and Anti-Corruption

Being a child with a grown-up mind and actions is not always bad if your mindset and actions are morally sound. And loving everybody does not mean believing everything. Additionally, you do not have to be like the bad or corrupted people you descended from. As an individual, you have the opportunity to do your best to change the corrupted history of humanity, your family, people, or nation, and you can start even being young.

The transition or development from puberty to adulthood can be very tempting not only physically and culturally but also psychologically. And being a youth with diversity, equity, and inclusion in mind can be very challenging in our world. God is a God of diversity, equity, and inclusion, yet He gave us moral laws to help us navigate life with a balanced, clean mindset, and heart, or spirit. You do not throw away moral values and refuse to defend them because of diversity, equity, and inclusion.

The company or the people you choose to have a close relationship or alliance with will surely influence your decisions and actions. Choose them wisely. Being an open-minded young man or woman should not be synonymous with going in the wrong direction in life, even if you know they are bad or wrong. An open-minded person does not believe everything, but carefully listens and analyzes others' opinions; loves, and respects them regardless of their differences or moral values. However, being open-minded should not also be a pass to corruption or compromise on your beliefs and moral values either, it should not appease you from believing in and doing the right things.

Be careful who you build relationships with, because many people who want to be in your company, befriend you, become your business partner and much more have ulterior motives.

> *"An open-minded person does not believe everything, but carefully listens and analyzes others' opinions; loves, and respects them regardless of their differences or moral values."*

FOOLISHNESS | The Madness of Genesis

According to historians, the Shunzhi Emperor was Emperor of the Qing dynasty from 1644 to 1661, and the first Qing Emperor to rule over China proper, from March 15, 1638, to February 5, 1661. Members of the prince's committee selected him to succeed his father after his death, and he was only five (5) years old at the time.

Due to his young age, most parts of the empire were ruled by his uncle Dorgan, who was the regent. Fulin, the young Emperor fully gained power and started ruling the empire at the age of twelve (12). Determined to crush his political enemies, he quickly developed an uncertain relationship and agreement with the influential court eunuchs.

The remarkable traits of the young Emperor were his tenacity to fight corruption and unite the various parts of the land under one Chinese empire. It was also noted that he was an open-minded person and interested in astronomy (The science that studies celestial objects and phenomena. Objects of interest include planets, moons, stars, nebulae, galaxies, and comets). He also was interested in technology, religion, and government. And one of his advisers was a German missionary, precisely a Jesuit missionary who was an astronomer himself.

"You do not throw away moral values and refuse to defend them because of diversity, equity, and inclusion."

Unfortunately, he died of smallpox at the very young age of 22 and was succeeded by his son, according to the tradition.

One of the characteristics of wisdom is open-mindedness. But if you cannot differentiate between open-mindedness and compromise, then open-mindedness will trap you. Unfortunately, in our world today, open-mindedness is synonymous with compromise. You do not have to compromise your values when you are open-minded. And being open-minded does not mean you have to accept and believe in everything contrary to your Godly and moral values. Be open-minded, meaning be receptive to new ideas, willing to think, evaluate, and consider new ideas, and not have distrust based on fixed or preconceived ideas. Have an open-minded approach to the views and knowledge of others. But do not compromise your values. This helps you to get clarity, learn new things, and know the differences between your values and other people's ideas and values. And to find common grounds that could benefit everyone. Moreover, there is no way you can convince anyone to believe in your ideas, values, and principles if you do not understand why they believe in what they believe.

> *"One of the characteristics of wisdom is open-mindedness."*

Corruption

Corrupted persons, businesses, nations, governments, or kingdoms do not last or remain without falling and being emersed in shame and disgrace — It might last for some time, but eventually will fall. Corruption is defined as "Any dishonest or fraudulent conduct by those in power, typically involving bribery, any form of dishonesty or criminal activity undertaken by a person or organization entrusted with a position of authority, to acquire illicit benefit or abuse power for one's private gain." This includes bribing someone with money, sex, material, or other forms of remittance to obtain a favor or something that you do not deserve. These activities always come to a revelation sooner or later.

The Bible's definition of corruption is not only limited to people in authority. God refers to the human heart as wicked or corrupted in the days of Noah and it's not different in our time. (Genesis 6: 5-7). He spoke through the prophet Jeremiah and declared, "The heart is deceitful above all things and beyond cure. Who can understand it?." (Jeremiah 17: 9, NKJV).

The world is corrupted. But it does not mean you must be corrupted to make it or see the fulfillment of your dreams and vision in life. The earlier you understand this and start building a clean foundation for your life, purpose, destiny, and lifetime achievements or legacy, the better it will be for you. Many older people find it difficult to change certain things in their lives because they have lived their entire lives practicing them, which developed into their character. And once something becomes a part of your character, it becomes difficult to be set free from it; and only God can deliver you from it. You have to learn how to make the right decisions earlier in life so it becomes easier for you to make the right choices in life. As a parent, it's important to guide your children and help them learn how to make the right decisions or choices, even in difficult conditions. You do not love your children if you do not show them how to make the right decisions even if they are not comfortable for them.

> *"The world is corrupted. But it does not mean you must be corrupted."*

Another thing we may learn from this young Emperor is that you can believe in science and technology, but never let them replace God in your life. We will later elaborate on this.

Tutankhamen: The Man-Made Glory

When you are a child or young, one of your favorite things is to hear stories, some of which are true and others are not. Some of the stories you may hear or read in books, apart from fables, which are to teach a moral lesson, can be fictional, meaning in the form of prose (written or spoken) that describes imaginary events and people.

Be careful in believing in imaginary events and people. One of the signs of growth is having an analytical mind. Examine things and people. This is not to say you have to be suspicious of people or everybody, but ensure that you do not leave room for the error in believing in events, things, and people you should have not, and regret it later. Most of the times, the consequences of such mistakes can take a longtime to terminate or be delivered from.

A Partial Truth

Man-made glory can be a story or event made up for self-glorification, to glorify someone else, or an idea. While they may not look dangerous superficially, they can be very deceiving and make you look and believe things you should otherwise not believe and make the right decisions or choices.

This can be an honest mistake on some people's part. However, sometimes, even the people promoting an idea are not sure about what they are promoting and convincing others to believe. Many times, you would hear someone, a team, or an organization deny or walk back something they have previously said, announced, or supported. Some of them would be honest about the fact that they got it wrong. Therefore, as an individual, you are responsible for doing your work, reviewing and validating what you are seeing and hearing.

Underestimating and Overestimating Things

Often, stubbornness and gullibility can be attributes of youth. As a young person, it may be difficult for you to change your attitude, understanding, and position when it comes to some things or life's realities. Simultaneously, you may also have the tendency to be easily persuaded by the wrong values, ideas, lies, unrealistic wishes and expectations, and ungodly beliefs.

> *"As an individual, you are responsible for doing your work, reviewing and validating what you are seeing and hearing."*

As a young person, you may either underestimate or overestimate some realities about life, and this can lead you to dangerous decisions. This may apply to some older people as well. But it's more evident when you are young and inexperienced with life's realities. As you grow older, life will teach you to take a second look or double-check things before believing them. Young age can also make you be terrified by things you are not to be afraid of. You will learn as well that some events in your life are not a sign of the end of life. You can still make the good out of the bad that has already happened if you are honest and willing to amend the bad or change the bad into good. To do this, you have to keep things real with yourself, and then you can keep it real with others. Get the facts, find the right ways to learn more about things and people before making conclusions and decisions about them. Do not underestimate or overestimate things because you may pay for it with your time, money, or peace of mind sooner or later.

Tutankhamun, an Egyptian pharaoh believed to have reigned for nine years in the 14th century B.C. Also known as "King Tut", he inherited the throne between the ages of eight and nine, or nine and ten, and at first ruled Egypt under the supervision of advisers because of his young age. While there are no certain answers to questions surrounding the cause of his death, it has been the subject of significant debates and extensive studies. Eventually, it was determined that his death was likely the result of the combination of his multiple weakening disorders, a leg fracture, maybe as the result of a fall, and a severe malarial infection.

While some of the powerful kings and rulers of the ancient world were the Pharaohs who thought about themselves as gods and representatives of the gods; and built pyramids as evidence or statements of their greatness and achievements, their glories were mostly man-made.

Considering many historical records, past and present, the fame of the young pharaoh is man-made. One would ask, what are the striking achievements that make him this famous, the discovery of his tomb, or what else? Did he just lie to make himself famous just like the other Pharaohs, or historians made him famous? And if so, why?

We all know that history's measure of a great ruler depends on the impact, size of his empire/kingdom, charisma, or forcefulness of personality, of which we will discuss the good and bad further in this book.

Never build your image on men's praise. Not every praise from men is authentic. You might be worthy of the praise, but if you let it carry you away from reality, sooner or later, it can become the cause of your downfall. And sometimes, you might not be even worthy of that praise, and sooner or later, people will know you for who you are, and what you have done, and not who people and you pretended to be.

> *"Never build your image on men's praise."*

Chapter 2

Rashness Clearance

"A wise man is cautious – but a fool is arrogant and careless."
Proverbs 14:16

I HAVE SEEN OLDER PEOPLE in various places and occasions get drunk. And when they do, they walk erratically while the alcohol controls their muscle coordination and balance, some with only one of their pair of shoes on one foot, some cry while singing, some curse everybody on their way – and that is if they can see them. And some quarrel with everybody around them. And as a child, I thought this phenomenon must be fun – I had to get drunk to experience this. Little did I know that getting drunk is not fun.

After several attempts of trying to get drunk unsuccessfully and being disappointed in not having enough wine to get drunk on other occasions or celebrations, I finally got the opportunity – the day my wish came true. I managed to drink the wine as much as possible to ensure I got drunk and waited patiently for the presumably fun moment – the moment I could feel like these older people. Several minutes later, the wine started overtaking my body. I sensed my wish had arrived – "I'm also drunk today." I was smiling very nicely because I have accomplished my long-time goal – getting drunk. Not knowing that was just the beginning of the effects. A few moments passed, and then my heart started palpitating, my vision became blurry, and my ears could not hear properly – I'm losing consciousness. "What's happening to me?" "Am I dying?" "I thought this would be fun, but it's not?" "Maybe my experience is just different from the older people's?" All these questions started running through my mind. Then, I realized I could not walk straight when I wanted. I felt like my feet were not touching the ground. "How can I reverse this experience?" I thought.

My young friends came to the rescue, "Go home and take a cold water shower; that will reduce the effect of the wine." They said. But how would I go home drunk? You already know what will happen. But then, how can I stay out drunk, not knowing what will be next? A decision has to be made. I had to stay out to avoid my parents knowing I was drunk, or I had to go home and face other consequences when my mom would secretly schedule a correction or discipline for the next morning with all doors closed while I woke up to a cane beating on me asking to get up for a question I certainly have no answers for, "Where were you yesterday?" That would have been the perfect moment to apply the Bible's truth, *"Foolishness is bound up in the heart of a child, but the rod of discipline drives it far from him."* (Proverbs 22:15, NKJV).

To concise a long story, I painfully realized that the only way to reverse that awful experience I was having was to wait till my body metabolized the wine and it got out of my bloodstream. It was one of the experiences that cleared my rashness. And never did I try to get drunk again since that day. And thankfully, I grew up not to like alcohol.

The only time natural laws, mathematics, reasoning, assessment, and validity are useless is when God performs a miracle, and without God's supernatural intervention in a matter, wisdom suggests that you assess the consequences of your choices before executing them.

> *"The only time natural laws — and validity are useless is when God performs a miracle."*

Rashness is undertaking without considering the consequences or being careless and unwise. Without taking some realities into account, you will make unwise decisions. And our ability to measure the results of the choices we make is not fixed or stable because of our humanity – the state of our mind, feelings, events, and times influences that.

The Power of Your Counsel

Who provides you with advice, and where do you get your action plan or behavior from? Every so often, the people close to us can surely give us the best counsel. While this could be true, the Bible and history reveal that some of the most ridiculous actions taken in human history were advised by spouses, parents, brothers or sisters, relatives, friends, co-workers, and partners. Ironically, as I will discuss further, sometimes the most intelligent person you know can provide you with the most ridiculous advice that can cost you a lifetime of work, pain, and loss to recover from — and that is if you survive it and are still alive.

> *"Sometimes the most intelligent person you know can provide you with the most ridiculous advice."*

Sometimes, all you need is wise counsel or advice, not money, and materials because God can provide them via wisdom. Wisdom has the power to transform bad situations into good, and negative values into positive ones.

Some of the powerful kings and rulers of the ancient world were the Pharaohs, the monarchs of ancient Egypt. They even considered themselves to be gods and representatives of the gods. They built pyramids as evidence or statements of their greatness and achievements. They represented themselves in writings and sculptured reliefs on temple walls, and often depicted themselves as warriors who courageously killed many enemies all by themselves and slaughtered a whole group of lions to support their identity as powerful rulers. But it's also believed by some scholars that an unspecified number of these are for publicity purposes to just make these kings look like heroes and respected by their people.

One of these kings, Pharoah, who had a pretty good leadership team according to their standards, which is composed of many others, such as magicians and wise men, had a terrifying dream. We read, "Pharoah had a dream: He was standing by the Nile, when out of the river there came up seven cows, sleek and fat, and they grazed among the reeds. After them, seven other cows, ugly and gaunt, came up out of the Nile and stood beside those on the riverbank. And the cows that were ugly and gaunt ate up the seven sleek, fat cows. Then Pharaoh woke up.

He fell asleep again and had a second dream: Seven heads of grain, healthy and good, were growing on a single stalk. After them, seven other heads of grain sprouted — thin and scorched by the east wind. The thin heads of grain swallowed up the seven healthy, full heads. Then Pharaoh woke up; it had been a dream." (Genesis 41:1-7, NIV).

Understanding that there is only a group of people who can help with his troubling dreams, Pharoah sent for those people; among them were wise men. (Genesis 41:1-8). But as you may know, the people Pharoah considered his wisemen could not interpret his dreams for him. Only Joseph, full of the Spirit of God and the wisdom of God could interpret his dreams. Stop telling everything to everyone. When you tell or share some things with the wrong people, you will get the wrong answers or results. First, Pharaoh did not start telling his dreams to everyone. He knew exactly who to send for – his magicians and wisemen. Second, the people he considered wise in his kingdom were less wise compared to Joseph. Who do you share the things that are troubling you with? Do you share them with the right people who can give you the right answers or with everyone who does not even have the knowledge and wisdom to give you the right advice or answers?

As much as I appreciate social media in our world and all the groups and communities you can join to share ideas and get answers, may I suggest to you that not everyone in those online and offline groups and communities has the same moral values and character as you do? You may easily lose your husband or wife, a potential spouse, money, business, relationships, and many other things because of the wrong advice from those groups. This is not to say that everything is wrong with those groups, but make sure you join the right ones, and double-check every piece of advice you receive from anyone before executing it, or you will regret it sooner or later.

Unfortunately, Pharaoh's magicians and wisemen could not give him answers, because the matter was beyond their wisest minds and power. (Genesis 41:8). But, Pharaoh didn't stop asking for help and answers.

"Then the chief cupbearer said to Pharaoh, "Today I am reminded of my shortcomings. Pharaoh was once angry with his servants, and he imprisoned me and the chief baker in the house of the captain of the guard. Each of us had a dream the same night, and each dream had a meaning of its own. Now a young Hebrew was there with us, a servant of the captain of the guard. We told him our dreams, and he interpreted them for us, giving each man the interpretation of his dream. And things turned out exactly as he interpreted them to us: I was restored to my position, and the other man was impaled."

"So Pharaoh sent for Joseph, and he was quickly brought from the dungeon. When he had shaved and changed his clothes, he came before Pharaoh." (Genesis 41:9-14, NIV)

A Wise Man Versus an Intelligent Woman

Intelligence can cause, or be used to inflict harm, but wisdom always wins. This story could be the other way around because there are also men who use their intelligence to manipulate and abuse women for selfish gains.

FOOLISHNESS | Rashness Clearance

According to the Bible, a few years before Pharaoh had those dreams, a young Hebrew named Joseph, a son of Jacob and Rachel (Genesis 30:25), was sold into slavery in Egypt by his own brothers. (Genesis 37:18-36). Upon arrival in Egypt, he was bought by Potiphar a captain of the palace guard, and became his servant. He quickly rose to a leadership position in the household of his master and everything he did was blessed. In fact, the master was abundantly blessed because of him. (Genesis 39:1-6).

> *"Intelligence can cause, or be used to inflict harm, but wisdom always wins."*

After some time, it was clear Joseph was marked by beauty (good look), intelligence, knowledge, wisdom, morals, and dignity. Everyone started noticing that there was something uncommon about the young man. Then, the test for his wisdom began. The wife of Potiphar got interested in him and wanted him to sleep with her. To the average young man, this might be a great opportunity and way to satisfy his ego and boast about his abilities and achievements. Little did Joseph know that it was the beginning of the test of his wisdom, but he proved to be the wise man who was able to run the household and all the properties of his master Potiphar. The same wisdom he used to lead and make the right decisions in the daily management and governance of his master's affairs, he used it to make the right decision concerning the quest of his master's wife – he refused to sleep with her, even though she repeatedly asked him to do so. The Bible says, "Although Potiphar's wife spoke to Joseph day after day, he refused to go to bed with her or even be near her." (Genesis 39:1)

He added, "My master does not concern himself with anything in the house; everything he owns he has entrusted to my care. No one is greater in this house than I am. My master has withheld nothing from me except you, because you are his wife. How then could I do such a wicked thing and sin against God?" (Genesis 39:8-10, NIV)

Joseph's judgment was right. He was able to apply the knowledge of God's moral laws to that situation and decided not to sacrifice his reputation, respect, peace, position, and life for a temporary sexual gratification by sleeping with his master's wife.

Treacherously, the wife of his master had a plan to lie to her husband and send Joseph to prison. It was her way of revenge because a young man full of wisdom and vision for his life was able to distinguish not only the evil in sleeping with his master's wife, but saw the bigger picture in that betrayal and what could be the long-term consequences of that one or multiple misjudgment and acts of sexual immorality.

One day he went into the house to do his duties, and none of the household servants was inside. His master's wife caught him by his cloak and said, "Come to bed with me!" But he left his cloak in her hand and ran out of the house.

When she saw that he had left his cloak in her hand and had run out of the house, she called her household servants. "Look," she said to them, "this Hebrew has been brought to us to make sport of us! He came in here to sleep with me, but I screamed. When he heard me scream for help, he left his cloak beside me and ran out of the house."

She kept his cloak beside her until his master came home. Then she told him this story: "That Hebrew slave you brought us came to me to make sport of me. But as soon as I screamed for help, he left his cloak beside me and ran out of the house."

When his master heard the story his wife told him, saying, "This is how your slave treated me," he burned with anger. Joseph's master took him and put him in prison, the place where the king's prisoners were confined.

But while Joseph was there in the prison, the Lord was with him; he showed him kindness and granted him favor in the eyes of the prison warden. So the warden put Joseph in charge of all those held in the prison, and he was made responsible for all that was done there. The warden paid no attention to anything under Joseph's care, because the Lord was with Joseph and gave him success in whatever he did.

Sometime later, the cupbearer and the baker of the king of Egypt offended their master, the king of Egypt. Pharaoh was angry with his two officials, the chief cupbearer and the chief baker, and put them in custody in the house of the captain of the guard, in the same prison where Joseph was confined. The captain of the guard assigned them to Joseph, and he attended them.

After they had been in custody for some time, each of the two men — the cupbearer and the baker of the king of Egypt, who were being held in prison had a dream the same night, and each dream had a meaning of its own.

When Joseph came to them the next morning, he saw that they were dejected. So he asked Pharaoh's officials who were in custody with him in his master's house, "Why do you look so sad today?"

"We both had dreams," they answered, "but there is no one to interpret them."

Then Joseph said to them, "Do not interpretations belong to God? Tell me your dreams."

So the chief cupbearer told Joseph his dream. He said to him, "In my dream I saw a vine in front of me, and on the vine were three branches. As soon as it budded, it blossomed, and its clusters ripened into grapes. Pharaoh's cup was in my hand, and I took the grapes, squeezed them into Pharaoh's cup and put the cup in his hand."

"This is what it means," Joseph said to him. "The three branches are three days. Within three days Pharaoh will lift up your head and restore you to your position, and you will put Pharaoh's cup in his hand, just as you used to do when you were his cupbearer. But when all goes well with you, remember me and show me kindness; mention me to Pharaoh and get me out of this prison. I was forcibly carried off from the land of the Hebrews, and even here I have done nothing to deserve being put in a dungeon."

When the chief baker saw that Joseph had given a favorable interpretation, he said to Joseph, "I too had a dream: On my head were three baskets of bread. In the top basket were all kinds of baked goods for Pharaoh, but the birds were eating them out of the basket on my head."

You may have noticed that the baker did not tell Joseph his dream until he realized that he was able to interpret the Cupbearer's dreams first. It was like, "Look, I'm not wasting my breath and time telling this guy (Joseph) my dream until I'm sure he can really interpret dreams." And as soon as Joseph interpreted the Cupbearer's dream, he said to Joseph, "I too had a dream." And he continued to share the dream with Joseph, and Joseph gave him the interpretation.

"This is what it means," Joseph said. "The three baskets are three days. Within three days Pharaoh will lift off your head and impale your body on a pole. And the birds will eat away your flesh."

Now the third day was Pharaoh's birthday, and he gave a feast for all his officials. He lifted up the heads of the chief cupbearer and the chief baker in the presence of his officials: He restored the chief cupbearer to his position, so that he once again put the cup into Pharaoh's hand — but he impaled the chief baker, just as Joseph had said to them in his interpretation.

The chief cupbearer, however, did not remember Joseph; he forgot him. (Genesis 40:1-23).

Wisdom Survives

People may assassinate your character, but not your gifts. And no matter how you try to kill wisdom, it will survive.

Some time had elapsed, notably two years when Joseph was put in jail based on false accusations and after he interpreted the dreams of his fellow prisoners. Everything seemed hopeless. The wife of his master lied about the incident and sent him to jail in revenge expecting he would live the rest of his life and die over there. The fellow he interpreted the dream for and who was restored to normal life has forgotten him. But God did not forget him. He had a plan to not only bring him out, but also make him a leader and put him in a position where he can fully exercise the wisdom he has always made use of from the beginning.

"People may assassinate your character, but not your gifts."

Staying true to the knowledge of your core values and morals guides your decisions because it becomes the foundation of your wisdom.

Little did Joseph know that while he was forgotten by a man he helped, God was giving Pharaoh dreams that only he can interpret. The wisemen of Pharaoh could not interpret the dreams. The Cupbearer remembered Joseph who interpreted their dreams for them in jail two years prior and suggested him to Pharaoh.

The Bible reports, "Then the chief cupbearer said to Pharaoh, "Today I am reminded of my shortcomings. Pharaoh was once angry with his servants, and he imprisoned me and the chief baker in the house of the captain of the guard. Each of us had a dream the same night, and each dream had a meaning of its own. Now a young Hebrew was there with us, a servant of the captain of the guard. We told him our dreams, and he interpreted them for us, giving each man the interpretation of his dream. And things turned out exactly as he interpreted them to us: I was restored to my position, and the other man was impaled."

So Pharaoh sent for Joseph, and he was quickly brought from the dungeon. When he had shaved and changed his clothes, he came before Pharaoh.

Pharaoh said to Joseph, "I had a dream, and no one can interpret it. But I have heard it said of you that when you hear a dream you can interpret it."

"I cannot do it," Joseph replied to Pharaoh, "but God will give Pharaoh the answer he desires."

Then Pharaoh said to Joseph, "In my dream I was standing on the bank of the Nile, when out of the river there came up seven cows, fat and sleek, and they grazed among the reeds. After them, seven other cows came up—scrawny and very ugly and lean. I had never seen such ugly cows in all the land of Egypt. The lean, ugly cows ate up the seven fat cows that came up first. But even after they ate them, no one could tell that they had done so; they looked just as ugly as before. Then I woke up.

"In my dream I saw seven heads of grain, full and good, growing on a single stalk. After them, seven other heads sprouted—withered and thin and scorched by the east wind. The thin heads of grain swallowed up the seven good heads. I told this to the magicians, but none of them could explain it to me."

Then Joseph said to Pharaoh, "The dreams of Pharaoh are one and the same. God has revealed to Pharaoh what he is about to do. The seven good cows are seven years, and the seven good heads of grain are seven years; it is one and the same dream. The seven lean, ugly cows that came up afterward are seven years, and so are the seven worthless heads of grain scorched by the east wind: They are seven years of famine.

"It is just as I said to Pharaoh: God has shown Pharaoh what he is about to do. Seven years of great abundance are coming throughout the land of Egypt, but seven years of famine will follow them. Then all the abundance in Egypt will be forgotten, and the famine will ravage the land. The abundance in the land will not be remembered, because the famine that follows it will be so severe. The reason the dream was given to Pharaoh in two forms is that the matter has been firmly decided by God, and God will do it soon.

"And now let Pharaoh look for a discerning and wise man and put him in charge of the land of Egypt. Let Pharaoh appoint commissioners over the land to take a fifth of the harvest of Egypt during the seven years of abundance. They should collect all the food of these good years that are coming and store up the grain under the authority of Pharaoh, to be kept in the cities for food. This food should be held in reserve for the country, to be used during the seven years of famine that will come upon Egypt, so that the country may not be ruined by the famine."

The plan seemed good to Pharaoh and to all his officials. So Pharaoh asked them, "Can we find anyone like this man, one in whom is the spirit of God?"

Then Pharaoh said to Joseph, "Since God has made all this known to you, there is no one so discerning and wise as you. You shall be in charge of my palace, and all my people are to submit to your orders. Only with respect to the throne will I be greater than you."

So Pharaoh said to Joseph, "I hereby put you in charge of the whole land of Egypt." Then Pharaoh took his signet ring from his finger and put it on Joseph's finger. He dressed him in robes of fine linen and put a gold chain around his neck. He had him ride in a chariot as his second-in-command, and people shouted before him, "Make way!" Thus he put him in charge of the whole land of Egypt.

Then Pharaoh said to Joseph, "I am Pharaoh, but without your word no one will lift hand or foot in all Egypt." Pharaoh gave Joseph the name Zaphenath-Paneah and gave him Asenath daughter of Potiphera, priest of On, to be his wife. And Joseph went throughout the land of Egypt.
Joseph was thirty years old when he entered the service of Pharaoh king of Egypt. And Joseph went out from Pharaoh's presence and traveled throughout Egypt. During the seven years of abundance the land produced plentifully. Joseph collected all the food produced in those seven years

of abundance in Egypt and stored it in the cities. In each city he put the food grown in the fields surrounding it. 49 Joseph stored up huge quantities of grain, like the sand of the sea; it was so much that he stopped keeping records because it was beyond measure.

Before the years of famine came, two sons were born to Joseph by Asenath daughter of Potiphera, priest of On. Joseph named his firstborn Manasseh and said, "It is because God has made me forget all my trouble and all my father's household." The second son he named Ephraim and said, "It is because God has made me fruitful in the land of my suffering."

The seven years of abundance in Egypt came to an end, and the seven years of famine began, just as Joseph had said. There was famine in all the other lands, but in the whole land of Egypt there was food. When all Egypt began to feel the famine, the people cried to Pharaoh for food. Then Pharaoh told all the Egyptians, "Go to Joseph and do what he tells you."

When the famine had spread over the whole country, Joseph opened all the storehouses and sold grain to the Egyptians, for the famine was severe throughout Egypt. And all the world came to Egypt to buy grain from Joseph, because the famine was severe everywhere." (Genesis 41:9-57).

The wisdom and discernment of Joseph to make the right decisions saved him from sexual immorality that could have destroyed his purpose and destiny, and a whole country and the neighboring inhabitants from famine, death, and destruction. Later, his own family would come to Egypt for food to survive the feminine his right decision-making prevented Egypt to experience. (Genesis Chapters 42-47).

Even though it looks like it, your decisions do not only affect you, no matter how insignificant and personal you think they are, they will affect everyone connected to you sooner or later. Sometimes, even when you are gone from the earth or this world.

While Egypt had food to survive the famine, other parts of the world suffered from it because of lack of wisdom. The truth may be that just as God gave the dreams to Pharaoh, he may have given them to other kings and leaders in different parts of the world during that time, but they could not do anything about it. Fortunately, because of the wisdom of a young man named Joseph to make the right decisions – Egypt was saved. Joseph helped the Pharaoh to make the right decisions to navigate even difficult moments in the history of a country.

The Prayer of Solomon

One of our problems today is that we seek pleasure and related things instead of essential and fundamental things on which we can build our lives, and experience peace, health, happiness, prosperity, stability, and security. Before anything, we tend to think about money, big house, the latest luxury car, dresses, and accessories — And nothing is wrong with the aforementioned things. But there are other necessary things that have the power to bring peaceful, good, safe, and lasting pleasures in our lives if we choose to have them first or instead. It is like the old saying, "Putting the cart before the horse" which suggests that everything in life has a place or should be in a particular order. There are certain things one should yearn for in life above all, because when you have these things, they easily bring others into your life without pain and heartbreak, and one of them is wisdom.

> *"We seek pleasure and related things instead of essential and fundamental things."*

Even though it is unconfirmed, traditionally, it is believed that Solomon became king when he was twelve or fourteen years old. There have been many discussions about the actual or approximate age of Solomon when he ascended to the throne as king because of other factors that are notable to consider, including the time he died, the age of his son Rehoboam, who succeeded him at the time he died (I Kings 11:42-43), the proper age for marriage at the time, which is around eighteen.

Personally, after putting many factors together, I also believe he was young when he ascended to the throne, but not at the age of twelve or fourteen. He might be a little older than twelve or fourteen, and I would agree with scholars and historians who believe he was around twenty (20) years old.

Nevertheless, what is true according to the records of the Bible is that Solomon became king at a young age as a promise his father David made to his mother Bathsheba, or according to the choice of the LORD Himself. (1 Kings 1:28-53). King David's own words confirm Solomon was young, and I quote, **"Then King David said to the whole assembly:**

"My son Solomon, the one whom God has chosen, is young and inexperienced." (1 Chronicle 29:1, NIV).

After Solomon became King, he invited all the people, "the commanders of thousands and commanders of hundreds, the judges and all the leaders, the heads of families — and Solomon and the whole assembly went to the high place at Gibeon, for God's tent of meeting was there, which Moses the Lord's servant had made in the wilderness -- So Solomon and the assembly inquired of him there. Solomon went up to the bronze altar before the Lord in the tent of meeting and offered a thousand burnt offerings on it." (2 Chronicles 1:1-6).

The Bible says, ***"That night God appeared to Solomon and said to him, "Ask for whatever you want me to give you."*** (2 Chronicles 1:7, NIV).

One may argue that Solomon did not need anything because his father King David left him with everything he needed. While this is true, there is also another truth that demands our attention. Enough, has never been enough for a human being, especially considering the era in which Solomon became king, when there were no advanced technologies and scientific discoveries, even in our ages — there is always a need for help with one thing or the other for a king. Moreover, some of the things that have been so important to us in our world today have also been important to the people who lived at that time. If there are no similarities between our current needs and theirs, at least things like health, longevity, peace, happiness, stability, and security are important at every point of time in history. Therefore, if Solomon could not ask for other things, because his father, King David already provided them for him, and he had enough of things that were necessary to him, he could have asked for health, longevity, peace, happiness, stability, and security in expectation of preserving what he already had. But surprisingly, he asked something else: *"Give me wisdom and knowledge"*, he replied. (2 Chronicles 1:10, NIV). Solomon asked for wisdom and knowledge to lead and govern.

"God said to Solomon, *"Since this is your heart's desire and you have not asked for wealth, possessions, or honor, nor for the death of your enemies, and since you have not asked for a long life but for wisdom and knowledge to govern my people over whom I have made you king, therefore wisdom and knowledge will be given you. And I will also give you wealth, possessions, and honor, such as no king who was before you ever had and none after you will have."* (2 Chronicles 1:11-12, NIV).

Solomon was not the only young man who ascended to a throne. In fact, some were even younger than he was when they became kings. Josiah was eight (8) years old when he became king. (2 Chronicles 34:1). Joash was seven (7) years old when he became king. (2 Chronicles 24:1, 2 Kings 12:1).
I wonder if Solomon was not wise before he prayed or asked God to grant him wisdom. The fact that he knew what he needed primarily tells me he was already wise. But when he prayed to God to grant him wisdom, his wisdom increased. This leads me to also believe that wisdom can increase in someone's life.

Wisdom Demonstrated

King Solomon was known throughout the world in ancient days for his wisdom, people, including kings and queens came to Israel to just glean from his wisdom; and still honored throughout our world today, even by non-Christians for his wisdom. He was considered the author of several biblical books, including the collections of Proverbs, Ecclesiastes, and Song of Solomon.

Arguably, the most powerful yet, humble demonstration of King Solomon's wisdom is found in 1 Kings 3:16-28, the story of his wise judgment between two women. This really reveals the essence or properties of wisdom.

You may already know the story but let us refresh it in our minds so we can clearly get what we need from it. We read from the Bible:

"Now two prostitutes came to the king and stood before him. One of them said, "Pardon me, my lord. This woman and I live in the same house, and I had a baby while she was there with me. The third day after my child was born, this woman also had a baby. We were alone; there was no one in the house but the two of us.

"During the night this woman's son died because she lay on him. So she got up in the middle of the night and took my son from my side while I your servant was asleep. She put him by her breast and put her dead son by my breast. The next morning, I got up to nurse my son – and he was dead! But when I looked at him closely in the morning light, I saw that it wasn't the son I had borne."

The other woman said, "No! The living one is my son; the dead one is yours."

But the first one insisted, "No! The dead one is yours; the living one is mine." And so they argued before the king.
The king said, "This one says, 'My son is alive and your son is dead,' while that one says, 'No! Your son is dead and mine is alive.'"

Then the king said, "Bring me a sword." So they brought a sword for the king. 25 He then gave an order: "Cut the living child in two and give half to one and half to the other."
The woman whose son was alive was deeply moved out of love for her son and said to the king, "Please, my lord, give her the living baby! Don't kill him!"

But the other said, "Neither I nor you shall have him. Cut him in two!"

Then the king gave his ruling: "Give the living baby to the first woman. Do not kill him; she is his mother."

When all Israel heard the verdict the king had given, they held the king in awe, because they saw that he had wisdom from God to administer justice." (1 Kings 3:16-28).

Absalom: The Aspiring King

Absalom was the son of King David and wished to become the successor of his father. There is nothing wrong about aspiring to become a king or leader one day or soon. There is nothing wrong with dreaming to become great, successful, or a public figure. There is nothing wrong about dreaming to become a president, prime minister, mayor, doctor, lawyer, judge, artist, athlete, or holding a public office in the future. But what matters is how you become one. The way you ascend to power or positions, get this or that job, and become this or that person in public, business, government, or leadership matters a lot and says a lot about who you really are, your character, and your heart.

Absalom the son of David wanted to become a King and would do anything, including trying to overthrow his own father, King David in order to become a King he so wanted to be.

Long story short, he noticed Solomon would be selected by his father instead of him. So, he set out to overthrow David, his father from the throne before he even announced his successor sooner or later.

The Bible accounts that "In the course of time, Absalom provided himself with a chariot and horses and with fifty men to run ahead of him. He would get up early and stand by the side of the road leading to the city gate. Whenever anyone came with a complaint to be placed before the king for a decision, Absalom would call out to him, "What town are you from?" He would answer, "Your servant is from one of the tribes of Israel." Then Absalom would say to him, "Look, your claims are valid and proper, but there is no representative of the king to hear you." And Absalom would add, "If only I were appointed judge in the land! Then everyone who has a complaint or case could come to me and I would see that they receive justice."

Also, whenever anyone approached him to bow down before him, Absalom would reach out his hand, take hold of him and kiss him. Absalom behaved in this way toward all the Israelites who came to the king asking for justice, and so he stole the hearts of the people of Israel.

At the end of four years, Absalom said to the king (David, his father), "Let me go to Hebron and fulfill a vow I made to the Lord. While your servant was living at Geshur in Aram, I made this vow: 'If the Lord takes me back to Jerusalem, I will worship the Lord in Hebron.'"

"The king said to him, "Go in peace." So he went to Hebron. Then Absalom sent secret messengers throughout the tribes of Israel to say, "As soon as you hear the sound of the trumpets, then say, 'Absalom is king in Hebron.'" Two hundred men from Jerusalem had accompanied Absalom.

They had been invited as guests and went quite innocently, knowing nothing about the matter. While Absalom was offering sacrifices, he also sent for Ahithophel the Gilonite, David's counselor, to come from Giloh, his hometown. And so the conspiracy gained strength, and Absalom's following kept on increasing." (2 Samuel 15:1-10, NIV).

The Prayer of David

At that moment, a messenger reached King David with the news that Absalom, his son had captured the heart of the people of Israel. King David could have decided to fight the rebels, instigated by his own son. After all, he's David, the man who killed giants and ferocious animals. His mighty men were even tougher. But he decided not to fight his own son and army. So, he went on the run. During his journey to exit the Kingdom God made him King over, and David received one of the worst news in his life: Ahithophel, his own advisor, whom without doubt David knew was full of wisdom, joined his son and the rebels. He was so devastated and much afraid of the man's wisdom, so much so that he prayed one of the most powerful prayers in his life, *"Lord, turn Ahithophel's counsel into foolishness."* (2 Samuel 15:31). Meaning, whatever Ahithophel, the wise man will advice the son, which he knew would have been the best advice, would be discarded by the King's counsel as foolishness. David knew he would have never survived the coup of his own son as long as Ahithophel was one of his counselors. It is recorded that *"In those days the advice Ahithophel gave was like that of one who inquires of God. That was how both David and Absalom regarded all of Ahithophel's advice."* (2 Samuel 16:23, NIV).

David went further to make one of the best decisions he has ever made in his life: He strategically sent back Hushai, one of his confidants to Jerusalem so he could work for his son, the new king, in order to prevent any plan or attempted action against David and his people from being accepted, progressing, succeeding, or being fulfilled. The Bible says, "When David arrived at the summit, where people used to worship God, Hushai the Arkite was there to meet him, his robe torn and dust on his head. David said to him, "If you go with me, you will be a burden to me. But if you return to the city and say to Absalom, 'Your Majesty, I will be your servant; I was your father's servant in the past, but now I will be your servant,' then you can help me by frustrating Ahithophel's advice. Won't the priests Zadok and Abiathar be there with you? Tell them anything you hear in the king's palace. Their two sons, Ahimaaz, son of Zadok, and Jonathan, son of Abiathar, are there with them. Send them to me with anything you hear.

So Hushai, David's confidant, arrived at Jerusalem as Absalom was entering the city." (2 Samuel 15:32-37).

When David ran away from his own son, Absalom, the Bible says, "Ziba, the steward of Mephibosheth, was waiting to meet him. He had a string of donkeys saddled and loaded with two hundred loaves of bread, a hundred cakes of raisins, a hundred cakes of figs and a skin of wine.
The king asked Ziba, "Why have you brought these?"

Ziba answered, "The donkeys are for the king's household to ride on, the bread and fruit are for the men to eat, and the wine is to refresh those who become exhausted in the wilderness."

The king then asked, "Where is your master's grandson?"

Ziba said to him, "He is staying in Jerusalem, because he thinks, 'Today the Israelites will restore to me my grandfather's kingdom.'"

Then the king said to Ziba, "All that belonged to Mephibosheth is now yours."

"I humbly bow," Ziba said. "May I find favor in your eyes, my lord the king." (2 Samuel 16:1-4).

This Mephibosheth was the son of Johnathan, son of King Saul, whom David ordered Ziba and all the members of his household to servants of Mephibosheth and was eating at the table of King David as a reward of his friendship to his father Jonathan. (2 Samuel 9:1-12). He now sees David being chased out of his palace by his own son for no justified reason and actually rejoiced over that, and expected the kingdom to be restored to him — Citing, "My grandfather's kingdom." He thought David was never returning to reign, so his real identity and foolishness surfaced; he was glad for the downfall of someone who had helped him, a king who let him eat at his table daily. But as you may know, the end of the story, David's wisdom and decisions prevailed, Absalom his son who was leading a coup against his father died, and King David was restored to the throne.

Keep in mind that the good you do for people does not guarantee your protection from them. There are ungrateful people in this world who would not consider how good you have been to them. Therefore, you should always consider your good deeds as a one-way or non-returnable service to others. Of course, there are good people who will remember your good deeds and do whatever it takes to also treat you well, but only a few do. It is troubling to notice that even while King David was running for his own life, he was still asking about Mephibosheth from Ziba, the servant he ordered to take care of him. But at the same time, the person (Mephiboshet) King David was concerned about his well-being, even in distress, was rejoicing over his downfall. Can you imagine that?

Never consider the downfall of people as an opportunity for you to reign; especially if they are unjustly facing troubles. God can restore them. Falls are not the end of people lives, purposes, and destinies. God can restore them to goodness if they were wrong or made a mistake, but obey and repent, even in their lowest level in life.

> *"Keep in mind that the good you do for people does not guarantee your protection from them."*

After all, David did not unjustly ascend to the throne. God chose him. (1 Samuel 16:1-23). And as you can notice, out of foolishness, Mephiboshet lost everything David willingly and favorably gave him as a friend of his father. Mephiboshet did not do anything to deserve the love and care David offered him. But he did it because of the friendship he had with his father, Jonathan.

David's decisions during his crisis teach us a few truths: First, not every battle is worth fighting. He was a man of war and could have decided to fight against his son, which he might have easily won with his mighty men, but he decided not to do so. And I believe because he analyzed and imagined what that war could have cost to the people of Israel. So, out of selflessness, he decided to let time and God work things out. Second, he left one of his confidants behind to help keep things under control. The lesson here is that, you should never leave the "Kingdom", and in your case, business, ministry, or office without not having a "confidant", a man of integrity who can be honest with you, and loyal to your God-given calling and vision.

"Not every battle is worth fighting."

The Battle of Wisdom

When David left behind Hushai, one of his confidants who was also a wise man, it threw the King's palace into a battle of wisdom. There was Ahithophel, whom David and his son Absalom knew was very wise, and he was David's advisor, who betrayed him and became loyal to his son. And Hushai, another wise man who remained loyal to David but agreed to stay behind to frustrate the wise advice of Ahithophel upon David's request. Notably, there must have been a war of wisdom. But the Bible only talks about two (2) major advice that Ahithophel gave Absalom to destroy his relationship with his father, David and gain the hearts or trust of the people of Israel. And another advice is to overtake his father, have him killed, and bring his followers back to serve him, the son.

"Absalom said to Ahithophel, "Give us your advice. What should we do?"

Ahithophel answered, "Sleep with your father's concubines whom he left to take care of the palace. Then all Israel will hear that you have made yourself obnoxious to your father, and the hands of everyone with you will be more resolute." So, they pitched a tent for Absalom on the roof, and he slept with his father's concubines in the sight of all Israel. (2 Samuel 16:20-21). Apparently, Hushai, the wise man, and confidant of King David who returned to the palace to secretly work on behalf of David in his son's government did not find that advice to be too destructive to David. After all, they were David's concubines and not wives. It was immoral, but not physically destructive to King David. He could dismiss the concubines once he returned, which was a normal thing Kings do at the time, and when polygamy was not discouraged under the law God gave to Moses in the Old Testament.

Following that, Ahithophel the wise man who was working against King David advised, "I would choose twelve thousand men and set out tonight in pursuit of David. I would attack him while he is weary and weak. I would strike him with terror, and then all the people with him will flee. I would strike down only the king and bring all the people back to you. The death of the man you seek will mean the return of all; all the people will be unharmed." This plan seemed good to Absalom and to all the elders of Israel.

But Absalom said, "Summon also Hushai the Arkite, so we can hear what he has to say as well." When Hushai came to him, Absalom said, "Ahithophel has given this advice. Should we do what he says? If not, give us your opinion."

Then Hushai the wise man working on behalf of David replied to Absalom, "The advice Ahithophel has given is not good this time. You know your father and his men; they are fighters, and as fierce as a wild bear robbed of her cubs. Besides, your father is an experienced fighter; he will not spend the night with the troops. Even now, he is hidden in a cave or some other place. If he should attack your troops first, whoever hears about it will say, 'There has been a slaughter among the troops who follow Absalom.' Then even the bravest soldier, whose heart is like the heart of a lion, will melt with fear, for all Israel knows that your father is a fighter and that those with him are brave.

"So I advise you: Let all Israel, from Dan to Beersheba — as numerous as the sand on the seashore — be gathered to you, with you yourself leading them into battle. Then we will attack him wherever he may be found, and we will fall on him as dew settles on the ground. Neither he nor any of his men will be left alive. If he withdraws into a city, then all Israel will bring ropes to that city, and we will drag it down to the valley until not so much as a pebble is left."

Absalom and all the men of Israel said, "The advice of Hushai the Arkite is better than that of Ahithophel." For the Lord had determined to frustrate the good advice of Ahithophel in order to bring disaster on Absalom.

Hushai told Zadok and Abiathar, the priests, "Ahithophel has advised Absalom and the elders of Israel to do such and such, but I have advised them to do so and so. Now send a message at once and tell David, 'Do not spend the night at the fords in the wilderness; cross over without fail, or the king and all the people with him will be swallowed up.'"

Jonathan and Ahimaaz were staying at En Rogel. A female servant was to go and inform them, and they were to go and tell King David, for they could not risk being seen entering the city. But a young man saw them and told Absalom. So the two of them left at once and went to the house of a man in Bahurim. He had a well in his courtyard, and they climbed down into it. His wife took a covering and spread it out over the opening of the well and scattered grain over it. No one knew anything about it.

When Absalom's men came to the woman at the house, they asked, "Where are Ahimaaz and Jonathan?"

The woman answered them, "They crossed over the brook." The men searched but found no one, so they returned to Jerusalem.

After they had gone, the two climbed out of the well and went to inform King David. They said to him, "Set out and cross the river at once; Ahithophel has advised such and such against you." So David and all the people with him set out and crossed the Jordan. By daybreak, no one was left who had not crossed the Jordan.

When Ahithophel saw that his advice had not been followed, he saddled his donkey and set out for his house in his hometown. He put his house in order and then hanged himself. So he died and was buried in his father's tomb." (2 Samuel 17:1-23, NIV).

Remember, this Ahithophel was a member of King David's counsel. But, as soon as David's position as the King became shaky, he easily forgot and changed his mind about him. Do not be surprised when people you consider as your closest friends, allies, teammates, or partners change their minds and follow others because your position or social status has changed. And keep in mind that not everyone will remain with you, or will be supporting you when things do not go the right ways they expected. So, you have to plan and always know that anybody can leave your support circle at anytime.

I believe you may have noticed that Ahithophel's advice was to surprise David and his people in the night, kill only him, and bring the rest of the people to come and serve Absalom, his son. But Hushai counterattacked that advice by offering another advice, which would have also led to Absalom being in the front of the battle against his father's mighty men who would kill him alone, and the rest of the people and the Kingdom should be restored to David, his father. Hushai's counter-advice won by God's grace, and it was not the right one in favor of Absalom. God made all the people supporting Absalom believe in the counter-advice and executed it instead. Surely, the LORD heard and granted David's prayer, and Ahithophel's advice was turned into foolishness, leading to the death of Absalom and the throne and Kingdom being restored to David.

The Bible says, "David mustered the men who were with him and appointed over them commanders of thousands and commanders of hundreds. David sent out his troops, a third under the command of Joab, a third under Joab's brother Abishai son of Zeruiah, and a third under Ittai the Gittite. The king told the troops, "I myself will surely march out with you."

But the men said, "You must not go out; if we are forced to flee, they won't care about us. Even if half of us die, they won't care; but you are worth ten thousand of us. It would be better now for you to give us support from the city."

The king answered, "I will do whatever seems best to you."

So the king stood beside the gate while all his men marched out in units of hundreds and of thousands. The king commanded Joab, Abishai and Ittai, "Be gentle with the young man Absalom for my sake." And all the troops heard the king giving orders concerning Absalom to each of the commanders.

David's army marched out of the city to fight Israel, and the battle took place in the forest of Ephraim. There Israel's troops were routed by David's men, and the casualties that day were great — twenty thousand men. The battle spread out over the whole countryside, and the forest swallowed up more men that day than the sword.

Now Absalom happened to meet David's men. He was riding his mule, and as the mule went under the thick branches of a large oak, Absalom's hair got caught in the tree. He was left hanging in midair, while the mule he was riding kept on going.

When one of the men saw what had happened, he told Joab, "I just saw Absalom hanging in an oak tree."
Joab said to the man who had told him this, "What! You saw him? Why didn't you strike him to the ground right there? Then I would have had to give you ten shekels of silver and a warrior's belt."

But the man replied, "Even if a thousand shekels[c] were weighed out into my hands, I would not lay a hand on the king's son. In our hearing the king commanded you and Abishai and Ittai, 'Protect the young man Absalom for my sake.' And if I had put my life in jeopardy — and nothing is hidden from the king — you would have kept your distance from me."

Joab said, "I'm not going to wait like this for you." So he took three javelins in his hand and plunged them into Absalom's heart while Absalom was still alive in the oak tree. And ten of Joab's armor-bearers surrounded Absalom, struck him and killed him.

Then Joab sounded the trumpet, and the troops stopped pursuing Israel, for Joab halted them. They took Absalom, threw him into a big pit in the forest and piled up a large heap of rocks over him. Meanwhile, all the Israelites fled to their homes.

During his lifetime Absalom had taken a pillar and erected it in the King's Valley as a monument to himself, for he thought, "I have no son to carry on the memory of my name." He named the pillar after himself, and it is called Absalom's Monument to this day." (2 Samuel 18:1-18, NIV).

I suggest that you keep in mind that the same people who are praising you now can turn over on you in the next moment or at any time. It is difficult to believe that, I know. But the history of humanity has revealed this truth several times. It is unbelievable that the same people who praised and danced when David killed Goliath and made him King (1 Samuel 18:6-18, 2 Samuel 5:1-25) are the same people who turned against him and supported his son's cause and were ready to fight and kill him for a very unjust reason (a son who wanted to become a King so bad that he wanted to overthrow and kill his father). Remember, the same thing happened to the Lord, the same people who ate the bread and fish he provided to them and wanted to make him their King, turned against him and shouted for His crucifixion (Matthew 14:13-21, John 6:15, Matthew 27:22-23). Trusting humans with all your heart is a dangerous thing.

> *"Trusting humans with all your heart is a dangerous thing."*

Intelligence Voided of Wisdom

Knowledge and intelligence without wisdom becomes dangerous. That is why you may know educated, intelligent and eminent people who make stupid decisions, and do things they thought can never be caught, and without not considering all the realities or facts surrounding their decisions and actions.

Because intelligence is only the ability to acquire and apply knowledge and skills. And though someone may have been able to gather knowledge and intelligence, that does not automatically make the latter wise.

Know this, and watch yourself about it, intelligence is not wisdom. And this reality tends to be ignored by many

> ***"Knowledge and intelligence without wisdom becomes dangerous."***

who think they are intelligent and never double-check their thoughts, decisions, and plans with wisdom before acting on it. Before you decide and act on any of your thoughts, or intelligence, ask yourself, where is the wisdom in it? Wisdom is a positive questioner, and not a doubter or lack of faith, because questions lead to information, discoveries, and preparations.

Intelligence and knowledge may tell you, "Now that is smart, no one will ever know." "You know you are smart." "Just do it for the first and last time." "You were able to get away with it several times." "Get that money." "Sleep with or rape that woman." "Kill that person." "That is a short cut." "You do not have to wait." "Why endure all these while you can just cheat." Wisdom would ask, "What will be the end results, a few minutes, hours, days, months, or years from now, after getting what I want, the pleasure, satisfaction, fame, money, position?"

Intelligence has been interpreted as the understanding, capacity for logic, self-awareness, learning, emotional knowledge, reasoning, planning, creativity, critical thinking, and problem-solving. Note, "Understanding for logic." So, your understanding of logic is different from the "Understanding," which is discernment and good judgment that equals wisdom, or wisdom provides you. This only confirms the truth that no matter how much understanding of logic, self-awareness, information, and knowledge you have in addition to your intelligence, planning, creativity, and problem-solving capacity and skills you have, it does not necessarily equate to wisdom, and you always need conscious thought and serious attention to analyze things with wisdom before deciding.

Even though knowledge and understanding can be considered as some of the properties of wisdom, they are not wisdom, and can make one proud, arrogant and lead to blind self-assurance and self-sufficiency that can be disastrous in decision-making. The skills you acquire through experience or education, the theoretical or practical understanding of any subject can create facts, and information, which is knowledge. But it is not wisdom, and you need wisdom to properly use it. And if you let your knowledge make you feel like you know it all, it can also be disastrous to your decision-making. Use your knowledge in your decision-making, but rely on a higher and more accurate discernment instead of just your knowledge.

You may philosophically justify your belief and certain understanding and gain some familiarity and awareness by the experience of some situations, but wisdom requires that you approach each belief, understanding, and situation as different in order to force your awareness to reset and refresh to handle every decision-making process properly. This helps you avoid the surprise of making decisions about things that look familiar but are actually different in essence before you realize that you made a mistake.

> *"Force your awareness to reset and refresh to handle every decision-making process properly."*

It may be unusual or exceptional, but your familiarity, awareness, or understanding of someone or something, which you obtained in different ways and from many sources, including but not only from perception, reason, memory, testimony, education, scientific examination, and practice, can change. Hence, it's important to approach every decision-making as new and standalone so you do not leave room for error.

Some of the world-known criminals and evil people were actually very intelligent. But when you think about their crimes and the horrors they inflicted on people, themselves, society, and the world, you can clearly notice that they were not wise. They never thought about what could happen, or the consequences of their actions, which would have surely been revealed sooner or later, and the fact that they think they are invincible.

Just like in ancient days, people have a misconception of wisdom in our current world. Wisdom is not malice or manipulation. Trying to influence the behavior or perception of others personally or socially through indirect, deceptive, or dishonest schemes and advancing your interests as a manipulator at the expense of others is not wisdom; it is exploitation and deviousness. It will become a shame and disgrace on you when it comes to revelation, and it surely does come to light sooner or later. Do not unjustly outsmart or take advantage of people. If you are wise, then you know it is a seed you are planting, and one day you will harvest it. The Bible says, "Don't be misled—you cannot mock the justice of God. You will always harvest what you plant." (Galatians 6:7, NLT).

> *"Wisdom is not malice or manipulation."*

A Corrupted Wisdom

A corrupted wisdom is just as foolishness. A corrupted wisdom is when wisdom is deviated to serve evil purposes. Ahithophel was in the counsel of King David and served him as a counselor. But when Absalom rebelled and chased his father out of the palace, he decided to use his wisdom for evil. If you consider a few things, you will realize that his decision came out of envy, jealousy, and pride – He thought David could not have made it without him. Note this, and never think anyone cannot make it without you. If God chose you to be someone's helper and you refused to do it or for one reason or another, you choose not to do what you are supposed to do, especially if the person is in the right or has not done anything wrong to you, God will surely use another person to fulfill his plans. While he thought David could not have made it without his wisdom, David eventually returned to his palace by the grace of God, and he ended up hanging himself and died. (2 Samuel 17:23).

A wise man uses his intelligence for good, and a fool uses his intelligence to destroy people and himself.

> *"A wise man uses his intelligence for good, and a fool uses his intelligence to destroy people and himself."*

Adolf Hitler and the 1000-year Reich

No destroyer is left undestroyed. No human can win a war against God, morality, and unjustly against humanity. Whenever you find yourself fighting or in any battle or war, ask yourself, "Who am I fighting, and what am I fighting for?" It is important that you ask yourself those questions because if your fight is against God, or the plan of God, and unjustly motivated against another human, you will surely fail sooner or later and be destroyed. Do not be fooled by your earlier successes when you are wrongfully fighting another human; it is just a matter of time before your downfall comes swiftly. The Bible says, "You will hear the cries of the oppressed and the orphans; you will judge in their favor, so that mortal men may cause terror no more." (Psalm 10:18, GNT).

> *"No destroyer is left undestroyed. No human can win a war against God, morality, and unjustly against humanity."*

Adolf Hitler was born on April 20th, 1889 and died, notably committed suicide on April 30th, 1945 by swallowing a cyanide capsule and shooting himself in the head. Eight (8) days later, Germany unconditionally surrendered to the Allied forces, putting an end to Adolf Hitler's vision or dream of a 1,000-year Reich or Empire.

Hitler was a German politician who was the leader of the Nazi Party, Chancellor of Germany from 1933 till the time he died in 1945, and Leader of Nazi Germany from 1934 to 1945. The dictator started World War II in Europe with the invasion of Poland in September 1939 and was the instigator of the Holocaust.

In short, Hitler's vision was to resurrect a dead Empire, The Holy Roman Empire or, in German, Heiliges Römisches Reich. His dream was to have a third Holy Roman Empire, which would last or stay in power for another thousand (1000) year. In all historical accounts, even the Second Reich or Holy Roman Empire lasted from 1871 to 1918.

What is very notable to me is that, at the time Hitler was trying to re-establish The Holy Roman Empire by World War II; I personally believe it was impossible for him to reach that vision regardless of the weaknesses of the countries he was invading. I know many historians suggested if this or that were to play in his favor, he would have won the war — I do not think so. His decision was foolish all the way from the beginning. But thank God also that the Allied Forces made the right decisions to stop a fool or madman from causing so much destruction to humanity and many other countries, including the Jews.

Before we move forward, what was The Holy Roman Empire? Someone who does not know may ask. The Holy Roman Empire Hitler envisioned re-establishing a multi-ethnic territory in Western and Central Europe that emerged during the Early Middle Ages and existed until its dissolution in 1806 during the Napoleonic Wars or when Francis II abdicated, following a military defeat by the French led by Napoleon Bonaparte.

When Otto I (Known as Otto the Great, the German king from 936 and Holy Roman Emperor from 962 until he died in 973) was crowned Emperor, the largest territory of the empire was the Kingdom of Germany. However, it also included the bordering Kingdom of Bohemia, the Kingdom of Italy, and many other territories; subsequently, the Kingdom of Burgundy was added, but later it was lost to France. In effect, by the end of the 15th century, the Empire was still constituted of three major territories: Italy, Germany, and Burgundy. Realistically, only the Kingdom of Germany remained, as the Burgundian territories were lost to France. The Italian territories, which were officially part of the empire, were disregarded in the Imperial Reform and broken into many independent territorial entities. At the end of the Napoleonic Wars (A series of major wars setting the French Empire and its allies, led by Napoleon I, against unstable European powers, formed into many confederacies) in 1815, most of the Holy Roman Empire was included in the German Confederation, except the Italian states.

Pope Leo III crowned the Frankish king Charlemagne as Emperor on December 25th, 800, and this action revived the title of Emperor in Western Europe, which was nonexistent for more than three centuries after the collapse of the earlier ancient Western Roman Empire in 476. It is to be noted that the Emperors at the time were considered "primus inter pares" (first among equals, who is the presiding bishop), meaning, they were regarded as first among equals among other Roman Catholic monarchs in Europe.

The relationship between the Holy Roman Empire and the Jews was not a good one. Some of the Emperors massacred them at the will of the people, and the ones who claimed to be their protectors found other ways to oppress them, such as taxation and other dubious ways.

There is no doubt that Hitler's vision was to become an Emperor, a world leader who also hated the Jews just as they were hated and maltreated by the Holy Roman Empires and the Crusaders (A series of religious wars believed to be launched, supported, and directed by the Roman Catholic Church in the Middle Ages against Islam and other religious groups). Nevertheless, his wish did not come true. He was stopped by the Allied Forces. And on April 30th, 1945, hiding in a bunker under his headquarters in Berlin, he committed suicide by swallowing a cyanide capsule and shooting himself in the head. His dream of becoming an Emperor at the cost of the blood of innocent human beings was crushed.

There is no doubt that Hitler was an intelligent individual, but when intelligence and knowledge is voided of wisdom, you make the wrong decisions and think you are above everybody, and invincible. Only the fool thinks he is invincible — especially when doing wrong against fellow human beings and violating God's moral laws.

When the Right Decisions Meet the Wrong Ones

When the right decisions meet the wrong ones, the right decisions simply win. We must also notice that Hitler's defeat, among many factors, including the supernatural working power of God, was determined by the decisions of the Allied countries, specifically their leaders and the main ones, which included the so-called "Big Three" central Allies, British's Prime Minister Winston Churchill, United

States President Franklin Roosevelt, and Soviet Union's General Secretary Joseph Stalin.

Hitler lost the war partly because not only did he make the wrong decision to go to war against the world, but also because many of his decisions throughout the whole war were not the right ones, including the timing of the start. Some historians believe had he waited a few years later before launching the war, that would have allowed him to be well prepared and develop some of the most powerful weapons the world had ever known to destroy his enemies. But he chose to prematurely start the war. Make no mistake, Hitler had some of the most intelligent and experienced scientists and engineers working on his weapons. We may say his bad decisions were also orchestrated by God to cause his downfall. But yes, he was not a wise man or leader. Wisemen know the importance of timing in everything they do. When you launch things prematurely without preparations, one thing is certain, you are just setting yourself up for failure.

> *"Wisemen know the importance of timing in everything they do."*

The Necessity of Preparation

If you carefully analyze different historical accounts, it is clear that Hitler had the drive and a dream to become an Emperor, world leader, and knew how to launch a war, but did not know how to be prepared, which also contributed to his loss. On the other hand, Winston Churchill, the former Prime Minister of the United Kingdom during the war, knew how to be prepared to win. So, he delayed the invasion of Normandy, France, while his Allies were anxious, especially as Russia was taking the impact or pressure of the war against Germany. Joseph Stalin of Russia had aggressively insisted on invading northern France. But Churchill holds out against it in the meantime. It was said, he believed that any premature second front of the war was likely to fail. Consequently, at the Tehran Conference, a date was finally set for June 1944 to execute that D-Day invasion of Normandy, France, which led the way for Hitler and Germany's nightmare during the war and was defeated by the Allied Forces.

While the invasion of Normandy, France, was still on hold, Prime Minister Winston Churchill was using that time to build relationships around the world and campaigning to win the rest of the world over to support the Allied Forces.

Whether is your marriage or relationship, family, vision or dream, business, ministry, product, service, or anything related to your purpose and destiny, if you prematurely launch it, it may fail not because it is not a good one, or the plan of God, or you do not have the ability and capacity to do so, but because the timing was wrong, and the preparedness standards were not met.

Whatever God has called you or laid on your heart to do, you cannot do it all by yourself. You need "Allies" supporters. You need people to support your dream and vision, so build good relationships and respect them. You are not better than them because you are the leader or visionary; you are a leader because they follow you. There would be no leader without followers, and without followers, there would be no need for a leader. When it comes to the calling, yes, you are called, but when it comes to humanity, you are human just as they are.

> *"You are not better than them because you are the leader or Visionary."*

Respect and Consider Opinions and Suggestions

While you do not have to execute every opinion and suggestion people may give you, learn how to take some time to think about opinions and suggestions to determine whether they are right or wrong. If they are right, why are they right? And if they are wrong, why are they wrong?

Thank God, Hitler lost the war because, first, his intentions for world control were not good. But, one thing we can also learn is that there have been speculations among historians that Hitler might have won the war had he let his generals lead the war in some cases. But up till the battle in which Berlin, the capital and where his movement was headquartered was besieged, he did not allow his generals to lead the battles and was the only one giving ideas and orders on how to fight the battles during the war.

As a leader or an individual, you are entitled to the ultimate or final decision in any given situation in your personal life, family, relationships, business, government, and ministry. However, wisdom suggests that you have an open mind and a listening ear to listen, analyze, and glean from the wisdom of the people surrounding you, especially the ones who tell you the truth, and have your best interest at heart. Surrounding yourself with people who only fear you, and do whatever you want them to do and tell you what you want to hear, even if it is questionable will only lead you to failure and the death of your dreams and legacy.

Generally, many battles would have been won, and crises, losses, pains, shame, disgrace, dishonor, imprisonment, debts, breakups, heartbreaks, missed opportunities, curses, and even death would have been avoided if only some people had listened and considered some truth someone had told them, and some good moral advice, suggestions, and opinions shared with them.

Peace, happiness, health, prosperity, victory, security, stability, and longevity are the portion of him who takes advice from God and is submitted to him, and listens, considers, and gleans from the morally sound advice of other Godly and wise people. The Bible says, "The way of fools seems right to them, but the wise listen to advice." (Proverb 12:15, NIV).

> *"Many battles would have been won, and — pains — avoided if only some people had listened."*

Keeping Your Advice Filters On

Should you take and execute every advice you receive from even your confidants? No. Even though it is wise to listen and consider the various advices you are given in specific situations, you are responsible for the exercise and the results it will produce in different areas of your personal life, career, business, government, and ministry. Having this in mind, you must keep your advice filters on to continually filter all the advice you are being given by many people, including the ones you trust. You should not forget that while it is wise to listen, consider, and glean from the wisdom of people you trust, and even strangers, wise people may not always be right, and may give the wrong advice on certain occasions. So, you have the full responsibility to examine every piece of advice before executing it to avoid physical and spiritual damage to the grace of God and the reputation of your life. Always try to get a second, third, or even more opinions on matters, and carefully analyze, compare, and weigh the results or consequences before making your final decisions.

> *"You have the full responsibility to examine every piece of advice before executing it."*

Why Bad Decisions Are Made

Bad decisions are made for several reasons, and I may not be able to mention or discuss all of them in this book. However, let us touch on a few of them, and that includes the lack of purpose, insecurity, fear (The fear of losing, the fear of being the last or late, the fear of being inferior in position or leadership, the fear of being who we are or lack of identity, the fear of servanthood, the fear of the unknown), evil dominance or ruling, impatience, lack of endurance, taking short cuts, selfishness, greed, pride, lack of discipline.

The Lack of Purpose

The dictionary defines "Purpose" as "The reason for which something is done or created or for which something exists." And to put it in a simple meaning to you, it is the reason you exist or were born into this world. Knowing why you are alive in this world influences your decisions — Good or bad.

When you know and understand your purpose in life, you will knowingly and unknowingly be making choices based on that. Knowing your purpose influences how you spend your time, energy, money, materials, properties, the person or who you spend it with, and where. When you believe you are just here in this world to get a job, eat food, have sex, or just for the pleasures of life, and die one day, your decisions will always be bad or poor because you do not have anything significant than yourself you are living for. Life is more than just pleasure and self-gratification, which are temporary things. When your life is all about pleasure, it influences the decisions of your relationships, jobs, and services. When you know your purpose, your decisions are not just based on pleasures, money, position, or fame.

> *"When you know and understand your purpose in life, you will — be making choices based on that."*

Instant gratification does not last. Yes, you will experience pleasure, but it's for a moment and ends soon after. So be careful about trading your lasting and eternal gratification with temporary ones.

The Fear of Losing Someone or Something

The fear of losing someone or something can cause you to make bad decisions. But before you let that fear force you to make a wrong decision, ask yourself if it is worth it. It is not new how many times people make all the wrong decisions because of someone or something, only to realize sooner or later that it was not worth it. As opposed to the advice some psychologists and manipulators would tell you, when your emotions are all caught up in someone or something, that might not be the right time to decide concerning that person or the thing. Give it some time for your emotions or feelings to fall back so you can use a clear judgment to make that choice. Even if you do not get the opportunity to decide on it or it has passed, sometimes missing someone or something can actually be a blessing instead.

"Instant gratification does not last."

The Fear of Being Last or Late

The fear of being the last can drive you into bad decision-making. You do not have to possess what someone else has or be who someone else became at your age, or the same time. Everybody has their life timeline. The Bible says, "There is a time for everything, and a season for every activity under the heavens…" (Ecclesiastes 3:1, NIV). Many times, people make the wrong choices because they want to be like somebody or accomplish something at the wrong time — not their time. Trying to force things to happen in your life at the wrong time because you are afraid of being seen as the last, or a loser can cause you to make the wrong choices just to show off, and you will surely pay for it sooner or later with pain and regret. The only person you are in competition with is yourself. Stop trying to force things to happen before their God-given or appointed time. Whether it's your relationships, marriage, business, or ministry, do not be afraid to wait for the right time, which can lead or bring the right people and things that will fulfill the plan of God for your life. You are never late with God and His plan for your life if you can obey and trust Him for the best with all your heart.

The Fear of Being Inferior in Position or Leadership

This is not an inferiority in humanity because we know God created all human beings, all races, genders (Male and Female) equally, but I'm talking about position or leadership. The fear of being inferior to people can lead you to bad decisions. You are born to be free, and you are not supposed to be a slave to anyone or anything. However, one of the principles of life is growth and promotion. When you don't want to grow and be promoted to your position or ranking in life or call anyone your senior, boss, mentor, pa, or coach before becoming one yourself, this can lead you to bad decisions. Humility is not stupidity and weakness, but a virtue and route that leads to greatness.

> *"One of the principles of life is growth and promotion."*

The most common ways to overnight, or quick success, promotion, and growth are cheating, stealing, betrayal, sexual immorality, and dishonorable and disrespectful behaviors.

There should be nothing to be afraid of if someone is your senior, elder, mentor, or coach. However, oppressive superiority is bad, and you should wisely and honorably move away from them and protect yourself. The ugly side of enduring ungodly leadership, relationships, and behaviors is that if you are not careful, you will become exactly like them and oppress others as well because at some point, it will become morally correct for you even though it's not right.

People are forced to accept everything and anything without understanding the consequences of it all. People think as long as they don't accept behaviors such as theft or murder, then the world will become a better place. What many don't realize is that not only theft, murder, or any other crime is immoral. And any immoral lifestyle or behavior you tolerate in a society will ruin it. If you know you cannot tolerate or accept one immorality, then do not tolerate the other one because gradually, before you know it, your whole life or the entire society will be plunged into a deep immorality era.

Immoral pleasures are for a given time, and they don't last forever. But when the pleasures leave, they leave with your self-worth, respect, and honor.

> *"When the pleasures leave, they leave with your self-worth, respect, and honor."*

The Fear of Being Who You Are

Your identity crisis will pressure you to make the wrong decisions. When you do not know who you are, or your value, first as a human being, and second, as a man or woman on a mission on earth or in this world regardless of your current status, you can easily sell out or trade your dignity, respect, and honor to temporary pleasures, money, sex, materials, or any kind of immorality.

Sex is a powerful emotional phenomenon and force that is irresistible to the body after it takes over your brain. It can overpower you at any time and anywhere if you don't safeguard yourself to avoid its first stages.

I strongly suggest you do anything sound to prevent yourself from falling into sexual immorality, but if it would happen, may it be with someone you will not regret having a child with. And I will elaborate. Many people later regret not only falling into sexual immorality because they didn't guide themselves wisely to avoid it, but also getting pregnant and having a child with someone they never wanted for some reason.

There is nothing like a Superman when it comes to sex. Once sexual feelings get to some stages in a moment, it's difficult to reverse it. So, your first prevention method for inappropriate or immoral sex with someone is guided relationships, interactions, and meetings, and if possible, staying away. If you have to be or work together for some reason, it should be in an open place where other people can see you, and you can also see them. Having at least a third person if you have to be somewhere can also help. The presence of the third person can increase the influence and attenuation of your feelings at some point.

People argue, "Why God created sex, but having or using it, is a sin?" The answer is that having sex is not a sin; it's sexual immorality that is a sin. There are other things we don't talk about. Eating food is not a sin, but gluttony is a sin. Can we call it food immorality? Yes. So think about sex just like any fulfilling or pleasurable thing God has created and given to human beings to enjoy. Morally sound sexual activities are not sins, but immoral sexual activities are sins. Think of it simply this way: Driving a car is not illegal, but driving it without the required licenses or authorizations is unlawful and punishable everywhere, at least in civilized societies governed by laws. These driving laws are carefully created and enacted with several safety concerns in mind, including age, physical competence, mental status, and the vehicles' capacities, volumes, or sizes. So why do you think human beings are wiser than God, who created sex, not to have moral laws to regulate how you can use it and experience the good fulfillment or pleasure for which He created it?

First, you are a human being. So, you think, understand, and form your judgments by processing your thoughts, feelings, and choices through logic, fact, and truth.

Your Self-Worth

Questioning your self-worth or belonging in this world can push you to make wrong choices or decisions. Physical appearance, title, position, financial, material, or social status are not measures for the value of who you are, or your identity.

> *"Questioning your self-worth or belonging in this world can push you to make wrong choices or decisions."*

If any, the only physical appearance enhancement or correction you may need, is physical deformity, distortion, or disfigurement, but again if necessary. Unfortunately, we are in a world now where you may feel it is necessary to change the look of your nose, mouth, buttock, breasts—

Because you think that is how you can get attention, identify yourself with a group of people, and feel good.

Keep in mind that while science has made some great discoveries and helping to manage our health, or well-being in so many ways better than ever before, there are many known and unknown side effects to these scientific accomplishments. Before you lay down on that surgical bed, drink, and apply those drugs to your body or skin, think again – You might just be putting yourself up for a progressive death, or damage to your physical body, which can also lead to serious psychological and spiritual issues, such as insomnia, body odor, and many other skin or body complications.

All your value or worth is not in what you look like, and how you feel about yourself and people think about you, but rather in your character, and in your purpose and destiny. And it does not matter whether others can see it or not. Know that you are valuable. You were born because you are needed here on earth. The Bible says, *"And even the very hairs of your head are all numbered. So do not be afraid; you are worth more than many sparrows."* (Matthew 10: 30-31). Your creator, God is telling you that you are more than a sparrow or animal. So, regard and treat yourself and other human beings as such. It all starts with your decisions or choices.

The Fear of Servanthood

Being a servant does not mean being a slave. Each time the word, "Servant" is mentioned, the first thing that comes to mind is "Someone who performs duties for others, especially a person employed in a house on domestic duties or as a personal attendant", which is the definition of the dictionary. However, being a servant does not definitively mean being a laborer or slave to someone else. The Lord Jesus gave us an example of what it really means to be a servant by washing the feet of His disciples. The Bible says, *"After that, he poured water into a basin and began to wash his disciples' feet, drying them with the towel that was wrapped around him."* (John 13:5). And he continued and said, "Do you understand what I have done for you?" he asked them. *"You call me 'Teacher' and 'Lord,' and rightly so, for that is what I am. Now that I, your Lord and Teacher, have washed your feet, you also should wash one another's feet. I have set you an example that you should do as I have done for you. Very truly I tell you, no servant is greater than his master, nor is a messenger greater than the one who sent him. Now that you know these things, you will be blessed if you do them."* (John 13:12-17, NIV).

"Being a servant does not mean being a slave."

When you don't want to serve or render a service to people or anyone, which comes from humility and selflessness, you can easily start making the wrong decisions because it's not about anyone, but you and your ego. And you want to be the center of all attention and beneficiary of every service in order to feel good.

History shows that people who tend not to be willing to render a good service to anyone end up making wrong decisions to either manipulate, take advantage, cheat, kill, rob, or oppress others.

The truth is, not only does rendering service to others show humility, but it also teaches and sets a good leadership example, that God and people have always approved and appreciated.

As I mentioned earlier, one of my favorite subjects is history. And having parents from two different countries has been a blessing culturally and intellectually.

I'm not a politician, nor am I defending any wrongdoings here. I do also know that for many Ghanaians, this is a very sensitive subject. But the world, Historians, Ghanaians, and others around the world may have mixed opinions about the Former Revolutionary, Coup Leader, and President of The Republic of Ghana, J.J. Rawlings, depending on the level of information and knowledge everybody has respectively now, or in times preceding the revolution and post-revolution; and maybe their relationship with the various individuals involved in the governments and the coup. Some people believe he was the man for the hour, or sent by God to deliver Ghana from corruption, injustice, and inequality, and forging a new avenue of justice, equality, freedom, and peace for Ghana. But then, some people also believe the revolution generated some excesses in killings, imprisonments, and disappearance of individuals in some instances in an attempt to stop bad government practices and promote accountability.

Personally, I do not also condone the killings, but as opposed to what some people may believe, I do not think some of the executions or killings he may have supported or ordered were disciplinary or punishment actions, but rather a military strategy to eliminate all their potential future rivals during and after the coup, and who can rise sooner or later to retaliate against them. I also understand that the group he led in the coup and during the revolution was composed mostly of junior military elements who were young, and they were somehow facing or overthrowing prominent Ghanaian Politicians and Military Generals. We should also note that these young military men, including himself as the leader, were influenced and guided by outside powers or governments who wanted a share in the country. Consequently, these young men were caught up in a turbulence of difficult decisions. On one hand, in their minds and hearts, they were leading a coup to save their beloved country from corruption. But on the other hand, they realized that the outside powers guiding them to succeed in the coup actually also wanted their share in the country as well. Therefore, they had two parties to satisfy, their beloved country and people, and the presumed outside powers and helpers who were certainly advising them on their next steps or actions to take to secure their lives and government. This fact, I believe, influenced or motivated their decision to kill all the prominent Ghanaian Politicians and Military Generals at the time, which they thought would have helped secure their revolution for a very long time. Was it necessary? I am not sure, and I would leave that part to Historians, witnesses, or people much more familiar with the situations at the time.

However, if we can lay aside other disagreements on the nature of his revolution, one thing that is undeniable about J.J. Rawlings, is his Servanthood Leadership. As a president, among many services he rendered to his country, he cleaned gutters, carried bags of products, joined in public group construction works and many other services that are unusual for a president of a country to do.

Even though this has been denied by his critics, I once heard him said when he left office as a president, he did not have any foreign bank account, and even ten (10) Dollar to their names (He and the wife) abroad. Whether this was verified or not, and if his statement was true, this is very unusual for an African president who rose to power like him. Many other African presidents and ministers embezzle money and take care of their own before anything and anyone else. But this man came to power, served the people in any way he could. He might not have been perfect, he might have made mistakes here and there as a human being, but after all, it is important to notice his selfless and servanthood character.

The Fear of the Unknown

Another reason human beings make the wrong decisions is the fear of the unknown. When you do not know what is ahead of you, you may be afraid, confused, and make wrong decisions. The unknown is a fearful thing for every human being. That is why many turn to divination, psychics, or occultism to be able to know the unknown. Demonic or satanic exercises will not change anything for the better about the unknown in your life. It can only maybe tell you, but never provide a real solution. However, you should not let the unknown terrify you. Be prepared for the unknown spiritually, physically, financially, and materially, but do not let it control and steer your decisions in the wrong direction. When the unknown becomes known, it will face your crisis management abilities, which are also based on your wisdom. The LORD said, *"And surely I am with you always, to the very end of the age."* (Matthew

28:20, NKJV). The "end of the age" not only means the end of the current world as humanity knows it but also means till or even in the unknown. When you are walking with a God who is omniscient (Who knows everything), you should put your hope and trust in him by wisdom. The word of God says, *"Trust in the Lord with all your heart and lean not on your own understanding; in all your ways acknowledge Him, and He will direct your paths."* (Proverbs 3:5-6). The unknown always becomes known sooner or later, and until then, keep trusting and making the right decisions based on what you know, and if possible, wait for time to reveal the unknown before you decide.

The plans of God are always good for you even when they seem to be bad and undesirable mostly. The Bible says, *"For I know the plans I have for you,"* declares the Lord, *"plans to prosper you and not to harm you, plans to give you hope and a future."* (Jeremiah 29:11, NIV).

The way you handle the unknown determines whether it can become a danger or a blessing to you.

> *"The way you handle the unknown determines whether it can become a danger or a blessing to you."*

Evil Dominance or Ruling

Bad decisions also emanate from the thoughts and desires to dominate others, especially in an evil way or reason. This could be in a government, organization, business, country, ministry, church, relationships, marriage, family, and many other areas of life. There is nothing wrong about wanting to become a leader of a people to serve or lead them to a better life, spiritually or physically. But when your desire is to put everybody or other races under your control, it becomes evil and leads to an unending chain of wrong decisions because to keep the first wrong decisions in place, you will continue making other wrong decisions. Sometimes, to keep what you got in a wrong decision and make people feel that you are doing alright, you will keep making other wrong decisions, so you will find yourself in an unending trap of making bad decisions, one after the other.

> *"To keep the first wrong decisions in place, will continue making other wrong decisions."*

Adolf Hitler's desire was to control the world and other races. Considering many historical facts, he knew at some point during the war that his dream could not come true. But out of arrogance, desperation, and evil mind, he chose to continue anyway. Do not let one wrong decision lead you to many other wrong decisions. It is better to stop at the first wrong decision, apologize, ask for forgiveness, reconcile, and maybe yes, you will be embarrassed, ashamed, or humiliated for it, but it is better than continuing to make other wrong decisions. Humanity and God will respect you for acknowledging your wrong decisions instead of continuously making other wrong decisions.

Taking Short Cutters and Quick Fixers

We all like shortcuts and quick fixes, but when the short cutter or quick fixer is sure to create another problem or danger to your peace, happiness, and safety sooner or later, it is not worth it. You do not want to create a problem to solve a problem. We live in a world where there is an ever-increasing desire to become or do this or that very quickly. Hard work and waiting are no more honorable. Everybody wants to become somebody, and have something overnight by all means, even if it is to break established protective laws and disobey the moral laws of God.

Taking the hard way or high roads, especially when the shortcut is potentially dangerous and problematic is a wise decision to make and the right thing to do. It will save you from apparent and hidden problems. The good thing about avoiding shortcuts sometimes is the lessons and experiences you will get along the journey of the hard work through or on the difficult road. It also builds your character and prepares you for future challenges, and gives you information, knowledge, and wisdom to handle defining events in your life, business, family, relationships, and leadership sooner or later.

> *"The good thing about avoiding shortcuts sometimes is the lessons and experiences you will get along the journey of the hard work through or on the difficult road."*

Impatience

We want to create a "Drive-Through" for everything in our lives. Already made, that is what many people are yearning for. We do not want to "waste time", we say. But in all actuality, it is not that we do not want to waste time, but rather, we do not want to spend time on anything that requires it. Spending time on something that needs or requires it, is not wasting time.

> *"Spending time on something that needs or requires it, is not wasting time."*

When you are not willing to spend time and earn what you want or need, you can make the wrong decisions because all you can see is what you want and how quickly you can get it. And in doing so, you ignore all the red flags or signs showing the dangers of what you are about to do.

It is interesting that mostly, the food that much time was spent on preparing or cooking is healthier when done. A research article published on September 18, 2014, by the American Journal of Preventive Medicine (Research Article, Volume 47, Issue 6, P796-802, December 01, 2014) shows that people who spend more time preparing and cooking meals are more likely to have healthier diets, the study found. And those who spent the least time on food preparation also spent much money on food away from home and were more likely to eat at fast food restaurants (which might not be a healthy food). If this is true about food or meals, how much more about other things in your life? Learn how to exercise patience when you want to eat, buy something, go into a relationship, get married, become rich, obtain a promotion or position, or build and lead a big business. Patience helps you to know and see what you did not know and see before, the blessings or dangers you are about to associate yourself with, and the potential good or bad results you will get by making that decision. These facts will play a significant role in whether you should ignore or accept them and move forward in preparation, or they are too dangerous to take a risk.

As you may have heard, the adage "Rome wasn't built in a day." This is just to substantiate the need for time to create or build great things. When you see others in the tenth stage of their endeavors, do not compare it to yours, which is in its first stage. It takes time to build distinguishable things in life. Do not be in a hurry and become blinded to the realities and risks in every decision that you want to make in any area of your life; otherwise, you will end up spending that time in pain and regret sooner or later.

The word of God admonishes us, *"Be patient, therefore, brothers--See how the farmer waits for the precious fruit of the earth, being patient about it, until it receives the early and the late rains. You also, be patient. Establish your hearts—"* (James 5:7-8, ESV). And also read, *"Whoever is patient has great understanding, but one who is quick-tempered displays folly."* (Proverb 14:29, NIV).

Lack of Endurance

Endurance is defined by the dictionary as, "the fact or power of enduring an unpleasant or difficult process or situation without giving way." The more science and technology are advancing in discoveries and inventions to make life easier and better, the more we as humans are losing our natural and spiritual endurance, knowingly or unknowingly. Humanity is becoming weaker and weaker rapidly in the way we endure things that life throws at us. We are becoming so sensible and quickly giving up on situations and processes that seem difficult. Our crisis survival capacity is quickly declining.

Therefore, whenever we find ourselves in a difficult situation where we have to endure a little hardship, or do some work we have not done before, spend the night or sleep time out of our comfortable beds, bear the heat of the sun for a while without Air Conditioning, ride in a public automobile, walk a certain distance, eat food we are not used to (Not bad food), wear clothes we consider inexpensive or not luxurious, we consider it as a punishment or curse. This weakness can lead you to make wrong decisions if you do not come to your common sense and remember that as God created you to enjoy all the beauties and luxuries of this world, He also equipped you with a survival capacity to endure and fight to get to the other end of every difficult situation in your life. Even if it takes longer than you expected, trust God and know He will surely make a way for your relief, deliverance, peace, happiness, stability, and security. I am not naïve about how some of these situations can feel because I have been there myself; even if mine cannot be compared to yours, I have observed and learned that God always delivers those who obey, trust, and hope in Him. Do not give in to wrong decisions because you do not want to endure any hardship because the end results and consequences will be more bitter than the trial itself. The Word of God says, *"—But his favor lasts a lifetime; weeping may stay for the night but rejoicing comes in the morning."* (Psalm 30:5, NIV).

"The more science and technology are advancing — the more we as humans

> *are losing our natural and spiritual endurance."*

When you are afraid of enduring any type of hardship, you can quickly make the wrong decisions just to escape rough times, knowing very well that your choices are not morally sound and will surely bear serious consequences sooner or later. Do not tie yourself into a relationship with someone because you think the person will save you from hardship or give you a job, position, or money if you know the latter is not the right person to be with. Do not engage yourself in immoral and fraudulent activities just because you want to avoid enduring hardship. Hardships are not permanent, but the results of some of your foolish decisions will last as long as you live, and even after you are dead.

Selfishness

When you see others as not having the same dignity and being concerned excessively or exclusively for yourself and your advantage, pleasure, or welfare, regardless of others, you begin making wrong decisions because all you can see is you.

When you think you are the only intelligent human being to exist in the universe, that becomes a real problem, not only to others, but even to yourself. When you believe you are the only one on planet earth who receives sensory information, or who has the five senses, sight, sound, smell, taste, and touch; and nobody else sees, hears, smells, tastes, and touches/feels, you become a danger to humanity, and even to yourself. The quickest way to become a fool, is to think that others are fools, and will never understand and know what you are about.

If you understand that others equally have the same rights, dignity, and respect, just as you, you will consider it before making your decisions to ensure that they reflect those values or morals. But if you do not value others in any way, your decisions will be all about you, your lust, what you want, hear, see, smell, taste, and feel.

> *"The quickest way to become a fool, is to think that others are fools, and will never understand and know what you are about."*

The Bible says, *"Do nothing out of selfish ambition or vain conceit. Rather, in humility value others above yourselves, not looking to your own interests but each of you to the interests of the others."* (Philippians 2:3-4, NIV). *"For where jealousy and selfish ambition exist, there is disorder and every evil thing."* (James 3:16).

Greed

You cannot separate selfishness from greed, the intense and selfish desire for attention, pleasure, position, power, money, materials, and even food. When you allow greed to override your morals, you will make the wrong decisions. Before you make your choices, be certain they are not motivated by greed.

Pride

Your pride may tell you the wrong way to handle things if you let it be so. But wisdom will tell you the right way to handle them, and sometimes, that means humbling yourself and treating others just as you would like to be treated. Sometimes, all that is needed to resolve a problem is recognizing that you are wrong and sincerely apologizing for your mistake. But pride will tell you, you are more than who they are, so you do not owe them any apologies. When you are on the wrong path to destruction, and someone notices that and tells you, wisdom tells you to listen, consider what they are saying, and check it to know whether it's true or false. But pride will tell you, you know better than them. Listen, some of the people who destroyed their own lives and others were actually intelligent people. So, understand that just because you are intelligent does not mean you will always get it right. So, try to at least listen to what others have to say to determine whether it's true and requires your attention to work on and implement good changes.

> *"Some of the people who destroyed their own lives and others were actually intelligent people."*

The word of God says, *"For all that is in the world—the lust of the flesh, the lust of the eyes, and the pride of life — is not of the Father but is of the world."* (1 John 2:16, NLV). And *"Pride goes before destruction, a haughty spirit before a fall."* (Proverb 16:18, NIV).

Lack of Discipline

Being able to control your behavior is a great blessing, and if you do not have it, you must pray for it. Discipline will save you from many bad decisions. It is not a surprise that the same word "Discipline" used for self-control, is the same "Discipline" used for correction. In other words, if you do not "discipline" yourself, someone else will "discipline" or "correct" you. I would rather discipline or control myself than give someone else the opportunity to control my life. Undiscipline can cause you to make all the wrong decisions or choices in the world if you let it be.

Before you give up the blessing and opportunity to control yourself to someone else to do it as a punishment, think again, and make the right decisions.

> *"Before you give up the blessing and opportunity to control yourself to someone else to do it as a punishment, think again."*

When you are caught doing wrong, and you know it is true, change your ways or stop it. Do not start trying to point out how much wrong other people are also doing to defend yours. This behavior makes you look low. This is not to say that others can do wrong, but you cannot. Trying to use other people's wrongs, especially the ones who are not concerned or related to your wrongdoings, to advocate for your bad decisions or mistakes is just not a mature way to handle mistakes in life. Instead, take responsibility, correct it, and do better to live up to the moral standards you are supposed to.

The Bible says, *"No discipline seems enjoyable at the time, but painful. Later on, however, it yields the peaceful fruit of righteousness to those who have been trained by it."* (Hebrews 12:11, CSB).

Public Sentiment

Public sentiment or opinion may help decision-making, or solve public or community problems, or help to bring solutions to specific issues that are relevant to a society, or even more to a personal problem. However, it is dangerous sometimes to rely on public opinion to make personal decisions because your values might not be the collective values of the public. There have been many instances when people relied on public opinion and made the wrong decisions, and when the consequences of the decisions started emerging, the public was nowhere to be found to come to the rescue. Listen and think about the public or majority's opinion or sentiment, but understand that you will be the one who will bear the consequences of your decisions if they turn out to be the wrong ones. Do not let the public pressure you into making decisions against your values or beliefs. Remember, the day you will be standing the judgment for it; no one will bear the effects with you.

> *"It is dangerous sometimes to rely on public opinion to make personal decisions."*

Avoid Curses

Do your best to avoid curses. One of the most dangerous things you must avoid in life is curses. They are so dangerous and can be in effect for generations even though you might not see their works immediately.

According to the Greek word "Katara" in the Bible, a curse are "penalties received due to condemnation, or a doomed one." And according to the Oxford English Dictionary, a "penalty" is "a punishment imposed for breaking a law, rule, or contract." This word is also synonymous with sanction and retribution. And the word "doom" is defined as "death, destruction, or some other terrible fate. "Doomed" is also defined as "likely to have an unfortunate and inescapable outcome; ill-fated."

The Merriam-Webster dictionary defines a curse as, "a calling for harm or injury to come to someone, a word or an expression used in cursing or swearing, evil or misfortune that comes as if in answer to a curse."

The only way to avoid curses is to live in righteousness. Curses are perilous because they do not only work against you alone, but sometimes even against people related to you and your descendants. While you may think you are getting away with mistreating people and being wicked, you are actually creating spiritual debts in the form of misfortune that you may not be able to finish paying off, and your descendants may have to deal with it one way or the other.

> *"The only way to avoid curses is to live in righteousness."*

Yes, Christ came to set you free from curses. (Galatians 3:13, Romans 5:18). However, if you continuously, irresponsibly, selfishly, and wickedly give the devil and his demons spiritual legal grounds by your behavior, character, or actions, curses can work against you.

To avoid curses, you have to adhere to the moral laws of God and practice them. Because the Bible says, *"An undeserved curse will be powerless to harm you. It may flutter over you like a bird, but it will find no place to land."* (Proverbs 26:2, TPT). This means if you do not deserve a curse, no matter who invokes it on you, it will not prosper or happen. So ensure that you do your best to be undeserving of any curse by your decisions and actions.

Godly Wisdom

The Bible says, *"For since in the wisdom of God the world through its wisdom did not know Him, God was pleased through the foolishness of what was preached to save those who believe."* (1 Corinthians 1:21). Considering this statement, according to the word of God, there are two kinds of wisdom, even though psychology and philosophy have their own interpretation and types of wisdom. The word of God mentions "The wisdom of God" and "The world's wisdom."

Godly wisdom is more than theoretical wisdom, Sophia or Sophia's, and practical wisdom, Phronesis, and Sapience, or Sagacity, and even what others refer to as Godly neocortical spirit wisdom, which is internal reasoning and has a good mental state that represents a commitment to always carry out a good judgment and decision. Godly wisdom is more than just being a wise individual who is morally virtuous and does not commit wickedness.

From my understanding of the word of God, Godly wisdom is not limited to just the capacity of perceiving the revelation of the truth in a matter, and making the right moral decisions, but it also includes the revelation, understanding, and interpretation of divine or spiritual things. I will elaborate on this a little further.

> *"Godly wisdom — also includes the revelation, understanding, and interpretation of divine or spiritual things."*

Wisdom Will Save You and Yours

The wisdom of Daniel is one to be considered. Among the people that Nebuchadnezzar, king of Babylon, came to Jerusalem, besieged, and took into captivity in Babylon were Daniel, Hananiah, Mishael, and Azariah of the tribe of Judah. They were to be fed with exceptional food because, after all, they must look youthful without blemish, have a good appearance and be skillful in all wisdom, endowed with knowledge, understanding learning, and competent to stand in the king's palace, and learn the literature and language of the Chaldeans. (Daniel 1:1-7). However, Daniel and his friends declined to the food of the king and suggested that they been served vegetables and water. When the time came to evaluate their appearance, they looked better and fatter in flesh than all the young men who ate the portion of the king's delicacies. (Daniel 1:15).

Then came the evaluation of their intelligence, understanding, knowledge, and wisdom, and they surpassed their fellows as well. The Bible says, *"As for these four young men, God gave them knowledge and skill in all literature and wisdom; and Daniel had understanding in all vi-*

sions and dreams." (Daniel 1:17). Furthermore, "Then the king interviewed them, and among them all none was found like Daniel, Hananiah, Mishael, and Azariah; therefore, they served before the king. And in all matters of wisdom and understanding about which the king examined them, he found them ten times better than all the magicians and astrologers who were in all his realm--" (Daniel 1:19-20).

Two years later, "Nebuchadnezzar had dreams; and his spirit was so troubled that his sleep left him. Then the king gave the command to call the magicians, the astrologers, the sorcerers, and the Chaldeans to tell the king his dreams. So, they came and stood before the king. And the king said to them, "I have had a dream, and my spirit is anxious to know the dream." (Daniel 2:1-3). The irony of this was that the king himself forgot his dream. So, not only did he need someone to interpret the dream, but also one who could even tell the king the dream he had and the meaning of it — that was a real challenge. And the king made up his mind to kill all magicians, astrologers, and sorcerers who worked for him if they were not able to tell him the dream he had, and it is meaning. Long story short, they were not able to handle the king's demand, so he ordered that they kill all of them, which would include Daniel and his friends, Hananiah, Mishael, and Azariah. The news of the execution command reached Daniel, but he managed to request more time from the king to tell him the dream he had and the meaning. He later told his friends about the king's order, the peril that awaits them if they failed to provide a solution to the king, and pleaded with them to join him in seeking God about the matter.

God heard their prayers, and the Bible says, *"Then the secret was revealed to Daniel in a night vision. So, Daniel blessed the God of heaven."* (Daniel 2:19, NKJV). Daniel was filled with gratitude, and replied to God with an exceptional prayer in Daniel 2:20-23:

"Blessed be the name of God forever and ever,
For wisdom and might are His.
And He changes the times and the seasons;
He removes kings and raises up kings;
He gives wisdom to the wise
And knowledge to those who have understanding.
He reveals deep and secret things;
He knows what is in the darkness,
And light dwells with Him.
"I thank You and praise You,
O God of my fathers;
You have given me wisdom and might,
And have now made known to me what we asked of You,
For You have made known to us the king's demand."

Daniel could not wait to see the king and tell him about his dream and the interpretation. So the Bible says, "Therefore Daniel went to Arioch, whom the king had appointed to destroy the wise men of Babylon. He went and said thus to him: "Do not destroy the wise men of Babylon; take me before the king, and I will tell the king the interpretation."

Then Arioch quickly brought Daniel before the king, and said thus to him, "I have found a man of the captives of Judah, who will make known to the king the interpretation." The king answered and said to Daniel, whose name was Belteshazzar, "Are you able to make known to me the dream which I have seen, and its interpretation?"

Daniel answered in the presence of the king, and said, "The secret which the king has demanded, the wise men, the astrologers, the magicians, and the soothsayers cannot declare to the king. But there is a God in heaven who reveals secrets, and He has made known to King Nebuchadnezzar what will be in the latter days. Your dream, and the visions of your head upon your bed, were these: As for you, O king, thoughts came to your mind while on your bed, about what would come to pass after this; and He who reveals secrets has made known to you what will be. But as for me, this secret has not been revealed to me because I have more wisdom than anyone living, but for our sakes who make known the interpretation to the king, and that you may know the thoughts of your heart.

"You, O king, were watching; and behold, a great image! This great image, whose splendor was excellent, stood before you; and its form was awesome. This image's head was of fine gold, its chest and arms of silver, its belly and thighs of bronze, its legs of iron, its feet partly of iron and partly of [l]clay. You watched while a stone was cut out without hands, which struck the image on its feet of iron and clay, and broke them in pieces. Then the iron, the clay, the bronze, the silver, and the gold were crushed together, and became like chaff from the summer threshing floors; the wind carried them away so that no trace of them was found. And the stone that struck the image became a great mountain and filled the whole earth.

"This is the dream. Now we will tell the interpretation of it before the king. You, O king, are a king of kings. For the God of heaven has given you a kingdom, power, strength, and glory; and wherever the children of men dwell, or the beasts of the field and the birds of the heaven, He has given them into your hand, and has made you ruler over them all—you are this head of gold. But after you shall arise another kingdom inferior to yours; then another, a third kingdom of bronze, which shall rule over all the earth. And the fourth kingdom shall be as strong as iron, inasmuch as iron breaks in pieces and shatters everything; and like iron that crushes, that kingdom will break in pieces and crush all the others. Whereas you saw the feet and toes, partly of potter's clay and partly of iron, the kingdom shall be divided; yet the strength of the iron shall be in it, just as you saw the iron mixed with ceramic clay. And as the toes of the feet were partly of iron and partly of clay, so the kingdom shall be partly strong and partly fragile. As you saw iron mixed with ceramic clay, they will mingle with the seed of men; but they will not adhere to one another, just as iron does not mix with clay. And in the days of these kings the God of heaven will set up a kingdom which shall never be destroyed, and the kingdom shall not be left to other people; it shall break in pieces and consume all these kingdoms, and it shall stand forever. Inasmuch as you saw that the stone was cut out of the mountain without hands and that it broke in pieces the iron, the bronze, the clay, the silver, and the gold—the great God has made known to the king what will come to pass after this. The dream is certain, and its interpretation is sure." (Daniel 2:24-45).

This was unbelievable to King Nebuchadnezzar. How can someone know exactly the dream another person had, and give the interpretation? Only the true God who is above all gods can do that. The king commanded that Daniel and his companions be promoted. (Daniel 2:46-49).

The God of Joseph Is the God of Solomon and Daniel

The situation Daniel and his friends found themselves in was not different from Joseph's, and so was their God. The God of Joseph is the God of Daniel and his companions. The remarkable thing about these young men is that their wisdom was not only the understanding, knowledge, and the right course to take in each matter, but they could also perceive, understand, and interpret spiritual events and matters.

Daniel did not interpret the king's dream with instinct but with the revelatory Spirit or wisdom of God. But before I proceed, even what you call instinct, is actually your human spirit sensing the invisible. Remember, when God first created humans (Adam and Eve) in the Garden of Eden, the Bible says, *"And the Lord God formed man of the dust of the ground, and breathed into his nostrils the breath of life; and man became a living soul."* (Genesis 2:7, KJV). The "breath of God" is the Spirit of God. We read, *"And the breath of the Almighty gives me life."* (Job 33:4). "A Living soul" also means a spirit. So, from the time God breathed into man, man had also become a spirit. Therefore, you are not only a body or flesh. You are a spirit living in a body. In effect, the human spirit is the one who senses invisible matters or events before they even happen, and that is what some people call "instinct." Therefore, when the Holy Spirit of God comes into you, it takes that sensor or capacity to sense invisible matters to another higher level. I will elaborate more on this later.

Pay attention to your human spirit sensor (instinct), the voice of God through the Holy Spirit, your dreams, and the Godly counselors God has placed in your life.

> *"Pay attention to your human spirit sensor (instinct), the voice of God through the Holy Spirit, your dreams, and the Godly counselors God has placed in your life."*

The wisdom of God is more than theoretical wisdom, or Sophia, and practical wisdom, or Phronesis, Sapience, or Sagacity, and even more than what some Theologians refer to as Godly neocortical spirit wisdom. In my understanding, the wisdom of God includes, but is not limited to those capacities, it also grants you enlightenment, a spiritual revelation, understanding, and knowledge about matters and situations in a Godly or divine way — it is a Divine Wisdom. Anyone who had it in the Bible was not only capable to rightly judge matters, but also understood, knew, and precisely interpreted divine events and warnings.

Kings and Queens, Kingdoms, Armies, Generals, and Captains have, and were surrounded by people filled with theoretical wisdom, practical wisdom, and sagacity, but they could not make it to victory, peace, happiness, prosperity, success, stability, and security because life is more than a physical or natural matter — it is spiritual as well.

Joseph had the wisdom of God, and nothing was able to stop him from fulfilling his dream, becoming dreams interpreter, and a sophisticated prime minister in Egypt. Solomon had the wisdom of God and became an effective King, the most prosperous man on earth, and intellectually respected as well. Daniel and his companions had the wisdom of God, and they were healthy, knowledgeable, skillful in all literature; and had understanding in all visions and dreams — it is Divine Wisdom or God's Wisdom.

> *"Divine Wisdom. Anyone who had it in the Bible was not only capable to rightly judge matters, but also understood, knew, and precisely interpreted divine events and warnings."*

Increasing In Wisdom

One of the attributes of wisdom is the thirst for increasing in wisdom. The wise continually learn and search for knowledge and understanding to fortify his wisdom and increase in it. But the fool thinks he knows it all and does nothing or has no interest to learn more and increase in wisdom.

Throughout the Bible, individuals noted as wise have some characteristics: They honored and served God, sought more information, knowledge, understanding, and were humble.

Even when the LORD was born, in a quest for information, knowledge, understanding, and increased wisdom, the Bible reveals to us that "Magi from the east arrived in Jerusalem." (Matthew 2:1-12). A few details are given about these men in the Bible; the record does not specifically say how many men they were or how much of what they brought, but analytically, scholars assumed they were three men according to the gifts they presented to the baby Jesus: gold, frankincense, and myrrh. Among many remarks, we also note that these men were wisemen. Not only that, but some traditions also identify the Magi as ancient kings, Balthasar of Arabia, Melchior of Persia, and Gaspar of India. If this traditional information is true, which could be true, since these traditions have been passed on from generation to generation, and for centuries, one may say God told or revealed to them the birth of Christ Jesus so they can go and worship him and announce it to the world. But I would argue differently that these kings, who were already identified as wise, were still searching for wisdom. They believed the birth of Christ was a supernatural event, which would have a greater impact on the world and humanity. So, they decided to go there to witness and offer gifts, which may be a good idea and plan to acquire more wisdom.

> *"One of the attributes of wisdom is the thirst for increasing in wisdom."*

The Bible says, *"And Jesus grew in wisdom and stature, and in favor with God and man."* (Luke 2:52, NIV). When He was born, wisemen went looking for him, knowing there was something special about Him — He was wise. So, they wanted to become wiser, and that is one of the reasons they went looking for Him. But with time, He grew wiser himself. Are you growing in wisdom or foolishness? You do not want to become a disrespected and dishonored old man or woman with gray hair.

Respect is earned by your character and behaviors, but honor is given to you by your position, status and age. That is why people can honor you for your position, status or age, but not respect you because of your character and behaviors. And don't mistake honor for respect, especially if you are in a high position or advanced in age. It is important to live well and exhibit good character, behaviors, and moral values to earn respect rather than honor. Seek respect rather than honor, and honor will surely follow the respect people give you, a respect that you have earned by your character and behaviors.

> *"You do not want to become a disrespected and dishonored old man or woman with gray hair."*

Power or Wisdom

Generally, there are two types of individuals in this world: those who search for power and those who search for wisdom — but you need both. In other words, some people are impressed by power, and some people are impressed by wisdom. Paul, the Apostle, wrote to the Corinthians, *"Jews demand signs and Greeks search for wisdom."* (1 Corinthians 1:22, BSB). He was trying to get them to understand that it will take a sign to convince a Jew about the authenticity of something, and it will take wisdom to convince a Greek about the reality of something. In theory, one looking for signs is also looking for power, because it takes power to produce a sign. And one looking for wisdom is looking for persuasive understanding, which sometimes comes from speech or oratory.

There is a difference between manpower and divine power. And I'm not absolutely talking about a workforce or people working or available for work or service. I'm referring to physical strength, resources, and weapons as manpower. And divine power is the supernatural working power of God.

> *"There are two types of individuals*

> *in this world: those who search for power and those who search for wisdom — but you need both."*

In my settled belief, you need both power, preferably divine power and wisdom. However, Godly wisdom can undoubtedly overcome, weaken, and destroy natural or manpower, whereas divine power is always supreme.

When Moses was sent to Egypt, it took power to demonstrate to Pharoah and his people that he was sent by God. (Exodus 4:17, Exodus chapters 7-11). When the Jews wanted Jesus to prove to them that He was sent by God, they said, **"What sign can you show us to prove your authority to do all this?"** (John 2:18, NIV). It is surprising to note that the disciples of the LORD believed in him after he turned water to wine in Cana of Galilee. One should think that, after all, they did not believe in Him until that miracle because the Bible says, **"What Jesus did here in Cana of Galilee was the first of the signs through which he revealed his glory; and his disciples believed in him."** (John 2:11, NIV).

The Greeks were much more interested in philosophy, precisely the "know-how" or "skill in execution". It could also be a carnal or human eloquence. Even back in the ancient world, many philosophical schools, all with fundamental disagreements, were inclined to seek power and political influence with their philosophical works. It is also important to note that Paul, the Apostle himself being a devoted Jew, was also a philosopher until He met the LORD on the road to Damascus. (Acts 9:1-17).

Philosophy is not necessarily Godly wisdom. The dictionary defines philosophy as "the study of the fundamental nature of knowledge, reality, and existence." If so, this is purely thinking, reasoning, thought, or knowledge, which are regarded as questions and problems to be studied and resolved.

You may have power, it may be a position, status, talent, spiritual or natural gift, beauty, intelligence, money, or ability to do or accomplish something, but lack wisdom. This power can sooner or later destroy you because of the lack of wisdom. Wisdom gives you the moral, physical, and spiritual measure, or "power" to control and monitor your "power." Therefore, power without wisdom is a recipe for a catastrophic life and existence.

> ## *"Power can sooner or later destroy you because of the lack of wisdom."*

There are many things attached to life, but none of them is the only one that there is to life. Food is to life, but it's not all that there is. Water is to life, but not all that there. Sleep is to life, but not all that there is. Work is to life, but not all that there is. Money is to life, but not all that there is. Marriage is to life, but not all that there is. Sex is to life, but not all there is. Children are to life, but not all there is. Success is to life, but not all there is.

Chapter 3
Captain of Your Vessel

"There are three things that are too amazing for me, four that I do not understand: the way of an eagle in the sky — the way of a ship on the high seas."
Proverb 30:18-19

WE ARE ALL CAPTAINS, and life is a voyage. As a Captain of your vessel, you have an honorable and enormous responsibility to lead your ship or flight to its intended destination.

As you may know, all evidence in history and science till now proves that Africa is the Cradle of humanity, and mankind migrated from Africa to all other continents one way or the other at a certain point in time either in pursuit of food, water, liberty, protection, security, defense, peace, prosperity, stability, happiness, expansion or religious freedom. Some of these migrations were undertaken by rivers or via the oceans. Since the beginning of ages, mankind has been a traveler, and every human being and animal has the natural gift of orientation to some degree. So, you are a naturally born captain, flight, voyage leader, or commander. And precisely put, you are the captain of your life.

As a captain of your life, you have the responsibility to lead your life to its intended destination, where food, water, liberty, protection, security, defense, peace, prosperity, stability, happiness, expansion, and religious freedom abound. And once you do, everything and everybody connected to you will be positively affected or will benefit from the results directly or indirectly.

Unlike the ship or flight loaded with dozens, hundreds, or thousands of passengers or goods, onboard your life's ship, are your soul, spirit, and body. And every decision you make directly or indirectly affects each one of these areas of your life, and others, eventually.

I'm always in awe when looking at the sea. My personal quest to understand some things about the ocean through the magnificent research works of oceanologists around the world continuously leaves me with more questions. A researcher stated, "Ninety-five percent (95%) of the ocean is unexplored, and we know more about space than the ocean." I also believe in the researcher's statement, "The ocean has unbelievable depths that are impossible to reach."

The ocean, as we know it, covers seventy-one percent (71%) of the Earth's surface and contains over 1.3 billion cubic km of water. Its average depth is about 4 km, 2.48 miles, or 3,688 meters (12,100 ft). The ocean is one of the most dangerous possessions of nature that anyone can deal with. The tides, currents, and rip currents often become violent and pose a high risk of drowning. However, long before the invention of modern sophisticated navigation systems, skilled navigators in the ancient world courageously navigated these vast and powerful oceans to reach their destinations, which were their goals. But it was not easy, they had to use some creative methods to find positioning, directions, and locations.

The Vikings ventured out from their homeland due to overpopulation or looking for riches, such as Leif Erikson, the Norse explorer from Iceland who is believed to have been the first European to have set foot on North America except Greenland, roughly five hundred years before Christopher Columbus and John Cabot. How did they do it?

The renowned explorer Christopher Columbus, the Italian explorer and navigator, completed four voyages across the Atlantic Ocean, which opened the way for the extensive European exploration and colonization of the Americas. How did they do it?

Ferdinand Magellan, the Portuguese explorer and Hispanic Monarchy's subject, is best known for planning and leading the Spanish expedition to the East Indies across the Pacific to open a maritime trade route in which he discovered the interoceanic passage and completed the first European navigation from the Atlantic to Asia. And his expedition teammates returned to Spain to mark the first navigation around the world after he was killed in a battle against the natives of Mactan Island, current Philippines. How did they do it?

Captain James Cook, the British explorer, navigator, and cartographer, was famous for his three voyages in the Pacific Ocean and to Australia particularly; and created detailed maps of Newfoundland, the present-day Canadian Province, before making three voyages to the Pacific, while completing the first registered European exposure to the eastern coastline of Australia and the Hawaiian Islands, plus the first noted complete navigation around New Zealand. How did they do it?

John Cabot, the Italian navigator and explorer's voyage to the coast of North America, which was under the commission of Henry VII of England, was the primarily known European exploration of coastal North America since the Norse of Norway, or Scandinavia visits to Vinland in the eleventh century. How did they do it?

Vasco da Gama, the Portuguese explorer was the first European to reach India by sea, and his first voyage to India was the first to connect Europe and Asia by an ocean way, connecting the Atlantic and the Indian oceans, in other words, Europe and Asia. How did they do it?

Jacques Cartier, the French-Breton maritime explorer for France, was the first European to describe and map the Gulf of Saint Lawrence and the shores of the Saint Lawrence River, which he named "The Country of Canadas" after the Iroquoian names for the two big settlements he saw at Stadacona, current Quebec City, and Hochelaga, current Montreal Island. How did they do it?

The Sense and Importance of Direction

No one can successfully reach a destination without good directions, whether from within (your heart/mind) or from outside (nature's elements, signs, instruments, or other people).

> *"No one can successfully reach a destination without good directions."*

Your sense of direction influences your sense of decision-making. When you know where you are going in life (your well-being, dreams, goals, and vision) and after-life (when you die) it becomes one of the fundamental elements or cornerstones of your decision-making.

> *"Your sense of direction influences your sense of decision-making."*

The first sense of direction in life is knowing where you are going. And your ambitions might not necessarily be the right ones, so they can give you the wrong directions that will lead you to the wrong destinations in life. Do you know where you want to go in life, and do you know if it is the right direction you are taking to the right destination? Do you know where you want to be? Figuratively, every moment in your life is a location or place you decided to be, or someone tricked you into being earlier, a few days, months, or years ago, directly, or indirectly. Every one of your feelings is a location, whether it's peace or trouble, happiness, or unhappiness. Unless it is God-ordained, every status in your life is a location you have already decided for, or you can also change by a decision before it is too late. Wherever you want to be, good or bad, your decisions or choices will take you there.

> *"Every moment in your life is a location or place you decided to be, or someone tricked you into being Earlier."*

Wrong decisions are made because of wrong directions, birthed by the wrong aspirations or desires. When you have the wrong directions, you make the wrong decisions. People make the wrong decisions because they have been given or believe in the wrong directions, which after all, produces the wrong aspirations in them. Directions come from information emanating from your own heart, or mind, someone, something, or God, and this information is received in the form of presentation, talk, display, lecture, reading, hearing, and instructions disguisedly via individuals, institutions, societies, governments, relatives, friends, books, radio, television, music, and education systems. Where do you get your directions from?

> *"Wherever you want to be, good or bad, your decisions or choices will take you there."*

The reason why you make bad decisions sometimes is not because of the gravity of your situation or condition that panics you. No matter how bad or heavy the situation may be, if you have the right information or direction, you can navigate yourself out of it. It may not be quick, but you will surely come out of it if only you can make the right decisions.

Ancient sailors, famous or infamous, did exploits by sea and discovered other lands, prosperity, peace, happiness, security, stability, and longevity in other places no one could have ever imaged, not because the oceans were calm, but because they had ways to find the right path. Ancient sailors or navigators used pointers, hints, or tips to navigate powerful oceans. Their method of finding directions could help us today to make good decision in our journey or navigation of life. Ancient sailors' pointers or hints include lands, odors, clouds, moon, stars, birds and waves, currents, wind, sun, and moon.

You may also think that what matters is getting to your destination, and it doesn't matter how you get there. No. "All roads lead to Rome" does not apply to everything in life. You may have good ambitions, but if the way you accomplish them or get to the realization is cluttered with bad decisions, or injustice and immorality, then your roads may lead you to the wrong destinations, or you may arrive, but will have to deal with all the troubles in the world.

What you have personally learned and know in life is never enough for you to live by and have a good and fulfilled life. Be humble and wise enough to borrow from the lessons, experiences, and knowledge of others. Do not be afraid and ashamed of admitting that you do not know or have limited knowledge or information about something. And never judge, denigrate, or belittle someone because they do not know what you know; because they may also know something you do not know, regardless of it is importance to you.

> *"Be humble and wise enough to borrow from the lessons, experiences, and knowledge of others."*

A wise person never knows everything; because everything has inexhaustible characteristics, meanings, mutations, or transformations over time under different circumstances, and is known by individuals and even nature in various ways according to their encounters and experiences with it.

What something is to you, and what you have learned from it may not be what it is to someone else, and what the person has learned from it, which could be profitable to you as well sooner or later.

> *"Never judge, denigrate, or belittle someone because they do not know what you know; because they may also know something you do not know."*

Questions are a friend of wisdom, and the wise asks questions because questions lead to discoveries or information, and information leads to preparedness, precautions, redirection, correction, growth, and fulfillment. However, you should also be aware of intrusive questions, or about private or sensitive topics, and only ask them when needed — but at least questions to get answers you need.

Foolishness or stupidity knows everything and never needs advice or considers one. The fool may be gifted but will waste all his life going in circles because he refuses to take advice. You may be gifted or anointed but may lack how to use your gift or anointing. Other gifts and talents are not wisdom, even though wisdom can be a gift. I have seen and met so many people who are gifted and anointed for many things yet, not wise. That is why you must be wise and open-minded to learn or take good and Godly counsel from others whenever necessarily.

> *"Questions are a friend of wisdom."*

Moses was one of the most anointed and gifted persons, but nearly killed himself with fatigue had he not listen to his father-in-law Jethro's advice. Jethro said to Moses, "Select capable men from all the people — men who fear God, trustworthy men who hate dishonest gain — and appoint them as officials over thousands, hundreds, fifties and tens. Have them serve as judges for the people at all times but have them bring every difficult case to you; the simple cases they can decide themselves. That will make your load lighter, because they will share it with you. If you do this and God so commands, you will be able to stand the strain, and all these people will go home satisfied." (Read full story in Exodus 18:13-26).

"A wise person never knows everything."

Nobody knows everything. Only God does. We may know some things about something, but not everything about everything.

It is a wise advice to welcome criticism, even if it hurts. And use it to improve yourself and the things that you are doing.

Let me tell you one of my short and funny stories: I used to struggle to open and close public restroom doors after using them and washing my hands. I often use my legs and feet to try opening and closing them because I do not want to dirty my hands after washing them. This, sometimes becomes a lot of work because I had to exercise so much strength and energy to accomplish it.

One day, I was standing outside a public restroom waiting for a lady to finish using it so I could also use it. While standing there, she finished using it and opened the door. To my dismay, she was holding the door with the tissue paper comfortably without struggle, got out, closed the door, and snugly threw the tissue paper away. Then I thought, "Why in the world have I never thought about doing it the way this lady just did?" "How long will I struggle with this simple task?" "Why was I trying to use my legs to open, hold, and close these doors?" I felt so unsmart about this. The lesson I learned that day was, no matter how smart you know you are, there are little things that your intelligence or smartness can miss. From that day on, I started using the unknown lady's method to open and close public restroom doors after using them and washing my hands.

I shared this short story with you to say that no matter how intelligent you are, you can easily flop in your choices or decision-making, and you must be aware of that and deal with matters or situations in a conscious way. And ask yourself, "Is there any safe, better, and morally sound way to do this?"

> *"No matter how intelligent you are, you can easily flop in your choices or decision-making."*

Ancient Navigation Tips

As I mentioned earlier, ancient sailors used pointers, hints, or tips to navigate dynamic oceans. And I believe their ocean navigation tips can figuratively help us navigate life, which is full of decision-making. They also used lands, in other words, they used dry grounds, and the coasts as a guide. They kept in sight and observed what they believed could lead them to their destinations.

Before we get to the metaphorical stages, let us enumerate the techniques they have used, such as dead reckoning, celestial navigation, and piloting that have endured until our modern days. In navigation, dead reckoning, is the process of calculating the current position of a moving object by using a previously determined position or fix and including estimations of speed, heading direction, and course over elapsed time. Celestial navigation, also known as astronavigation, is the ancient and modern navigation practice of position fixing using stars and other celestial bodies that enables a navigator to precisely determine the current physical position or location in space or on Earth. Piloting is navigating using fixed points of reference on the sea or on land, usually with reference to a nautical chart or aeronautical chart to obtain a fix of the position of the vessel or aircraft according to a desired course or location.

Even though ancient sailors did not perfect these navigation techniques, it is to be noted that even modern navigation instruments such as the GPS (Global Positioning System) which is a satellite-based navigation system funded and controlled by the U.S. government's Department of Defense, and launched between 1978 and 1985 with eleven (11) satellites, and now includes about 24 satellites that orbit the Earth and send radio signals from space has been built with these very ancients navigation concepts or techniques.

Remember, your human spirit, led by the Holy Spirit, who is a the greatest communicator, can convey information or talk to you through by and with anything, anywhere, and anytime. He can warn and encourage you about something, especially when you are about to make some crucial decisions. He's always with you as a child of God, and His mission or responsibility in your life even here on earth, is to guide you if only you would let him. Jesus said, *"But when he, the Spirit of truth, comes, he will guide you into all the truth. He will not speak on his own; he will speak only what he hears, and he will tell you what is yet to come."* (John 16:13, NIV).

I informed you earlier that this book is not from a mere natural, psychological, or philosophical understanding; rather, Biblical and spiritual, even though I may use them to help you understand these truths. So, in the following few paragraphs, I will also use phrases or expressions that typically represent a figurative, or non-literal meanings. There will be comparisons, mutations, or transfigurations to help you break into the realities surrounding your decision-making.

The Land: Your Defense, Thriving Place and Position

The Bible says in the beginning, "The waters covered the earth." (Genesis 1:1-2). God knew that human beings and some animals He was about to create could only thrive on the ground or land. So, before He created him, He had to create the ground or dry land. (Genesis 1:9).

Land or ground is a safety element for humankind. Man is made from the dust or ground and lives, thrives, safeguards, and defends himself on the ground better than anywhere else on Earth. Man is not aquatic, and any experience in the water will require extra effort for him to survive. Ancient sailors and vessel captains knew that as long as they kept the land in sight, primarily, they could quickly get to the soar in case of peril, recharge themselves, and plan for their next move or the journey ahead.

In decision-making, figuratively, the ground represents your place or position of defense, security, and stability. When you are making decisions, ensure that you keep the land or ground (Your positioning) in sight. Make sure the results of your decision will not push you away from a place (position) where you cannot better safeguard, protect, and defend yourself. Before deciding about anything in your life, relationship, career, business, and ministry, ask yourself, "Will the consequences take away my safety net?" What is your safety net? It is anything, location, place, position, possession, or item that you know, you can better defend yourself and fight from in a Godly way or even legally. And if yes, when, and how long?

The location where you are making and revealing your decision is also very important. There are some decisions that you have to be prepared before making them known or announcing them; otherwise, it will cost you time, money, properties, or even your life. Wisdom suggests that you know how, when, and where to make your decisions known.

Any constitution, agreement, partnership, or collaboration that will drive or take you out of your position or ground from which you can better defend yourself is to be reviewed and changed in order for you to keep a hundred or at least fifty percent of your ground or fighting position. Giving out a hundred percent of your figurative ground, defense or fighting position to someone, an organization, or a company, is like giving out a hundred percent of your power out – you may regret it sooner or later, except it is to God.

Before we even get to the next chapter, let me remind you that, an ancient war strategy has been to lure or drive your opponent out of his defense zone, or territory, or find a way to take it from him in order to effectively attack and overpower him. This strategy has been used in wars in Bible days, and in history to conquer cities, territories, and kingdoms, and many individuals, organizations, and companies continue to use that in various ways. For example, in constitutions, agreements, or contracts to tie the other party in case there arises a dispute, or something goes wrong, and they have to fight back one way or the other. Before you sign any papers, ask yourself, "Where am I situated in case something goes wrong?" And if your land, ground, or positioning of defense and fight is nowhere to be found in it, or it is taken away by the agreement or contract, or whatever it is you are about to do, think twice. Just don't do it.

This is not to advocate for leadership, or leaders who misbehave, or not let others lead an organization if there is evidence of such conduct.

Steve Jobs, the entrepreneur, industrial designer, investor, and media proprietor, became a household name in America and worldwide. After all, he was a co-founder of Apple, Inc. In fact, there are two sides to the story, because Steve Jobs had his side, and the former CEO of Apple John Sculley, also has his side of the story. Many do not adore him because of his radical business understanding and strategies. However, the lesson is, in 1985, Steve Jobs was forced or fired from Apple after a long power struggle with the company's board and its then CEO John Sculley, and would not return until 1997 to become the new CEO of the company, following the acquisition of NeXT, the new company he started after he left Apple. He then helped revive

Apple, which had been on the verge of bankruptcy and led it to where it was before he died in 2011.

The question is, if Steve Jobs' side of the story is true, and he was initially fired from Apple, which is different from then CEO John Sculley account, and who stated that Steve Jobs voluntarily left the company, then what was in the constitution or bylaws of the company? I'm not sure, since I have not read their Bylaws. But, I think had he, Steve Jobs, assured that his safety, defense, and fighting positioning or ground in the constitution of the Apple company right from the beginning was protected, they would not been able to fire or let him go as it happened; especially on the wrong basis. The lesson was, to never give out a hundred percent of your safety, defense, and fighting positioning or ground to anyone, except you are, or know you might be physically incapacitated — even then, think twice. Do not give a hundred percent of your ground to anyone in any kind of relationship, to an investor, or CEO of a company you founded even in case you have to step down or hold another position in a new venture —Just. Don't. Do it. Always make sure your ground is protected. If you ignore this, you may see your vision for the company or entity collapse in front of your eyes, and there will be nothing much you can do to save it. This is also true with every area of your life.

Odors or Scents: Your Alerts or Warnings

Ancient sailors used odors or scents as their navigation guides, which can travel far away into the sea. An odor is a distinctive smell, meaning the smell can reveal its source or what it is coming from. A smell can bring joy or irritation.

When you smell good food, it brings you excitement. But when you smell a dead fish, it prompts for annoyance, right?

Odors in the air generally inform you that you are exposed to something good or bad, dangerous or safe, familiar or unfamiliar. Ancient sailors usually follow these distinctive odors to find lands, shores, or islands. The odors can also alert them of nearby dangers, which helps them to be prepared and deal with them accordingly.

> *"Odors in the air generally inform you that you are exposed to something good or bad, dangerous or safe, familiar or unfamiliar."*

Scientifically, when we smell something, our nose and brain work together to make sense of hundreds of tiny invisible particles, known as molecules or chemicals floating in the air. If we inhale or sniff, more of these molecules get to the top inner surface of our nostrils and enable us to easily smell a scent.

It is amazing how the human body is physically able to store or memorize odors or scents, which sometimes helps us as humans to be able to distinguish where we are, what is close, and what is about to happen. Olfactory neurons, which are composed of tiny cells, have long connections like cable that send electrical messages to a spot at the front of the brain, also known as the olfactory bulb. Every one of the olfactory neurons connects with a different neuron in the olfactory bulb, that subsequently sends this information to other areas of the brain. The parts of the brain that receive these signals also do other things, such as storing memories and arousing emotions. These natural and human settings enable us as humans to experience and feel old memories or get emotional when we smell familiar scents.

I have noted that some people literally hate some perfumes and fragrances because their ex-husband or wife whom they divorced used to wear them. They hate those scents not because they are not good scents, but because their former lover uses them. This reveals to us how powerful and significant a scent could be.

> *"Some people literally hate some perfumes — because their ex-husband or wife whom they divorced used to wear them — This reveals to us how powerful and significant a scent could be."*

The sense of smell is very significant to animals as well because it leads and helps them find food, recognize their family members, and keep away from potential dangers. Even though not all animals have an active sense of smell like dolphins and whales who cannot smell due to the form and position of their nostrils, it is to be noted that some animals even have a very high-level sense of smell, and that is why till now, many hunters will go hunting with their dogs which can smell other animals' scents better than them. Security forces around the world use animals to detect illegal drugs, foods, explosives, and human traces.

The sense of smell is very powerful and was not of less value to ancient sailors, so they track or follow scents as guides to get to where they wanted to go and discover new lands.

This olfactory system, or sense of smell, is the sensory system used for smelling, or olfaction. And the olfactory language refers to language associated with the sense of smell. Interestingly, this involves the naming and categorization of odors by humans according to each odor's kind source or characteristics. This fact proves to us that scents are actually a language, and a language is a system of communication.

> *"Scents are actually a language, and a language is a system of communication."*

If we can consider odors or scents as a language, and a language is a system of communication, then just as the ancient sailors who have done great exploits through the oceans, by just mastering their physical sense of smell, we can also wisely navigate life with a mastery of how to intuitively and spiritually smell problems far away before they reach us.

When making decisions, pay attention to the "Odor/scent" that you can instinctively or spiritually smell without your conscious reasoning. Most importantly as a child of God, His Spirit would impact those strange or familiar figurative odors of problems to your spirit. At some point, you will be so familiar with the odor of problems to the extent that you will know that the decision you are making or you have just made will produce bad or good results. What I meant by all the above is, whenever you want to make a decision, double-check for "problem odors" figuratively.

Remember, you cannot see odors, and neither can you see problems until they start unfolding; and that's when you can know that there are problems. The truth is, odors are always generated by something that has become decomposed, rotten, decayed, or caused to decay. Similarly, in a figurative sense, odors in decision-making represent the already spoiled elements about the matter or concern you are making the decision about — Pay attention to things you cannot see, but have a feeling or sense that they exist or can happen.

> *"We can also wisely navigate life with a mastery of how to intuitively and spiritually smell problems far away before they reach us."*

The Clouds: Observe them, But Do Not Trust Them

Ancient sailors followed the clouds as a navigational guide. According to the Oxford English Dictionary, a cloud is "a visible mass of condensed water vapor floating in the atmosphere, typically high above the ground." But when it comes to your decision-making, the clouds represent the images of the matter or concern you are deciding about. What can your imagination see? Can you see anything in your imagination? And if yes, what are they?

Sometimes, figuratively, the state of the invisible atmosphere at the time you are about to make a decision can tell the outcome of the decision you are about to make. Whether the results or consequences of the decision you are about to make will be good or bad, you can feel it in the atmosphere.

Just as there are many different clouds and atmospheres, the results of your decisions are not the same, and you may feel that at the time you are deciding to say or do something. We will not deepen into meteorology, atmospheric sciences, or weather forecasting. However, it is to be noted that there are ten main clouds, and each one of the clouds has different shapes, and colors and predicts different weather. While you and I might see a cloud and not know what is about to happen, an experienced meteorologist or a weather forecaster knows what is about to happen when he sees these different clouds, Altocumulus, Altostratus, Cirrocumulus, Cirrostratus, Cirrus, Cumulonimbus, Cumulus, Nimbostratus, and Stratocumulus. As a non-meteorologist, it can be challenging to keep track of cloud names and the main types because it is not your field of profession unless you have an interest to learn and know weather forecasting. Interestingly, it is not too difficult to study how to easily identify most clouds. Clouds can be identified by their shapes, height, and accompanying weather.

> *"Sometimes, figuratively, the state of the invisible atmosphere at the time you are about to make a decision can tell the outcome of the decision."*

Consider that clouds can look very similar, and it requires attention and expertise to identify similar clouds. All the same, situations or events in your life, family, business, or ministry can look similar, and the physical and spiritual atmosphere can look and feel very similar so if you are not careful, you can easily make the wrong decision believing it will just produce the same good results it provided a few days, months or years ago when you made a similar decision. Therefore, you would have to handle each decision-making on a case-by-case basis even if the matters look very familiar. There are various tips you can use to differentiate between two types of clouds that look similar.

All ten major clouds have their heights (The position or where in the sky the cloud commonly appears, low-level, mid-level, or high-level), colors (The color of the cloud), shape (The form of the cloud), and weather (The weather the cloud is normally associated with, forecast or predicts). The different clouds can predict various kinds of weather: warmer weather with the possibility of light precipitation, sunny and cold weather, warm front weather approaching, thunderstorms, just sunny weather, steady rain or snow weather, weak convection in the atmosphere, and gloomy weather.

For ancient sailors to know where they were, and what was about to happen in the atmosphere, they checked the clouds. First, they figure out the shape of the clouds; second, where they are in the clouds; and third, they observe the weather. However, they also know that clouds cannot be trusted.

"Clouds cannot be trusted."

Clouds Are Not Stable and Very Tricky

While you may metaphorically observe the clouds or the atmosphere when making a crucial decision, do not trust them because they can change at any given moment.

There is a proverb in the Ewe language (Ewe is a language spoken in Togo and southeastern Ghana as a first language) that says, "Do not put your hope in a cloudy sky expecting it will rain and throw away your dirty water." The message in that is, do not throw your dirty water away because it looks like it will rain. When you throw your presumably dirty water that you think you do not need away because the sky looks rainy, you might be wrong because it might not rain, and you will end up losing even the water you think was not a good one. In other words, be careful when relying on what is not, or has not yet materialized to make decisions, unless you are dealing with God. Yes, the Bible says, *"Now faith is the substance of things hoped for, the evidence of things not seen."* (Hebrews 11:1, KJV). This only applies when dealing with God and expecting something from God, not humans.

Do not make crucial decisions based on human promises because there is no guarantee they will keep their words, or things will happen as promised. Always keep the little that you have and stay where you are until what you have been promised, hoped for, and expected comes true before discarding the old one or moving forward. Hebrews 11:1, is not related to you trusting men, or even nature, but God.

> *"Do not make crucial decisions based on human promises without a backup plan."*

Ancient sailors were able to identify clouds by figuring out the shapes of the clouds, looking at their location and position in the sky, and considering the weather. They were able to easily identify different types of clouds by looking at their shapes, because identifying the shape helped them narrow down their options of interpretation before moving to other steps and identifiers to determine which particular cloud it was. The location and position of the cloud in the sky, low, mid, or high level also helped them narrow down on what it meant to their trip and where they were in the oceans. Last, but not least, the current or coming weather helped them with the cloud identification, which notifies them of what should be their next action to make their journey successful.

Emergency and Non-emergency Decisions

Do not handle time-sensitive decisions, or emergency decisions as non-emergency ones, and non-emergency ones as emergency. Emergency decisions are decisions you have to quickly review facts and truths, weigh the consequences or results as a measure, and take to stop life-threatening events or problems. Non-emergency decisions are decisions you can take time and request or search for more information, analyze facts and truths, and weigh the consequences or results as a measure before making them. The truth is, when it comes to goodness or fortune, wanting to see it before you believe it might not be problematic or dangerous. But when it comes to the dangers of life, trying to see it before you believe it will be a mistake. Therefore, you have to take every life-threatening warning or notification as seriously as it could be. It is necessary to make a quick decision to quickly take the next life-saving action, otherwise, you or someone will perish, and lose money or properties. Do not drag emergency decisions and handle them as non-emergency decisions. You must make that decision right away. Figuratively, turn right or left immediately before it is too late.

> *"When it comes to the dangers of life, trying to see it before you believe it will be a mistake."*

When the clouds show it will rain, you better prepare for rain, and if it does not rain, you will still count it as a win or be fine. But if you think the clouds are not stable, so even when it looks like it will rain and you do not prepare for it, but then it rains, that can cost you losses. Remember the idiom, "Better safe, than sorry." Meaning, you should be cautious — if you are not, you may regret it." You can be prepared for rain without throwing away your dirty water. You can be prepared for the coming events without discarding what you already have, then maybe discard it later after assuring it is safe to do so.

Clouds Serve as a Guide

When the children of Israel left Egypt, they were led by the prophet of God, Moses. Little did they know how long and difficult their journey to the promised land would be. (Exodus 12:31-33). Surprisingly, they finally realized it would take them more time than they ever thought. But how long? A few years? No. Actually, forty (40) good years. How can a whole nation or thousands of people traverse through a desert for forty (40) years without getting lost? They did not have a modern-day compass or GPS (Global Positioning System). The answer is simple: God Himself was leading them by the clouds. The Bible says, "And the LORD went ahead of them in a pillar of cloud to guide them on their way and by night in a pillar of fire to give them light so that they could travel by day or night." (Exodus 13: 21). God himself would confirm this to them by saying, "I have led you forty years in the desert. Your clothes did not wear out. And your shoes did not wear out on your feet." (Deuteronomy 29:5).

Wise decision-making suggests that you observe the figurative or symbolic images, pictures in the situation or matter, but be flexible because they can change and may not be exactly what they look like or produce what you think they will generate — Observe the clouds but do not trust them, yet prepare for the rain so in case it rains, you will still be fine anyways. A clear or sunny sky does not necessarily mean it will not rain, and a cloudy or dark sky does not necessarily mean it will surely rain, but sometimes it does. So, be prepared in a way that when the predictions of the clouds turn out to be true or exactly that, you will win, and if they do not, you will still win.

Missing the Odors and Clouds

It is important to also note that sometimes, just like you may not smell an odor literally, or see something coming regardless of your spiritual level or anointing and the grace of God over your life, other people can smell and see it coming. The Bible is full of examples of highly anointed men and women of God who were not able to detect problems their decisions would cause until the problems were manifested. So, as an individual or a leader, even though you are not obligated to take every piece of advice or suggestion from people around, working with you, or God has placed in your life, business, or ministry, it is very important that you pay attention and carefully evaluate their suggestions because they can smell or see a problem or something you may not smell or see regardless of your spiritual level. That is just the sovereignty of God. He reveals things to whom He wants. Many leaders and individuals have lost time, money, and in some cases, their lives simply because they did not pay attention to the good, God-inspired suggestions people around them have given them. I will discuss more about this in another chapter.

The Moon, Stars, and Sun: Foreseeing Bad Moments

Ancient sailors used the moon, stars, and sun to navigate, find locations, and tell time.

Making the right decision at the wrong time, too early or too late, can turn your good decision into a bad one. Executing a good decision at the wrong time can turn your good action or act into a bad one, and you may not be able to correct the damages. Make sure you make the right decision at the right time and you execute that decision at the right time.

> *"Making the right decision at the wrong time, too early or too late, can turn your good decision into a bad one."*

While making crucial decisions, be time conscious, but not time-pressured. The weight of the decision will not push the clock backward or forward. As I stated before, if the decision is a non-emergency decision, do not rush it. But even if it is time-sensitive, be aware of the deadline, but do not let the time pressure you into making a wrong decision. One of the worst things that can happen to you in your decision-making process is making a decision and realizing a few days, hours, minutes, or seconds later that you could have made it otherwise, which would have been the best.

> *"While making crucial decisions, be time conscious, but not time-pressured."*

As I mentioned earlier, the location where you announce your decision is also very important. There are some decisions you have to be prepared for before making them known or announcing them; otherwise, it will cost you time, money, property, or even your life. Wisdom suggests that you know how, when, and where to make your decisions known and to whom it may concern.

For example, you do not tell your violent husband, boyfriend, or business partner your intention of leaving the toxic relationship while you are by yourself. He may hurt you. Or do not tell an abusive employer that you got a new job until you are hired by another employer – Common sense right?

Thousands of years before 360-degree panoramic photography, 360-degree view, and Virtual Reality (VR) technologies emerged, the ancient world used the same fundamentals, techniques, and tips to achieve great things, including navigation.

A 3D panoramic photography, or as some call it, wide-angle shot or view, or ultra-wide-angle shot or view, is a three-dimensional wide-angle view or rendering of a physical space. A 360-degree shot or view is a 3D panorama that covers the full horizontal and vertical fields of view around something or a person, while virtual reality (VR) is a simulated experience that can be like the real world – It seems almost real.

Mathematically, 360 degrees is a full circle, but in the physical world, a 360-degree view is the ability to see everything around you without blind spots. Like a full 360-degree panoramic photography or video, which enables the viewer to view any part of a location or object, up or down, left or right, wisdom suggests that you view every matter or situation in a 360-degree view to be able to see everything concerning it before making a decision. Do not just view one side of a matter or situation and rush to make decisions. Viewing the matter in a 360 degree allows you to rule in realities or truths, intentions, and purpose, then rule out feelings, pride, arrogance, selfishness, greed, and many other elements that lead to bad decisions.

Let us play a little in geography: As you may know, the Earth in spherical coordinates is Geographic or Unprojected. The lines running North to South are called lines of longitude, while the lines running East to West are called lines of latitude. When you move East-West, you change through 360 degrees. So, the Earth is 360 degrees around. But when you move North-South, you change through 180 degrees. So, going from the North Pole to the South Pole is 180 degrees.

One of the applications of human creative skill and imagination that ancient sailors utilized to travel is called Celestial Navigation, which is the art and science of finding ways by the sun, moon, stars, and planets. Sailors used this creative technique in navigation when needed instead of dead reckoning, which is the process of calculating the current position of some moving object by using a previously determined position, or fix, and then including estimations of speed, heading direction, and course over elapsed time. The Celestial Navigation technique uses the stars, moon, sun, and horizon to calculate position. It has been proven to be very useful on the open ocean, where there are no landmarks. In other words, this navigation technique consists of the observation of celestial bodies to determine a navigator's position.

It is also interesting to note that Ocean tides are caused by the Moon's gravitational pull. The Moon and the Sun influence the ocean tides, but the Moon plays the biggest role. This also reveals to us that the Celestial Navigation technique not only helped ancient sailors to reach destinations, but also assisted them in detecting and foreseeing bad moments in Oceans or what challenges to expect next in their navigation.

It is necessary to do your best to foresee the bad moments that could arise after your decisions. This does not mean you will not move forward with your decision if you believe it is the right one, however it will help you to be prepared to deal with the bad moments. Sometimes, you cannot separate some decisions from bad moments, but you have to make that decision to prevent other ugly and worse situations or problems. But if you can foresee the upcoming bad moments, you can fully be prepared to deal with them properly.

The Sooner or Later Effects

When deciding, you have to keep in mind that what you are expecting to happen or not after you make and execute it, may happen sooner or later, so you have to be prepared for the sooner or later positive or negative effects or results of your decisions. I hear people sometimes say, "I knew that it will happen, but I did not know it could happen this fast." Or, "I thought it would happen later." When you are dealing with everything in the natural realm, expect the sooner or later effects. The only person or thing that is fixed is God. The Creation, Nature, and everything in it, or this world can change, so you have to prepare for the sooner or later effects and surprises. Having faith does not mean ignoring to have a plan. God is a master planner.

Use faith where it's due, and use common sense and wisdom where they are due.

> *"Use faith where it's due, and common sense and wisdom where they are due."*

Small Preparations May Deliver From Big Challenges

Five thousand men, according to the Bible, went to listen to the LORD Jesus Christ and witness the miracles, healings, signs, and wonders He was doing. Traditionally, women and children were not counted or numbered. So, we may estimate roughly that these men either brought their whole family, including children and wives, or at least one of their children if possible. So let us assume that five thousand men took their children and wives to a remote place for an event and did not prepare or plan for food and probably water. And when it was too late for them to leave and go back home, they were hungry and needed something to eat, but had none. The Gospel according to John reports, "Andrew, Simon Peter's brother, spoke up, *"Here is a boy with five small barley loaves and two small fish, but how far will they go among so many?"* (John 6:9, NIV). Clearly, a boy or his parents were wise enough to know that it is not good to go to such a remote place without food, knowing it may be late by the time he comes back home and surely will thirst and hunger since it was not a fasting meeting. But as the story unfolds, we understand that had it not been for that boy who was prepared and took five small barley loaves and two small fish with him to the meeting, there would not been a multiplication of bread and fish, which fed all the crowd.

You may argue that the Lord Jesus Christ could have performed the miracle without the bread and fish of the boy anyway. But if you have to understand that, while God can create and bring anything into existence nothing, He likes doing things in collaboration with humanity or humans. Faith or the belief that God can do it does not exclude Godly wisdom or consideration of realities as long as it does not violate the word or commandment of God. If God directly commands you to do anything in a particular way without consideration of natural laws, then do it exactly like that because He will surely intervene supernaturally to miraculously change the natural laws in favor of His commandment, or rhema — His "utterance" or what He said to you specifically. But if He does not tell you specifically to do something against logic or natural laws, just do not do it without putting logic and realities into consideration. That does not make you less of a Christian or a man of faith, but it makes you wise because you understand the sovereignty of God in the circumstances of humanity.

Jesus could have raised His hands towards heaven and prayed for bread and fish ready to eat from the skies for the people to eat and enjoy; after all, God did it exactly like that when the children of Israel were in the desert coming from Egypt. (Exodus 16:1-36). But that time, He used what a little boy or his parents thought about provisioning as preparation for the event.

Decision results or consequences may materialize or happen sooner or later than you think, so you must be wisely prepared. Perhaps, the payment, money, property, or access to whatever it is, will not come immediately. So, you have to plan for that. Sometimes the opposite may even come or happen sooner; the attack, cancellation, betrayal, separation, or the bad may happen immediately, so you have to be prepared to counter-attack or protect yourself, everybody, and everything that needs to be protected at the maximum.

Being prepared for things does not mean you do not trust God. Even though we are more than conquerors (Romans 8:31-37) and conscious of our spiritual being and life on earth, we live in a natural or physical world. The Lord himself warned us, he said to the disciples, *"I have told you these things, so that in me you may have peace. In this world you will have trouble. But take heart! I have overcome the world."* (John 16:33, NIV).

We may have all learned from this: When Mr. Joe Biden took office as the 46th President of the United States, he tried to keep a promise he made in his campaign to end America's longest war overseas in Afghanistan and withdraw the army. As many stated, and mentioned, Mr. Donald Trump, the 45th President of the United States, also committed to do the same before he took office. So, on April 14, 2021, President Biden announced the full U.S. Troop withdrawal from Afghanistan by September 11, 2021, which would have been the 20th anniversary of September

11, 2001. In short, US intelligence analysts predicted that it would probably take many weeks before Afghanistan's civilian government in Kabul fell to Taliban fighters. But surprisingly, it only took a few days. Taliban militants retook Afghanistan's capital, almost two decades after the US military forces drove them out of Kabul, the capital city.

The United States revealed the fact that Afghan security forces were well funded and equipped, but did not resist the Taliban militants till they seized many parts of the country after the withdrawal of US troops, which began earlier. President Ashraf Ghani fled the country and abandoned the presidential palace to the Taliban fighters.

In effect, the US officials finally acknowledged that they miscalculated how fast the Taliban were able to advance across the country and take over. Unfortunately, more people were killed, including civilians and US military service members.

I do not want to talk about politics here, but I believe we can all learn a very important lesson: What follows after we make decisions can actually happen sooner than we thought or calculated. So, we must always put this fact into consideration, and be prepared in several ways in case the results of our decisions happen sooner or later than we expected.

Additionally, as I mentioned earlier, the execution of your decisions is another step you must evaluate before acting. Think about the time, the place or location, the how, and what will follow. Otherwise, your good decision might turn into a bad one because your plan of action is miscalculated.

Knowing Your Position In Time During Decisions

Many have destroyed their lives and others by making the wrong decisions because someone made the same decision the same way in the past and got good results. What they missed is that the time in which they were making their decisions was not identical to when the previous person decided on the same matter. Things and people change in times or seasons, so make your decisions in consideration of the times and seasons. Do not make decisions just based on history, but evaluate your position, time, or season as well.

> *"Make your decisions in consideration of the times and seasons."*

Figuratively, knowing your time and position, right from your left, so to speak, meaning the era, generation, year or season you are making your decision helps you make better decisions as well. You cannot make a decision in 2019 as it was made in 1845.

Time is defined as the progression of events from the past to the present into the future. The reason nothing in our world is timeless, except God, is because our world, or solar system, which consists of our star or the Sun, and everything associated with it by gravity, including the planets Mercury, Venus, Earth, Mars, Jupiter, Saturn, Uranus and Neptune, and dwarf planets such as Pluto, in addition to dozens of moons and millions of asteroids, comets and meteoroids is actually in time or live in time. So, if you live on Earth, which is in our solar system and the physical and natural realm, you also live in time.

The modern international unit of time, which is second, is determined by the electronic transition of the cesium atom. Clocks run like the solar system. The Sun controls our concept of time, and the moon, which is four hundred times closer to us than the Sun and moves around the earth, our planet like the hand of a clock can help us tell time if we know how – and the ancient people, including the sailors knew how.

As you may know, our present-day clocks are established in seconds, minutes, and hours. In fact, the fundamentals for these units have long existed throughout history, and they can be traced back to some of the earliest known civilizations in the historical region of southern Mesopotamia, emerging during the Chalcolithic and early Bronze Ages between the sixth and fifth millennium BC.

Time, as defined by science or physics, is not something you and I can see, touch, or taste, but we can measure its passage. And it's the progression of events from the past into the future. Meaning, time moves only in one direction. It's possible to move forward in time, but not backward, and Scientists believe memory development or formation is the basis for human perception of time.

Navigators who use the Celestial Navigation technique used tools such as the sextant, backstaff, and cross-staff to measure the angle between objects in the sky and the horizon. According to it's definition by the dictionary and various navigation schools, a sextant is a doubly reflecting navigation instrument that measures the angular distance between two visible objects. It is primarily used to measure the angle between an astronomical object and the horizon for the purposes of celestial navigation. The sextant allows celestial objects to be measured relative to the horizon rather than relative to the instrument. It has been known that, unlike the backstaff, the sextant allows direct observations of stars, which enables the use of the sextant at night when a backstaff is difficult to use. The backstaff is also a navigational instrument that was used to measure the altitude of a celestial body, especially the Sun or Moon. When observing the Sun, users kept the Sun to their back, where its name originated from, and observed the shadow cast by the upper vane on a horizon vane. The cross-staff just like the sextant and backstaff, was a navigational tool used to measure the angle between the horizon and a celestial body such as the sun or stars; and by knowing this angle, a navigator could easily determine his latitude and direction. The cross-staff is also referred to as the fore-staff and the Jacob's staff.

Geography reveals to us why it is important for navigators or sailors to know their latitude and longitude. The longitude and latitude helped them to locate their position on a map. To know their location, navigators determine their latitude and longitude.

Longitude is a geographic coordinate that specifies the east–west position of a point on the Earth's surface, or the surface of a celestial body. It is an angular measurement, usually expressed in degrees. Meridians connect points with the same longitude.

Latitude is a geographic coordinate that specifies the north–south position of a point on the Earth's surface. It is an angle which ranges from 0° at the Equator to 90° at the poles. Lines of constant latitude, or parallels, run east–west as circles parallel to the equator.

Geography teaches us that the distance around the Earth measures 360 degrees. The meridian that runs through Greenwich, England, is internationally accepted as the line of 0 degrees longitude, or prime meridian. The antimeridian is halfway around the world, at 180 degrees. It is the basis for the International Date Line.

Cardinal directions are probably the most important directions in geography: north, south, east, and west.
Additionally, the quality of being morally right or justifiable is a key in decision-making. Ask yourself, "How can I morally or rightfully justify my decision?" If you cannot morally justify your decision, it means something is wrong with it. Any decision you cannot justify morally will result in troubles, and some will last for years. Moreover, as yourself, "Is there any truth, facts, or evidence in the cause of my decision?"

> *"If you cannot morally justify your decision, it means something is wrong with it."*

How can you make the right decision if you do not know the way to righteousness, good, injustice, or wickedness? The only sure way to know right from wrong is from the word of God. Jesus said, **"I am the way and the truth and the life."** (John 14:6, ESV).

In a recognizable way, knowing your part in a matter also can help you make the right decision if you have to make any. Sometimes, you might be tricked into matters that do not concern you in any way, and getting involved could be a matter of choice. While it's a human responsibility to defend and protect others, this may come with heavy consequences or prices, so you must properly evaluate how and when you should be involved in matters, and the required preparations before getting involved to rescue or save other people. You might also be careful and know your limits because sometimes trying to save everybody might not be successful, or end well for you. I'm not saying you should be selfish or egoistic, but just be vigilant and well-prepared to do that. If you are not well-prepared, you can cause too much trouble to yourself and others and be exhausted without really helping. Remember, you can also find creative ways to rescue people from various problems and dangers without not getting fully involved.

Seizing the Momentum and Monitoring Time

During one of the most difficult conquests in the history of the world by the children of Israel, when they conquered the promised land, and Jerusalem as what will become today's most coveted city in the world, the Bible accounts, when "Adoni-Zedek king of Jerusalem heard that Joshua had taken Ai and totally destroyed it, doing to Ai and its king as he had done to Jericho and its King, and that the people of Gibeon had made a treaty of peace with Israel and had become their allies. He and his people were very much alarmed at this, because Gibeon was an important city, like one of the royal cities; it was larger than Ai, and all its men were good fighters. So Adoni-Zedek king of Jerusalem appealed to Hoham king of Hebron, Piram king of Jarmuth, Japhia king of Lachish and Debir king of Eglon. "Come up and help me attack Gibeon," he said, "because it has made peace with Joshua and the Israelites." (Joshua 10:1-4, NIV).

"So Joshua marched up from Gilgal with his entire army, including all the best fighting men. The Lord said to Joshua,

"Do not be afraid of them; I have given them into your hand. Not one of them will be able to withstand you."

"After an all-night march from Gilgal, Joshua took them by surprise. The Lord threw them into confusion before Israel, so Joshua and the Israelites defeated them completely at Gibeon. Israel pursued them along the road going up to Beth Horon and cut them down all the way to Azekah and Makkedah. As they fled before Israel on the road down from Beth Horon to Azekah, the Lord hurled large hailstones down on them, and more of them died from the hail than were killed by the swords of the Israelites.

On the day the Lord gave the Amorites over to Israel, Joshua said to the Lord in the presence of Israel:
"Sun, stand still over Gibeon,
   and you, moon, over the Valley of Aijalon."
   So the sun stood still,
   and the moon stopped,
   till the nation avenged itself on its enemies,
as it is written in the Book of Jashar.
The sun stopped in the middle of the sky and delayed going down about a full day. 14 There has never been a day like it before or since, a day when the Lord listened to a human being. Surely the Lord was fighting for Israel!
Then Joshua returned with all Israel to the camp at Gilgal." (Joshua 10:7-15)

Joshua knew if he held back and stopped fighting because of the sun going down, and the night and darkness coming upon them, they probably would lose momentum. So, he prayed a prayer no one had ever prayed before and believed God to answer it. He wanted the sun to stop. In other words, time to stop, and it did. It was a major factor that determined their victory.

Try to detect what is about to destroy or stop your victory halfway before it does. Joshua quickly knew the going down of the sun or the coming of the night was about to limit their victory and turn it into a lost or uncompleted victory. So, he prayed a prayer no one prayed before and the result was that what never happened occurred – the sun stopped, and time stopped.

You do not make decisions and then forget about it or without monitoring the results. When you make decisions even at the right time, announce it at right time, and at the right location, you still have to monitor the outcome because even if it turns out to be favorable to your personal life, and the people around you, your team, organization, ministry, or country, there may be some little things that can still go wrong and become bigger challenges or problems. So, you must keep your eyes on them to monitor and control the results before they get out of hand. Your initial win does not necessarily guarantee your permanent victory if you do not monitor situations along the way and make sure they are under control and a perpetual defeat or submission, which yields a lasting peace of mind, a sense of security, happiness, and stability.

> *"You do not make decisions and then forget about it or without monitoring the results."*

Keep in mind that, circumstances, including natural events, can affect the execution of your decisions, so it might take more than what you estimated it will take to bring your decision to fruition successfully.

Do not be a blind supporter, either. Always try to properly listen to both sides in a conflict before you draw a conclusion. Do not be the parent, wife, husband, brother, sister, friend, relative, or teammate who is not honest and does not tell the truth to their child, spouse, friend, brother, sister, relative, or teammate. The main reason why God places you in someone's life is for you to support them one way or the other to reach their full potential. But with that comes two main responsibilities in order to be an effective supporter: You have to be able to cheer them on when they are doing the right thing, and also be honest and tell them the truth when they are wrong. Love the person you are related to one way or the other, but be honest and tell them the truth when they are wrong. Do not support them in wrongdoings against others just because you are related to them. God will judge one day for that.

> *"Always try to properly listen to both sides in a conflict before you draw a conclusion."*

When two people or parties have a misunderstanding or conflict, each side tends to narrate the story in its favor in order to convince you and gain your support. So, you must use your intelligence and wisdom to properly listen to both sides of the story before drawing conclusion. Do not unwisely support someone against the other. You can still love and support someone while telling them the truth.

The Birds: Follow Your God-given Signals

Ancient sailors follow birds, especially seabirds, to determine their direction and reach land. They navigated by watching the flight of birds. For instance, when they see a seabird with a fish in its mouth, they know the bird was most likely flying back toward land after catching a fish to eat; and when they see a bird with an empty beak, they know the bird was likely flying to deep sea to catch a fish. So, ancient sailors would usually follow the seabirds to reach the shore.

For years, scientific researchers have tried to understand several things about birds, and the findings have been very intriguing. Among many other species, birds migrate thousands of miles or kilometers each year either to escape weather deemed to be bad for them just like humans, or to find food in other areas or regions.

Birds migrate to mild or moderate regions during Spring in search of food and where they can securely create a habitat. During the Fall season, birds migrate to warmer regions in search of food and comfort. During the Winter season, some birds move from the North to the South, and others move from the South to the North. This also means some birds like the cold weather, and others also like warm weather.

The annual migrations of birds, or flyways are flight path used by several birds in their migration between their breeding grounds and their overwintering quarters. Researchers noted that flyways generally stretch across continents and usually the oceans. It is also interesting to know that there are four major north-to-south flyways in North America and six overlaying Europe and Asia, Africa, New

Zealand, and other close islands. In other words, birds travel the world and fly over oceans without getting lost or going in the wrong direction to find themselves in the wrong place. So, how do they do that? How do they know or detect the four cardinal directions: north, east, south, and west?

To date, researchers are unable to fully tell how birds can navigate their vast flyways every season of the year. However, they concluded that it is safe to believe that birds have an internal Global Positioning System (GPS), which enables them to follow the same pattern every season of the year to go where they need to be for food and comfort. Findings also include the fact that young birds recognize or imprint on the sun and stars, and use them to detect their global positioning. Another intriguing fact is that, birds recognize landmarks, and could use that as navigational help.

Naturally, birds' eyes are connected and communicate with their brain in a region called "cluster N" which helps them to detect their orientation to the north. Additionally, birds have small amounts of iron in the neurons of their inner ear that help them to recognize their global positioning as well.

It is also believed that birds' beaks help them in their navigation. Their beak helps them determine their positioning. The trigeminal nerve, which connects birds' beaks to their brain, helps them evaluate their exact situation on the map. Scientists believe the trigeminal nerve of birds can help them detect the strength of the Earth's magnetic field, which is stronger at the poles and weaker at the Equator.

It is important to also note that birds can smell their way through their flyways. This helps them to easily find lands and their arrangement, natural, artificial, and physical forms.

God's Natural Gifts

If birds are naturally hatched or born with a built-in (or should I say created-in) Global Position System (GPS), which ancient sailors follow to navigate, believe that human beings are also born with the ability or natural features to know wrong, right, and detect upcoming dangers, lies, and deceptions. And as a child of God, when you receive the Holy Spirit, it even gets better as He uses these natural gifts coupled with the spiritual gifts of God to guide, protect, and deliver you from problems and dangers. The problem is that we, human beings do not develop these natural gifts, nor do we observe and use them to our advantage to navigate life, and in decision-making processes. Believe it or not, you were born with a natural ability to make the right decisions. But many times, these human natural and spiritual abilities or sensors are suppressed by our desires, pleasures, greed, selfishness, and ego.

> *"Believe it or not, you were born with a natural ability to make the right decisions."*

Wisely use your natural and spiritual God-given gifts to evaluate truth and fact, and measure the expected results before deciding. Each time you are about to make a crucial decision, pay attention to what is happening in your heart or spirit; even though the feelings might be similar, with time, you will master and know the difference between the feeling and what you sense when your decision is a bad or good one. These signals are not the same for everybody, but they are very similar, and once you get familiar with yours, then you can personally interpret them for yourself. They become one of the tools God uses to help you make the right decisions, even with the supernatural help of the Holy Spirit.

> *"Many times — human natural and spiritual abilities or sensors are suppressed by our desires, pleasures, greed, selfishness, and ego."*

Noah, the Raven and the Dove: Use the Right Things to Measure Your Decisions

Do not use the wrong things to measure or evaluate your decision-making. When you use the wrong things to measure your decision-making, you will surely end up making the wrong decisions. Do not use mere desire, selfishness, greed, envy, jealousy, pride, money, riches, beauty, and fame to evaluate your decision-making. While those things are good to have, they can blur your understanding, judgment, or common sense, and not help you to have an open mind, clear judgment, and good morals to make the right decisions.

When God decided to destroy humanity, He remembered Noah and saved him and his immediate family. But after the rain and flood, God used to destroy wickedness on earth stopped, Noah needed to know whether the water had receded or not before coming out of the ark. That was a decision Noah had to make because if the water did not recede and he tried to get out of the ark, he could have drowned and died in the water. So, staying on or coming out of the ark at a particular time after the flood was another crucial decision Noah should make. So, Noah thought about finding a way to check if the water had receded from the earth. And the Bible says, "After forty days Noah opened a window he had made in the ark and sent out a raven, and it kept flying back and forth until the water had dried up from the earth. Then he sent out a dove to see if the water had receded from the surface of the ground. But the dove could find nowhere to perch because there was water over all the surface of the earth; so it returned to Noah in the ark. He reached out his hand and took the dove and brought it back to himself in the ark. He waited seven more days and again sent out the dove from the ark. When the dove returned to him in the evening, there in its beak was a freshly plucked olive leaf! Then Noah knew that the water had receded from the earth. He waited seven more days and sent the dove out again, but this time it did not return to him. (Genesis 8:1-12).

> *"Do not use the wrong things to measure or evaluate your decision-making."*

Simply, Noah used the wrong bird to check and get the information he needed for his decision-making, whether he should come out or stay on the ark. First, he sent a raven that never came back to him, and did not even care about who sent him. It was like as soon as the raven was released out of the ark by Noah, it said, "Mind you. I'm out, and it is up to you to find your way out." But when he finally sent the dove out to check, at least it did the work Noah sent it out to do first: It returned to him in the evening, and there in its beak was a freshly plucked olive leaf! Then Noah knew that the water had receded from the earth."

Your wrong decision-making measure might not be the wrong bird as Noah, but anything that is not morally sound and God-fearing, and does not have the potential or ability to indicate what the results could probably be in checking your decision-making is the wrong thing to rely on, and you should not use it to detect or predict what the results of your decision could be.

The Currents and Prevailing Winds

Ocean currents also referred to as gyres are forms of water movement that control climate zones and weather around the world. They are fundamentally driven by winds and were the fortune or misfortune of ancient sailors due to their moving power. They used it to navigate to their destinations, or it prevented them from reaching their destination safely. As far as when human started navigating oceans, undersea winds have helped or destroyed their journeys. Several ships were lost because of currents and some made it to their destination with the help of currents as well. In other words, depending on the type, currents are good and bad servants for sailors. It's good for them if their ship can ride it, or bad if it's working against their ship and direction.

There are primarily two categories of ocean currents: The surface and deep-water currents. These two major currents advice in defining the nature and flow of ocean waters across the globe. And there are five main ocean-wide currents or gyres: The North Atlantic, South Atlantic, North Pacific, South Pacific, and Indian Ocean gyres.

The fact is, all these different currents or winds were discovered and studied by ancient sailors and modern scientists and experts to know their advantages and disadvantages.

Trade or prevailing winds have been necessary to ancient sailors. To make their ocean trips a good experience, they ride on prevailing winds. Prevailing winds are surface winds that blow principally from a particular direction. The dominant winds are the trends in the direction of wind with the highest speed over a particular point on the Earth's surface at a specific time.

Riding the Currents, Winds, and Waves: Follow the Leads to the Truth

Early sailors used the wind and ocean currents to confirm or even control their directions and speed during navigation. In fact, these seven or even eight principal winds were named, and the directions of these winds have become the points of the wind rose that was noted on early ocean charts, and became the eight points of the compass in geography. One thing you may have observed about inventions is that they are just an upgrade or improved version of older creations, and built on ancient ideas.

In order to make good decisions, you need truth and facts. The dictionary defines truth as "the true or actual state of a matter, conformity with fact or reality, a verified or indisputable fact," "the body of real things, events, and facts," "a judgment, proposition, or idea that is true or accepted as true."

Truth has been generalized or made widely applicable to anything in our current world. People describe truth as something that looks like it and does not aim to represent truth, morality, and Godliness. Truth does not look like truth; it is truth (actual or real), or it is not. Maybe because of things such as beliefs, values, and religions, everybody has his own definition of truth. Truth is the opposite of falsehood, which is lies and fabrications. This tells us that we have a world full of lies and fabrications, and many of the things we are being told and taught that are true "truth" are falsehoods.

> *"In order to make good decisions, you need truth and facts."*

Values Determine Validations

Your values control your validations. The measure of what is acceptable to you is embedded in your morals, ethics, and principles, or a fundamental truth, and this, is what influences your recognition or affirmation of what is valuable or important to you. For instance, if money is everything to you more than character and God, no matter what actions, who or what character is behind the money, fame, or luxury, you will choose that and accept it because money is everything to you — even if it's terrible or immoral money, it's valid or worthwhile to you. When beauty is everything to you, no matter what character is behind it, you recognize and confirm it as good, even if the beautiful thing or person has a horrible character.

As children of God, we view and validate truth based on the word of God. In other words, we see truth and what is true according to the word of God, the Bible.

Let us check "fact" now. The Merriam-Webster dictionary also defines fact as "Something that has actual existence," "an actual occurrence," or "a piece of information presented as having objective reality." With these definitions in mind, we may conclude that a fact is a happening or incident in the existing state of things, as opposed to one that is imaginary, simulated, or theoretical. And the only way to validate a fact is to verify it. However, how are facts verified? They are checked against experience correspondence or a close similarity, connection, or equivalence, and standard reference works are also used to check facts. Arguably, if facts can be checked based on experiences, similarity, connection, and equivalence, then it is possible to be actually misled in trying to validate a fact. Considering this, it is not a surprise that people have "different facts."

"Your values control your validations."

The point is, that facts are provided by human beings and machines, or computers as a result of evidence from experiments, experiences, and discoveries, which is the available body of facts or information indicating whether a belief or proposition is true or valid -- and that can be fabricated by human beings. Undisputably, truth is provided by truth itself, and by God through his word, and truth overrides fact. So, follow the lead, and it will take you to the destination, or the truth you are looking for.

God is the Truth. And the Lord said, "I am the way, and the truth, and the life." (John 14:6). And that's why even though it's a blessing to leave money and material things to your children and descendants, the best and first inheritance you should strive to leave them is the Truth, and Truth is GOD.

> *"Facts are provided by human beings — and that can be fabricated — Indisputably, truth is provided by truth itself."*

To make good decisions, you have to follow the truth while keeping your eyes on the facts to make sure they are not fabricated to support a lie or deception.

The points of the compass are an evenly spaced set of horizontal directions, or azimuths in Greek, used in navigation and geography. The four cardinal directions, or cardinal points, are the four main compass directions: north, east, south, and west, usually indicated by their initials N, E, S, and W. The ordinal directions (also known as the intercardinal directions) are northeast (NE), southeast (SE), southwest (SW), and northwest (NW). The intermediate direction of every set of intercardinal and cardinal directions is called a secondary intercardinal direction.

Science reveals that ocean currents are continuous and a directed movement of seawater generated by some forces or considerable overall patterns of atmospheric circulation acting on the seawater; these include wind, the Coriolis effect, breaking waves, cabbeling, temperature, and salinity differences. And the ocean waves are generated by winds.

Ancient navigators observed the direction and type of the current, wind, and wave to obtain information about their situation at sea. Not only that, they follow and flow with the currents, winds, and waves to get to their destination. They also tracked regional and seasonal weather patterns to successfully navigate the vast oceans.

In short, there is a lead effect in the winds, waves, and currents. Simply put, figuratively, navigating toward the direction of the wind, wave, or current means, you have something to follow that can lead you to your destination (the truth you are looking for) to help you make the right decision.

The Investigative Mind and Truth Leads

This, is not to encourage nosy people. Do not try to get into people's personal lives. By all means, avoid trying to know what has nothing to do with you. Do not be prying; being intrusive is a sickness. Spying on people to satisfy your mere curiosity and low self-esteem is stupidity and a mental illness. Only try to get information on people when it is necessary for you to make a crucial decision or your life is threatened.

> *"Spying on people to satisfy your mere curiosity and low self-esteem is stupidity and a mental illness."*

One of the hardest things in a crime investigation or any type of investigation is when the wrongdoer is not known. So, investigators have to rely on the information the victim and witnesses can provide, then meticulously analyze it to determine the truth and the suspect, who may be the offender. However, if the victim or witnesses are able to truly name an individual with certainty, the case is easily solved; otherwise, investigators must use some techniques to trace and find the truth and the offender. One of these investigation tips or techniques is called "Investigative Lead Development." This consists of developing investigative leads through trace evidence. Meaning that investigators must supplement the fundamental investigative leads to try to discover the identity of the wrongdoer.

The primary lead usually comes from the victim, dead or alive; but better if the latter is still alive to talk to investigators. Investigators can develop a lead by learning more about what the victim was doing prior to the incident, people who have contact with the victim, and may profit from the crime. The possessions of the victim, fingerprints on items, or other evidence at the scene can also help prove, lead, and discover the criminal's identity.

Investigators also look for leads in the manner in which the crime was committed and double-check to find out if it matches the way other crimes were committed earlier. The sequence may reveal the suspect, or information from previous crimes can be put together to present leads. In other cases, recovered stolen items may be tracked back to the thief. And as the old saying puts it, "A picture is worth a thousand words." Therefore, in some cases, investigators may present the victim with known criminals' pictures to see if they can identify their assailant.

Time is very influential in investigations. Every investigation is time-sensitive or influenced by time. The amount of time it takes to gather information and evidence in a case can highly affect the results of the investigations. So, investigators always take this fact into account and do not play with the essence of time in their works. Wasted time in investigations means evidence can be tempered, witnesses and victims can forget what exactly they have heard, seen, and felt, and the criminal can get away and fabricate justification or defense before they identify him.

Despite the fact that some leads can yield good results, including the arrest of the criminal, and some do not, investigators always utilize this technique anytime they do not have established evidence for charges, arrest, and prosecution.

It is important also to note that, leads may not be the only sure foundation to build a case against someone because sometimes the person of interest might not be the offender because they have just been mistaken by the victim and the witnesses. However, surprisingly, sometimes they may be related to the criminal one way or the other. So, investigators may use the first person of interest just as a starting point of contact for the criminal or offender they are looking for.

What Could be the Leads and Tips

Depending on the crime, the leads that can help investigators to solve the crime may vary. But it could be what some people would consider insignificant. It could be a word, body language, phrase, item, action... Etc.

Follow the leads in matters before you draw conclusions and judgments or decide. Listen carefully to what the person is saying, watch his body language, and actions; these will help you intelligently discover their intentions. After all, intentions are what they are hosting in their mind and hearts, either out of selfishness or malice, which will sooner or later materialize or happen.

> *"Follow the leads in matters before you draw conclusions and judgments or decide."*

You can easily trace truth with leads coming out of the mouth of the person in question or in the events surrounding the thing about which you have to decide.

Have you ever listened to someone tell you their side of a story, and your mind is just suspended in the air, asking yourself so many questions internally? These are the very questions you should ask the person.

Fortunately, there is always a seed of the truth in the lie someone is telling you.

Do not make people your enemies because of what you heard about them without finding out the truth yourself. Do not become a fool by believing what someone is telling you about another person without reasoning with the latter and confirming the truth yourself. When something is not clear to you, ask questions. People usually react to what others say or do to them. Some people will tell you their side of the story to gain your support. But when you use your intelligence and wisdom, you would realize that whatever negative they were narrating about the other person they are in conflict with was a result or reaction to what they did or said to the other person..

FOOLISHNESS | Captain of Your Vessel

The Titanic: Bad Decisions On The Mighty Oceans

As famous as it's even today, the tragedy of the Titanic is one of history's most analyzed or evaluated events by experts and researchers from all industries. However, the findings on the cause of this tragedy are almost identical with very little disagreement. Everybody wonders if this tragedy could have been prevented in any way. Some experts believe it could have been prevented for one reason or the other. But above all, it is clear, and we may all agree, that bad decisions led to the sinking of the Titanic. I will clarify a few of them since it will take too much in this book to elaborate on all the worng decisions that were taken and led to the ruin of one of the world's largest passenger ships. I chose to use these examples because I mentioned some things earlier that I think these examples can narrowly clarify or explain.

I believe you may know or have heard about the history of the Titanic. But for the sake of those who do not know or remember the history of the Titanic, what was it?

The Titanic was a British passenger liner run by the White Star (The Oceanic Steam Navigation Company Line), headquartered in Liverpool, United Kingdom. It was one of the largest passenger ships of its era. But it sank in the North Atlantic Ocean on April 15, 1912, after striking an iceberg during her maiden trip from Southampton to New York City. The event and news shook the world when among the approximately 2,224 passengers and crew aboard, more than 1,500 died, setting the sinking accident the deadliest ever in the history of a passenger shipwreck, the deadliest of a single ship, and the deadliest peacetime sinking of a superliner to date according to experts. The infuriated public mourned the victims and cried for changes in regulations surrounding ocean travel by ship. Since then, the calamity has been expressed through many artistic works, including paintings, movies, books, and more.

But what really happened? Records show that after leaving Southampton on April 10th, 1912, the ship called at Cherbourg in France and Queenstown, now Cobh in Ireland, before sailing towards New York. On April 14, four days after crossing and traveling about 375 miles, or roughly 600 km, the Titanic hit an iceberg at 11:40 pm. The accident caused the hull plates to buckle inwards along her starboard, notably the right side, and opened five of the Titanic's sixteen watertight compartments, allowing seawater into it while it could only take four floodings and resist sinking.

Survivor attempts were able to evacuate passengers and some crew members with lifeboats. However, it was also reported that many of the lifeboats were not fully loaded. So, a number of men were left onboard while evacuating women and children was prioritized according to the regulations.

Unfortunately, the Titanic could not survive the seawater pouring into her and broke apart at 2:20 am, taking the lives of approximately a thousand people who were still onboard and were hopefully waiting to be rescued.

In 1985, the Titanic's wreckage was found in the deep waters of the sea at a depth of 12,415 feet (2,069.2 fathoms; 3,784 m) by a Franco-American expedition funded by the United States Navy. And her remains amounted to thousands of artifacts that have been recovered and displayed at museums around the world. Unfortunately, the Titanic has gone down in history as a synonym of tragedy and fame at the same time. Today, she is more popular than ever in countless projects, including children's books, songs, and movies.

Even though the mistakes leading to the wreck of the Titanic are generally different from expert to expert or historian to historian, there are certain suggestions that are common and have strong familiarity and need to be frankly considered and learned from. It seems there were several bad decisions that were made knowingly and unknowingly, which led to the destruction of the once believed to be unsinkable mighty Titanic.

Do Not Play with the Weather

Unless you receive a direct word from the LORD to go against the weather, do not do it. Apostle Peter received a word from the LORD to walk on water, and he did according to His word. (Matthew 14:22-33). At another time, Jesus spoke to the storm, and it calmed down. (Matthew 8:23-27). God made a way in the Red Sea for the children of Israel to cross it. (Exodus 14:1-30). All these were God's supernatural interventions in human's affairs or miracles, and God can do it again today. But, wisdom suggests that you use common sense to observe and work with the weather or nature, especially when there are other Godly, logical, and morally sound alternative ways to achieve the same expected end.

Remember, we talked about how ancient sailors or navigators observed and used tips from the climate and weather, including ocean tides and currents, to successfully navigate and reach their destinations? Could it be true that ocean tides and currents contributed to the sinking of the Titanic?

According to an article published by the University of Texas and posted by Jayme Blaschke, on March 5, 2012, on their website, ocean tides could have turned the icebergs in the sea into a dangerous route for the ship. A team of astronomers from the University of Texas found that there were unusually high ocean tides in January 1912. They theorized that the high ocean tides could have moved icebergs from other areas of the sea and sent them on the way of the Titanic, which eventually caused her demise.

No matter how good your weather devices or equipment are, always take into account the surprises the climate and weather can bring and be prepared not only spiritually, but physically as well. Watch out for what the sophisticated machines could not detect, predict, or find. Pay attention to what the weather is telling you, and do not go against it unless you are directly asked by God to do so, which is very rare – rarely does God ask human beings to do such things.

> *"No matter how good your weather devices or equipment are, always take into account the surprises the climate and weather can bring—"*

Beware of Show-offs or Challenges

Some believe the captain of the Titanic, Edward J. Smith was trying to maximize the speed of the ship in comparison to another one, which was owned by the same company, the White Star. This is believed to have caused the ship to be traveling at a very high speed, and could not have enough time to dodge the icebergs. If this finding is true, what was the whole purpose of trying to pilot the ship at that high speed? Was it a sincere speed test? And if so, was it supposed to be done while passengers were on board? Or was it just a completely erroneous power showdown?

Avoid unnecessary challenges or showdowns of power; what you or what you have can do. There is nothing wrong with testing things or machines out, but if you would have to do it at the peril of your life and others, then your decision lacks wisdom, morals, and Godliness. You do not have to prove anything to anyone; these types of situations usually result in failure, loss of time, money, or lives. Remember when the devil came to the LORD after he fasted for forty (40) days and nights and asked him if he was really the son of God to turn a stone into bread? The LORD knew it was unnecessary, even though he could do it.

> *"Avoid unnecessary challenges or showdowns of power; what you or what you have can do."*

The Bible says, "After fasting forty days and forty nights, he was hungry. The tempter came to him and said, "If you are the Son of God, tell these stones to become bread." Jesus answered, "It is written: 'Man shall not live on bread alone, but on every word that comes from the mouth of God." (Matthew 4:2-4). The LORD's answer was not only relevant spiritually, but he was also saying to the devil, "It is unnecessary to prove to you that I am who I am because I am who I am, and I can do what I have the power to do."

Do Not Ignore Signs and Warnings

As we are blessed with the advancement of technology and can mostly predict with a high probability what is coming with the weather and climate, ancient people did not have any of that, but they made use of what they had and used common sense to avoid dangers caused by weather and climate.

When you have been notified of an event that indicates a possible or impending danger, problem, or other unpleasant situation, do not panic, but take it seriously; and while you are praying for God's guidance and protection, be prepared, take immediate action to protect yourself and the people with you. Unless God gives you a direct word to stay where you are, continue in the same direction, or do nothing, do what you know best with common sense to protect yourself and people.

Consider When, Where, and How to Execute a Good Thought

Remember, earlier, I mentioned that executing your good decision at the wrong time and place could turn your good decision into a bad one. I also noted that there is nothing like a little decision, and what you may consider as a little decision can amount to serious devastating severe consequences.

Perhaps, such a decision made earlier on the Titanic, which led to another issue that other analysts believed contributed to the destruction of the Titanic.

On August 29, 2007, an article published on the Guardian UK's website entitled, "Key that Could Have Saved the Titanic Goes up for Auction." It was about the key of the Titanic's crow's nest locker containing binoculars that people believed could have saved the ship. And it was sold at an auction for £90,000 in 2007.

In that article, believed to have been written by Steven Morris, a Guardian news reporter, a revelation on a key that was set to go on an auction the following month, September 22 of the same year, was a news or something that one must ponder on.

I will paraphrase this story to give you a concise version to save you time. It was narrated that the key of a crow's nest locker containing binoculars that the Lookouts used to watch out for hazardous objects, including icebergs, during their voyage was with an officer named David Blair, who was among the crew of the ship. But, when the big ship set sail towards her next destination before she sank, David Blair, the officer, was probably ordered off the ship for an undisclosed reason and accidentally took the key away with him.

Some individuals who have a close relationship with the story of the Titanic, especially in Britain, noted that Mr. David Blair left the ship because he was "surplus to requirements," which means he was no longer needed or his service was no longer needed onboard the ship and had become surplus to requirements.

Consequently, the lookouts were left without the use of binoculars, which could have helped them to easily identify hazardous objects in the sea from far away.

May I also note that other experts argued that the event had an insignificant impact or did not contribute to the sinking of the ship because there were other greater causes? But in my understanding, if the binoculars were integrated into the ship to be able to discover hazardous objects, including icebergs, but at the time the ship sank they were not in use, then it contributed to the sinking of the ship, and maybe we could say it was not the only fault, but suggesting that it was insignificant error does not make sense. I will side with the researchers who believe the Lookouts not having their binoculars on hand to properly do their job onboard the ship was a significant and grave mistake caused by a wrong decision. I would prefer having one man being surplus on a ship than a wreck that killed hundreds of people.

Remember, I suggested to you earlier to never discard something or people without proper evaluation, even if you do not need them anymore. Not only you may need them again, but remember to account for the support or help they provided to you in the past or in times of need, and treat them well. Furthermore, if you ever need to replace something or someone for one good reason or the other, do it in an honorable way and at the right time and place. If indeed, replacing or getting Mr. David Blair, the officer who had the key to a crow's nest locker containing binoculars that the Lookouts used to watch out for hazardous objects, including icebergs, during their navigation contributed to the accident of the Titanic, then my argument would be, they made a wrong decision or executed a good decision at the wrong time, which turned their good decision in a bad one. Can you see that? If Mr. David Blair, whom they got off the ship earlier, was still on it with the key to the crow's nest locker containing binoculars, and the lookouts were able to use them to see the icebergs a little earlier or far away, maybe the ship could have avoided or dodged them before it got too close to them.

> *"Never discard something or people without proper evaluation, even if you do not need them anymore."*

Do not get rid of things or people without considering upcoming possible needs and events. Do not execute your decision at the wrong time and place.

Take the Right Course and Double-Check Things

In a novel entitled "Good as Gold." originally published in 2010, authored by Louise Patten, the granddaughter of Charles Herbert Lightoller, a British naval officer and the second officer on board the Titanic, she revealed that the truth left behind by her grandfather about the wreck of the Titanic was that, the steersman turned the ship into the wrong direction, which was toward the iceberg, and causing her to run into the danger.

The granddaughter brought to light that her grandfather, Second Officer Charles Lightoller, covered up the mistake because he was worried it would damage the reputation and business of the owners of the Titanic.

According to her revelation, the ship had enough time to dodge the iceberg, but the pilot, either out of panic or confusion about what I would call the difference between the old and new navigation technology, misunderstood the command of turning to dodge the iceberg after it was seen ahead, and turned in the wrong direction. She added that the mistake was soon after realized, but there was not enough time to reverse it and avoid the crash. Another interesting thing she indicated was that, if the ship had stopped at the location where she crashed, seawater would not have gained access to multiple interior compartments, which precipitated the sinking of the ship. However, due to the fact that the Titanic was considered an unsinkable ship, and the owners did not want people to perceive it as a weak vessel, they decided to keep it moving, and that was another wrong decision.

Do not put your life, family, relatives, business, ministry, or properties at risk in a bid to impress others. At the end of it all, you will not be the only one bearing the consequences. Additionally, keep in mind that humbly admitting a partial defeat and learning from it for your next adventure or journey in life is better than trying to show how strong you are and continuing in the wrong decision, direction, strategy, or approach and ending up losing it all.

> *"Humbly admitting a partial defeat and learning from it for your next adventure or journey in life is better than trying to show how strong you are."*

Double-checking things is one of the most significant responsibilities you have any time, anywhere, in everything you do. Double-checking and reviewing your thoughts, speech, actions, and decisions are so important because they can save you time, life, money, property, energy, job, business, ministry, and any other things related to you. Double-checking things can help you catch errors and correct them before they become bigger problems – it will save you and others from loss and many other dangers.

If the argument of Louise Patten is true, that the command given to turn the ship in the other direction to dodge the iceberg was misunderstood, and the opposite was executed, the only simple yet vital thing that could have saved the Titanic from her accident should have been a review or double-checking of the command and it's execution by the captain or the person in charge who gave the command. It is clear in this revelation that there was never a review or double-checking of that important command until the worst had happened. Had they reviewed or double-checked the command and how it was executed, they would have known it was not executed or done the way it was supposed to be – they would have known that the contrary of what was needed and commanded was done instead, and could have quickly corrected it, to avoid the iceberg or at least slightly running into it.

> *"Double-checking things is one of the most significant responsibilities you have any time, anywhere, in everything you do."*

When you ask, order, or delegate people to do things for you, always double-check how it is going. Do you remember? One of the simplest pieces of advice you may have received since your Kindergarten or Elementary School days is, when you finish writing your test, read it a couple of times to check for errors, and if there are any, correct them before you turn over the test papers to your teacher. It is a very simple advice, but highly useful in any area of life. When you do not have the habit of following up, double-checking, or reviewing things, you leave room for minor errors that can sooner or later cause bigger problems.

The easiest and quickest way to stop human errors, or something that was not done intentionally, or has been done that was not intended by the author, and resulting in problems and unexpected dangers is to follow up, double-check, review, and confirm if the action will, or is producing the right results – the expected results.

You do not have to wake up and go about life scared, but be alert for warnings or signs of dangers that you can feel, see, and hear. What you do not know, God will take care of it, including the ones you know, but wisdom suggests that you heed warnings or signs of dangers in any form.

> *"You do not have to wake up and go about life scared, but be alert for warnings or signs of dangers."*

Do Not Sacrifice Quality and Safety for Cheapness

Savings. We all like them. Living on a budget, we all try it. But when it comes to quality and safety to protect the life that God gave you and others, be careful what you decide to eat and drink, where you choose to stay, and what you decide to use. I do not believe expensive always means quality. But sometimes, it is essential to check the state or quality of what you are paying or buying cheaply. You have to ask yourself, "Does it meet the level of quality and safety that is required for me to be safe?" This does not mean you do not have faith; use the wisdom and the Holy Spirit God gave you as a human being to make the right choices.

> *"Does it meet the level of quality*

and safety that is required for me to be safe?"

Adequate preparations do not mean weakness or lack of faith either. For example, making sure you have spare parts or tires and anything you might need if you have a car, especially when you are traveling does not mean you lack faith. While you are praying and believing for the best, peace, protection, safety, light, and food to abound in your life and home, try to keep anything you might need in your car, home, and work in place.

The Miracle On the Hudson River, New York, NY

Earlier, I mentioned that there are emergency and non-emergency decisions. And, you have to treat each one as such. While you may have many seconds, minutes, hours, days, months, or years to make a final decision about some things, in some situations, you may only have a few seconds to do so – and delay may cause other serious complications or problems. I will use the following story to give you a very close example.

You may be familiar with what has become known to those familiar with the story, or what could have become a severe plane crash in New York City, New York, "The Miracle On the Hudson River."

It was on January 15, 2009, when a US Airways Flight 1549, which was an Airbus A320 took off from New York City's airport LaGuardia en route to Charlotte, North Carolina. A short moment after taking off, the plane struck a flock of birds, leading it to lose all engine power. Scary situation, isn't it? One of the options they had was to quickly reach a nearby airport for an emergency landing, but due to the plane's low altitude, the pilots, Chesley known as "Sully" Sullenberger, and Jeffrey Skiles, decided to glide or make an unpowered flight and ditch, or bring the aircraft down on the Hudson River in New York City, New York. and the ditching was successful! It was reported that all the 155 people onboard were safely rescued by a nearby boat, with a few injuries to note.

This swift and wise decision and landing of a powerless engine plane has been noted by a National Transportation Safety Board official as "the most successful ditching in aviation history."

To honor the pilots and flight attendants, they were awarded the Master's Medal of the Guild of Air Pilots and Air Navigators in recognition of their "heroic and unique aviation achievement." This accident turned into joy because of the way it ended, and was dramatized in a 2016 film entitled "Sully."

Some experts argued that the pilots could have avoided ditching the aircraft on the Hudson River by returning to LaGuardia, where they took off, or diverting to nearby Teterboro Airport. Regardless of others' opinions, the fact is, these pilots were in the air with a powerless engine plane, and it was scary. They only had a few seconds or minutes to decide what to do to save their lives and the passengers. They made a quick decision that saved their lives and other people. I'm not an aviation expert, but I think one of the elements that helped to keep them sane and realistic to make the right decision was courage; they did not panic. They stayed calm yet swiftly took the right decision. Had they waited for several more seconds or minutes to make a decision, they might have lost the aircraft and their lives.

Dangers or unpleasant situations do not necessarily mean panic. The dictionary defines Panic as "a sudden uncontrollable fear or anxiety that causes wildly unthinking behavior." Panic can press you to make the wrong decisions in dangerous or unpleasant situations. No matter how scary and dangerous a situation is, take a quick breath, calm down, and quickly think through all the possible solutions or ways out of the situation. Do not let fear and panic cause you to make the wrong decisions or actually run into a dangerous or unpleasant situation. There might be a better way to escape the situation, and that can only surface within your heart, mind, or spirit under controllable fear or calm behavior.

> *"Dangers or unpleasant situations do not necessarily mean panic."*

Life's Panics

There are some things in life that can detonate your panic and force you to make the wrong choices. Some of them can be your age, when you hit a certain age without a stable income, career, financial stability, marriage, or children, or do not see your life as you have expected it then in your life. These realities can pressure you to make the wrong choices that will destroy your life. Letting life's panics force you into making the wrong decisions will not help you in any way, it will actually complicate your life and potentially create bigger problems or obstacles to prevent you from being where you would like to be in life and create unpleasant circumstances altogether.

Chapter 4
General of Your Army

*"As commander of the army of the Lord,
I have now come."*
Joshua 5:14

THE ULTIMATE RESPONSIBILITY of an army General is to command and lead his units to victory. And it takes more than an army of valor and elite with sophisticated weapons to win battles during a war. It takes wisdom.

General Joshua: Tricks and Regrets

Joshua understood that he was leading a mighty army; nonetheless, he needed wisdom, good judgment, or understanding to win the war against their enemies to possess the promised land. In effect, when he got the opportunity, after confirming that the individual he just saw was an angel of the Lord, he immediately asked if he had a message for him. We read, "Now when Joshua was near Jericho, he looked up and saw a man standing in front of him with a drawn sword in his hand. Joshua went up to him and asked, "Are you for us or for our enemies?" "Neither," he replied, "but as commander of the army of the Lord I have now come." Then Joshua fell facedown to the ground in reverence, and asked him, *"What message does my Lord have for his servant?"* (Joshua 5:13-14, NIV).

Joshua quickly understood that he had an opportunity to get spiritual guidance or wisdom from the angel to win the battle, and essentially the whole war to conquer the land. Remember, the Bible says, *"For lack of guidance a nation falls, but victory is won through many advisers."* (Proverb 11:14, NIV). And I should add, good advisers, because not everybody can give you the right advice. I will explain this later.

One of the ultimate goals in your life should be to lead yourself, your life, everything, and everybody related to you to victory. And this requires making the right decisions.

Your life is the army, and you are the General. Unlike an army of many battalions, several companies, infantry, cavalry, artillery, and armored forces, however, in your life's army are your soul, spirit, and body.

> *"Your life is the army — in your life's army are your soul, spirit, and body."*

You must take charge of your life, relationship, business, profession, ministry, purpose, and destiny as an impressive or capable General and lead it to victory by the grace, power, and wisdom of God despite all the challenges you may face.

Tricked by the Trickers

No matter how powerful and even wise you are, your power, force, or strength becomes useless when you get tricked. Because when you get tricked, you are trapped, and when you are trapped, you are powerless. We know this even about Samson as well. (Judges 16:1-31). That's why you should never forget to have and consult with wisdom at every point in time before making decisions. Regrettably, your past successes in various areas of your life, business, or organization can give you some elusive confidence to make decisions sometimes without consulting or checking up with wisdom. And General Joshua was a victim of such a thing.

What happened to the formidable and wise General Joshua, who was leading difficult and vicious battles and wars and winning? He got tricked. People who use clever ways to cheat others out of something or for something are everywhere, and if you get overconfident and ignore tapping into your wisdom, you will make the wrong decisions before you realize it. Trickery or creative acts intended to dupe you can easily evade your wisdom radar.

Maybe this has been around for some time, but the first time I heard that was from my dad, "A tricker cannot play a tricker." Well, maybe we should say not in all cases because I have witnessed trickers playing trickers, and I would just have a good laugh and think, "Look at these trickers playing each other." However, the most dangerous part is finding yourself caught up on a farm of trickers playing each other, and you happen to be the morally sound person who does not want to play and get hurt by their tricks – it becomes a complex situation.

We should also remember that making decisions without consulting the word of God and letting the Spirit of God, the Holy Spirit, lead us will eventually result in the wrong choices.

The Spirit of God is given to mankind for a beneficial reason. There are things that even technology, psychologists, medical professionals, money, and materials can never help you with, but the power of the Holy Spirit, the Spirit of God, can.

> ## *"The Spirit of God is given to mankind for a beneficial reason."*

Never get to the point where you don't need God to make the right decisions. Life has surprises, and the most minor decisions can go wrong and result in more significant problems and complications. Always depend on God when you're making decisions. Even if you don't need a whole prayer and fasting session for a decision that you think you can make with your judgment or understanding, always have your spirit, mind, or heart connected and tuned in to the Holy Spirit to quickly sense His leading so you can sharply make changes if necessary to get it right before it's too late.

The story of Joshua, the Children of Israel, and the Gibeonites is a perfect example of how tricky, wrong decision-making can turn into a lifetime problem if you leave God out. (Joshua chapter 9). The successor of Moses and the children of Israel made a treaty with the Gibeonite before they realized that they made a mistake without consulting the LORD. When the Gibeonites learned how Joshua and the children of Israel were defeating the nations on their way to the promised land, they devised a plan to preserve their lives. They dressed up in old clothes and used supplies to make it look like they came from a faraway place and tricked Joshua and the children of Israel into making an agreement with them to spare their lives.

> *"Wrong decision-making can turn into a lifetime problem."*

Joshua, the wise General, as his decisions, actions, and results have demonstrated even when Moses, the servant of God, was alive, unfortunately at that moment, did not ask God for discernment, and he went along with their deception. When he found out he had been tricked and could not destroy the Gibeonites because of the covenant he made with them, he ordered them to become servants to the Israelites. However, throughout history, these people became a thorn in the lives of the children of Israel.

Tapping Into Wisdom

I consider wisdom as a property that you may have but often forget to use or misuse it. There is no doubt that General Joshua was wise, but when the Gibeonite came to meet them, he did not tap into that — he decided just by looking at the facts they presented to him and the Israelites. He decided based on the old clothes and used supplies they showed them. As I will elaborate further in another chapter, facts can be fabricated, and that's precisely how General Joshua and the Israelites got tricked.

The Four Kingdoms

It's significant to note that each one of the kingdoms, empires, and their reigns that God revealed to Daniel, and which already played and will play a major role in the history of humanity spiritually and physically, were all led and attained power and dominance by extraordinary ancient Generals who are all categorized as some of the best Generals in history. Let's take a quick look at the Book of Daniel in the Bible, which introduces us to the four (4) kingdoms that would rule the world according to Nebuchadnezzar's dream that Daniel interpreted. What is known among Biblical scholars and Christians as the four kingdoms of Daniel, are four kingdoms, which according to the Book of Daniel precede the "end-times" and the establishment of the "Kingdom of God" on planet earth.

In the book of Daniel chapter 2, Nebuchadnezzar had a dream of a statue composed of four different materials, which represent four kingdoms: The head was gold. It represents King Nebuchadnezzar of Babylon and his kingdom (verses 37–38). The chest and arms were silver. It represents what many believe is a small kingdom that followed the kingdom of Nebuchadnezzar (verse 39). The belly and thighs were bronze. It represents a third kingdom that would rule over all the world (verse 39). The legs were iron, and the feet were a mix of iron and clay. This represents a fourth kingdom, strong as iron but the feet and toes are of a mix of clay and iron means, it will be divided. (verse 41).
In summary, the four empires are the Babylonian Empire, the Medo-Persian Empire, the Greek Empire, and the Roman Empire.

This revelation was followed by other ones in the same

book of Daniel chapters seven (7) and eight (8). But since we are not talking about eschatology or the apocalypse, I will not go into details about them. I only mentioned these revelations of Daniel so you can understand the connection between these revelations and some of the greatest military generals the world has ever known.

Throughout history, there have been excellent and bad army Generals, and what makes the difference between them, or sets them apart, are their achievements in the forms of victory through offensive and defensive decisions they have made.

Since Biblical times, there have been great Generals, like Joab, who commanded the army of King David and under whom David's army captured Jerusalem. (2 Samuel 5:6-8; 1 Chronicles 11:4-6). He was pivotal in many victories attributed to King David. He was a son of Zeruiah, the sister of King David, so he was King David's nephew. (1 Chronicles 2:13–17). In fact, two other brothers of Joab were in David's army, and one of them, including Joab, was among the mighty men of David. (2 Samuel 23:8-39). Joab was an excellent military leader, a skilled fighter, and an insightful strategist. He also led the resistance and battle against Absalom, the rebellious son of David, and his army crushed them and killed Absalom. (2 Samuel, chapters 13-19).

Abner also was a remarkable army General and was actually a cousin of King Saul who commanded his army and later his son Ish-bosheth until he finally sided with King David. (1 Samuel 17:55, 1 Samuel 14:51).

From Alexander the Great, King of Macedon from B.C.E. 336 to 323, who is considered the greatest military leader or General the world has ever known, to Quintus Servilius

Caepio, who is considered the worst military leader or General of all times, it is consequential to note that, between the swords, arrows, horses, chariots, elephants and all the other ancients weapons, stand their decisions. Their sophisticated ancient weapons and mighty men alone would not have given them those huge or historical victories.

> *"It is consequential to note that, between the swords, arrows, horses, chariots, elephants and all the other ancients weapons, stand their decisions."*

A General, according to the dictionary, is "a senior army officer, usually one who commands units larger than a regiment or its equivalent or units consisting of more than one arm of the service. Frequently, however, a General is a staff officer who does not command troops but who plans their operations in the field."

Universally, Army Generals are also responsible for the preparation and leadership in wars. Remember, soldiers do not achieve the rank of General just because they are good-looking or cute in their uniform, have money, know how to talk, entertain, and use a weapon, rather, they have achieved certain characteristics that show their effectiveness to prepare and lead a unit of soldiers.

The same responsibility applies to you, your life, purpose, destiny, business, or ministry. God has made you the General of your life, everything and anyone connected to you, and it is your responsibility to make the right decisions and strategically lead your life, dreams, and visions to fruition or victory. The decisions you make will literally determine either the victory or the loss of the battle of your life and potentially others.

While I was writing this book and got to this point, I wanted to know more about the qualifications of soldiers before they are promoted to the rank of General, and my findings just confirmed my belief and what I wanted to remind you in this chapter.

From ancient times, the army in every nation has requirements and tests that anyone who is joining must have and pass, such as Survival, Role-playing, Courage, Discipline, Clear Communication, Levels of Responsibility, Order, Vision, Empathy, Attentiveness, Self-Awareness, Self-Esteem, Emotional Intelligence, Moderation or Balance, Conflict Resolution, Sense of Belonging, and Justice.

However, when it comes to a soldier attaining the rank of General, more qualifications are required. An effective Army General must have the following characteristics: Leadership, Selflessness, Ethics, Self-confidence, Good planning, Quick thinking, People Skills (Good communication, ability to interact effectively with others and with one's own emotions, reactions, and motivations), Cool Temperament, Lead by Example, and Intelligence.

If you are serious about your life, purpose, and destiny, and everything under your care, your own life, family, business, ministry, and government, then you have to figuratively look at it as you are a soldier and a General altogether, fighting for your life, purpose, and destiny in order to successfully be who God created you to be, and accomplish what He sent you in this world to achieve. This requires making the right decisions in everything, everywhere, and every time.

Survival

The dictionary defines the word "Survival" as "the state or fact of continuing to live or exist, typically in spite of an accident, ordeal, or difficult circumstances."

Earlier, I mentioned that one of the reasons why the wrong decisions are made is because people tend not to be ready to endure hardships. I am not advocating for perpetual hardships in life; you must fight or do your best to get out of unnecessary suffering. However, sometimes, that is the road to your authentic and lasting solutions, peace, happiness, security, prosperity, and stability.

When you are afraid of hardships or endurance, long wait, and want to take unsafe or dangerous ways to the solutions of your problems, you may end up making the wrong decisions, which will create bigger problems for you, people who are related to you, your family, children, and grandchildren sooner or later. It may be what the majority of people around you are doing, and some may even encourage you to do the same by giving you all the reasons why you should also do it like that and the benefits of it. Do not let difficult moments force you into making the wrong decisions in a bid to get quick solutions. Remember, sometimes fast and easy solutions in some situations in real life do not last; they are just a mirage and will eventually put you in other disheartening circumstances. They will later hunt and shame you or people related to you. If you understand that first, you are a soldier, and second, a General of your army, meaning your life, you will know and easily prefer to endure the hardship or discomfort till you win and conquer the solution to your challenge without not making and executing the wrong decisions.

As a soldier, and particularly a General, you are ready to survive any challenge and wisely fight until you win or conquer.

Manufacturers, including automobile makers, intend, design, and create their products for use in harsh conditions for survivability. All the same, God created you to survive even in uncomfortable conditions for the greater good of yourself, the people related to you, and the whole of humanity. Do not let uncomfortable situations push you to make the wrong decisions.

> *"When you are afraid of hardships or endurance — you may end up making the wrong decisions."*

We are taught at a very young age, either by parents or in school, that to survive in the outdoors, certain items are needed, or you have to prepare and equip yourself with what is called a "Survival or Emergency Kit." For example, First Aid Kit, Outdoor Trauma Bag, Tactical Flashlight, Knife, Pliers, Pen, Blanket Bracelets, Compass… Etc. To survive in situations life throws at you in your personal life, job, business, or ministry, you have to be prepared and equip yourself with things you might need to survive. Primarily, make sure you equip yourself with the knowledge of the Word of God, prayer, and fellowship with the Holy Spirit of God who knows how to better lead you out of any bad situation. Additionally, learn any skill you can, never have only one degree or career, use and save money properly, eat right to strengthen your immune system and energy, learn stress management, and the list goes on. As insignificant as these habits may sound to you, they are very important and may affect your decision-making. In fact, many studies show that stress can affect human valuation, risk-taking, and learning. Meaning that stress can influence your decision-making. When you are stressed, your judgment is under pressure and lacks clarity to make the right decisions.

> *"Do not let uncomfortable situations push you to make the wrong decisions."*

Courage

Courage is defined as "the ability to do something that frightens one." But the definition continues and says, "Strength in the face of pain or grief." Another interpretation of courage also reads, "Courage is the choice and willingness to confront agony, pain, danger, uncertainty, or intimidation. And in a battle, courage is valor or bravery."

In my observations, I noticed that usually, we tend to have the courage to do things that are frightening, but we feel like doing them, and eventually do them, and they cause us problems. However, we lack the courage to do good things that are frightening but will be beneficial for our spiritual and physical lives, and maybe because we think it will humble us or shake our ego. And it all comes down to making decisions.

Throughout history, the outcomes of wars have defined the greatness of Army Generals, but in actuality, what defined them all were their decision-making skills, the way they were able to see through or have a deep insight into their battles and make critical decisions. Whether we like or dislike them because of their beliefs, values, or lifestyle, their good or bad decision-making lessons can serve as examples and warnings to everyone.

> *"We lack the courage to do good things that are frightening but will be beneficial for our spiritual and physical lives."*

Alexander The Great: Potent Will and Adaptable Mind

Alexander the Great has been considered throughout history as the greatest Military Leader of all time. His successful military exploits are so notable to the extent that Military academies all over the world still teach his battle tactics. Alexander the Great conquered most of the known world at his time. His Military achievements have endured and stood against the test of time and culture. But what exactly made him that great? Was it just his military tactics? But then, even so, how do we interpret that? In my opinion, Alexander the Great was not just a great Military Leader or tactician, but he was a great military decision-maker. An army can have the best soldiers and weapons and be in the best condition to win battles in every war, but if it has the wrong General who makes the wrong decisions, it will lose every battle. Even though some historians attributed some of his success to his father King Philip II because of the way he paved the way for his son, I do not think he could have been militarily successful if he was not a good military decision-maker. There have been many kings who did similar things for their heirs, but they ascended to the throne only to make one wrong decision after another and destroy what their parents left behind or their legacy.

Behind every action, there is a decision. And the first

battles of Alexander against the Persian king Darius, which were very pivotal in winning many of the battles that followed and the conquest of a vast territory cutting into multiple continents, were not only won because of his military tactics but because of the right military decisions he made as a General in both offense and defense during those wars. You may call them tactics, but behind those tactics were decisions. Alexander the Great fought three crucial battles against the Persian Empire, and those three battles were the battle of Granicus, the battle of Issus, and the battle of Gaugamela. All these three battles somehow determined who was going to be the next ruler of the known world. But his right offensive and defensive decisions yielded great victories, which turned Alexander into "Alexander the Great."

Who was Alexander the Great? He was commonly known as Alexander the Great and ruled the ancient Greek kingdom of Macedon. He was born in Pella, a city located in Ancient Greece likely in 356 BC. His life and accomplishments span from around 20-21 July 356 BC to 10-11 June 323 BC. He ascended to the throne at the young age of 20, and spent a very long time of his early reign as king in military campaigns throughout West Asia and North Africa. History recorded that by the age of thirty (30), he had already conquered the majority of the world in those days, stretching from Greece to northwestern India.

"Behind every action, there is a decision."

We may disagree on many things about his quick temper or anger, his folie with the belief that he is a god or the son of a god. According to my examination, I believe he was a religiously confused man who worshiped a little bit of any god at his time.

The intriguing question I have asked myself for a while about Alexander the Great is, "Would some of the greatest Generals and leaders, including Alexander, who existed before the birth of Christ, have believed in Christ or the God of the Bible, assuming they existed after Christ?" Only God can answer this question. So, I would leave it as such. However, may I present that, in my opinion, I would side with some scholars. And you may disagree with me – but I do believe that God had used Alexander the Great unknowingly to pave the way or enable the propagation of the Gospel and save it in a region and world that the majority related to less commonality.

Furthermore, I believe that his remarkable battles and war victories, including the expansion of his dominance from Greece to Anatolia, Syria, Phoenicia, Egypt, Mesopotamia, Persia, Afghanistan, Pakistan, and India were not natural. There is no doubt that he was a charismatic General and leader. Although, I believe his conquests were powered by supernatural interventions. Many historians talk about his spiritual life, the gods he believed in, and all the rituals he practiced before going to battles in wars and note that these must be the forces behind his unbelievable victories and ruling. I would dispute that by saying that if his victories and dominance somehow created a way for the propagation and keeping of the Good News of the Lord Jesus Christ centuries before the birth, crucifixion, and resurrection of Christ, then God Himself was assisting his victories and Empire knowing that He will use it indirectly for the benefit of saving humanity through the proclamation of the Gospel.

As I mentioned earlier, there are pertinent questions that only God can answer. Considering the fact that Abraham was called to leave Haran, today's Turkey around 2091 BC, it suggests to me that the world before God revealed Himself to Abraham was really a confused religious place. For example, when I think about Abram, later known as Abraham, who was called by God to leave his father's house and go to a land He will show him. (Genesis 12:1). Abraham's father was an idol worshiper and trader. If Abraham's father later followed in the path of his son and worshiped the God who called him, the Bible does not mention that. Biblical records are unclear about how Abraham's life and relationship with God were before He called and told him to leave his father's house. But we would all believe that he must have had some sort of relationship with Him one way or the other before God called and gave him the instructions.

Why am I bringing all this to your attention? I just want to clarify that maybe several people, including Alexander the Great served other gods and practiced idolatry in the past, especially before Christ, because that was all they knew. And if maybe they were born after Christ, they would have believed in Him. This is just my opinion.

However, I agree with many historians who also believe that his conquests played an important role in the economic development of the known world at the time, and the spread of Greek culture, including the language. Remember, the New Testament was recorded in the Greek and Aramaic languages and helped the propagation of Christianity in the region and the world, and the conquests of Alexander the Great paved the way for that.

In relation to my remarks, one of Alexander's valuable

attributes is his strong will. It takes a potent will to be a soldier and an army General. Conquering challenges in life requires a dominant will. It's not questionable that he was also adaptable to conditions he did not necessarily like but knew were needed for the common good. He was good at visualizing or seeing "The big picture" in circumstances and riding or using them to his advantage or victory, whether in war or governance of the vast territory he had conquered.

Some Historians and Christian Scholars believe that his reign and exploits, which happened long before Christ came to Earth, may have impacted Christianity positively in the earlier days. Nonetheless, he was a worshiper of the Greek Ancient Greece's religion, which is now known as the Greek Mythology. He believed in the Macedonian-Greek worship of a pantheon of celestial deities zeus, son god. These religions have nothing to do with the God of the Bible or Christianity. It is recorded that Alexander the Great even considered himself the son of god zeus. But I don't want to go into those details now so we can focus on our subject.

I do not believe any of the aforementioned religions or gods helped Alexander the Great to conquer the world, but God, because it was needed for the proclamation of the Gospel. Nevertheless, I believe it was ultimately achieved through his right decisions at the right times and charismatic skills. His war decision-making skills as a General was unmatched and anyone could learn from it.

Richard the Lionheart and Philip II: Two Generals with Ulterior Motives

Born with skills for war, but lived with a hunger for kingship or a desire to be a king. One may ask, "Are these two things not interconnected?" The answer is no. Warriors are not always born kings, and kings are not always born skilled warriors. Sometimes, trying to be and do too many things simultaneously, especially the ones you are not born and talented to be and do, can be your downfall and destroy your life, morals, and reputation. It takes wise decisions to effectively operate under your calling or stay with your spiritual or natural gifts without not trying to become who God has not created you to be and do the things God has not created you to do. In my opinion, this was the story of Richard the Lionheart. I believe he was born a warrior, but not a king.

Richard the Lionheart was known for his political and military exploits, including perhaps the most intriguing one, which was the fight against the Muslim General Saladin to conquer Jerusalem back; nevertheless, he finally made a peace treaty and ended the crusade or movement after several battles against his opponent General Saladin and his army.

But before Richard the Lionheart became a hero, crusader, and recognized by Christians, and Christian leaders of his time, and even now, he had quite a troublesome past.
From an early age, Richard demonstrated remarkable political and military potential and without a doubt, turned out to be a courageous and strong-willed warrior who fought to keep control of his domain as a ruler against a rebellious group of nobles.

History reveals that by the age of 16, Richard was already in charge of his own army, and fighting against his own father as a rebel. Many historical sources confirmed that his mother was encouraging him and his brothers to rebel against their father, King Henry II.

When I was analyzing the childhood of Richard, who became King Richard, or Richard the Lionheart, several things got my attention, and one of them was his unending battle against his own father, King Henry II of England. One would ask, "Why?" Though many historians may have their own different opinions about the reasons why Richard was fighting his father till his death, and his mother Eleanor being the instigator, I think the final battles and agreements he made with his father revealed his main intention – becoming the king.

Among many rebellious actions against his father King Henry II, it has been recorded that Richard tried to take the throne of England for himself by joining the efforts of King Philip IV of France to conquer England, hence fighting against his own father, King Henry II of England. It seems Richard was the type of son Absalom has been to King David in the Bible. Remember, Absalom wanted to overthrow his father, King David to become King of Israel. (2 Samuel chapter 15). I have heard this several times, "Some children, parents wish they never had." It's troublesome how sometimes you witness children trying to undercut their parents, kill or betray them just to have their way, inherit money, properties, or insurance benefits sooner.

On July 4th, 1189, the forces of Richard and Philip defeated his father, King Henry's army at Ballans. In effect, King Henry, with the approval of Richard's brother John, accepted a deal to name him as his heir apparent. And out of pain, as many historians believe, his father, King Henry II died two days later in Chinon. Eventually, Richard became King of England, Duke of Normandy, and Count of Anjou.

Using your talents or skills to inappropriately gain power, especially by overthrowing one's own father is not a morally sound way to become who God created you to be and do what He created you to do. I believe Richard could have still accomplished the things he had done even by not fighting continuously against his father and forcibly taking the throne from his brother John, making his father, King Henry, name him his heir apparent. The irony is that his decisions and actions following his ascension to the throne as King of England revealed that he was not born a king but rather a warrior or soldier. Therefore, his position should have been that of an army General, not a king. If you closely analyze Richard's life, you will notice that he performed poorly as a king, but highly as an army General. What is the difference, you may ask? I will clarify further.

For instance, a Commander in Chief is the supreme commander of a nation, and in most cases, is the president. In the United States, the Commander in Chief is the president, who commands the various departments of the armed forces. But do you think the president is the one who commands the army directly in wars on the field? No, it's the army officers who are skilled as soldiers and know how to fight wars, and that would be the Chairman of the Joint Chiefs of Staff, the nation's highest-ranking military officer, the principal military advisor to the president, and the secretary of defense. The decisions and strategies are securely passed on to the Generals for execution. Of course, there are protocols concerning when, and what requires the president's approval before execution.

There is a difference between briefings, holding meetings, delegating authority, and responsibility to people, and fighting in battles as a soldier in wars. There is a difference between administration or the executive, described as a decision-making body, and generalship, which is the skill or practice of exercising military commands. In effect, I think Richard the Lionheart was born and skilled for the generalship, but not for the administrative or executive.

> *"Born and skilled for the generalship, but not for the administrative or executive."*

Yes, back in the old days, and even in the Bible, kings were warriors, but how many of them were really good at fighting? Many of their significant victories in wars were attributed to their army generals.

As it's said, "Give credit to whom credit is due." You should commend someone on something when they deserve it, even if you dislike some things about him. When Richard became King of England, one of the impressive things he did was to become a defender of the Jewish population. Before him, many kings failed to protect the Jews. But Richard has done his best to protect the Jews and even distributed a writ, or a formal written order, demanding that the Jews should not be maltreated. This is where I think Richard's decisions started changing from negative to positive or from bad to good. He has already made too many bad decisions, you would say, or this might not be significant. But God has sworn several times in the Bible to bless whoever blesses the Jews, the children of Israel, and curse whoever curses the Jews. In Genesis 12: 3, He declared, *"I will bless those who bless you, and whoever curses you I will curse; and all peoples on earth will be blessed through you."* In Deuteronomy 30:7, He reiterated, *"The Lord your God will put all these curses on your enemies who hate and persecute you."*

However, King Richard's edit was not successfully enforced, leading to more violence against the Jews in the land. Eventually, his stand and demonstrated action as a King who defended the Jews may have progressively helped in the reduction or cessation of violence against the Jews.

The Third Crusade Cold Feet

At this point, Richard seems to be shifting from wickedness to his moral obligations. In 1187, he had already taken the cross as Count of Poitou as his father, and Philip II did at Gisors on January 21, 1188, when they received the news that Jerusalem had fallen to the Muslim General Saladin. After Richard became king, he and King Philip agreed to go on what is known as the "Third Crusade." But was this agreement a genuine one? History reveals that each of these kings was afraid the other could rise to take possession of his land in his absence or while fighting in the Middle East to regain possession of Jerusalem. This uncertainty or fear to undertake the mission of Jerusalem's liberation apparently never left either of them.

From a deep observation, these two individuals Richard and Philip were only using each other to their own advantage all those times. If they were real friends as it looked in the past till Richard also became King, why would they worry? Friends trust each other, but in their case, they did not trust each other. Be careful of people who pretend to be your friends just to use you to gain what they want. Sometimes, your feelings about some people, including the ones who seem to be your friends, may be a good indication that you should not trust them with some things. God would always warn you about dangers one way or the other, and He would not always use the same method or ways to warn you. He has thousands of ways to talk to or reveal dangers to you. So just pay attention, consider that unsettling in your spirit, and pray about it.

> *"Be careful of people who pretend to be your friends just to use you to gain what they want."*

I fully understand these two Generals being concerned about the fact that the other could plan and take his territory while fighting in Jerusalem, but this is due to their personal ulterior motives. From Jerusalem to the United Kingdom and France there is a long way to travel back to do damage control if there was a setup to overthrow you as a king. And remember, there was not a first-class flight to quickly return to your kingdom or office to stop and reverse the coup.

The Lord Jesus stated to His disciples, *"I no longer call you servants, because a servant does not know his master's business. Instead, I have called you friends, for everything that I learned from my Father I have made known to you."* (John 15:15, NIV). He said this to them about spiritual things. However, He also was helping them to understand the main characteristics of a true friendship. It's summed up in one word, "trust." If you cannot trust someone regardless of the amount of time you have known him, obviously, he's not your friend. We usually make the mistake of considering people as friends of ours based on how long we have known them. However, the Lord told us what we can use to measure a relationship or validate it to be a true friendship or not. Trust is defined by the dictionary as, a "firm belief in the reliability, truth, ability, or strength of someone or something." That means before you can confirm that someone is your friend, you can firmly believe in what he says and does; he's reliable, tells you the truth, and you can also tell him the truth without being afraid; he serves you with his abilities just as you serve him with your potentials, he strengths or power you up in weaknesses, and lack spiritually and physically.

Clearly, these two Generals have ulterior motives in what seems to be a constant support for each other. One may argue that they were just being wise, of course. But how can you call someone a friend or relative, if you cannot trust the person with your territory or land? I charge more to what happens behind you, or in your absence. Real friendship and partnership do not exclude vigilance and wisdom. However, they should surely include trust. If you cannot trust someone with your absence, or your ignorance, that person is clearly not a real friend or partner. I care less about what they do or say in your presence and at your knowledge.

When King Richard was preparing to embark on his Jerusalem liberation journey, he religiously renounced his dark and wicked past in order to show he was worthy to take the cross. He also started forming his army for the task ahead. By that time, his father King Henry had already raised some funds called "The Saladin tithe" for that particular purpose. If you recall, liberating Jerusalem was his father's heart's desire as well.

History tells us that, to raise more funds for the war of conquering Jerusalem back as the holy city of God from the Muslims, King Richard started selling official positions, lands, and many other governmental offices and privileges to people interested in buying them. Meaning, if you had a lot of money at the time, you could buy an office or position in the government of the kingdom, and if you were already holding a position that you could not pay to keep, you were forced to leave it to another person who can pay for it. Imagine you have to pay to be a mayor or governor. We might just have to say, "Offices and positions for sale." It is recorded that when King Richard was raising funds for the war in Jerusalem, he said, "I would have sold London if I could find a buyer."

At first thought, one may think it was a good idea because, after all, he was raising funds to go and take back Jerusalem, the holy city of God from captivity. But then the danger in selling government positions in any kingdom, country, state, business, or ministry could be devastating because, at that point the positions are not being delegated based on qualifications, but on offers. And that's how mischievous people get into position. And when evil people occupy government offices, the land or organization is controlled by evil or immorality.

Do not be so desperate to sacrifice leadership, ethics, and morality to achieve your goals, even if it's concerning what you believe belongs to God and must happen. When God calls you or assigns you a task, you do not have to disobey him to do his work. You do not have to go against the moral laws of God in order to achieve your purpose and destiny. If you do, you will regret it because you are setting yourself up for spiritual and physical problems.

After planning and modifying his army, and determining which part was going with him for the war to reclaim Jerusalem and the one remaining behind to protect his French possessions, Richard undertook his expedition to go and conquer Jerusalem in the summer of 1190.

However, getting to Jerusalem was not easy and did not happen smoothly. He had to go through Sicily to defend and rescue his sister Joan who lost her husband King William II of Sicily, and was imprisoned by Tancred of Lecce who illegitimately ceased power as king of Sicily. Upon his arrival to Sicily, King Richard demanded that his sister Joan be released, and given her inheritance. Eventually, she was released but was not given the inheritance that her husband King William II allocated to her in his will.

King Richard, with his army, managed to capture Messina in Sicily on October 4th, 1190, and used it as a base to continue his plans. This victory apparently secured him the attention of King Tancred, who realized that making a deal with King Richard might be a better option for him. So, he entered an agreement with him on conditions that, first, his sister Joan would receive twenty thousand (20,000) ounces or five hundred and seventy (570) kilograms of gold as compensation for her inheritance, a benefit the illegitimate king Tancred kept for himself. Second, King Richard officially proclaimed his nephew Arthur of Brittany, who was the son of Geoffrey, his deceased brother, as his heir. Third, King Tancred promised to marry one of his daughters to Arthur when he came of age and would give an additional twenty thousand (20,000) ounces or five hundred and seventy (570) kilogram of gold that should be returned by Richard in case Arthur his nephew did not marry Tancred's daughter.

Dangerous and Trappy Transactions

Life is all about transactions, spiritual, physical, financial, and material transactions. And behind each transaction, there is a loss or benefit. And the most dangerous ones are the transactions that can promise and give you the world, but take away your soul – making you disobey God or break away from Him. Be careful about such transactions. The Lord asked, *"For what profit is it to a man if he gains the whole world, and loses his own soul? Or what will a man give in exchange for his soul?"* (Matthew 16: 26, NKJV).

Losing your soul is more than going to hell; it involves experiencing hell even in this world. It means you are losing or exchanging your authentic peace and happiness with temporary and fictitious pleasures. Remember the old saying, "All that glitters is not gold." Meaning that not everything that looks precious or true turns out to be so."

> *"Losing your soul is more than going to hell; it involves experiencing hell even in this world."*

In short, after Tancred finally agreed to sign the treaty on March 4th, 1191, the treaty was signed by Richard, Philip, and Tancred. But after some time, the true intentions of each one of them started manifesting.

When a friendship, or generally any relationship, is created and maintained by just self-interests and not by purpose and the pursuit of the will of God, sooner or later, it will collapse and reveal the true intentions of the various parties when the interests or benefits are not obtained by either one of the parties or the selfish one. Stay away from any relationship that only stands on self-benefit and not on purpose and the pursuit of the will of God. These types of relationships keep records and are built on numbers, counts, and measurements. For example, if you give them one glass of water, they will give you one glass of water. If you give them a Dollar, they will give you a Dollar not because that's what they can afford, but because that's what you gave them according to your capacity.

There are people who would never want to do something for someone unless the person has done something for them first, so their good deeds toward people are always a reward for what the person has given or done for them first. The Bible says, *"It is more blessed to give than to receive."* (Act 20:35).

Do you remember the Lord's declaration about the widow during the offering? The Bible says, "Jesus sat down opposite the place where the offerings were put and watched the crowd putting their money into the temple treasury. Many rich people threw in large amounts. But a poor widow came and put in two very small copper coins, worth only a few cents.

Calling his disciples to him, Jesus said, *"Truly I tell you, this poor widow has put more into the treasury than all the others. They all gave out of their wealth; but she, out of her poverty, put in everything—all she had to live on."* (Mark 12:41-44, NIV). This tells us that it's not how much we give or do, but how much we have in proportion to how much we give or do.

Such relationships in any way are always and just built on self-interest, and not on purpose, the will, and the plan of God. These types of people tend to lose focus on the big picture, the plan, the will, and the purpose of God. They are always looking for their benefits or what they can get or profit from the relationship. Anything that doesn't profit them, but serves God's purpose and plan, will not be supported by them regardless of what benefit it could be for others and the world – These people always pick what is their personal interest and pretend as if they are doing it for God and others until they see it will not be fully their benefit, and that's when they plainly or secretly pull away their support.

This is not to say you have to invest your energy, time, money, and materials in the wrong place or people. But keep in mind that not everything you can support should be for your own interest or benefit. If you only give or support people and things based on your personal interest, and not on God's purpose and plan or interest, you will miss the full mark of being and doing what or who God sent you on earth to be and do. It should be about God's purpose, plan, and interest first.

Before the kings reached Acre on their way to fight for Jerusalem, they also passed through Cyprus, conquered it, and spent some time over there in preparation for the big battle which was their main objective. To reach their destination, they decided to capture and go through Acre according to their strategy, so they embarked on Acre with their allies, and King Richard and his allies successfully captured Acre.

After many unexpected deals with his allies, he faced

some difficult decisions, including King Philip's demands of getting half of Cyprus, the island they conquered earlier, and the most unrealistic one – the kingship of Jerusalem. This is where things got really disturbing. How do you demand even the kingship of Jerusalem that has not been captured yet? Was it in the agreement, and if they had any? The lesson here is, unless you are investing your energy, time, money, and materials into some ministry or mission endeavors, or just to support, always make sure you have an agreement on the revenue or benefit of your investments, that is, if you are clearly doing it for profit.

There are times in life when you will do something as a non-profit endeavor, and there are also times when you have to make profits, for example, in business endeavors. Always make sure there is a signed agreement. Don't embark on a business or for-profit journey without a clear signed agreement. There are wicked people in the world who only look for their interests and nothing else, and even though signing an agreement is not a hundred percent guarantee to have a business deal, at least you have something to show as evidence should the law require it.

Good decisions might not always look, or be an apparent victory, but they will save you from losses. Never keep your eyes too much on the benefits and forget the possible dangers that can come out of your decisions and actions.
Richard was not a perfect man, but we can learn from his military decisions as an army general.

> *"Good decisions might not always look, or be an apparent victory, but they will save you from losses."*

At some point, the Muslim General Saladin, who held control of Jerusalem, tried to pressure and trick King Richard's army and break its formation in order to attack them by unit. But the tactical General King Richard didn't move according to their expectation, he rather maintained his defensive formation. This gave an opportunity to the Knights Hospitaller (an Order of Knights of the Hospital of Saint John of Jerusalem, a medieval and early modern Catholic military order), who were allies of King Richard in the battle for Jerusalem to break the ranks, attack, and drive away the right wing of Saladin forces.

Do not give in to pressure orchestrated to force you to make the wrong decisions. Some people are masters of using pressure to push you to make the wrong decisions, either to take something from you, get access to something, or make you enter an agreement unwillingly or prematurely. Be quick to recognize such pressure and relax in your solid defense and protection position or mind.

> *"Do not give in to pressure orchestrated to force you to make the wrong decisions."*

King Richard, the General ordered an extensive counterattack against the army of Saladin and won the battle of Arsu. This was a key victory for him, his army, and the allies who desperately wanted to capture Jerusalem back from the Muslims.

Despite the defeat of Saladin's army, the Muslims still held onto Jerusalem and a few lands. However, this moment of victory was very encouraging to the Crusaders, who took advantage of it and moved towards Jerusalem after conquering Jaffa as well.

The momentum was used by Richard and the other Crusaders, and they trooped to Beit Nuba, which was only twelve (12) miles away from Jerusalem. What an advancement! Pretty close, right? By this time the inhabitants of Jerusalem and surrounding cities have lost hope. Their resistance is folding at each defeat.

But nature had a surprise for Richard's army and allies who were on the move to cease Jerusalem: The weather got bad, it was cold and heavily raining hailstorms. Additionally, they realized that if they attempted to besiege Jerusalem, their army could be confined in between, in case a backup unit of Saladin's soldiers descended from behind. So they wisely decided to retrieve to the coast, and not to move in to attack Jerusalem.

Do not be too desperate to get what is in front of you to the extent that you forget what could come behind you, happen, or later overtake you by surprise. Always consider the other realities surrounding the matter before making decisions and executing them. Had Richard and his army only seen how close they were to Jerusalem and could possess it, and never thought about what could happen from behind or later, surely, Saladin's army would have trapped and killed them, which would have turned into a big victory for them and have possibly ended the war for Jerusalem in favor of Saladin and his army altogether.

> *"Do not be too desperate to get what is in front of you to the extent that you forget what could come behind you, happen, or later overtake you by surprise."*

When negotiations failed between Richard and Saladin, he organized and fortified Ascalon. Following that, they made another attempt to capture Jerusalem but failed and retrieved themselves again. However, their actual failure was because there was a division among the army leaders about the tactics they were to employ to conquer the Holy City. Some of the military leaders wanted to invade Egypt to cut the supply for Saladin and his army to force them to surrender, and some of them also wanted to descend directly on Jerusalem to capture it. This misunderstanding weakened the Crusaders, of which Richard and his army were a part in the campaign to conquer Jerusalem. Eventually, none of the divided forces was able to execute an effective assault on its target, hence their failure to capture Jerusalem again.

The Bible says, *"Every kingdom divided against itself is brought to desolation, and every city or house divided against itself will not stand."* (Matthew 12:25, NKJV).

It's important to make sure that people in your life, business, or ministry's army not only understand the vision, but also understand each other, including you, and you also understand them. That doesn't necessarily mean you would always agree on the means to do things. But if there is mutual respect, understanding, and humility, you would find a common ground by reasoning with each other spiritually and intellectually to form or find a strong way to combine the differences and make the most and best out of them for the common good, goal, or purpose.

> *"It's important to make sure that people in your life, business — not*

only understand the vision, but also understand each other, including you, and you also understand them."

Richard and his army tried a few other attacks here and there to defeat Saladin and his army, but couldn't succeed in taking Jerusalem back. Finally, as he was running out of time, considering the fact that his brother John and King Philip were planning against him back home in England and France, he made a last desperate attempt to attack Egypt to increase his occupation and win a better bargain with his opponent the Muslim General Saladin. Unfortunately, the invasion attempt failed.

As King and General Richard ran out of all possible options to capture Jerusalem from the Muslims, he succumbed to a settlement as his last option to at least secure part of the land. In effect, on September 2, 1192, the two Generals settled on terms that each other believed he deserved. The terms provided for the destruction of Ascalon's fortifications, while allowing Christian pilgrims and merchants access to Jerusalem, and would initiate a three-year truce.

King Richard, being worn out, sick, and fearing his brother and King Philip II plan to overthrow him may come true, embarked on a return journey to go back to England. He did encounter a few challenges on his way back home and was even imprisoned at some point, but he finally made it back home.

If nothing is learned from these two individuals or Generals (King Richard and General Saladin), at least we have learned how you could believe in God and what you believe He has entrusted you with to accomplish, and never give up on it. Both Generals believed Jerusalem is a Holy City of God in their different respective, different religion or way of serving God. And each one believed it was supposed to belong to them and fought vigorously for it.

If you do believe your purpose, and destiny, your life, business, ministry, or anything you believe must change for the better and the glory of God, be a General; a courageous, tactical, and wise General to lead your life, purpose and destiny, family, business, and ministry to victory. And understand, each and every one of your decisions matters, and will either contribute to your loss or victory.

> *"Be a General; a courageous, tactical, and wise General to lead your life, purpose and destiny, family, business, and ministry to victory."*

Additionally, be careful of people who come to what you are doing, leading, or managing as if they want to support you to bring the vision or dream to come to pass, but have ulterior motives. They just want to use you to get their own agendas to come to pass. This is not to say that you can't help others to reach their purpose and destiny, but when they are not clear about their intentions sooner or later, and just want to outsmart, and use you mischievously, that's something to watch out for. Because these people usually can wickedly ruin your work or accomplishments in a bid to just build their own, while maintaining the innocence of any wrong-doings. These types of people are careless about what you have done for them, and wouldn't mind hurting you to satisfy their selfishness.

Your life is the army, and you are the General; lead it to

victory with the right decisions.

Hannibal: The Path Finder and Defeats Survivor

"We shall find a way, or we shall make one." This quote is synonymous with an ancient military leader, a General you may have heard of. His name is Hannibal, and regarded as one of the toughest and best military Generals.

Although Hannibal's vision of putting the Romans out of power was not fulfilled, his audacity and military strategies have left everyone in suspense to date. He was dubbed, "The Father of Strategy" by historians.

As I mentioned earlier, we will fetch from history to learn lessons. I want us to learn something about these Generals, including their mistakes. Maybe we could remember them in a way that would help us make better decisions and not repeat their mistakes. The strategies they employed, which have decisions behind every one of them, and their competence as Generals or leaders.

In short, what started as a childhood dream became one of history's most celebrated military exploits of all time. Historically, when Hannibal was just a youngster, his father made him swear to him that he would never become a friend of the Romans, who were his enemies. Surely, he grew up to witness the rivalry between his father Hamilcar Barca, a General and Statesman himself who was assassinated, and the Roman empire.

At the end of it all, Plutarch, a Greek Middle Platonist philosopher, historian, biographer, and essayist, recorded that Scipio Africanus, a Roman General who is often also regarded as one of the greatest military Generals or commanders, asked General Hannibal, "who are the greatest generals?" He replied, "Either Alexander, or Pyrrus, and himself (Hannibal)." This shows that the man was not only regarded by others as one of the greatest military leaders, but he knew he was one, and even had confidence that he was in the second position when it comes to the greatest Generals of all time.

Amazingly, this also reveals that Hannibal, even after he was defeated in battles, was never defeated in his mind or heart. Many of the things that look like defeat in your life often are not defeats, or they are just defeats in your mind or heart – they look like defeat, but they are not one. Remember, one thing that looks like something is not necessarily it. It just looks like it. Many situations you would experience in life will look like defeats and losses, but might not be one. In fact, every impact the devil may have on your life here and there is never victory for him. He has never won any battle before, even to say he will win a war. Do not panic at any attack of the enemy, even if they hit you one way or the other. God will surely turn it into your good. The Bible says, *"And we know that in all things God works for the good of those who love him, who have been called according to his purpose."* (Romans 8:28, NKJV).

I believe Hannibal made up his mind at a very early age to walk in the footsteps of his father, hence at some point, he would defiantly utter these words, "I swear so soon as age will permit – I will use fire and steel to arrest the destiny of Rome." "What?" Some older soldiers would have exclaimed, because the Roman empire at the time was not a joke or game box for anyone to play with. Certainly, this young man was not settling for less, and will not take defeat for an answer.

This passion and vision to put the Romans out of power

would turn Hannibal into one of the greatest military strategists the world has ever known, the one who would attempt an ambitious military expedition and combat that seemed impossible at his time and age. But how did he do all that? The plan was to take the war and the battles to the doorsteps of the enemy and fight them on his terms instead of waiting for the enemy to attack as some historians and military experts explained.

But, to do this, he had to go all the way to Rome, and getting to Rome with an army without the knowledge of the Romans seemed impossible. The Roman Empire was not a weak government and organization. They were in to rule the world or at least the known world or territories. As we would say in our modern-day's language, "surveillance and security were tight." He would have to pass through the Roman and allied garrisons and the water routes, which were saturated by the Roman naval forces and strategic checkpoints. However, he went against the odds and traversed through the Alps, bypassing the Roman and allied troops stationed in particular locations, and succeeded at least to reach the Roman Republic.

This route took about five (5) months, but some historians also suggested six (6) months, and a thousand (1000) miles or 1609 kilometers. The Alps are the highest and most extensive mountain range system; however, against all challenges, he made it to Rome, to the doorsteps of the enemy for a series of battles that the world would remember for centuries to come.

Endless speculations and research sometimes cast more shadow or confusion about how Hannibal was able to traverse the Alps to Italy with that many soldiers, horses, African war elephants. And of course, supplies for his army – to date, at the time I'm writing this book, there has not been any sure answer to the question, "which route would most likely be the one Hannibal used to get to Rome via the Alps?" As much as it's impossible to confirm their route today, so was their entire journey to Rome to fight the Romans on their own land or territories – impossible.

The Toughest, Yet Sure Route

When you look at the map, even considering the various known routes to Rome in ancient times, there were shorter and easier ways to get to Rome. However, General Hannibal knew that even though using one of those routes might be the easiest and shortest to Rome, he would surely be detected, and his vision or destiny would be arrested by the Romans instead. And his goal and expected results will not be fulfilled – they will fail. In effect, he chose the toughest yet sure one, the most difficult one. Don't be fooled by the easiest and shortest ways to do, get, or achieve things. And I'm not saying you should always choose the toughest way to accomplish things: Your dreams, visions, purpose, and destiny. But make sure that if the easiest way puts your plans, goals, peace, happiness, security, and stability at risk, then choose the toughest, yet sure way to accomplish or get it.

Remember the idiom that says, "Better late than never." It's interpreted as the delayed occurrence or achievement of something that one desires, and is better than it not happening at all." I would paraphrase that and say, "It's better to take the toughest yet sure route to successfully reach your goals rather than choosing the easiest and shortest route and never reaching them, or experiencing peace, happiness, security, and stability. Remember, the world is full of fabricated happiness. Many people you see here and there are just pretending to be happy – but they are not. No, they don't have authentic happiness – they are just faking it to impress others.

While the vision of General Hannibal Barca never fully came to pass, the battles he won with his army in the second major Punic War were remarkable, and to date, many military leaders and historians respect him for those victories, especially the way he strategically fought them, and even called those defeats of the Romans, the "perfect defeat." History remembers this African army General, Hannibal, as the greatest tactical commander or General.

> *"It's better to take the toughest yet sure route to successfully reach your goals rather than choosing the easiest — route and never reaching them."*

Stopping the "Hannibalists" or the Art of Confusion

While we can learn a great deal from the military leadership of General Hannibal, it's also very important to wisely watch out for people who are identical to Hannibal in some ways; these people tend to handle their wives, children, family members, friends, co-workers, employees, and other people with some Hannibal characteristics. These individuals will manipulate you one way or the other for their own interest, and before you know it, you have unwillingly and unknowingly given them what they wanted out of confusion.

Don't Flow In Confusions

Hannibal is known to have used many types of tactics, which in real-life experiences, would be considered inappropriate because they are not morally sound and Godly. Among many of his tactics, maneuvers, including double pincer or envelopment, rapid movements, rushes, and ambushes; he would surprise the Romans many times and take advantage of their confusion.

Keep this in mind, when you are confused, you have a blind spot. Remember, I mentioned earlier that you should not make decisions when you're confused. Look at all areas of your life, family, business, and career carefully to detect and correct confusion and blind spots before someone who would take advantage of them does. Chaos is a setup for defeat and loss. When any area of your life or organization is in chaos, that's always a perfect time for the enemy to strike. So don't play with confusion, misunderstandings, and internal quarrels because it can be costly to you, but profitable to your common enemy. Make it a practice to quickly sort out misunderstandings and clarify confusions before the attacker takes advantage of that.

> *"When you are confused, you have a blind spot."*

In my opinion, there are two main types of confusion in the world or our lives: Internal and influential confusion. Internal confusion is our own misunderstanding about matters, and influential confusion is other people's understanding of matters that directly or indirectly impact us. Our internal confusions start from our misunderstanding of God, the universe, and our identity or who we are, what we can and cannot do, and what is good or bad for us.

When you are not able to resolve your internal confusions, influential confusions are highly effective on you, meaning, other people can easily convince you to believe in anything. While education may help clarify some matters for you and resolve some of your internal confusion, it does not resolve all of them, especially the spiritual ones. That's why you can easily and erroneously propagate ideas and theories that are not true, or you can easily believe in one because you think the person disseminating it is highly educated, intelligent, specialist, expert, scientist, president, doctor, or lawyer. While I encourage you to consider what experts tell you, I would also encourage you to always verify or check what they are saying yourself or against what many other experts are saying.

> *"Internal confusion is our own misunderstanding about matters, and influential confusion is other people's understanding of matters that directly or indirectly impact us."*

For instance, Steve Hawking, an English theoretical physicist, cosmologist, and author and director of research at the Centre for Theoretical Cosmology at the University of Cambridge, was well respected in the scientific domain. In his book "The Theory of Everything: The Origin and Fate of the Universe," he stated, and I quote, "If you believe in science, like I do, you believe that there are certain laws that are always obeyed. If you like, you can say the laws are the work of God, but that is more a definition of God than a proof of his existence." "We are each free to believe what we want and it's my view that the simplest explanation is there is no God." "No one created the universe and no one directs our fate. This leads me to a profound realization, there's probably no Heaven and no afterlife, either. "We have this one life to appreciate the grand design of the universe and for that I am extremely grateful." End of quote.

Honestly, I have one or two questions: First, how do you define something that does not exist, or someone who does not exist, whether visible or invisible? Steve Hawking wrote, "If you like, you can say the laws are the work of God, but that is more a definition of God than a proof of his existence." Let's look at what "Definition" means.

The Oxford English Dictionary says, "Definition" is "a precise statement of the essential nature of a thing; a statement or form of words by which anything is defined." Dictionary.com, the online Dictionary whose proprietary source is the Random House Unabridged Dictionary, and accepted sources including American Heritage and Harper Collins says, "Definition" is "a statement expressing the essential nature of something."

Hereby, with all due respect, I believe Mr. Steve Hawking contradicted himself. If you believe that the laws of the universe are the definition of God rather than His existence, either way, according to his statement, the laws of the universe prove the existence of God because you cannot "define" something that does not exist – visible or invisible. And even if we have to understand Mr. Hawking's statement the other way around (which I do not think was what he meant), which would be that the universe is actually a god. That also takes me to another question, did he believe that there is a Higher Power? Considering the following, and I quote, "If you believe in science, like I do, you believe that there are certain laws that are always obeyed." What is the power making the universe always obey certain laws? I believe it is the "Higher Power."

Uncertainty Has a Cure

In his biography with Walter Isaacson, Steve Job stated, "I think religions are many doors to one house; sometimes I think the house exists, and sometimes I don't."

The cure for confusion and uncertainty is knowledge. And note that there are different types of knowledge that can also refer to a collection of knowledge. Unfortunately, we want to know about everything, but God. We spend time, money, and many other resources to know about the universe more than its Creator. Even when people do, they do not wholeheartedly. The Bible says, *"You will seek me and find me when you seek me with all your heart."* (Jeremiah 29:13, NIV).

> *"The cure for confusion and uncertainty is knowledge. And note that there are different types of knowledge."*

According to dictionaries and psychological terms, the word "uncertainty" has other definitions. However, uncertainty is generally caused by our limited knowledge about events, things, and times. This means that whenever we know and understand something, our uncertainty about it becomes non-existent. Therefore, I believe that the only way we can build certainty and confidence about something is by educating ourselves concerning it. And the Oxford Languages Dictionary defines "Education" as "the process of receiving or giving systematic instruction." In effect, I wonder why, when people are either confused or uncertain about God, they do not systematically search for Him according to the plan and book available to humanity to know about Him. I believe anyone who can systematically (according to the fixed plan given to humanity in the Bible) search for God, will find and know Him personally. And their confusion and uncertainty about Him will vanish.

The Bible Says, *"Ask and it will be given to you; seek and you will find; knock and the door will be opened to you. For everyone who asks receives; the one who seeks finds; and to the one who knocks, the door will be opened."* (Matthew 7:7-8, NIV).

This is where the confusion is for some people, and understand this, "GOD" is a name. Once more, the Dictionary defines a "Name" as "a word or set of words by which a person, animal, place, or thing is known, addressed, or referred to." And "GOD" is a name we use to refer to a being. However, that being is more than just a "name." The reality is, whether you believe in that "name" or not, you surely do believe that there is a Higher Power, law, or being in control of the universe. So, if you can be honest with yourself, the problem is not that you do not believe in a Higher Power or Supernatural Being who is in charge of the universe, but the issue is that you do not believe that the Higher Power or Being should be called "GOD." In effect, call that Being any reasonable and honorable name you want – and He does exist even in your conscience.

You may say, "There are several ways to do things." or "Many roads lead to Rome." While this idiom is true of many achievements, when it comes to your relationship with God, many roads do not lead to Him. Do you say or do things any way you think or believe it can be done and ignore the civil and criminal laws of your residential, citizenship, or naturalization country? If earthly governments have a particular way you should do things in this world, then God ultimately has a particular way for you to connect, communicate, and fellowship with Him. And the Lord Jesus Christ declared, *"I am the way and the truth and the life. No one comes to the Father except through me."* (John 14:6, NIV).

Either way, alive or dead on earth, you live in the universe of the Higher Power, Force, or Being. So, who must set the rules or laws of connecting to Him, you or Him?

Protect Your Information

Intelligence-gathering has been a practice for kingdoms, empires, countries, and armies for centuries. One of the strategies Hannibal used was the gathering of information through intelligence activities. He would often send spies among the enemy's territories and camps to gather important and sensitive information about the Romans. The gathering of intelligence is not a new thing. Every government on earth has a certain level of intelligence-gathering activities. Some are immature or at an entry level, while some are very advanced with modern-day technologies. As insignificant as the gathering of intelligence could be to the ordinary person, it's vital to nations who understand that their survival depends on it.

Sadly, criminals are using the same methods and technologies to steal people's sensitive information or data. To the ordinary person, modern-day technologies have made it difficult to maintain a certain level of privacy, but that doesn't mean you should not do your best to protect your vital information one way or the other. Security and privacy are no longer optional to anyone but necessary. Cyber-threats are ever-increasing, and everybody is at risk of having personal, family, and business information or data stolen or accessed against their will.

Be careful with what information you share with who, where, and when. I wish the world was full of Godly and all-loving people, but it's not, so you have to be careful with your information. There is nothing like a total or hundred percent security because the more technology advances, the less secure the world will become. Of course, modern-day technology is providing us with various ways to secure and protect our lives and belongings. However, if we turn the other side of the coin, and if we can only be honest with ourselves, technology always creates both ends of the rope – the good and bad. To sum it up, try your best not to say, write, print, or post online and offline needlessly.

> *"Be careful with what information you share with who, where, and when."*

Sometimes, laziness and blind trust can cause you loss, pain, and many other troubles. But you better spend a little time making sure that your properties, including your electronic devices and important documents, are secured at some level with Passwords, PINs, Locks, Software, and Encryption, and doing what you are supposed to do vigilantly with a high level of care and watchfulness, and constantly attentive to respond and review signs of activities, or dangers to your sensitive information. This will minimize the risk of your properties and sensitive information being stolen.

Watch out for any items that contain your sensitive information at home, office, or workplace. It amazes me to see many people leaving their devices and documents to go and use the restroom, even when they are in public places, airports, coffee shops, restaurants, and hotels, without taking it with them. Remember, it's better to inconvenience yourself having your devices and bags with you when you want to ease yourself in the restroom rather than returning and finding out that they have been stolen, or someone has intentionally installed malware or virus on them to later use it as a backdoor to get into your computer or phone remotely. Even hotels are not to be trusted with your sensitive information. Make sure to at least you have hardened the access to your sensitive information and devices with a safe or a security means before leaving for your conference or meeting. I have heard stories about people hiring hotel workers who have access to almost every room on the premises to steal the sensitive information of guests or customers who stay there.

Don't forget to have someone you trust watching your food and drink before going to ease yourself in the restroom. If you live in a shared house or work in a shared office or space, especially when you notice that there are people who don't like you, homeowner, roommate, or co-worker — make sure to secure your food and drinks before leaving. There are wicked people in the world. Someone can pour poison or some chemicals into your food or drink, which can cause you a disease that can progressively kill you.

One of the biggest challenges many companies are facing now, including the financial industry, is the fact that criminals are now infiltrating them and becoming their employees and working as agents of criminal groups who can easily get your information to a criminal and get paid for it. So, instead of just thinking these companies are watching your sensitive information and no one can steal it, you have to actively check your accounts to notice and report or complain about unusual activities to them so they can look into that before the worst happens. The companies mean well, but it's difficult for them to catch every malicious activity on your account. So, you have to help them with that as well.

Poverty is also adding to these cyber threats in many areas of the world. Needy people feel like they have the right to hack and steal other people's money because rich people don't help them, and they are left behind in everything. I remember having a conversation with a man about cyber threats and telling him how this is bad. Unfortunately, he quoted me from the Bible and said, **"From the days of John the Baptist until now the kingdom of heaven suffers violence, and the violent take it by force."** (Matthew 11:12, NKJV). And he added, "We have to take it by force from the people who have it, and don't want to give it out." I was standing there looking at him and wondering where they were getting these erroneous thoughts from.

I should also remind you not to be greedy – don't be looking for free or quick money to the extent that you play yourself into the hands of criminals. When someone tells you that there is money somewhere they want to transfer into your bank account or mobile money account, and know you haven't worked for that money, and nobody died and put you in their will to receive such a huge amount of money, but you give out your banking information to receive it – that's greed. Or someone sends you a message or calls you that you have won a lottery, and you know you haven't played any lottery, but you give out your financial information to get that money – that's greed. The criminals have many ways to illegally gain access to your information by luring you to freely give it to them, including fake police, sheriff, judge, court, lawyer, attorney, FBI or investigative calls, text messages, and mails to cause you to panic and return their calls, text messages, or mails with your sensitive information. You should always directly go in person to these local or federal offices to confirm these messages because, unfortunately, many of them are fake and from criminals or someone who is trying to illegally access your sensitive information.

> *"I should also remind you not to be greedy – don't be looking for free or quick money to the extent that you play yourself into the hands of criminals."*

Illusive and Nosy People

Be mindful of illusive and nosy people, who are always trying to know more than they should about your personal and private affairs – some of them just want to help, but many others are just nosy and want to know so they can share with other people to satisfy their ill-intentions or to their advantage. And if you are managing an enterprise or organization, be careful and watch out for people who come not to sincerely contribute to what you are building as an individual or team, but to steal information and use it to their own advantage while they try to destroy what you are building. This is not to say you can't share profitable information with others. When you're blessed or have good information, you can share it with people to benefit them as well. After all, that's part of being human and Godly. However, watch out for destroyers, people motivated by jealousy, greed, and selfishness because they usually just don't want information that will benefit them, but your downfall, which you should avoid.

People who want your downfall don't mind spending their time, resources, money, materials, and energy to make sure their wish comes true. So you shouldn't hold back on doing your best to protect your sensitive information by all affordable and good means possible.

> *"People who want your downfall don't mind spending their time, resources, money, materials, and energy to make sure their wish comes true."*

As God-fearing people, we want to share everything and anything with anybody, which is the way it should be. However, experiences have shown that sometimes, it's just not the right thing to do until you trust the person or receiver. Sometimes, you give information no one has asked you, and sometimes you give too much information when asked. Either way, you should be wise about how much information you give out, and don't give out information unnecessarily. The problem is, that not everybody is Godly and morally sound. Believe it or not, there are selfish and evil people in this world. People will go to any extent just to do evil to satisfy their ego and selfishness, and some of them are even in churches or religious organizations. The Bible says, *"No weapon formed against you shall prosper, And every tongue which rises against you in judgment You shall condemn. This is the heritage of the servants of the LORD, And their righteousness is from Me,"* Says the LORD." (Isaiah 54:17, NKJV). They will not prevail, but you have to learn not to spend or waste your time on every battle because you have so many other things that you can spend that time on. Save yourself from unnecessary work and battles by keeping your information to yourself, and only share it when necessary or with trusted and Godly people.

> *"As God-fearing people, we want to share everything and anything with anybody — However, experiences have shown that sometimes, it's just not the right thing to do until you trust the person or receiver."*

There are people who will use your own resources to take you down. Before you accept anyone to work for you in any capacity, ensure they are not up to using your own resources, including a position you gave them, to destroy you or what you are building. This doesn't mean people can't have their own as they work for you, or collaborate with you, but it's the wickedness and selfishness of some human beings' hearts that you have to be mindful of and avoid falling prey to.

It amazes me how some people think they are so intelligent, but you realize they are not wise. I have dealt with people or found myself in various situations where some people will be doing some things against me, and just because I pretended that I didn't know about it, they continued doing it. So, at some point, I would just judge it's even better not to let them know I know about their malice because trying to reason with them will rather make me look stupid like them.

In business, and even in ministry, I have dealt with people who would lie to me and just turn themselves in right away, or contradict what they have just said in the same conversations just a few seconds or minutes later. And I would be holding my head, thinking, "Really, is this smartness or stupidity?"

A group of people was, and still very intrusive, trying relentlessly to steal my personal and business information, attempting to hack my network, computers, or devices, eavesdropping, intercepting my phone calls and messages, attempting to access my bank accounts, servers, websites, and breaching or opening my door when I'm not around. And even doing the same to people they knew were related to me, trying to steal business information they wanted since they were unsuccessful in getting it directly. I pretended I didn't know, and they really believed I didn't know anything about it, so they kept doing it, thinking I was suspecting some outsiders were conducting these activities.

You have to keep in mind that you cannot outsmart everybody. Some people are naturally born detectives, and others are by training, and the acute ones are people who have the Holy Spirit of God in addition to them being naturally born or trained detectives. They will either catch you right away or just a few moments later. They are that sharp detective. Personally, I will surely find out one way or the other, and in most cases will not even ask you. You can reverse things and cover up your back exactly the way they were, and that cannot still stop me from knowing. Additionally, I have used several ways of finding out what people with evil intentions do with my belongings when I'm not around.

Security risk is inherent and does not depend on you alone, but also on organizations or entities and individuals you deal with in every area of your life, including your banks, medical professionals, property managers, landlords, hotels, travel agencies, restaurants, schools, stores, and even religious organizations. However, you have to try and do your best to harden access to your properties and make it so that in the event someone still tries to access them, you can know and take the appropriate technical, legal, and official measures to protect yourself and yours.

Even though criminals can still try to bypass the following, it's better than not having and doing them at all -- at least it gives you a certain level of protection. Legally leave cameras, audio recorders, fleece or signs, and other custom-made detectors and recorders that are difficult for intruders to notice, jam, and turn back on after their criminal activities.

I remember the night before I moved to that place, I had a dream and knew that God was telling me about what would happen over there. In effect, I was watchful, and just a few days after I got there, I started seeing their activities.

You have to take your dreams seriously, otherwise, you will regret so many decisions. I will elaborate on this later.

Note that I do not put cameras or recorders in common areas but in my private places where I have personal items. And if I put it in a common area, even at the office, I always post a notice that "Camera is in use," so anyone who comes to that area knows there is a camera there due to their privacy.

When you get to some point in life, and you think you know all a human being can be and do, another demonstrates by his character, attitude, and morals that you haven't seen anything yet. So, you cannot trust a human being until it's proven you can.

> *"You cannot trust a human being until it's proven you can."*

I have personally learned that there is nothing you can do humanly or naturally to change criminal minds. Being kind, gracious, and loving to them is Godly, but remember that they can still do what they want regardless of your kindness. Therefore, be cautious while you are trying your best to be kind to them, and take all precautions to ultimately protect and defend yourself against them.

Criminals always think they are smart and can outsmart everybody, but often, their activities prove that they are not wise. Their criminal minds make them believe everyone is stupid, and because the other person couldn't catch them, this or that person also cannot catch them. Or because they got away with their criminal activities before, they can get away with it again.

A smart and wise person understands the consequences

of his decisions and actions, not the one who is talented or able. In other words, if you're smart or intelligent, and wise, you must know or understand the results, or consequences of what will come out of your bad decisions and actions, and not do it. Being able or talented to do something wrong does not make you smart until you know how to refrain or restrain yourself from doing it.

> *"A smart and wise person understands the consequences of his decisions and actions, not the one who is talented or able."*

Catching a Surprise Before It Becomes One

One of General Hannibal's strategies was surprise. He was willing and worked hard with his army to use unimaginable means to surprise his opponents. This was clear when he sacrificed so much time, energy, materials, money (silver), animals, and even the lives of his soldiers to cross the Alps in harsh weather or Winter in order to appear at the doorsteps of the Romans — something they never expected.

"Never say never." It's an idiom that you have surely heard. And maybe the closest parallel to it would be, "Never say it's impossible." The Bible says, **"With men this is impossible, but with God all things are possible."** (Matthew 19:26, NKJV). This passage of the Bible refers to God – Nothing is impossible to him. But you have to understand also that when it comes to human beings who don't fear God and practice his commandment of love,

"You shall love your neighbor as yourself—" (Mark 12:30-31), they can do anything that will surprise you without the fear of God. When someone loves God first, then his fellow as himself, he watches to not be wicked. But if he doesn't, then he can do any unimaginable evil to others that would usually surprise them because they never thought that person could treat them in that manner. That's one of the reasons the Bible says, *"Do not put your trust in princes, in human beings–"* (Psalm 146:2-4).

You don't have to be sleepless and suspicious of everything and everybody, but cultivating the art of detecting problems or surprises before they become one or happen might be very helpful in your life, business, or organization. Watch out for strange behaviors, languages or words, sudden changes in various things, reactions, responses, or replies… Etc. As I mentioned earlier, just as God has given birds a natural built-in Global Positioning System (GPS) that helps them orient themselves, He has also given every human being an inner abnormality detector, and each one of us has to learn how to use it, or how it works for you through the Spirit of God, the Holy Spirit.

> *"You don't have to be sleepless and suspicious of everything and everybody, but cultivating the art of detecting problems or surprises before they become one or happen might be very helpful in your life, business, or organization."*

Be Careful of Enticements

General Hannibal would usually lure his enemies to a place and time where and when he could easily use nature to his advantage to defeat them. He would sometimes lure his enemies to either fight in the night, by the lake, where there was a thick mist above the lake that obscured visibility for the Romans, opposite the sun, and sandy winds to blow into their faces while his army strategically fought them.

The dictionary defines "Enticement" as "something used to attract or to tempt someone." Behind every bait, is your downfall, loss, or death. Your enemies would usually lure you directly or indirectly through other people with things they believe you will follow or that can get your attention — Sending, showing, or saying things that can easily anger you, or attract you, including money, positions, job offers, sex, and materials. It's not a new thing. Do you remember Samson in the Bible? All it took for the Philistines to get him, their enemy was Delilah, whom they used as a sexual bait to get the secret of his strength and eventually arrested him, plugged out his eyes, and made him a slave to grind in their mills. (Judges chapter 16).

People will entice you in different ways, knowingly or unknowingly to pick up unnecessary fights with you, push you to make the wrong decisions, and do the things you are not supposed to do in order to use those mistakes to their advantage. Be wise and do not let yourself be fooled into unnecessary fights, money, time, and material expenses. Spend your time, energy, money, and materials wisely.

> *"Behind every bait, is your downfall, loss, or death."*

The Fear Factor

General Hannibal was a master of psychological warfare (PSYWAR), or the basic aspects of modern psychological operations (PsyOp), also known by many other names or terms. According to military sources, this includes Military Information Support Operations, political warfare, "Hearts and Minds," and propaganda." The expected end is "to convey selected information and indicators to audiences to influence their emotions, motives, and objective reasoning, and ultimately the behavior of governments, organizations, groups, and individuals."

The tactic eventually confuses people's minds, sends fear into their hearts, weakens their confidence, will, morale, alertness, and energy level, and easily makes them fall into traps. Be wise to recognize such manipulations in your relationships, business, or organization's affairs when dealing with people, especially people and entities you know are looking for your downfall or overcoming you in any way.
This is not to encourage you to disregard dangers. Wisdom helps you understand whether you steer away from danger or fight and overcome it. But be alert to detect when someone or an entity is just trying to bully you into fear in order to take advantage of you. Wisely and safely resist them strategically.
In 1933, when the depression, unlike any other, hit the world including the United States of America after World War II, and threatened people's jobs, savings, and even their homes and farms at its peak, then President Franklin D. Roosevelt, in a speech uttered, "So, first of all, let me assert my firm belief that the only thing we have to fear is fear itself – nameless, unreasoning, unjustified terror which par-

alyzes needed efforts to convert retreat into advance." There are many bullies out there who will always try to terrorize you, even when you are right, and they are wrong, and just take advantage of you because of your seeming lack of knowledge, education, influence, race, or background. You should know how to wisely, safely, and strategically resist and push back the predatory actions of these bullies.

It's Not About the Size, But How You Use It

Remarkably, General Hannibal's army was mostly outnumbered by his opponent or the Romans'. But he would manage to use it to fight critical battles against them multiple times and kept them restless and fearful. His ability to use what he has teaches that you can achieve great things in life, business, or organization with little or small things at your disposal. You can use the small things or possessions as stepping stones to start and reach bigger and better things and places. Don't wait for the big things to start working on the dream, vision, or goal; start now with the little things.

Looking at the Danger

Like anyone, most of your parents' teachings to you are not given in a classroom setting, but in daily conversations, activities, and instructions between parents and children. One of those instructions my mother gave us since I was a child that I never forgot was, "Never walk along a street in the same direction as the vehicles, in case something goes wrong, and they are about to hit or crash into you, you can't see them. But when you're walking in the opposite direction of the traffic, you can see all the oncoming vehicles and dodge them in case they are out of control." That advice became evident to me one Saturday morning: A mechanic shop that many knew in the small town I grew up in was test-driving an old LandRover on the main street of the town; and for some mechanical fault, the vehicle got out of control and ran over about three to five people from their behind. Unfortunately, some of them didn't make it back to life but died. The whole town, especially the area where the incident occurred, which was a few meters away from our home, was in mourning about that beautiful group of farmers who were just peacefully and happily going to the market to sell their produce, make some money and return home to their families by the evening, but couldn't make it – their lives in this world were shorten, and their families livelihood changed forever.

I would say it was a trauma for many who witnessed the accident. And to many children, it was very scary. But then, to me personally, in addition to the fear and sadness, it was also a reminder or sign of how important it is to listen to one's parents' good and Godly instructions. I thought, "If they were walking on the other side of the street, facing the oncoming traffic, the vehicle wouldn't have crashed into them. And if the vehicle was coming in the opposite direction, they would have seen it and at least tried to dodge it, and perhaps would have escaped the accident — It was a moment of mixed feeling — what could have happened if this or that was done?

There are so many dangers hovering in the world, in or around your personal life, job or profession, business, organization, ministry, and various relationships one way or the other. If you ignore and turn your back to them, they may reach and crash into you. Figuratively, do not turn your back on dangers or anything you know is a threat to your physical and spiritual life, peace, security, stability, prosperity, and longevity. Keep your eyes on them — monitor them. I hate to tell you this, but there are some battles you may have to fight all your life to keep yourself and yours safe or protected. Never assume that some bad people will leave you alone, they may not stop trying to do wrong to you. So, you have to be alert all the time, and in everything. This doesn't mean you have to live in a phobia, or an uncontrollable, irrational, and lasting fear of something, situation, or activity. But when you know something is a danger to you and yours, handle it as such — Pray about it, ask for the LORD's protection, but also take wise precautions or measures against it so that in case the enemy wants to use it to disturb or destroy your life, peace, security, prosperity, stability, and longevity, you can counter-attack or dodge it effectively.

Unusual and Unnoticed Traps

Making the right decisions also requires the ability to detect, recognize, and predict the possible outcome of your actions in order to be prepared to handle them properly, counter-attack, and stop, reverse, or defeat them. There may be many traps on your way to growth, liberation, success, and stability, but it's how you handle them that matters. Epictetus, a Greek Philosopher said, "It's not what happens to you, but how you react to it that matters." I agree, but it's also important to consider that before it happens to you, you detect or know and possibly escape or avoid it. It's not only how you react to it, but how quickly you may be able to know that it's a danger or a trap and avoid playing with the bait. Understand that the devil keeps using old tricks, but some of the old tweaked tricks may completely catch you off-guard because they look different or come in different formats or ways. And every tactic the devil uses to even combat you is just a simulation of physical war and battle strategies.

> *"Every tactic the devil uses to even combat you is just a simulation of physical war and battle strategies."*

To date, one of General Hannibal's battle strategies has been a considerable subject among military experts and non-military analysts. But the question you and I must ask ourselves, and what we must be curious to know and understand is, are these strategies new? And how do they apply to our physical and spiritual lives? To my understanding, the Bible declares, **"What has been will be again, what has been done will be done again; there is nothing new under the sun."** (Ecclesiastes 1:9, NIV).

"Double envelopment," as it's called, was one of Hannibal's favorite war tactics. Even though some military historians disagree on who invented and used it the first time in a war, the fact is that General Hannibal was the one who was able to successfully use it to destroy his enemies or the Romans in a great number. A few military historians noted that it could have been first used as early as 490 B.C. by Miltiades, the Athenian General who defeated the Persians at the Battle of Marathon, which caused the story of a messenger by the name Pheidippides to run twenty-five (25) miles, from Marathon to Athens to announce the good news of the victory — This was what inspired the creation of the modern sporting event, the Marathon Race.

The "Double envelopment" was used by General Hannibal to defeat nearly eighty-five thousand (85,000) Roman soldiers at the Battle of Cannae. The tactic consists of forcing or tricking the enemy to commit more soldiers to a forward or front attack, allowing your own troops to foldback in the center, then having a hidden heavy armed force attack the enemy's troops from the sides or flanks, and the back, preventing them from maneuvering and escaping.

According to the Oxford English Dictionary, a "trap" is "a device or enclosure designed to catch and retain animals, typically by allowing entry but not exit or by getting/catching hold of a part of the body." However, it also defines a "trap" as "a situation in which people lie in wait to make a surprise attack."

Once more, do not be too focused on what is in front of you to the extent that you forget what may come from your sides and behind; I mean other important things you should take care of or focus on as well. When one thing takes all your attention, you may have a blind spot that the enemy can hit or take advantage of before you wake up or realize it. "Tunnel vision," we called it. "I'm just focused on this or that right now," we usually say. That's great! But while you are focused on something, ensure that you do not entirely take your attention off other essential things until they are out of control before you realize it. The enemy, the devil, would usually bring things into your life, business, or organization to get your attention – and sometimes good things, but is only to deviate your attention from other important things so he can attack you from there.

While there are priorities in life, everything about your spiritual and physical life that is taking too much of your attention and causing you to neglect all other important things become traps. Making money is important, but caring for your health also is important. You ought to have longevity in order to do, and enjoy more.

Traps come into our lives and retain us in different forms, in relationships, partnerships, jobs or professions, ministry, food, drink, sex, and many other things. The evil thing about traps is that you don't even notice or recognize them as one. They are effective because they can easily escape your logic, intelligence, and wisdom. Traps are primarily in the form of what you like, want, or expect, and that's why when they arrive one way or the other to you, or you get to them, your pre-set desire or need easily pushes you into them. Traps are also very pleasurable, so the good feeling they give you kills your desire to get out of them, and in some cases, even when they are hurting you in other areas. Traps give you false promises that will never be fulfilled. You think it will change for the better, but it will not change for the better, but it will worsen.

The first step to take in dealing with traps is to see them as what they are – they are traps, and traps are not a blessing, because they come into your life to destroy, kill, or waste your time, energy, money, purpose and destiny.

> *"The evil thing about traps is that you don't even notice or recognize them as one."*

Sometimes, traps are not holding your entire life captive, but just a part of it, so you might not know because you only see it as a very insignificant thing, but remember, when one tiny piece is missing in a puzzle, it's never completed. So, get serious about the little things that you are missing in your life, but are supposed to be in the big picture, and take a very honest or transparent evaluation of them to confirm.

Traps also can be hidden in your life in the form of disorder. The Bible says, ***"God is not a God of disorder."*** (1 Corinthians 14:33). You may be caught up in various disorderly things and not realize they are traps. When things are not running in an orderly way, it may be a sign that you are trapped in something that you have to identify and untrap yourself by the grace of God before it's too late or it becomes a bigger and stronger trap.

As I mentioned earlier, in addition to prayer and faith, always provision your plan and necessities for escape when you are doing things. In effect, if they become an identified threat, danger, or trap, you can escape to save your physical or spiritual life, as well as resources. Faith is not ignorance and stupidity.

General Hannibal understood the importance of location and position. Remember earlier, we discussed the importance of your location and position because it contributes to your success or victory as well. This could be physical or figurative. When you are wrongly positioned, it can affect your ability to win battles in any area of your life. Your location or position also can be a trap and facilitate an ambush of your enemies or life's dangers. Where are you located in your life, marriage, business, ministry, and projects? Evaluate what you are doing now, and see if in case something goes wrong, you are protected. This is not a lack of faith, but wisdom. For example, you better have an insurance policy from the insurance company and never use it by the grace of God, rather than not having it at all. And when something goes wrong, you have to spend too much money out of your own pocket. Glory be to God if you have enough to spend that way, but that surplus can help others who don't even have food to eat or are in other needs. I have heard some Christians say that they believe in divine health so they don't have any health insurance, and don't plan to get one. I'm not sure how they came to this conclusion by faith. In case you don't have the means to get insurance is one thing, but if you do, and refuse to get it because you believe in divine health, that's another. But I would say that's not wise. That gives opportunity to some medical establishments and others to ambush you with bills in case you need medical treatments.

> *"The first step to take in dealing with traps is to see them as what they are – they are traps."*

May I repeat, that your position can also be your legal bindings or grounds, including agreements and rights. Are you positioned so that you can't be spiritually, physically, and business-wise be ambushed by life or what you are doing? Review every area of your life constantly to check your positioning before life ambushes you.

General Hannibal took advantage of other Generals' ignorance and lack of experience to win battles. It's essential to understand and know that you don't know everything. And what you don't know can become a danger to you. While most people learn in schools, you have to make it a personal responsibility to grow your knowledge outside or in addition to your school learning and all the degrees you have acquired. It's only by learning that you actually discover what you don't know. And you have to educate yourself about things you don't know, so you can discover and know them before someone tries to use them to their advantage to hurt you, waste your time, or delay your projects, vision, purpose, and destiny.

It's very important to reiterate that humility is a good thing and is never weakness or stupidity. Looking back in history, and how Hannibal is celebrated in military and non-military sectors, you would be tempted to believe that no other Generals in history were like him. But the truth is, the General who actually defeated Hannibal, who was Publius Cornelius Scipio Africanus, or just as he's referred to as "Scipio", must have been one great General as well, and probably skilled more than Hannibal. This General was humble enough to learn or glean from the genius of Hannibal whom he defeated.

Historians noted that General Scipio may have learned how to implement some war and battle tactics from Hannibal. When you think you know so much that you don't need anyone's advice or glean from the intelligence, knowledge, and wisdom of other smart people, sooner or later it can cause your downfall. Even though it's clear that people are born with some natural talents and spiritual gifts, it's obvious that looking through history, you can realize that many great people, knowingly or unknowingly emulated other great people who came before them one way or the other, spiritually or physically. History reveals that many of the greatest army Generals tried to mirror or reproduce Hannibal at a certain level, including Julius Caesar, Charlemagne, Napoleon, and many others. It is as, "Mention one great General, and I would tell you who he emulated — from Attila, Marius, Alaric, Cyrus, Sun Tzu, Trajan, and up to the eighteen hundreds (1800s). Generals like Ulysses S. Grant, the American Union army commander during the American Civil War, and Johannes E. E. Rommel, who was a German General and a propaganda figure during World War II, and was known as the Desert Fox, and served Nazi Germany. Of course, not all of them served good causes. But the point here is that they emulated other Generals to achieve their good or bad goals. And the lesson or understanding here is that you should never get to a point in life where you think you know it all and don't need to learn from anyone.

As I mentioned earlier, even though I don't command many of the activities and lifestyle of these Generals, there are many things that occurred under their leadership and could be lessons we can learn from to prevent similar things from happening to us, or someone trying to use them to destroy our lives, purposes, and destinies.

Take charge of your life, relationship, business, profession, ministry, purpose, and destiny as a good and formidable General and lead it to victory by the grace, power, and wisdom of God.

> *"Take charge of your life — as a good and formidable General and lead it to victory by the grace, power, and wisdom of God."*

Chapter 5
King of Your Kingdom

"You are a chosen people, a royal priesthood – God's special possession."
I Peter 2:29

IF YOU WERE NATURALLY BORN into a royal family in this world, and become a King or Queen, how would you rule your Kingdom? The Bible states that you are a royal.

One of a King's responsibilities is to make decisions. History reveals to us that some Kings and Queens in the past made good decisions, while others made wrong decisions. Good decisions bring or crown you respect and honor, and bad decisions bring or crown you with disrespect and dishonor.

Imagine yourself being a King or Queen sitting on your throne while they bring you difficult matters to judge. The same reality applies to your life. You are the King, and your life is the Kingdom. Life will bring you its pains and pleasures, challenges and successes. But how will you use your understanding and judgment to make the right decisions in your life, relationships, business, career, and leadership?

As a king, your skills and competence will be tested on several levels, including your wisdom. The wisdom of the king is tested by wars, famine, pestilence, insurrection, or social and economic events.

The Bible says, ***"Moreover, Solomon has taken his seat on the royal throne."*** (1 Kings 1:46, NIV). May I say to you as well, "Please, now take your seat on the royal throne of your life."

The Oxford Dictionary defines a kingdom as "a country, state, or territory ruled by a King or Queen." And a King or Queen is the "Ruler of an independent state, especially one who inherits the position by right of birth." However, it also noted that it is "A person or thing regarded as the finest or most important in its sphere or group." The dictionary also goes more profoundly on the word's definition and states that it also means a "Leading light, star or superstar." Unlike an actual earthly Kingdom, or a piece of land inhabited by people and ruled by a King or a Queen, in your life's Kingdom, are your soul, spirit, and body.

We like the idea of being called a King or Queen in our modern world, but we miss the essence of what a real King or Queen is. We like the title, but our behaviors, decisions, and lifestyles are completely opposite of those of a true King or Queen. There are things that qualify someone to be enthroned as a King or Queen, and Kings or Queens have specific ways of carrying themselves.

In ancient Biblical days, the Kings of Israel and Judah were divinely selected by God to serve and rule His people as His representatives. And so was the case with King Saul. Let's read from the Bible: "Then Samuel took a flask of oil and poured it on his head and kissed him and said, "Has not the Lord anointed you to be prince over his people Israel? And you shall reign over the people of the Lord and you will save them from the hand of their surrounding enemies. And this shall be the sign to you that the Lord has anointed you to be prince over his heritage. When you depart from me today, you will meet two men by Rachel's tomb in the territory of Benjamin at Zelzah, and they will say to you, 'The donkeys that you went to seek are found, and now your father has ceased to care about the donkeys and is anxious about you, saying, "What shall I do about my son?"' Then you shall go on from there farther and come to the oak of Tabor. Three men going up to God at Bethel will meet you there, one carrying three young goats, another carrying three loaves of bread, and another carrying a skin of wine. And they will greet you and give you two loaves of bread, which you shall accept from their hand. After that you shall come to Gibeath-elohim, where there is a garrison of the Philistines. And there, as soon as you come to the city, you will meet a group of prophets coming down from the high place with harp, tambourine, flute, and lyre before them, prophesying. Then the Spirit of the Lord will rush upon you, and you will prophesy with them and be turned into another man. Now when these signs meet you, do what your hand finds to do, for God is with you." (I Samuel 10:1-7).

> *"We like the idea of being called a King or Queen in our modern world, but we miss the essence of what a real King or Queen is."*

After God rejected King Saul because of his disobedience, He selected another king to rule over his people, and His name was David. We read, "The Lord said to Samuel, "How long will you mourn for Saul, since I have rejected him as king over Israel? Fill your horn with oil and be on your way; I am sending you to Jesse of Bethlehem. I have chosen one of his sons to be king—."

"So Samuel took the horn of oil and anointed him in the presence of his brothers, and from that day on the Spirit of the Lord came powerfully upon David. Samuel then went to Ramah." (I Samuel 16:1-13, NIV).

The roles of a king in Bible days were clear: they were to reign over the people of God, and protect, and save them from their enemies with the help of God himself. When we hear the word "reign," the first thing that comes to mind is "power and control." But when you look a little closer, you understand that the original intent of God about the kings He selected to reign over his people was to provide them with good judgment and leadership, and not just leadership that other nations' kings were able to offer the land or territories they ruled – Godly leadership. He wanted a man who could guide and direct his people to follow His laws and ordinances. He wanted a man who could influence His people to behave and reflect the characteristics of the God of Abraham, Isaac, Jacob, Joseph, and Moses. In doing so, they were expected to keep the covenants and laws of God in conjunction with, or help of the priests and prophets.

> *"The original intent of God about the kings He selected to reign over his people was to provide them with good judgment (Wisdom) and leadership."*

It is to be noted that these kings, at some point, could also prophesy, but not sacrifice. As a matter of fact, this was the sin and the beginning of King Saul's fall. Instead of waiting for Samuel to come and make the sacrifice, he decided to do it himself while he was tired of waiting for Samuel to arrive. (I Samuel 13:8-14). This was a sacrificial and priestly restriction, but King Saul decided to violate it because he thought he was the King and could do anything he wished. But the repercussions were painful and devastating.

One of the troubles in the world today is that every man believes he's a king, and every woman believes she's a queen, so they can do anything that pleases them. The husband thinks he's a king so he can do anything that pleases him, and the wife cannot hold him accountable. The wife also believes she's a queen so she can do anything that pleases her and the husband cannot hold her accountable. The children believe they are princes and princesses, so they can do whatever they please, and nobody can hold them accountable – Everybody now is royal without self-restrictions or discipline.

> *"One of the troubles in the world today is that every man believes he's a king, and every woman believes she's a queen, so they can do anything that pleases them."*

A royalty without moral restriction is not wise. In effect, it will cause you pain, losses, and destroy or kill you sooner or later.

The belief that you are a king or queen is great! And in

fact, you should think about yourself as a king or queen. However, there are characteristics, and duties or responsibilities that come with kingship or royalty. And as a king or queen, one of the things you should learn is restriction. No matter how assertive, or powerful and in control you feel, there are things you cannot do just because of your position. Yes, you can, but it will destroy the trust the people have in you, the people you rule, and eventually yourself. Moreover, as a king, you must understand that you are not exempt from God's correction and punishment. A king who cannot control or restrict himself is useless. Throughout history, kings and queens who couldn't restrict themselves did not end well.

> *"A royalty without moral restriction is not wise. In effect, it will cause you pain, losses, and destroy or kill you sooner or later."*

Since ancient days, once someone is considered the heir presumptive, the royal house or family starts educating and grooming the latter in matters of the state and kingdom as preparation to take over at the needed time.

Needless to note, this preparation includes teaching the heir the core characteristics of a king or queen, which are very fundamental, such as his birthright to ascend to the throne, his absolute authority, the power of his words and decrees, his possessions and wealth, his power over the people he rules and the government of the kingdom, the influence of his presence, his decisiveness and the power of his decisions, and integrity.

Generally, among other responsibilities of a king, which

we will talk about further, he has to work and find ways to protect the well-being of his people and increase territory and wealth. This requires special skills and anointing to campaign, motivate, and rally the people for dangerous activities such as defensive and offensive wars to protect the Kingdom or conquer other territories to expand it.

Titles Without Merit: Self-proclaimed Kings and Emperors Without the Merit

One of the worst things you can do to yourself is placing a title on yourself without merit – it will stress, destroy, and possibly kill you.

With other exceptions, Kingship is inherited by birthright, and I must add that it's also confirmed by merit, because not everybody from the bloodline or has historical ties to a monarchy can become a king or queen. Notably, a king or queen without moral characteristics is a voided one, disrespected and dishonored.

Our world is full of self-proclaimed kings, queens, princes, and princesses. We like the idea of being referred to as kings and queens but lack the exhibition of the essences.
Napoléon Bonaparte, the First Consul (Premier Consul) in France proclaimed himself as "Emperor Napoléon I" in 1804. The French First Consul thought that he would be accepted by European monarchs as one of them by changing his title and being referenced to as one. Obviously, he was not – they rejected him despite his military exploits and power consolidation.

Ironically, Napoleon's nephew, Louis-Napoléon Bonaparte, was elected in 1848 as President of France. Then, in 1852, he declared himself "Emperor Napoleon III" and was deposed in 1870.

Orélie-Antoine de Tounens, a French adventurer declared the "Kingdom of Araucanía" in Chile with the support of the local Mapuche chiefs in 1860, named himself "Orélie-Antoine I." But he quickly learned a lesson – in 1862, the Chilean government arrested and deported him.

China had a very interesting monarchy, from the first monarch Qin Shi Huang to the last Xuantong Emperor who reigned from December 2nd, 1908 to February 12th, 1912, and abdicated due to the Xinhai Revolution. Puyi, also known as Yaozhi, was the last emperor of China, and the eleventh and final Qing dynasty ruler. He became the Xuantong Emperor at the age of two in 1908.

Surprisingly, in 1915, the president of China, Yuan Shi-kai proclaimed the restoration of the Chinese monarchy; not only that, he made himself an emperor. His plan was unsuccessful and he was forced to leave power.

A Divine Royal Bloodline

The Bible declares, *"Jesus Christ, the faithful witness, the firstborn from the dead, and the ruler over the kings of the earth. To Him who loved us and washed us from our sins in His own blood, and has made us kings and priests to His God and Father, to Him be glory and dominion forever and ever. Amen."* (Revelation 1:5-6, NKJV). And in I Peter 2:9, NIV we read, *"But you are a chosen people, a royal priesthood, a holy nation, God's special possession, that you may declare the praises of him who called you out of darkness into his wonderful light."*

According to the word of God, Christ paid the price and has given the whole of humanity an opportunity to become a royal, even if you are not of, or relating to kingly ancestry, or lineage. Under the New Covenant or Testament, everyone who accepts the LORD Jesus-Christ as his personal Savior and Lord is no longer a commoner anymore. Therefore, you are a King or Queen. So behave, act, talk, walk, and dress like one. You may be born as a commoner or non-royal, but you can live and die as a King or Queen through Christ Jesus.

There Is a King or Queen In You

As I mentioned earlier, unlike an earthly kingdom, or a piece of land inhabited by people and ruled by a king or a queen, in your life's kingdom, are your soul, spirit, body, and the world. And you have an honorable responsibility to lead or conduct your life to peace, joy, health, security, prosperity, and stability.

It's great to be called a King or Queen, but do you live like one? I'm not talking about your financial, material, and social status. Does your life reflect that of a real King morally? Anyone can put a title on himself, but if the behaviors are not reflecting the title, then it is void.

The King's Wisdom

Throughout history, there have been good and bad Kings and Queens. One of the criteria that makes a king a successful one, is his wisdom. King Solomon's wisdom earned him respect and honor, even after he passed away. The Bible says, "God gave Solomon wisdom and very great insight, and a breadth of understanding as measureless as the sand on the seashore. Solomon's wisdom was greater than the wisdom of all the people of the East, and greater than all the wisdom of Egypt. He was wiser than anyone else, including Ethan the Ezrahite — wiser than Heman, Kalkol and Darda, the sons of Mahol. And his fame spread to all the surrounding nations." (1 Kings 4:29-31, NIV).

Looking through the past, you can notice that all kings who failed either didn't have wisdom or had bad advisers. Remember, earlier we discussed King Solomon's wisdom, which prompted him to ask for more wisdom. And I remarked that wise people seek more wisdom, and fools think they already know everything and have enough wisdom.

> *"Looking through the past, you can notice that all kings who failed either didn't have wisdom or had bad advisers."*

Once more, as a king, your skills and competence will be tested on several levels, including your wisdom. The wisdom of the king is tested by wars, famine, pestilence, insurrection, or social and economic events. The way you handle these occurrences matters to the people you are leading. Just as a king's leadership is trusted by his people when he can demonstrate the ability to lead and protect their well-being, you have to evaluate your judgment as an individual to ensure you can trust your own judgment and decision-making. You have to lead your own life or yourself, family, business, or organization as a king and with a king's capacity. Ancient kings who only had charisma, or were gifted naturally just to fight and win wars, but lacked wisdom usually were able to conquer vast territories, but failed to sustain and rule them effectively. This reality prompted the fall of many kings and emperors. Do you trust your wisdom? Do you trust your judgment? You may ask, "How can I measure or rate my own wisdom or judgment?" You can start with an evaluation of the results you got out of your past decisions. And if you realize that the results are not encouraging, you must recalibrate your decision-making procedures. Ask yourself honest questions: Why did you miss it last time? And what evaded your understanding, and how did it escape it? You may have gotten it wrong a few times, but promise yourself that next time, you will do better.

> *"As a king, your skills and competence will be tested on several levels, including your wisdom."*

The King's Council: Bad and Good Advisers

From ancient days, kings surrounded themselves with wisemen or a council of advisers and administrators who served them. The reason being that they know they might not have all the answers to the challenges the kingdom will face, and with the help of the advisers, they can successfully navigate troubles and win with them. No matter how intelligent and wise you believe you are, there will be times when the true composition of a problem will evade your knowledge and understanding, and only the wise people around you can catch it. So if you surround yourself with incompetent people, you will play into the hands of dangers and regrettable decisions.

To be good at decision-making, you need not only to be

wise, but also surround yourself with wise people. Each time a king faces challenges, he calls on his wisemen for advice and answers. But if the king's entourage is composed of fools, he will eventually be making foolish decisions. As an individual, family, or organization, you need a King's wisdom and surround yourself with wise people who can honestly tll you the truth. Who do you call or go to when you are faced with troubles? Kings usually incorporate wiser people into their administrations. The Bible says, ***"Walk with the wise and become wise, for a companion of fools suffers harm."*** (Proverbs 13:20, NIV).

When you have parents, relatives, friends, and co-workers who will never tell you the truth – it's dangerous. Do not run away from people who tell you the truth, even if you do not like the way they speak it, just work with them on the way they deliver the truth to you; and even if that doesn't change, keep them in your court, because sooner or later, you will thank them for their brutal truths.

Be careful of people, a spouse, parent, brother or sister, relative, friend, co-worker, or teammate who never tells you the truth. Have you ever shared a situation with someone for advice and you even realized at the end that they were not bold enough to tell you the truth? Sometimes you just need a bit of truth to enforce good morals and ethics to yourself, or say a "no" or "yes" to something, but the person you thought could have given you that honest strike actually did not, and supported your bad understanding and decision? Never make a decision without understanding the matter, unless it's God instructing, and leading you to do so. Seek understanding before making decisions.

And if you are a parent, sister, brother, relative, friend, or teammate, try your best to be honest with people you are connected to. God placed you in their lives for some reasons, and one of them, is to serve as a referee. You are like an official who is watching the games of their lives closely to ensure that the rules are adhered to for their own protection, happiness, health, prosperity, and longevity. Sometimes, this role may be difficult to play; especially when the fellow is stubborn, but that's part of being related or connected to someone by blood, friendship or naturalization.

> *"Be careful of people — who never tells you the truth."*

The King's Throne: A Higher Position and Permission

There are several things we can discuss here, but let's just look at the most relevant to our subject.

The throne of the king is always at a higher position, and sitting on a platform. And the Bible qualifies the throne of Solomon as a unique throne on all the earth. We read, *"Then the king made a great throne covered with ivory and overlaid with fine gold. The throne had six steps, and it's back had a rounded top. On both sides of the seat were armrests, with a lion standing beside each of them. Twelve lions stood on the six steps, one at either end of each step. Nothing like it had ever been made for any other kingdom."* (1 Kings 10:18-20, NIV)

One of the facts about sitting at a higher position is being able to see what others are not seeing. The ability to see beyond what others are seeing is very important to make the right decisions. Most of the time, one of the reasons we make the wrong decisions is because we cannot see what is hiding behind that can come after our decisions. However, if you can see the benefits of your decision one way or the other, you will surely decide for the good results and not the bad ones. If you know when you say "yes" to something, the results will be devastating, you can easily say "no." But if you cannot see or imagine what is to come or the consequences, the situation, things, or people can easily influence you to make the wrong decisions. Therefore, each time you are facing a pending decision, ask yourself, "Is there anything about this matter that I can see that others are not seeing?" Or "Is there anything about this matter that others are seeing, but I cannot see?" When I say "See," that doesn't necessarily mean you have to see it with your physical sight, but your spiritual sight.

A throne indicates or signifies sovereign power. It's one of the most important assets of a King, or Ruler. Even though this may differ at certain time and location, the King may have everything, but if he doesn't have the throne, his power and sovereignty are incomplete. And until someone is enthroned, he's not a King.

Pharaoh gave Joseph much power over Egypt to the extent that no one had authority more than him, except Pharaoh himself. And how did he do that? He never gave him the throne. We read, "Then Pharaoh said to Joseph, "Since God has made all this known to you, there is no one so discerning and wise as you. You shall be in charge of my palace, and all my people are to submit to your orders. Only with respect to the throne will I be greater than you." (Genesis 41:39-40, NIV).

Pharaoh knew what he did. He needed the help and service of Joseph because he recognized his ability to do what he could not do. So, he provided him with all the power he needed to help him and his nation, but not the supreme power to remove him as a Pharaoh. Be careful when you are delegating power and authority to people to help you. Only give them the amount of power they need to help you, and not all the power to hurt you when they want to. Before you decide to entrust someone or a group of people with power or permission that belongs to you, think about the level or amount of permission that you are giving them over your life, family, business, or organization.

The King's Crown: Honor or Fear

The crown of a king or queen does not only represent royalty, nobility, power, authority, dominance, glory, righteousness, justice, wealth, and leadership; nor is it only a fancy ornament he wears for beauty or to look good, but it also calls for honor. While all the aforementioned attributes can be acquired by force and manipulation by humans, unlike trust, honor is given. But trust and respect are earned from people. People do not respect you by force. They may fear you by force because you may be a threat to them, but they can only respect you out of admiration or estimation. Just because someone fears you does not mean he respects you, even though he can honor you as a moral obligation. Honor and fear are two different states, conditions, or positions; and each one of them has an influence that contributes to a result or outcome.

Nonetheless, honor can also be a production of high respect. I mean you can earn honor out of respect, but you cannot earn respect out of honor if you do not live an honarable or moral life. This truth calls for you to seek respect with living by morals and ethics instead of causing fear to people to respect you; because honor without respect is useless. When people or someone has great esteem for you, it subconsciously turns into honor – so they honor you.

One of the delusions you have to do your best to avoid in life is believing that some people or someone respects and honors you while they actually just fear you. And one of the indicators of people who respect you is that they talk about you in your absence just as in your presence. Whether you are there or not, the respect they have for you never leaves them. And even when they disagree with you on some ways, solutions, and results concerning some matters, they will handle that disagreement with respect and honorably. But people who just honor you but do not respect you, or respect you out of fear will say nice things about you in your presence, but ugly things at your absence.

In my understanding, honor is based on the moral values and Godly character of the giver. Meaning, I honor someone because of my moral values regardless of who they are or have done. However, I respect people for their moral values and character. I understand honor like love – it's unconditional. But respect, just as trust is earned. If you would understand this, that's why God did not say, **"Respect your father and your mother."** But He said, **"Honor your father and your mother."** Why? Because He knows many parents cannot earn the respect of their children due to some mistakes they may have made in their lives, and these children may have less concern for them. Therefore, God said, **"Honor your father and your mother, so that you may live long in the land the Lord your God is giving you."** (Exodus 20:12). So, as a child, regardless of what your parents have done, God is commanding you to honor, love and cherish them – this commandment is not based on how well your parents behaved, but because they are your parents and you came in this world through them. In other words, there are no qualifiers for your parents to receive your honor – as long as they are your parents, God says, "Honor" them.

Respect is measured by your moral conduct, and not by the fear you can instill in people, and how much power, riches, or wealth you have. People may pretend they respect you because they do not want to lose their daily bread or what they can get from you. In effect, it's critical to make sure that you earn the true respect, trust, and honor of people, instead of them just fearing you for one reason or the other.

Throughout history, Kings who instilled fear into their people instead of earning their respect, trust, and honor, sooner or later were either betrayed or assassinated by their own people. Not that I condone this, but sometimes it's a sign of disrespect or hatred.

I hear people say, "They fear me." Well, it sounds great, but people only fear you until they know you do not have power and authority over them anymore. But when they truly respect you, even when they know you do not have power and authority over them anymore, they will still respect, trust, and honor you. Respect makes people love you and willingly submit to you, while fear forces people to only submit to you; and submission without love is delusional, and a quick road to false and temporary control and stability. When people truly respect you, they honor and love you, and will do everything they can to keep your relationship with them lasting and stable. If you want to be the King, Queen, Boss, Manager, CEO, Pastor, Supervisor, and Employer of someone for life, earn their respect with your moral conduct – They will not only honor you, but respect you wherever and whenever they find themselves, even when they are no more in direct contact, or close relationship, or leadership with you, they will respect and honor you. Yes, there might be exceptions – some people can still have false accusations against you due to their own moral failure. But the majority who are honest will respect you.

A real King must watch his moral conduct, decisions, and actions. Being a king or royal is not just a title; it's a conduct. Is your moral behavior showing the characteristics of a real King or Queen? Are the people metaphorically bowing down to you in respect or fear?

A true King handles things honorably. Whether it is a misunderstanding, conflict, or even war, authentic Kings or Rulers handled their opponents with dignity and honor. There were instances when ancient kings either put their defeated opponents in charge of a conquered territory or buried their killed foes with dignity after battles. Of course, they carefully made those decisions to ensure their own safety. But the beauty of those actions was in the respect they showed towards their rivals or opponents. Whatever is going on between you and an opponent, be careful to show respect towards them. There may be moments when you will be consumed by their bad behaviors and morals, and get angry, emotional, and ready to cross the lines or boundaries of your values and moral laws, but always re-calibrate back to your best and true personality and characteristics. Do not let bad people turn you into a bad person by their actions.

One of the responsibilities of a King is to lead his people to victory. And a crown is also set on the head of champions or winners. As a King of your kingdom or domain, meaning a ruler of your life, you are responsible for leading your life to victory, and becoming your own champion. A champion is not the only one playing a sports game. Every little battle you can win in every area of your life is a victory and qualifies you as a champion or at least a winner, and worth celebrating. Your decision, supported by action to quit smoking, using drugs, and alcohol, living in sexual immorality, eating disorders, greed, selfishness, and theft, will make you a champion worthy of an award and crown.

> *"Do not let bad people turn you into a bad person by their actions."*

Crowns are made and decorated with precious metals, stones, or jewels. For a precious metal or stone to be able to fit a crown, it has to be cut into shapes, flat, facets, or smoothed and polished in order to be suitable as an ornament. You are so valuable, but your worth is not completed until you are able to fit in your purpose and destiny in this world. And until you behave like a true King, Queen, Prince, or Princess, your title is invalid, and your royal status is incomplete.

The King's Scepter: Life or Death

In our modern world, what we know about the King's scepter, is a staff or wand held in the hand by a ruling monarch as an object of royal sign of rank, or title. But it's more than that. Throughout the Bible, it's clear that the scepter, just as other royal signs, has a spiritual meaning.

Thousands of years ago, when Jacob, renamed by God, Israel, was preparing to transition from this world, he uttered some powerful prayers or blessings over all his children. What was alarming is that, he wasn't just praying and blessing his children, but also prophesying. When he got to Judah, his fourth son, he spoke these words, ***"The scepter will not depart from Judah, nor the ruler's staff from between his feet, until he to whom it belongs shall come and the obedience of the nations shall be his."*** (Genesis 49:10, NIV).

Jacob was prophesying in two dimensions, or his prophecy was not just about Judah physically, but also spiritually. First, Judah's descendants became the rulers of the nation or people of Israel, from King David to Zedekiah. Judah's descendants became the royal family tree and line of succession. This confirms that the scepter did not depart from the tribe or descendants of Judah. Second, Jacob prophesied, maybe unknowingly, about the coming of the King of all kings, the Messiah, the LORD Jesus-Christ who will come to this world via the descendants or tribe of Judah to save humanity and rule the world. So he added, ***"Until he to whom it belongs shall come and the obedience of the nations shall be his."*** (Genesis 49:10, NIV).

We can confirm the fulfillment of this prophecy in II Samuel 7:8–16; II Peter 1:11. And in Revelation 5:5, the Bible reveals the completion of the spiritual side of Jacob's prophecy, "Then one of the elders said to me, "Do not weep! See, the Lion of the tribe of Judah, the Root of David, has triumphed. He is able to open the scroll and its seven seals." This was a win or victory for humanity. But we will fast forward to the understanding we need here.

We have to keep in mind also that the scepter could actually be a staff in ancient days, and with the evolution of art, design, and metal works, has evolved into beautiful pieces of artwork that Kings and Queens hold in our world today. A scepter represents a ruler's absolute power and authority over a people, territory, or kingdom.

The Rod of Moses

When God called Moses to go to Egypt for the deliverance of the children of Israel, He sent him with a staff or rod, and with that rod, He demonstrated His power to destroy the Egyptians and to deliver and save the children of Israel. With the same rod, Moses turned water into blood, produced frogs, lice, flies, livestock pestilence, boils, hail, locusts, and darkness, and caused the death of all Egyptians' firstborns. (Exodus chapters 7-11). But then Moses used that same staff, under the instruction of God, to help do many good things for the children of Israel, including parting the Red Sea and providing water. (Exodus 14:1-31; 17: 1-5). We can note that the rod of Moses was able to give life or death. The rod of Moses was able to destroy, but also provided, protected, and restored.

However, one thing that also got my attention is the fact that the same rod indirectly prevented Moses from reaching the Promised Land. I know we blame the children of Israel for it. But it's the rod's significance, the authority and power that it carries that also influenced Moses to do more than what God told him to do. God told Moses to show his rod to the rock, and water would come out of it, but like he was instructed before, He hit the rock with his rod. These were two different instructions: Show the rod to the rock, and not hit the rock with the rod. (Numbers 20:10-12). The Bible says because of that God told Moses, *"Although you shall see from a distance the land that I am giving the Israelites, you shall not enter it."* (Deuteronomy 32:52).

That was a difficult moment. The rod (the power and authority) that delivered, provided, protected, and restored the children of Israel, including Moses himself, is the same rod that caused Moses not to reach the Promised Land that he had so much expected to reach, and was so close to. Be careful, do not let your scepter as a King or Queen destroy you. Your scepter as a King, figuratively is your position, power, and authority, talent, spiritual and natural gifts, success, beauty, and riches that can destroy you. Use it wisely. Do not let anything that God has blessed you with destroy you – because it can destroy you when you misuse use it, or immorally use it.

> *"The rod (the power and authority) that delivered, provided, protected, and restored the children of Israel, including Moses himself, is the same rod that caused Moses not to reach the Promised Land."*

A Scepter Saved Esther and the Jews

The Book of Esther is an extraordinary compilation of a true story of an orphan who loved God and his people and rose to become a Queen, her challenges, courage, wisdom, and ultimate sacrifice, nearly cost her execution. (Esther Chapters 1-7)

Haman was promoted by King Xerxes of Persia, and given a seat of honor higher than that of all the other nobles. His promotion became a trap that would later destroy his life and family. He became so powerful that all the royal officials at the king's gate were afraid of him, knelt down, and paid honor to him, for the king had commanded this concerning him. But Mordecai, a Jew, would not kneel down or pay him honor. This incident didn't translate well to Hamanan, so he plotted to kill all the Jews in the kingdom by misleading the king that Jews were disobeying all his laws.

> ## *"Be careful, do not let your scepter as a King or Queen destroy you."*

Earlier, Esther who became the Queen, was raised and assisted by her uncle Mordecai who became the primary target of Haman out of pride and arrogance. Remember, we talked earlier about fear, respect, trust, or honor, and concluded that it's better for people to respect than fear you. Haman didn't earn the respect and honor of Mordecai, so he wanted to terrorize him by instigating the killing of the whole Jewish population, including him. But what he didn't know is that Esther the Queen, who was the niece of the man he was trying to terrify and kill could do something about the t situation. In short, Mordecai sent messages to his niece Queen Esther about the plot of Haman, and the Queen did the unimaginable to save her people.

What do you do when your people, including your own uncle, are about to be exterminated on an appointed date permitted by the King while you're the Queen? "Talk to the king and defend them", you would say. But it was more complicated than that. Esther the Queen could not just go and talk to the King without permission or except it was her turn to go in to the King. According to the regulations, whoever steps into the king's court without his prior invitation or permission would have been killed. But Esther tried to do what many would not do. She went to talk to the King after requesting Mordecai to tell all the Jews, including her female servants to fast and pray. When the fasting and prayer were done, then came the defining moment–Esther was supposed to go and face life or death to wisely talk to the King and invite him to dinner in an attempt to plead with him about his people and uncle.

The Bible says, "On the third day Esther put on her royal robes and stood in the inner court of the palace, in front of the king's hall. The king was sitting on his royal throne in the hall, facing the entrance. When he saw Queen Esther standing in the court, he was pleased with her and held out to her the gold scepter that was in his hand. So Esther approached and touched the tip of the scepter. Then the king asked, "What is it, Queen Esther? What is your request? Even up to half the kingdom, it will be given to you." (Esther 5:1-3).

Let's read it again, the King "Held out to her the golden scepter that was in his hand." If that scepter was not held out to Queen Esther, she would have been killed. But God was with her and prospered on her journey to save her uncle and people from death. Esther was able to talk to the King and invited him and their enemy to a banquet, where she revealed to the king the plans of Haman to kill the Jews. The King was angry, and eventually gave another order to help the Jews defend themselves against their attackers because he couldn't reverse his first edict to kill the Jews as a King because that was the law, a king could not change his decree. When the day of the first decree of the king to annihilate the Jews came, the Jews fought their enemies and won to survive. (Esther 8: 1-17).

Wisely use your scepter as a King or Queen. Use your

blessings, spiritual and natural gifts, position, platform, title, fame, money, and beauty to do good. Use it for the service of God, and the well-being of humanity. Use it for the greater good. Don't destroy people with it, build with it instead. Use it to establish peace, security, prosperity, healing, and stability. And moreover, do not let it destroy you, your purpose, and destiny.

> *"Wisely use your scepter as a King or Queen. Use your blessings, spiritual and natural gifts, position, platform, title, fame, money, and beauty to do good."*

The King's Dress: Glorious or Shameful

A royal robe, mantle, or garment, is worn by emperors, kings, or queens as an emblem of authority. However, the robe of a king also symbolizes his glory.

In Isaiah chapter six, verse one (Isaiah 6:1) we read, "In the year that King Uzziah died, I saw the lord high and exalted, seated on a throne, and the train of his robe filled the temple." The prophet described what the robe of the LORD looks like, and then what he saw and happened next. He said, "Above him were seraphim, each with six wings: With two wings they covered their faces, with two they covered their feet, and with two they were flying. And they were calling to one another:
"Holy, holy, holy is the Lord Almighty;
the whole earth is full of his glory."
At the sound of their voices, the doorposts and thresholds shook and the temple was filled with smoke." (Isaiah 1:2-4).

What preceded the revelation of the glory of the LORD was the train of the robe that filled the temple – the robe symbolizes glory.

History reveals that back in the ancient days, kings had their own royal robes, and these mantles commanded more respect, honor, and power if other defeated kings' robes pieces were sewn to the train of a king. Notably, whenever a king defeated another king, he would cut a piece of the defeated king's robe train and attach it to his own garment's train. This is one of the ways kings demonstrated their power, and the number of other kings and territories they were able to conquer. And the longer a king's robes train, the more glorious, powerful, and fearful he was.

King Nebuchadnezzar

Always remember that God is the greatest, respect and honor Him, and never take for granted any possession and position he has given you and elevated you to; or you will quickly learn you are not the one in control, but Him.

King Nebuchadnezzar was blessed and established more than any king at his time with a vast territory, wealth, and power. But unfortunately, he began to pridefully boast and perceive himself as the almighty. Then God warned him through a dream, but he wouldn't still refrain from his vain and wrong understanding of how he became so powerful, wealthy, and honored. (Daniel 4:1-27). In effect, God decided to give him a lesson – The dream came through, and he lost his mind, had to live in the bush, and ate grass like an animal for seven years. We read directly from the Bible:
"All this happened to King Nebuchadnezzar. Twelve months later, as the king was walking on the roof of the

royal palace of Babylon, he said, "Is not this the great Babylon I have built as the royal residence, by my mighty power and for the glory of my majesty?"

Even as the words were on his lips, a voice came from heaven, "This is what is decreed for you, King Nebuchadnezzar: Your royal authority has been taken from you. You will be driven away from people and will live with the wild animals; you will eat grass like the ox. Seven times will pass by for you until you acknowledge that the Most High is sovereign over all kingdoms on earth and gives them to anyone he wishes."

Immediately what had been said about Nebuchadnezzar was fulfilled. He was driven away from people and ate grass like the ox. His body was drenched with the dew of heaven until his hair grew like the feathers of an eagle and his nails like the claws of a bird.

At the end of that time, I, Nebuchadnezzar, raised my eyes toward heaven, and my sanity was restored. Then I praised the Most High; I honored and glorified him who lives forever.

His dominion is an eternal dominion;
his kingdom endures from generation to generation.

    All the peoples of the earth
    are regarded as nothing.
He does as he pleases
    with the powers of heaven
    and the peoples of the earth.
No one can hold back his hand
    or say to him: "What have you done?"

At the same time that my sanity was restored, my honor and splendor were returned to me for the glory of my kingdom. My advisers and nobles sought me out, and I was restored to my throne and became even greater than before. Now I, Nebuchadnezzar, praise and exalt and glorify the King of heaven, because everything he does is right and all his ways are just. And those who walk in pride he is able to humble." (Daniel 4:28-37).

Don't eat grass like Nebuchadnezzar before you learn how to be humble. Remember the Bible says, *"Pride goes before destruction, a haughty spirit before a fall."* (Proverbs 16: 18, NIV).

"Always remember that God is the greatest, respect and honor Him."

King Herod

Herod obviously was a Roman client king of Judea, which was also referred to as the Herodian kingdom. He obtained the position to rule over Judea. And in time he thought extremely highly of himself, and was careless about "The Way " or Christianity and Christians. He imprisoned Apostle Peter but by the supernatural intervention of God, he could not kill him. Unfortunately, the people believed in his delusion. In effect, it only took a few minutes for God to show who was in charge. We read directly from the Bible:
"At break of day, there was consternation among the soldiers about what had become of Peter. Herod made a search for him, but didn't find him, so then he examined the guards, and commanded that they be executed. Herod then went down from Judea to Caesarea, and spent time there." (Acts 12:18-19).

"Now Herod was very angry with the people of Tyre and Sidon. Their country depended on the king's country for food, so they came to him with a united front to make peace —they'd been able to win over Blastus, the king's personal aide. On an appointed day, Herod dressed himself in royal clothing, sat on the throne, and made a speech to them. The people shouted, 'The voice of God, and not of a man!' Immediately, an angel of the Lord struck him, because he didn't give God the glory. He was eaten by worms and died." (Acts 12:20-23).

The Emperor's New Robe: Hypocrisy, Stubbornness, and Gullibility

If the clothes or dress of a king or emperor signifies glory and can be glorious, then it can also be ugly and shameful. Apart from the Bible, Hans Christian Andersen, the Danish author, has demonstrated that very well with his literary fairy tale translated into over a hundred languages, "The Emperor's New Clothes." Although there are some controversies surrounding the lifestyle or behavior of the author, which some people believe and some do not, I'm not talking about the lifestyle or behavior of the latter here. I'm discussing the lesson we could learn from one of the fairy tales he wrote. In fact, Klara Bom and Anya Aarenstrup from the H.C. Andersen Center of the University of Southern Denmark disagreed with people's conclusions about his lifestyle. They stated, and I quote, "He did not. Indeed, that would have been entirely contrary to his moral and religious ideas–" Whether people's conclusions about his lifestyle are valid or not, God only knows.

The author wrote, and I may paraphrase when needed: "Once upon a time, there was an Emperor who extremely adored new clothes to the extent that he spent all his money on clothes to dress very well. He is careless about evaluating his soldiers, going to the theater, or riding his carriage unless it's to display his new clothes.

> *"If the clothes or dress of a king or emperor signifies glory and can be glorious, then it can also be ugly and shameful."*

He had a coat arranged to change hourly throughout the day. While many kings and rulers are mostly in council, the Emperor spends most of his time in his dressing room.

The city where the Emperor lived was always cheerful, and visited by many people from nearby and far; and among these visitors were two fraudsters. They announced that they were weavers and could weave an impressively beautiful, elaborate, extravagant, or superb full-color fabric. And the best about the fabric is that clothes made of the fabric have the power to become invisible to anyone who is incompetent in his office, or exceptionally stupid.

The Emperor gladly responded, "Those are exactly the clothes I want. When I wear them, I can find out every incompetent officer or person working for me in my empire. I could differentiate between the fool and the wise. Surely, I have to order this woven material immediately." Then, he paid the tricksters a huge amount of money to start their job.

These men set up the looms and pretended they were weaving (the magical fabric), but they were doing nothing because it was all fake and deceptive. Instead, they packed all the high-quality silk and sparkling materials they requested into their bags and ran the unloaded looms until late at night.

At some point, the Emperor wanted to know the status of the fabric the fake weavers were working on. But when he recalled that it was said those who were incompetent and extremely foolish would not be able to see it, and perhaps out of fear of being known as unqualified and foolish himself, he sent someone else to go check on the extraordinary clothes that the whole city knew about and was impatiently waiting for to reveal the people who were unfit and foolish around them. He finally decided to send one of his officers, whom he trusted, and said, "I will send my trustworthy minister to check on the weavers. He will be the right person, he handles his responsibilities pretty well, so he can tell what the material looks like."

Then came the critical moment: When the Emperor's minister got to the scene where the trickers were operating the vacant looms, he couldn't believe his eyes. He said, "Heaven help me. I can't see anything at all." But he did not reveal that.

The two deceptive weavers pleaded with the minister of the Emperor to come near, check, and approve the nice colorful, and magical material's pattern (which was invisible). They pointed to the empty looms and the minister tried his eyes any way he could to see the material, but he couldn't because there was nothing on the looms anyway. Then he thought, "Heaven have mercy! Can it be that I'm a fool? I'd have never thought about it, and nobody should know. Am I unfit to be the minister? It would never be appropriate that I can't see the cloth."

"Don't hesitate to tell us what you think about the cloth." The fraudulent weavers said to the minister."

"Oh, it's magnificent. It's charming." The old minister exclaimed while peering through his eyeglasses. "What a pattern and colors!" "I will make sure to inform the Emperor how impressed I am with it."

The fraudsters replied, "We are pleased to hear that." They continued to mention all the colors and detailed patterns. And the minister carefully listened to them so he could report to the Emperor. He returned and reported.

To this, the fraudsters immediately requested more money, silk, and gold textile, so they could continue their job. But they kept all the supplies in their bags. They were not using any of it to weave any cloth. The looms were empty, but they pretended to work as hard as they could.

The Emperor sent yet another official he trusted to go and check on the progress made in the weaving of his cloth and the time it could be completed. Unfortunately, the same thing happened, he could not see any clothes after looking as much as his eyes could see.

But they asked the official, "Isn't it a beautiful material?" While they showed and described their imaginary pattern.
The Official thought, "I believe I'm not stupid. So it must be that I'm not competent enough to hold my office or position. That's bizarre. Nobody should know this." So he applauded the fabric he could not see; and went on to mention how impressed he was with the colors and the elegant pattern. He also went and reported to the Emperor, "It was fascinating."

The whole city was talking about the wonderful cloth in making, and the Emperor desired to go and see it for himself. Accompanied by his old trusted officials, including the ones he sent earlier to check on the progress of the cloth, he departed to go and see the fraudulent weavers. He arrived and saw them pretending to weave with all their strength, but there was no textile on the looms.

The Emperor thought, "Am I a fool? Am I incompetent? What happened to me among all people!" And without also not seeing the cloth, he said, "Oh! It's very beautiful. It has my ultimate approval." As he nodded approval at the empty loom. He never said the truth that he couldn't see anything either in fear of being considered a fool and incompetent.

His entire staff and group of advisers gazed at the empty loom and looked at each other, and said, "Oh! It's very beautiful," and advised him to wear clothes made of the fabric none of them was able to see; and proposed to him to wear it for the upcoming parade he would soon conduct.

"Superb! Outstanding! Very good!" They were all exclaiming and seemed to be content. And the Emperor gave each of the crooks a cross to wear in his buttonhole, and the title of "Sir Weaver."

The night before the parade, the fraudsters burned more than six candles just to fool the Emperor and his people that they were very busy trying to finish his clothes. Then they pretended to take the cloth off the loom. They made cuts in the air with big scissors. And finally, they said, "The emperor's new clothes are ready now."

Then the Emperor himself came with his noblest noblemen, and the fraudsters raised their arms like they were holding something, and said, "These are the trousers, here's the coat, and this is the mantle," naming each outfit; and added, "All of them are as light as a spider web. One would almost think he had nothing on, but that's what makes them so wonderful."

All the noblemen accompanying the Emperor exclaimed with one accord, "Exactly," while they could not see anything, because there were no clothes.

Then the fraudsters said, "Your Majesty, would you please take your clothes off? We will help you put on your new clothes right here in front of the long mirror." The Emperor undressed, and they pretended to put his new clothes on him, one outfit after another. They took him around the waist and seemed to be fastening something like his train; and the Emperor turned around and around in front of the mirror.

The fraudsters asked the Emperor, "How well your Majesty's new clothes look? Aren't they elegant?" Every one of his officials said, "That pattern is so perfect! Those colors are so fitting! It is a wonderful outfit."

"Your Majesty, the canopy is waiting outside." Said the minister of the public parade.

"Well, I'm supposed to be ready," the Emperor said and turned again for one last look in the mirror. "It is a remarkable fit, isn't it?" He seemed to be fascinated by his (invisible) costume.

His noble assistants who were supposed to bear the train of his robe bowed down and pretended like they were picking it up from the floor; then held it up high and never acknowledged that there were no clothes.

The Emperor started the parade with his magnificent canopy while everyone watching by the roadside and from home out through the windows exclaimed, "Oh, how exceptional are the Emperor's new clothes! Are they not so suitable and perfect? And look at his long garment train!" Not even one person was honest enough to confess that they could not see anything or the clothes out of fear of being considered incompetent and a fool. The Emperor had never worn such a delightful cloth before.

Then, a little child said, "But he has nothing on."

The father said, "Have you ever heard such an innocent prattle?" Then every person started whispering to one another what the child just said., "He has nothing on. A child says he has nothing on."

Finally, the whole town started crying out, "He has nothing on!"

The Emperor had the impression they were right and trembled. But he believed, "The parade must continue." So he continued marching proudly as never before while his noble assistants held the train of his robe that never existed. Hans Christian Andersen's fairytale teaches us about some of the problems our world has today: How delusional, dishonest, unreal, prideful, and the degree of belief in vanity in our societies. Remember, I mentioned earlier that one of the worst things you could do to yourself is to surround yourself with people who will not dare or be honest enough to tell you the truth. It only took two fraudsters to fool a whole empire or town, and some of the smartest officials of an Emperor. But it only took a child to innocently confess the truth, "But he (the Emperor) has nothing on." or "He's naked."

> *"One of the worst things you could do to yourself is to surround yourself with people who will not dare or be honest enough to tell you the truth."*

Therefore, as a King or Queen, your clothes may bring you honor, glory, or disgrace. Your clothes are supposed to cover your nakedness – physically and figuratively, but when you wear the wrong clothes, they will instead reveal your nakedness and shame you publicly. Figuratively, this includes things you allow yourself into and things you allow on yourself. You may ask what I mean by that? I meant wrong self-gratification or pleasure, pride, selfishness, and greed. These things can quickly entangle and shame you.

Be Responsible For Your Responsibility

According to the Oxford Languages Dictionary, responsibility is "having an obligation to do something, or having control over or care for someone, as part of one's job or role." Responsibility is "the state or fact of having a duty to deal with something or having control over someone." You have an obligation to tell people or someone you are serving or leading the truth or the true state of things because it's the highest honor and the best gift you can give them, and the work ethic you must offer them. Even if they hate you at the moment for it, they will understand and appreciate it sooner or later and might not even confess to you.

This is even true for you as a parent. You may support, do, or allow your children to do some things thinking you just love them and supporting or doing it for their best interest. But let me tell you, if it is wrong or immoral, one day they will blame and hate you for it — I have witnessed many of these between parents and children who grow up to be morally sound than their parents, or realize that their parents did not raise them well.

One time, a young adult was talking to me about some issues she was having with her parents. After narrating all the issues, she ended with, "But they are the ones who raised me like this, and now they are blaming me for being the way I am." I can give you many other examples of children who grow up and realize that their parents did not raise them well by allowing and supporting some of their bad behaviors and decisions, even at the house or in the family. Teach and tell your children about moral values and truths about God and life. If you don't teach them the truth, one day, they will discover it and find out that, what you thought was love you were showing them as a parent was actually not true and has ruined their lives instead. Therefore, if you are a parent, note this: One day, your children and God will hold you accountable for any bad and immoral decisions you have supported in their lives, as children.

God sends people or individuals in this world as children through parents, but it does not mean you own them or they are yours. No, they are individuals whom God sent into this world through you to protect, raise, guide, and teach them until they are grown up, and know about right, wrong, or moral values from His word and not what you think. And if you do not do it according to His will, precepts, values, or commandments, He will hold you accountable for it one day.

Fashion, Style and Fantasy

According to The Oxford Languages Dictionary, fantasy is "the faculty or activity of imagining things, especially things that are impossible or improbable." The Emperor, being a person who liked clothes and was so fascinated by them, was easily and relatively fooled by it. Watch out for things you like, because they will be exactly what the devil and people will use to get, hurt, and disgrace you. When you like something, after some time, you will knowingly or unknowingly develop a fashion or a way of relating to it, and this could be good or bad. It's not a bad thing to be interested, explore, and enjoy morally sound or good and healthy things, but when they start controlling your behavior and negatively influencing your judgment and reasoning, it becomes dangerous to you and everybody related to you. Keep in mind that an interest can quickly lead you to delusion and fantasy if you let it be. You have to be alert to quickly detect and correct your interests that are turning into fantasy and delusion before they overtake, destroy, and shame you. Your fascination or obsession with something or someone can rapidly cause you to make ridiculous decisions.

> *"Your fascination or obsession with something or someone can rapidly cause you to make ridiculous decisions."*

While fashion and style tend to be the same, most experts in the beauty, personal care, and appearance industry agree that the slight difference between fashion and style is that fashion is general or collective, while style is personal or individual. Consequently, I would think about style as a person's signature way of dressing and way of life.

But the dictionary defines fashion as "a popular trend, especially in styles of dress and ornament or manners of behavior." Either way, be careful and do not let foolishness overtake you individually or collectively. Whether it is a common thing, or something just about you personally, and it is clear to you that it's not right, Godly, or morally sound. Be honest and tell yourself and people the truth so you can save yourself or others from bad decisions and fantasies.

Clothes of Respect and Honor

Kings and Queens dress for respect and honor. While everybody wants to be called king or queen, the clothes you may see people wear in public are so disrespectful and dishonorable to themselves, and unfortunately, they take pride in them. Adults and young men with sagging pants, tight clothing exposing body parts. And women with tight, revealing, and incomplete clothes that expose the most private parts and shapes of their bodies. No matter how a woman dresses, it should not be permission for harassment or rape by any man. However, keep this in mind, especially if you are a lady: The reason some things or materials are so expensive in this world is because they are rarely seen, touched, and used. It takes time and work to get to them before seeing, touching, possessing, and using them. When men are used to seeing the private parts of your body in public, with time, you become invaluable regardless of your social status, especially to the serious, purpose, destiny, and value-minded men. You may argue men are attracted to females' outer parts when they see it. Yes, they are, and it's a natural reaction. But keep in mind there is a difference between lust, attraction, value, honor, and ultimately, value and honor can earn you a lasting attraction that leads to a lasting commitment rather than a short-term lust, which only earns you a temporary interest and positions you to become a utility for men to quench their lustful desires and throw you away afterward like a disposable item.

Kings and Queens do not dress to expose their private

parts and body shapes. If you expect to be a respectable and honorable person, dress like one. Most likely, you have heard the saying, "Dress like you want to be addressed." Clothing is not the only attribute of a respectable person, but the way you dress reveals your characteristics to some degree.

> *"Kings and Queens dress for respect and honor."*

Look Beyond the Dress and Perfume

Stupidity was welcomed in our world, entertained, and exercised by Adam and Eve in the Garden of Eden, and since then, the beginning of the fall of man in the Garden of Eden, he continues to manifest in various forms, places, and times. He sat on thrones with Kings and princes, led generals in wars, counseled leaders, and above all, mocked them all in the end.

Foolishness dresses and walks in suits and ties as well. Don't forget foolishness also knows the dress codes, so he dresses well. Don't be fooled by how people look or dress, and talk; mind what is in their heart and character as well.

> *"Foolishness dresses and walks in suits and ties as well. Don't forget foolishness also knows the dress codes, so he dresses well."*

A King Who Knows the King of Kings

Throughout the Bible and history, only kings who acknowledged the King of kings, God almighty, lasted. And It's obvious that even ancient kings who didn't have a clean relationship with God claimed and believed they were his representatives in this world. The understanding of these kings is partially believed to have started the "Divine Right of Kings," which was a Christian political doctrine in defense of monarchical absolutism in Europe. The belief is that kings obtain their authority from God and will only be accountable to God and not men. The theory was that God gave power to the king or political ruler compared with the Church's authority. But it was not long before the kings started trying to authoritatively mingle themselves with the spiritual matters of the Church. King James I of England was the prime or leading advocate of the theory. Eventually, it slowly declined after what is known as the "Glorious Revolution," or "The Revolution of 1688," and "The Bloodless Revolution," which happened from 1688 to 1689 in England. This revolt involved the removal of the Catholic King James II, who was replaced by his Protestant daughter Mary and her Dutch husband, known as William of Orange.

It's not enough to just know God, or believe He created you to be His representative in this world. As a king or Queen of your kingdom or life, you cannot have a good, fulfilled, stable, lasting, and indelible impact in this world without God, the King of kings. Your close relationship with God will mirror your life, career, vision, purpose and destiny with His own power, authority, and characteristics that will be turned into a remarkable blessing one way or the other.

A King Without the Spirit of God

Pharaoh, king of Egypt, didn't have the Spirit of God. So he couldn't figure out what his dream was, and handle the famine that was about to befall Egypt. But Joseph had the Spirit of God, so he was not only able to understand and interpret the king's dreams, but also provided wisdom for preparation or a survival plan. (Genesis 41:37-57). The Bible says after Pharaoh listened to Joseph, "The plan seemed good to Pharaoh and to all his officials. So Pharaoh asked them, "Can we find anyone like this man, one in whom is the spirit of God?" (Genesis 41:37-38, NIV).

> *"As a king or Queen of your kingdom or life, you cannot have a good, fulfilled, stable, lasting, and indelible impact in this world without God, the King of kings."*

Do you have the Spirit of God? Do you have the Holy Spirit? The Spirit of God is a free gift of God to humanity. Note this, He's indispensable to you to successfully live in this world. Remember, I mentioned earlier that success is not only limited to the amount of money and materials you have, but also includes real peace, and happiness. When you have the Spirit of God, He will give you the same things. We read, "The Spirit of the LORD will rest on him — the Spirit of wisdom and of understanding, the Spirit of counsel and of might, the Spirit of the knowledge and fear of the LORD — and he will delight in the fear of the LORD. He will not judge by what he sees with his eyes, or decide by what he hears with his ears." (Isaiah 11:2-3, NIV).

These paragraphs will not be enough for me to elaborate

on how much you need the Spirit of God, or the Holy Spirit to lead you in your decision-making as a King or Queen. We will leave this subject for another occasion. All I can say to you here is to seek and get to know Him personally, He will take you far beyond your imagination and help you with crucial decisions.

The Bible says, *"His divine power has given us everything we need for life and godliness through our knowledge of him who called us by his own glory and goodness."* (2 Peter 1:3, NIV).

Chapter 6
Keeping the Balance

"The Lord detests dishonest scales, but accurate weights find favor with him."
Proverb 11:1

"**YOU ARE DOING TOO MUCH** – did you know that the man who introduced hygiene to the world was killed by a truck of feces?" My dad would jokingly tell my mom, a cleanliness extremist (Don't tell her I said that). I'm not sure where my dad got that joke from, but neither Ignaz Semmelweis, Louis Pasteur, or even Joseph Lister, whose contributions to the medical field have helped promote hygienic methods, practices, and infection control over the centuries, were killed by a truck of feces. Don't say or write this in your school exam – you will fail.

My mom is a cleanliness extremist, but my dad was a balanced, clean person. He keeps everything clean, but not extremely like my mom. My mom goes to places with her own drinking cup, spoon, and fork in her purse or bag because she hates using the ones somebody has already used, even if they are washed and sanitized. Our household cooking, eating, and drinking utensils have to go through boiled water sanitizing periodically just in case they fall on the ground, even in a clean place. When you wake up in our home, you have to do three things before you can eat: Brush or clean your teeth, take a shower, and do your core (whatever was assigned to you at the house). This consists of washing dishes, cleaning the rooms, and sweeping the court of the house. That was a real pressure for us as children. And you know, as a child, when you wake up, the first thing you think about is food, but if you have to do all that before you can even have your breakfast and school lunch allowance – it was painful.

Yes, as a child, I did refuse to take a shower before having my breakfast, but not now though. And don't be reading this, and pretend like you don't have any childhood secrets as well. Tell me where all those cookies that disappeared from the cookie jar went. What happened to the sweetened condensed milk, the powdered chocolate, and the toothpaste you eagerly ate, thinking it was like candy, but found out it wasn't that good and spat it quickly? Tell me why your parents called you and you couldn't answer. Was it not because the food you stole, knowing it wasn't time to eat, was still in your mouth? Don't let me tell too many of your childhood secrets.

When you look back on some of these childhood behaviors, you wonder why – just why? I remember the few times I would overeat while my parents warned me, then later start crying in the middle of the night because my belly hurt and I could not sleep. And it has been said that when you overeat and your stomach hurts, you can use the broom to sweep your belly, and the food will go down for you to feel better. So, it would be the time to let the broom do its magic. I do not remember if that ever worked though. Sometimes, I'm curious about where these older people got all these lies from.

Often, we had to strike against my mom's rules by refusing to do all of them before we even ate breakfast, which always didn't end well, or in our favor. My mom would lock all the food and refuse to give us any money for allowance. But if we were fortunate enough that our father was at home, he would beg her for mercy so we could eat before showering.

When my mom is cooking, you don't want to wait to eat before going to sleep; you would rather go to sleep and wake up to eat because what is supposed to be done in five minutes would be on the cooker for hours until everybody, including my dad, starts dozing, and is tired of waiting. And when everybody starts complaining of being hungry and sleepy, she would say, "A few more minutes – is not done yet." As if there was something in the food that had to die before she could serve it. My dad often would say, "All the nutrients in the food are dead by now." I honestly also believe all the vitamins were deactivated or leached out of the food during those cooking processes.

My dad's jokes about the contributors of medical and hygienic methods, practices, and infection control over the centuries might not be correct. However, we may agree with him that using too much of the cleaning agents we have in our homes today can cause other health issues, just as experts are telling us. Many cleaning agents can get you sick and kill you gradually if you misuse them. And I have gotten myself sickened a few times by using too much bleach or air freshener. Oops! I couldn't keep the balance.

To understand the necessity of balance, let us consider the weight, mass, or force scale. In our current world, we have so many different weighing scales; some in stores, gyms, health centers or clinics and hospitals, and our homes, in the kitchens and bathrooms. The different categories of weighing scales themselves have many other subcategories, but for time's sake, I would not like to elaborate on them. As you may know, whether mechanical, programable, analytical, or electronic, which could be digital or analog balance, their common purpose is to measure weight, mass, or force.

Balance and Extremism

One of the problems of humanity is extremism. Human beings tend to either be on the far right or left on anything pertaining to God, life, money, wealth, health, food, work, pleasure, sex, peace, and happiness. And balance or moderation seems to easily evade our understanding, belief, and acceptance.

Indifference, or lack of interest, concern is also unbalanced and makes people and things unsteady so they tip or fall. The truth is, lack of balance or even stability just on one side or one thing can cause unbalance everywhere in your life, family, business, organization, ministry, government, country, and society.

Balance, even though it is synonymous with the following, I believe rather produces them – Balance produces fairness or justice, self-control, assurance, peace, and some level of security.

The dictionary defines extremism as "the holding of extreme political or religious views; fanaticism." But it is more than just political and religious extreme views, despite the fact that these also are very dangerous.

Balance Is Power

To better understand this, let us go back a little in history: The weighing scale usage dates back to ancient times by Egyptians, Assyrians, and Indians, in North Africa, the Middle East, and the Romans in Europe, and the Chinese in Asia. However, according to history, it's believed that beam balance was the first mass-measuring instrument invented.

A conventional scale includes two plates or bowls hanging at the same interval from a fulcrum (a pivotal or central point); usually, one side bearing a known weight or mass (example: 1, 2, 3, 4, 5 pounds or kgs), while unknown weight or masses are added to equal or till it reaches a static equilibrium, or level off. In other words, a known weight is used to know or discover the unknown weight of an item or object.

Even though there are other scales that make use of different physical principles to determine the weight, mass, or force of an item or object like the spring scale, which uses a spring of known stiffness to detect the weight, they all reveal an unknown truth – the weight.

The "Weight" of an item is also considered as the "Force" of the item. And "Force" is synonymous with strength and power. This gives the understanding that the level of balance of an individual determines the strength or power of the latter.

One of the reasons why there is a lack of balance in many lives is because there is nothing to look up to or a refusal to look up to a Godly role model and existing principles, morals, and ethics. Having something authentic and Godly that you are aiming to be like or reach helps you keep the balance in your life. And for you as a child of God, your role model is Christ, God, and your principles should be the word or precepts of God. The Bible says, *"Love the Lord your God and keep his requirements, his decrees, his laws and his commands always."* (Deuteronomy 11:1, NIV).

> *"The level of balance of an individual determines the strength or power of the latter."*

It has been proven that "The perfect scale rests at neutral." Being neutral is being objective, and being objective is having a balanced judgment or understanding, and as the Oxford Languages Dictionary puts it, is "not influenced by personal feelings or opinions in considering and representing facts." While your feelings are telling you one thing, the facts and moreover the truth could be telling you another thing, which one should you believe? The truth will surely survive every suppression and manipulation, and sooner or later will be revealed and prevail. Unlike the truth, feelings are not stable or balanced and can be influenced by sight and hearing and circumstances.

I like to believe that balance is pushing back and keeping at bay anything that tries to master you. Why? Because the Bible says, *"For 'people are slaves to whatever has mastered them."* (2 Peter 2:19, NKJV). Everything that masters your life in other words controls your life, and everything that controls your life, controls your peace, happiness, and everything that controls your happiness holds your death and life because it has power over you.

> *"Having something authentic and Godly that you are aiming to be like or reach helps you keep the balance in your life."*

The Electrical Circuit and Circuit of Foolishness

Don't kill yourself, your purpose and destiny, relationships, career, business, progress, or success with your own energy or power (intelligence, talent, natural, and spiritual gifts). Use your best attributes to build and fulfill your purpose and destiny and people's, not destroy them. And if you are on the receiving end, meaning you are the one being fooled, make sure you are grounded, so no matter what the hazards from someone may be, you can be safe.

One of the devil's strategies is to kill or destroy you with what you are actually good at. Look around, and you will see so many people destroying themselves and their blessings with the very things God gifted them, including their intelligence, beauty, money, position, and career – Keep the balance. For instance, don't use your intelligence to become a professional liar, cheater, manipulator, oppressor, or criminal; it will only destroy you. As a law enforcement agent said some time ago, "The jails are full of intelligent people." In other words, some of the brightest people are the ones who make some of the stupidest decisions or choices.

Every professional Electrician knows that the earth wire is primarily used to avoid electric shocks. And the ground is primarily used for unbalancing when the electric system overloads.

> *"I like to believe that balance is pushing back and keeping at bay anything that tries to master you."*

An Electrical Circuit or Cable is usually composed of four, and popularly, three conductors, live, neutral, and ground wires. The live wire circuit is typically red and is at a high voltage. The neutral wire is black and has nearly the same voltage as that of the ground. The power capacity difference between the live and neutral wires is estimated to be about 220 to 230V, depending on your country's electrical power voltage.

The truth is, all the wires are important for a safe and good electrical circuit to supply power in order to run our machines, devices, and meet our energy needs. When one is malfunctioning or missing, this can lead to catastrophic electrical accidents or events. Why? Because while the neutral and ground wires serve two distinct purposes, the earth and ground wires provide safety against faults and current leaks. This is also a safety property or precaution in case the black or neutral wires come in contact one way or the other. Interestingly, as mentioned, connecting to the earth or ground eliminates the shock hazard in the event of a short circuit. Short-circuiting occurs when an electric current flows down the wrong or unintended route with little to no electrical resistance, which can cause serious damage.

When you are not grounded, and observe strong moral values in life, you are set to be damaged by your own gifts and talents, and other people. Remember, the Bible also says, *"Do not be deceived: God cannot be mocked. A man reaps what he sows. Whoever sows to please their flesh, from the flesh will reap destruction—".* (Galatians 6:7-8, NIV).

> *"One of the devil's strategies is to kill or destroy you with what you are actually good at."*

Don't use your gifts or talents to take advantage of people, and just for personal pleasure. Instead, use it to serve God and people. This is not to say that your talents are not meant to benefit you, but when you become the only beneficiary of your talent while it becomes dangerous to others, it will eventually become dangerous to you and destroy you as well sooner or later.

Have you ever seen a beautiful woman that all the men in the neighborhood, on the job, and at school end up sleeping with? Or a handsome or well-to-do man who ends up sleeping with all the women in the church? Use your beauty wisely.

God loves all His children, but also knows them individually and will do everything to protect the good ones against the bad ones. Think about this: As a parent, you know all your children very well, the good ones and the bad ones, or the ones with good character and the ones with bad character. Will you watch the bad ones destroy the good ones in a deal or any type of venture while you already know the truth about them? Absolutely not. You love all of them, but at the same time, you want the good ones to be safe as well.

Balance, sometimes, may look like a compromise or accommodation, but does not necessarily have to undermine or weaken your values and belief — It's a state of understanding where the excess or extremes are avoided.

> *"Some of the brightest people are the ones who make some of the stupidest decisions or choices."*

Keep Breathing or Die

There are situations or events that may occur in your life with the potential to break your heart or spirit, numb your feelings, kill your desire to keep living and force you into undesirable behaviors. Nevertheless, if you allow them, they will lead you to an unexpected and regrettable end. You have to resist the temptations of trying to use short-term solutions to fix long-term dilemmas and hurt. And you have to keep the courage and hope as a light for your darkest roads and days in life. Otherwise, you will enable life's negative events to turn you into a fool, and I'm sure you are not one.

We read, *"Then the LORD God formed man from the dust of the ground and breathed the breath of life into his nostrils, and the man became a living being."* (Genesis 2:7, NIV).

The above Bible mention is deep, but I would like us to consider the element that concerns this subject. The Bible says God breathed into man after forming him, and he became a living being. Being a living being is more than just living in this world or realm. But from that day on, whenever a man stops breathing, he dies. And to live in this world, you have to continue breathing.

I'm not just talking about physical death, but spiritual and psychological death. You will be amazed how many people you meet or pass by daily who are walking around but are actually dead. They might be dead because their hearts or spirits are broken, heavy, painful, bitter, angry, and hopeless.

> *"When you are not grounded, and observe strong moral values in life, you are set to be damaged by your own gifts and talents, and other people."*

Breathing In and Out

Scientists have done and are doing their best to explain the breathing process to better help humanity medically. However, I think breathing is a phenomenon that no matter how we try to explain it, there will not be enough human experiments and discoveries to fully explain it, especially if we do not understand its spiritual mystery.

When you breathe in or inhale, air enters your lungs, and oxygen from that air travels to your blood. When you breathe out or exhale, carbon dioxide, known as a waste gas, travels from your blood to the lungs, which takes care of that. This vital process is also called gas exchange.

Medical experts, especially respiratory therapists, know much about it, and you know and can tell that without this process or an artificial way to keep oxygen flowing in and out of your blood and lungs, you will be dead.

I have heard and learned a little bit about asthma, which is a chronic obstructive pulmonary disease. But the day I witnessed the son of one of our sisters in ministry suffer from this, I thought nobody should ever have to experience this. It was horrible and very painful to just even witness. The latter was just trying to breathe the same air we were breathing but could not. And you could see the mother literally feeling like breathing for him. It was horrible. And if you are reading this and suffering from it, I pray that you be free from it even now.

My point here is this, life itself as we know it, is all about a bi-directional exchange, and each of them is important. Each one of them keeps life flowing and running within you.

Peace Is Priceless

Most of the time, for one reason or the other, we underestimate peace. Consequently, peace of mind and soul is so important that it was one of the biggest things the Lord promised His followers. He said, *"Peace I leave with you; my peace I give to you. Not as the world gives do I give to you. Let not your hearts be troubled, neither let them be afraid."* (John 14: 27, ESV).

> *"Peace of mind and soul is so important that it was one of the biggest things the Lord promised His followers."*

In the absence of peace, your mind and spiritual man are choked, and gradually, it starts affecting your body, and sooner or later, your body starts deteriorating knowingly or unknowingly. This can lead to serious health issues over time and untimely death.

Sometimes, we mistake the absence of peace for stress. No, even though stress can be one of the results of a lack of peace, it is different from the absence of peace. You cannot function effectively when peace is lacking. I know everybody tries to learn survival strategies, even in wars or difficult times. But we are not talking about war as we know it. Stress can be explained as a condition we all experience when our mind or body is under pressure or in difficult situations. And it can be gracefully managed. But you cannot manage the absence of peace like you manage stress because these are two different entities.

> *"Sometimes, we mistake the absence of peace for stress."*

Peace, is something you choose or decide for in many areas of your life, so choose carefully. Whenever you have the options, always choose peace over power, money, materials, positions, luxury, and beauty. Always ask yourself, "Will this decision I'm about to make, the action I'm about to take, or what I'm about to do bring me and others peace sooner or later?" And unless you have no other options, always choose peace.

When there is a lack of peace at home, in your relationship or marriage, family, friendship, workplace, neighborhood, city, state, country, or in the world, life becomes unpleasant. And it's your responsibility to do your best to create peace through the choices you make here and there throughout your lifetime.

The truth about peace is that it's bi-directional: When you create and give peace through your decisions, words, and actions, not only other people benefit from it, you also benefit from it. And when you create troubles, you also benefit from the troubles. So give peace, so you can have it as well.

> *"Peace, is something you choose or decide for in many areas of your life, so choose carefully."*

If you are doing the wrong things, marrying the wrong person, choosing the wrong job, misusing your money, living at the wrong place, and eating the wrong foods, you will not have peace of mind and soul. Yes, you may think it's just food. But even food can cause troubles to your body, spirit, and soul or peace.

The Balanced God Created a Balanced Universe

You cannot doubt the fact that God is a balanced God who created a balanced universe. The universe was created with balance. (Genesis Chapters 1 to 3). Throughout the universe, every spiritual and physical being, every visible and invisible entity, has a distinctive element or substance, partially or completely different from the others. Science explains how we have daylight and night as the earth rotates around the sun. However it works, which time will not permit us to elaborate, and since we are not in a Solar System Exploration, the truth is that we have what you and I refer to as day and night. And all the eight discovered planets in our Solar System at the time I'm writing this book (There may be many other planets that we have yet to discover, and will never discover) have their respective characteristics, elements, or substances, fully or partially different from others. The existence of day and night, fire and water, heat and cold reality is a very simple explanation of how balanced God, the Creator of the universe and humanity is, and these elements reveal his personality or characteristics.

> *"God is a balanced God who created a balanced universe. The universe was created with balance."*

The Unbalanced World

While God created a balanced universe or world in the beginning, man has changed it to an unbalanced world starting with Adam and Eve in the Garden of Eden (Genesis 3:1-24). Thereafter, human beings have continued to be so self-destructive with pride or ego, arrogance, selfishness, and greed, which generate unprovoked anger, false happiness, gluttony, harmful medication, immoral sex, dictatorship, distorted self-esteem, and the worship of false gods or deities.

To understand our unbalanced inner drives, we have to go back to when and where it all started. Our unbalanced problems started in the Garden of Eden. And we have to remember that it all started with greed, in the sense that Adam and Eve were not content with the beautiful life that God created for them to live in the Garden of Eden, so they wanted more. They wanted to ***"be like God, knowing good and evil."*** (Genesis 3:5).

"Any excess is harmful", says a proverb in French. For example, do you have a measure for your thoughts? You have to know when it's time to stop thinking in a certain way because every action starts with a thought. If you can stop any unbalance in your mind before it becomes an act, then you are a hero. You have to congratulate yourself each time you arrest a negative thought in your mind before it becomes an action. You do take pride in so many things, right? Well, you should be proud of yourself when you don't act on a negative thought.

Unbalanced thoughts start with what seems to be logic quests, while supported by false reasoning, and false or unrealistic reasoning, or delusion leads to bad decisions. There is never a seed of truth in unbalance. It can make you feel good and offer you some pleasure, but just temporarily; and the consequences are always more devastating and long-term than the good feeling. The Bible says, ***"We demolish arguments and every pretension that sets itself up against the knowledge of God, and we take captive every thought to make it obedient to Christ."*** (2 Corinthians 10:5, NIV). Unbalance starts from the mind, and heart, so if you don't stop it at the early stage, it will overcome your other senses and pollute your spirit.

> *"There is never a seed of truth in unbalance."*

Keeping Situations Measure In Your Head

Let me start by saying, every win is not a win, and every loss is not a loss. In effect, your ability to quickly measure or evaluate situations and respond or react properly and accordingly will save you from many troubles, and save you time, energy, money, materials, and above all, your peace, and yet, lead you to a real win sooner or later.

> ## *"Every win is not a win, and every loss is not a loss."*

The LORD Jesus was a master of balance. And in everything he was doing here on earth, He has us in mind. In order words, He was giving us the perfect examples of how to handle things, human beings, and situations.

When the Pharisees wanted to trap Him with tax payment and sent their disciples and Herodians to question him whether they should pay taxes or not, His answer was simple and balanced, "Whose image is this?", he asked. They answered, "Caesar." Then He said, "So give back to Caesar what belongs to Caesar." We may have various interpretations for this declaration, but let us learn the simplest thing from his answer.

The deep thought here is, while the Lord said, "Give back to Caesar what belongs to Caesar", He never meant you belong to Caesar either — So how do you give back to Caesar what belongs to Caesar without not becoming a property of Caesar?

We read, "Then the Pharisees went out and laid plans to trap him in his words. They sent their disciples to him along with the Herodians. "Teacher," they said, "we know that you are a man of integrity and that you teach the way of God in accordance with the truth. You aren't swayed by others because you pay no attention to who they are. Tell us then, what is your opinion? Is it right to pay the imperial tax to Caesar or not?"

"But Jesus, knowing their evil intent, said, "You hypocrites, why are you trying to trap me? Show me the coin used for paying the tax." They brought him a denarius, and he asked them, "Whose image is this? And whose inscription?"

"Caesar's," they replied."

"Then he said to them, "So give back to Caesar what is Caesar's, and to God what is God's."

"When they heard this, they were amazed. So they left him and went away." (Mathew 22:15-22).

Remember, the whole idea of the Pharisees as we read above is to trap the Lord with his own words just as the Bible makes it clear, and proceed to hurt or kill him based on His own words. We read again, *"Then the Pharisees went out and laid plans to trap him in his words."* (Matthew 22:15, NIV). However, notice the Lord measured the situation, tipped the scale, balanced what was the most important thing, and escaped their trap. Measuring or evaluating situations to know what is the most important thing, tipping the scale, and keeping the balance will always protect and help you escape men's evil plans and foolishness to destroy you sooner or later. When you keep the balance, you never give out too much control, information, and emotional intelligence, which is your ability to perceive, use, understand, manage, and handle your emotions.

> *"When you keep the balance, you never give out too much control, information, and emotional intelligence."*

There are times when showing your emotion is recommended, especially when dealing with someone who is Godly, honest, understanding, and willing to help change a bad situation, when you know you are wrong and have to apologize, or when you are going through some problems and need help – you have to be honest with your human state. However, showing your emotions to someone who cares less about you, and is determined to hurt or destroy you will only empower them to do so. Always carry your situation measuring instrument in your head. Quickly measure or evaluate situations to determine how you can tip the scale to be safe and avoid being trapped by fools, evil planners, and doers.

The Difficult Stop and Return Point

Stopping the wrong decision or mistake late is better than never, and correcting it late is better than never.

There is a difficult stop-and-return point in everything in life; this is the level you get to in anything you are dealing with or handling, and it may be good or bad. And you must learn how to stop and reverse or correct it when you realize it's a bad decision you have made, the wrong direction you are taking, or a bad goal you are pursuing. Anytime is a good time to stop and reverse a wrong decision, and bad things. Don't let your ego, shame, and the devil use how far you have already gone and too bad you have already done to push you to continue something you know is the wrong thing to do. It's a good thing to honorably stop the wrong before it is too late, but stopping it late is also better than never, and correcting it late is better than never. And make sure you stop and correct it well.

If your decision is the right one, then the no-return point should instead facilitate and support you to continue and finish the good deeds, and even encourage you to do it one or several more times. Only know when it's enough, so you won't hurt yourself or cause yourself problems. While doing good is a good thing, you must also know how much you can do and when to stop in order to avoid regrettable problems or consequences.

> *"Anytime is a good time to stop and reverse a wrong decision, and bad things."*

Mind the Existing Truths and Principles

Do not let the pursuit of a "better" takes away the "good" that you already have.

Observe and learn from existing realities or truths, principles, and obviously, the consequences other people experienced when they made the same wrong decisions.

I believe you have heard the saying, "If it's not broken, don't fix it." The world is changing so rapidly that we want everything new and changed, even if it's good or not broken. While some things can be changed for better usage and implementation in our modern world, life's truths and principles constitute a solid foundation that you cannot change, or change and expect lasting peace, happiness, security, and stability. Every time you violate those truths and principles, you will unfortunately pay the price sooner or later with your peace, joy, health, and sometimes with your life in some forms.

Be careful, and don't let your ego, greed, selfishness, and lust seduce you to try to make changes that are not necessities to destroy your life and other people's one way or the other.

If you are careless, in pursuit of the "better", you may destroy the "good" you already have. Looking for better is encouraged, but ensure that the pursuit of the better does not eventually affect the good you already have. It is true that sometimes, to have the better, you have to let go of the existing one. However, the other truth is that as humans, we tend to always think of things in delusion; we do not properly evaluate things and confirm before judging the quality or level of their potential, and this leads us to the wrong desires, expectations, and fantasies.

> *"Do not let the pursuit of a "better" takes away the "good" that you already have."*

If the old is still working and provides you with the necessary and maximum need, peace, protection, happiness, and stability, then do not try to change it. It's better to have the good and keep it than try to have the "better" or "best" that does not exist and will never exist, which means it only exists in your head or mind. Not all things in this life are what they look like, and sometimes even not like what they feel like. Remember the old saying, "All that glitters is not gold."

Many times, we are caught up in how we feel, or what we want to feel, and what we think and want to believe, and forget about how others feel, and what they think. Trying to "walk in people's shoes" will help you better understand and avoid making selfish decisions that are just focused on you and not the well-being of other people as well or the collective good.

It's important to care about moral values when you are laying foundations for your life, and any endeavor in life.

When you lay the wrong foundation in anything you're doing in life, not only will you have to deal with the spiritual, physical, and psychological consequences, but even your children and descendants will have to deal with things they have never decided or signed up for. If you make decisions without considering your children born or unborn, your descendants, anyone related to you, and other people, you are selfish. Money, materials, position, and fame are good, but if you have to ignore the precepts of God, moral values, and the potential negative, spiritual, physical, and psychological consequences that it will cause to others, you are selfish.

> *"Life's truths and principles constitute a solid foundation that you cannot change."*

A good foundation does not necessarily mean a perfect foundation, or an error-free foundation. However, do your best to ensure that the foundations you are laying in everything you do are good.

You are either born in an already-made environment with the finances and materials you need to build and reach your purpose and destiny, or you are born in a lack or poverty and have to search, find, and create that platform or environment for yourself and your descendants to come, to fulfill your purpose and destiny. Either way, you have to make sure that you do it right to avoid bringing curses over yourself and your descendants.

Make Authentication Your Best Friend

FOOLISHNESS | Keeping the Balance

I rushed to an ATM one evening to make a payment on a credit card and had a pleasant experience. I prefer paying my credit card bills online, but I forgot to pay the bill online on one of the accounts, and since an auto payment was not set up for the card, I had to race to the ATM to make the payment and beat the late fee. But what I didn't realize is that the ATM was not set up like one of my other financial institutions with which I have another credit card. I was expecting the machine to ask me to set up a cash advance PIN first, and then proceed to make a payment just like what I had experienced with my other credit card a few months earlier. But to my surprise, when I slid the card into the machine, it just asked me what I wanted to do with two options, which one was to make a credit card payment. In effect, I selected the option to make payment and the machine asked me immediately to insert the cash. I waited for a while thinking it would give me another prompt until I realized that the next step was actually what the machine presented me with, so I either had to continue or cancel the transaction. For a moment, I thought the machine was out of order, but then I proceeded to insert the cash payment. The machine counted, added it to my account as payment, and finalized the transaction. I printed the receipt, then stood there for a while asking myself, "What have I done to myself? This machine must be out of order?"

Then, I thought while laughing so hard all by myself, "Who cares if you were paying the credit card bill of someone else?" "The machine didn't ask you for any authentication because you were making a payment." It was like, "Sir, you are welcome to pay that credit card bill without questions asked." "Who would be that creditor that would turn away a good Samaritan who wanted to pay the credit card bill of others?" Everything started making sense to me: Had I wanted to do a cash advance on the credit card, the machine would have asked me for authentication. However, since it was to pay the card, authentication was not required. It seemed, "Just pay the bill, my friend. By the way, you're welcome!"

When you are entering many countries, immigration is tough: Your paperwork, including passport, visa, and medical requirements are thoroughly checked and authenticated. But when you are leaving, except in oppressed countries, nobody cares much about whether your travel documents are in good status or not. After all, you are leaving the country or going out somewhere. But then, when you return to the same port of entry, everything must be authenticated.

One of the things I have learned the hard way over time to take care of before anything else when it comes to systems and properties is security. Being in the Information Technology industry, security risk is inherent, and things can get very stressful as you must go through some procedures at every step of your workflow to ensure the safety of the systems, platforms, networks, applications, and accounts –and that's when authentication comes in at every critical point of work. As we discussed earlier, this is also true for your personal sensitive information, such as your identification, financial accounts, credit, and medical information. And when it comes to your day-to-day life, at your own risk, you may easily let the validation or authentication of things and even people slide in without even knowing. This can initiate and create big problems in your life sooner or later.

According to the Oxford Language Dictionary,

"Authentication is the process or action of proving or showing something to be true, genuine, or valid." But I like the computing definition better, which is, "The process or action of verifying the identity of a user or process." In more clarification, it "Is the act of proving an assertion, such as the identity of a computer system user. In contrast with identification, the act of indicating a person or thing's identity, and authentication is the process of verifying that identity."

Considering the above definitions, let's say authentication is the process of verifying something or someone is true, real, or genuine. The Bible says, "Beware of false prophets, who come to you in sheep's clothing, but inwardly they are ravenous wolves. You will know them by their fruits. Do men gather grapes from thornbushes or figs from thistles? Even so, every good tree bears good fruit, but a bad tree bears bad fruit. A good tree cannot bear bad fruit, nor can a bad tree bear good fruit." (Matthew 7:15-18, KJV). The Lord warned about false prophets, but this applies to people and things in general as well. Sometimes, you don't need to wait to see a fruit, behavior, or character before you can know whether things or people are genuine, true, or real. Listen to the sensors God put in you by His Spirit. Pay attention to the first signs, and if something doesn't match for you, require more time to validate things, and confirm what was not clicking right in your spirit. Don't be in a rush to say, "Yes" or "No" to something you haven't authenticated or validated yet.

The Bible says, *"There are six things that the LORD hates, seven that are an abomination to him: haughty eyes, a lying tongue, and hands that shed innocent blood, a heart that devises wicked plans, feet that make haste to run to*

evil, a false witness who breathes out lies, and one who sows discord among brothers." (Proverbs 6:16-19, ESV).

The reason the Bible makes these characters, behaviors, or attitudes as major evils is because many other evils start from them. So, wisdom requires that you check things and people on these major characters:

Haughty eyes: Is the person prideful?

Lying tongue: Does the person tell the truth?

Hands that shed innocent blood: Does the person value life, and care about other people's needs?

A heart that devises wicked plans: Does the person plan evil against others?

Feet that make haste to run to evil: Does the person entice and support evil?

A false witness who breathes out lies: Does the person bear false witness, and tell lies for reward?

One who sows discord among brothers: Does the person sow trouble among people?

If some, or all the answers to the above questions are yes, then you need to be careful before they do it or it happens to you.

The Abraham Trap and Extending Grace

What I refer to as the Abraham traps are situations that force or push good people to make terrible mistakes without evil intentions. And this, is not an advocacy for any misjudgment or bad decision. But to remind you to deal with people on a case-by-case basis when it comes to your relationship with people generally. Truly, you have the responsibility also to review situations properly before deciding if someone is worth keeping in your life, business, or any type of relationship. You have to know when someone's bad decision is an error, behavior, or character.

Moreover, sometimes if you are not careful, you can make or create liars around you by your behaviors or the way you handle errors and truth. When people know that you do not like or appreciate the truth, or if they make a mistake, you handle it in extreme ways, they will not tell you the truth, and they will lie out of fear of the consequences. Therefore, handling errors and truth properly is also beneficial to you because it will help people to be honest with you, and tell you the truth, which will benefit everybody in the end.

> *"If you are not careful, you can make or create liars around you by your behaviors or the way you handle errors and truth."*

Keep in mind that human beings are naturally defensive. So, when you start using people's vulnerabilities and mistakes against them, they will stop being honest, or transparent with you. The best way to encourage people to be honest with you is to disagree with them on their mistakes yet, show them respect, love, and understanding, grace and compassion.

Abraham lied to Abimelek that Sarah, his wife, was his sister because he was afraid that he could be killed because of her beauty.

In Genesis 20:2-12, we read:
"And there Abraham said of his wife Sarah, "She is my sister." Then Abimelek king of Gerar sent for Sarah and took her.

But God came to Abimelek in a dream one night and said to him, "You are as good as dead because of the woman you have taken; she is a married woman."

Now Abimelek had not gone near her, so he said, "Lord, will you destroy an innocent nation? Did he not say to me, 'She is my sister,' and didn't she also say, 'He is my brother'? I have done this with a clear conscience and clean hands."

Then God said to him in the dream, "Yes, I know you did this with a clear conscience, and so I have kept you from sinning against me. That is why I did not let you touch her. Now return the man's wife, for he is a prophet, and he will pray for you and you will live. But if you do not return her, you may be sure that you and all who belong to you will die."

Early the next morning Abimelek summoned all his officials, and when he told them all that had happened, they were very much afraid. Then Abimelek called Abraham in and said, "What have you done to us? How have I wronged you that you have brought such great guilt upon me and my kingdom? You have done things to me that should never be done." And Abimelek asked Abraham, "What was your reason for doing this?"

Abraham replied, "I said to myself, 'There is surely no fear of God in this place, and they will kill me because of my wife'."

One of the notable things about this story is that God extended grace to Abraham and Sarah and still came to their rescue even when they lied. And I believe because He knew Abraham lied out of fear for his life – it was a trap and a mistake. Be careful about the things you lie about because you might not be able to recover some of them, except by divine intervention like in this story of Abraham and Sarah. Abraham could have lost his wife by not telling the truth.

Nevertheless, if you can put yourself in God's position in this story, you may ask yourself, what you can do to help people who fall short of truth or honesty without evil intentions. We all fall short of some standards now and then. The Bible says, *"For all have sinned and fall short of the glory of God."* (Romans 3:23, NIV). However, when evil intentions are the force behind actions and behaviors, you have to be cautious and protect yourself and yours against malicious, criminal, immoral, and ungodly people.

You cannot extend grace without being sympathetic, which is compassion. Compassion is that feeling that you have to go out of your way to relieve the pains or suffering of others.

> *"When evil intentions are the force behind actions and behaviors, you have to be cautious and protect yourself and yours."*

Considering realities in exceptional cases, you may securely extend grace to people just as God extends grace to you. The Bible says, *"Forgive us our sins, for we also forgive everyone who sins against us. And lead us not into temptation."* (Luke 11:4, NIV). Wisely and properly evaluate the situation to know and decide whether you can extend grace to the offender in some ways. I should also note that there are many ways of extending grace to people, which might not necessarily be the same for everybody. You must consider if you should extend grace to the latter, and how. For example, there may be cases in which you can discuss the ramifications with the person and still keep him in the same position. However, sometimes it may be dangerous to do so, and you can give him some allowance and let him experience the consequences of his actions to learn from them. It will all depend on the realities you find in the situation, and you should be honest with yourself and the person and avoid being fooled again.

Difficult, But Purposeful Decisions

There are decisions that you make against your wishes, but they are unselfish and beneficial to others as well. You have not matured in making the right decisions until you can make wise and unselfish decisions, and sometimes many that will not even profit you anything, but benefit others that you dearly care for.

Sometimes in life, you will have to make difficult decisions, that are the right ones. In other words, these decisions may cause you deep pain, but they may end up correcting some problems, or at least be the consequences of someone's continuous bad decision-making. At some point, you have to let the person experience the consequences to learn or get an understanding of the effects of their bad decisions.

> *"Wisely and properly evaluate the situation to know and decide whether you can extend grace to the offender in some ways."*

Keeping the Balance with Your Body and Appearance

God created your body and appearance. And while you should keep yourself looking and smelling good, don't go too far by trying to change your natural and biological features. And if you ever need to do it, be mindful of the consequences that can arise from it.

Statistics show that invasive procedures and anesthesia involved in cosmetic surgery-related result in death rates are very concerning. The truth is that no matter how human beings advance in anything in this world, it can never be as natural, organic, and safe as what God originally created. And that's why unless a feature of your body is malfunctioning, or becomes unbearable, it's not wise to want to take some medications or go through some surgical procedures to change it. As much as the medical industry can assure you about the safety of a medication you can take or a surgical procedure you can undertake, you have to be aware of the fact that not even one thing humanity invented or created is as safe as what God originally created.

Be careful with your overall health and beauty practices, many from statistics end up with various diseases and malaises, including sleep deprivation, restlessness, skin and eye diseases, and other serious illnesses such as different types of cancer while they continuously try to change one thing or the other about their physical appearance. Moderation in everything helps prevent if not much harm, at least destruction to some extent.

> *"Be careful with your overall health and beauty practices."*

Being Average or Trying to Equalize with the Crowd

Conventionally, when you are adding more to the item you are trying to measure weight for, it may even outweigh the original or existing weight you are using to determine the current or unknown weight. So intelligently, you reduce it till it balances or equals the existing weight. This is to say that while you're trying to know, gain, or experience something, be careful not to do too much to outweigh what is necessary. Many things in life become problematic when they reach over the limit. Don't be afraid of keeping the balance and if necessary, the average if that is safe, healthy, and Godly. We are used to thinking that anything average is not good enough. But sometimes, the average is actually what is safe for you. Don't follow the crowd. You don't have to do or have it the way everybody else is doing or having it. Your body, health, strength, time, purpose, destiny, and God's plan for your life are generally different. Be clever and avoid letting the weight of things and people push you to do what you are not supposed to do and is not suitable or good for you, ultimately according to God's precepts.

> *"We are used to thinking that*

anything average is not good enough."

Accepting God's purpose and plan for your life is not a defeat. It's just as Christ accepted the Father's will, *"Father, if you are willing, take this cup from me; yet not my will, but yours be done."* (Luke 42:22, NKJV). This doesn't also mean you have to settle for mediocrity, but accepting the will and plan of God when it's clear to you that what you want, is not what He wants.

Tipping Back to Equilibrium

Watching the scale tip back when you put the right amount to the falling side is amazing. Likewise, making the necessary changes or amendments in your life could tip it back from destruction to safety, stability, peace, and joy. Remember, it's always a good thing to make the right decision on time because sooner or later, it could turn the right decision into a wrong one. Timing is very important in the execution and process of your decision and plan. But it's also true that being late is better than never. When you finally make the right decision by admitting and correcting the wrong one, it has the power to instantly or progressively change a bad situation into a good or better one, even if you have to pay some price or experience some pain for the mistake. Your timely right decision can change your formerly wrong decision and hopefully help the balance to tip back to equilibrium sooner or later.

"Accepting God's purpose and plan for your life is not a defeat."

In effect, you have to be willing to put in the work in order for the scale to tip back. Ask yourself, "What can I do to make a good thing come out of the mistake or wrong decision I have made?" "How can I correct my wrong decision?" Then, seriously get to work to create something good out of the bad.

Trying to make good out of the bad does not mean you have to continue in the wrong. Do not try to polish a mistake to make it look good. It's dangerous to not be humble and change or redirect yourself when you find yourself on the wrong path and try to make or polish it to look good. It's disturbing to find out how people make mistakes and try to impress others with them, which clearly shows the level of their delusion. Why try to polish a wrong decision to make it look good while you know deep down in your heart that you are not at peace, and your ground is shaky? If you don't humbly admit, and retrieve from your wrong decisions and actions, but try to cover, polish, and make it look good to unnecessarily impress others, sooner or later, you will regret it. It will potentially cause you pain and destruction down the road.

Don't Let One Mistake Lead You to Another

It's a good thing to amend or correct things to put them in the right order. But sometimes, the best thing to do is to leave things where you stopped, and reverse course or redirect yourself to the right path if you really care about fulfilling your purpose and destiny, have peace, and real happiness.

For instance, if you know the man or woman you mistakenly have a child with is not the right person to marry, don't force yourself into marriage with the latter otherwise, you will regret it. Yes, it may be a good thing to consider marriage to amend your mistake of having a child out of wedlock. However, let it only be if you are convinced that the man or woman is your right or God ordained husband or wife. Too many people force themselves into a relationship or marriage with someone they have a child with, and only cry later about their decision to marry someone because they mistakenly have a child with the latter.

This is not to encourage vagabondage, but prayerfully be honest with yourself before marrying someone because you have a child with him or her.

It Takes Balance to Keep the Balance

How far can you go before it becomes too much? The answer to this question is always different because everybody has a personal measure of what is too much and too little for them. The fact is, there will always be differences in anything and everywhere, but when we understand and know how we can keep the balance, it becomes the stabilizer of our lives, families, businesses, country, government, and the world at large. There is always a middle ground that you can stand on while still keeping the things that are dear or valuable and pleasurable to you. The problem is when you always want the whole ground for yourself or in your favor, even if it will hurt you, and it's not what God wants and will cause pain or suffering to others and eventually destroy you as well.

"There will always be differences

> *in anything and everywhere, but when we understand and know how we can keep the balance, it becomes the stabilizer."*

Violating the balance in many areas of your life is like someone who blows a nuclear plant or arm, thinking it is in his way and not understanding that it will kill him as well. When you don't keep the balance in anything you think, say, do, eat, and drink, it may look under some circumstances that is to hurt other people, but believe it or not, it will hurt you as well sooner or later, one way or the other.

Self-balance produces self-accountability and restrictions. When you keep the balance, you become your own police or law enforcement. You start enforcing moral, civic, etiquette, and natural laws to yourself. In other words, you even double-check your thoughts before putting them into action, and continuously review the course of your actions and results or consequences to know whether to continue or stop, and revert them.

> *"Self-balance produces self-accountability and restrictions."*

Balance, just as boundary does not just happen by itself in any area of your life, it's believed, created, or established, and then respected by you first. And until you can imagine the consequences of unbalance, and they become true to you, and you honestly and firmly decide to avoid them, there will be a lack of balance.

It takes courage and inner strength to pursue and gain

balance in every area of your life. The irony is that, just as our mind tricks us to believe that all good things must be easy to attain, our mind tricks us as well to believe that balance in anything or any area of our lives should be easy. But the answer is no; balance is not easy; it will cost you something, and it will cost you self-denial. You will have to say no to some things, and yes to some things, and this, is against your feelings. Our feelings are always ready to support choices or decisions that feel good. However, when it comes to anything that does not feel good, our feelings do not support it. Therefore, it's our crucial responsibility to keep our feelings in check and measure the physical and spiritual effects or consequences of our decisions in advance, especially to confirm whether they are Godly, selfish, or wrong. Just because it feels good doesn't mean it's a good decision, and just because it doesn't feel good doesn't mean it's not a good decision. For instance, it doesn't always feel good when you are giving because it comes out of what you have, but the Bible says, *"It is more blessed to give than to receive."* (Acts 20: 35, NIV).

> *"Balance is not easy; it will cost you something, and it will cost you self-denial."*

The results are what validate the decision, even though sometimes it might take a while to confirm that.

The flesh always wants pleasurable things, things that feel good. And to keep feeling good, you have to keep doing what is making you feel good, and that's where the trap is.

I was not a coffee drinker until I started working night

shifts, and when I started my own companies and had to work many hours and around the clock in order to be able to keep up with my business demands. At some point, my amount of caffeine and sugar consumption was increasing too much because I had to drink several cups of coffee in order to stay awake and force myself to work even when I'm tired and sleepy.

I decided to cut down on coffee and sugar consumption. However, my focus primarily was on reducing the amount of sugar I was taking. So, I would only add sugar to my coffee on Sundays, but Monday through Saturday I would take my coffee without sugar. The next thing that occurred to me was that while I was trying to reduce the amount of sugar I was consuming at the time, unknowingly, my coffee intake also significantly reduced because I was not able to drink so much of the bitter coffee which has no sugar in it. In effect, I realized that the reasons why I was drinking so much coffee were not only because I was tired and sleepy; but also because it was sweet and easy to drink due to the sugar and milk in it. The lesson I learned was that when we decide to pursue balance in one area of our lives, the benefits affect other areas of our lives, and automatically start correcting other things that need corrections as well. The truth is that if we can start and keep the balance in some areas of our lives, then the balance will keep affecting and correcting many things that are out of balance in other areas of our lives.

> *"Because it feels good doesn't mean it's a good decision, and just because it doesn't feel good doesn't mean it's not a good decision."*

Human beings are never satisfied – we always want the next or other one of what we acquire or possess, or not. I'm not saying you should not yearn and work for the better and best, but when aiming for the next or what you would call sometimes the best may cause you and others pain and suffering sooner or later, and eventually destroy you, then it is not the best, even for yourself. It is an unbalanced wish; and it will sooner or later destroy you. It will later affect your sanity, morale, peace of mind, happiness, and health.

Is It a Strength or Weakness?

"The abuse of all things is a weakness," says a French proverb. Each time you fall off the balance by abusing or misusing, mishandling, exploiting, or perverting something, someone, or even yourself, it's a weakness, not a strength. And it means your weakness has scored, your weakness has overcome you. Unbalance knows where to start from, and it always starts by poking your weaknesses.

"If we can start and keep the balance — the balance will keep affecting and correcting many things that are out of balance in other areas of our lives."

One of the battle and war strategies is to fortify, protect, and defend the weak parts of your territory. In other words, put or set more fighters there. This has not only been a strategy in territorial wars and battles, but also in self-defense. Knowing how to defend yourself in case you are physically attacked is a class many attend. And in these classes, several things are taught, including how to master counter-attacking by the Human Weak Points, which are the eyes, nose, temples, ears, throat, jaw, solar plexus, ribs, spine, groin, knees, shin, toes and others. While you may be taught how to counter-attack by hitting these body parts, it's highly suggested that you use your intuition to know which one to adapt to in specific situations in order to effectively use it and set yourself free from your aggressor.

The same concept applies to your moral, physical, and spiritual weaknesses. You have to put more effort, apply several, and different strategies, and set boundaries that can help you withstand your weaknesses that push you out of balance.

We all have weaknesses – every human being has weaknesses, but it is how you handle your weaknesses that makes the difference: It will either use you to help others be free from them or destroy everybody and everything close to you one way or the other.

Keeping the balance starts from a sincere, or honest cry of the heart like the apostle Paul cried out, *"What a wretched man I am! Who will rescue me from this body of death?"* (Romans 7:24, CSB). Until you realize that your life is out of balance, your weaknesses will continue ruling your life and everything related to it. And it's in the pursuit of a sincere, and positive change that we actually start developing honest resistance, guidelines, and strategies to beat our unbalances.

> *"Each time you fall off the balance — it's a weakness, not a strength — Unbalance knows where to start from, and it always starts by*

poking your weaknesses."

The Tricks of Our Feelings

Feeling has been defined by the Oxford Languages Dictionary as "an emotional state or reaction." It's also noted as synonymous with "love, care, affection, fondness, tenderness, warmth, emotion, sentiment, passion, eagerness, desire, lust, infatuation, adulation, adoration, reverence, devotion, compassion, sympathy, empathy, understanding, concern, solicitude."

Feeling is also used to express sentience overall, and sentience as believed by scientists and philosophers, is the capacity to experience feelings and sensations. In other words, it is a multi-dimensional occurrence and level of awareness or responsiveness.

The truth is, responsiveness might not always be positive, even though the dictionary defines it as "the quality of reacting quickly and positively." Additionally, I believe our minds, thoughts or opinions, can influence our feelings, which can lead to a positive or negative responsiveness.

"We all have weaknesses – every human being has weaknesses, but it is how you handle your weaknesses that makes the difference."

Also, a positive or negative responsiveness can be judged and considered as one, depending on the perception of the person it's directed toward. So, let's get this out of the way before we continue. You have to be aware of the fact that you may receive back the type of feeling you sow into people. In other words, most people will respond or react to you based on the feeling you fuel into them. It's also true that some people can develop the wrong feelings towards you while you keep trying to stay positive in your feelings towards them.

The concept of the ability to feel that was given the name sentience, which came from the Latin word "Sentientem," meaning "feeling," was adapted in order to differentiate feeling from the ability to think or reason. This brings us to the truth that the difference between "feeling" and "reasoning" can never be compromised, and whenever we do, it will surely be to our own detriment sooner or later when the "feeling" recesses. And truly, human beings' feelings are never stable or fixed. So, if you just follow your feelings and discard your reasoning, you will become a fool. To avoid making the wrong decisions, you have to learn how to reason with your feelings or evaluate them.

While sometimes your feelings can communicate and confirm the truth about your reasoning, or you can feel the reality, you cannot only rely on your feelings to make decisions. Impressions are just the beginning of truth or lie, and you must validate them to confirm whether what you are feeling is the truth or not. Therefore, sometimes, you will have to disconnect yourself from your feelings in order to use your reasoning to validate the truth.

> *"Responsiveness might not always be positive."*

So many people have made the wrong decisions because they have just followed their mere feelings and have not evaluated and challenged them with their reasoning or judgment. Many people got married to the wrong person, chose a job, signed bad business deals, declared wars, committed murder, stole something, cheated, damaged their health with the wrong foods, and lived at the wrong places because of the way they felt. Simultaneously, many also divorced the right spouses, changed jobs, friends, and many other things because of the way they felt, and only to realize after all that they made one of the worst decisions in their lives. While our feelings sometimes could be an indicator of danger, we must also be very cautious not to let them fool us into dangers or things that could destroy our lives, reputation, integrity, and legacy.

One truth about feelings is that they don't last or run continuously in your being for a very long time – they decrease with time or at least temporarily. And that's why everything you build or venture into based on your mere feelings will never last.

One of the strongest tests of our feelings is done through time — let time confirm it or speak. Give it some time. And just as with your anger management skills, you should give all your feelings some relaxation: Take a deep breath, and imagine the before, during, and after the execution of your feelings. Try to imagine the consequences, even if they are offering you pleasure or satisfaction, boosting your pride or ego, or benefiting you one way or the other in the immediate scene.

> *"The difference between "feeling" and "reasoning" can never be compromised, and whenever we do, it will surely be to our own detriment."*

Some of our feelings are just not real. They come from infatuation, lust, selfishness, greed, and frustration. Remember, many of the satisfactions that your wrong feelings promise you will never last; they will never make you feel better for a long time, they are temporary.

Lust drains you, and you will never be able to quench it with the things it leads you to do. Let me say it again: You can never satisfy your lust. The road on which your lust will take you is endless – you will be lost in an eternal mirage.

When you keep making decisions based on your temporary wants and pleasures, you will always regret it sooner or later. Temporary means temporary, it is just for a moment. Making good choices or decisions by considering the purpose, the long-term benefits, and the bad consequences will help you make the right decisions and bring you peace. You don't want to be caught up in a circle of divorces. This is not an advocacy for cheaters and abusers. But before you decide to divorce, make sure it's the right thing to do at that point. I have observed people, men and women, who end up in a circle of divorces, one after another, because they couldn't work things out in their previous relationship or marriage. Some people choose to divorce their spouses because of what people will think about them or trying to gratify themselves based on their own past statements about other people's relationships.

> *"One truth about feelings is that they don't last or run continuously in your being for a very long time – they decrease with time*

or at least temporarily."

When you decide to divorce, let it not be for the wrong reasons. For example, people swear they will never keep their spouse if he or she ever cheated on them. So, when it happens, they want to prove to people that they are men or women of their word and file for divorce even if the relationship is repairable. After all, what are the benefits of trying to please people or prove a point to people by letting go of something you can repair or fix? It might not be easy, but what are the benefits of divorcing to prove a point and find yourself in a circle of divorces because the new relationships you will run into can be worse than the previous one you threw away because of a mistake or a childish decision on the part of your spouse? Cheating, infidelity, or any type of bad behavior in a relationship is painful to the loyal partner and breaks trust. However, if you know your partner very well and know that the relationship can be fixed, then try that instead of trying to please the crowd or people. Keep in mind that some of the people encouraging you to divorce your spouse because of infidelity wish they could have your spouse. Remember the old saying, "The devil you know, is better than the angel you don't know." And the proverb I mentioned to you earlier, "Don't sell a thief to buy a witch."

"Lust drains you — You can never satisfy your lust. The road on which your lust will take you is endless – you will be lost in an eternal mirage."

It's important to note that sentience, or our feeling, level of self-awareness, or consciousness, is connected to our wisdom, understanding, deep insight, judgment, and intelligence, which some thinkers or philosophers call sagacity. But remember, earlier I explained how I believe Godly wisdom is more than just sagacity because it gives you a spiritual aspect and understanding of things and situations or events that philosophy, natural intelligence, and understanding cannot give you. This Godly wisdom was what Joseph and Daniel had in the Bible, and it's beyond sagacity.

While growing up as a young Christian several years ago, one of the books I read on love was by Walter Trobisch, entitled "Love Is a Feeling to Be Learned." In that book, the author did a great job of shedding light on what love really is. The title of the book itself tells a lot about what love is. In conclusion – it's a feeling to be learned.

A few years ago, I was watching Rev. Kenneth Copeland on TV, and he said something so impactful. He said, "Love is a commandment, not a feeling. So it doesn't matter how you feel sometimes – the commandment is to love and continue loving regardless of your feeling." And I thought how true is that? If we just follow our feelings, we will definitively not go to work some days, but we do go because we don't want to lose our job. If we follow our feelings sometimes we may not go to the grocery store, but we do go because we are hungry and have to eat. I realized that we easily give in to our feelings when we think we have nothing to lose, but that has never been the truth, maybe at the moment we are about to make the wrong decisions, but we always and quickly learn then, and after that, we have so much to lose and it might be too late to undo what we have decided and already done.

Protective Establishments

Protective establishments are anything capable of or intended to protect someone or something, and everyone should have some protective establishments.

Every country, government, or society has ways or establishments to protect their well-being, including defense, law enforcement, financial, medical, education, employment, research... Etc.

For you as an individual, your protective establishments could be your family, marriage, job, business, relationships, finances, community, church, or organization.

It's obvious that sometimes, societies or individuals tend to decide to completely eradicate a protective establishment for things that go wrong here and there while ignoring the very main reasons why the establishment was introduced in the first place. We may all agree that if the intention behind an establishment is immoral, abusive, inhumane, racial, and ungodly, then it should be neutralized. However, it's wise to consider a review and reformation instead of completely neutralizing your protective establishment. Canceling your whole protective establishment is like throwing all the food in your house away because one apple got bad, and you know that's all the food you have and go hungry. Or you find out that one bill in your money is counterfeit so you burn all your money to go broke.

Don't throw away any of your protective establishments, plans, or strategies in life because of faulty incidents; instead, evaluate the incidents to fix the problems if possible, and leave the protective establishment in place to continue protecting you and others. When you cancel a structure, substance, or essence that keeps you alive, supported financially, materially, medically, or healthy, and Godly because of something that accidentally happened here or there, you may regret it sooner or later. Whenever something accidentally goes wrong with your protective establishments, sit down, think, and fix what is wrong to keep it in place and reformed instead of completely removing or leaving it.

Also remember, the most satisfying feeling and sense of belonging you can have besides God, is your family, the people you share blood with, and the closest you have bonded with as friends. So before you cut them off your life, think twice.

God is a God of relationship. Sometimes, He creates needs in people's lives so that He can connect them one way or the other because, needs create relationships. If you look back in your life, you will realize that the people you know today, except the ones you met randomly somewhere, came into your life because you either needed them for something, or they needed you for something, or both of you needed something, and it could have been a service, help or support, or even love. Regardless of the nature of the need, it has made you both met and know each other and having a type of relationship today.

> *"God is a God of relationship — He creates needs in people's lives so that He can connect them — needs create relationships."*

The Foolishness of Anger

Anger is generally natural and a human reaction to displeasure or dislike. However, it can also be demonic as well. The dictionary actually defines it as "a strong feeling of annoyance, displeasure, or hostility."

Anger becomes dangerous when it turns into a rage, which is violent and uncontrollable. The Bible says, *"In your anger do not sin": "Do not let the sun go down while you are still angry, and do not give the devil a foothold."* (Ephesians 4:26-27, NIV).

We feel angry when there is a sense of discomfort, cooperation refusal, provocation, hurt, threat, or injustice. The Lord was angry when people turned the temple, which was supposed to be a place of prayer into a marketplace. And the Bible says, *"So he made a whip out of cords, and drove all from the temple courts, both sheep and cattle; he scattered the coins of the money changers and overturned their tables. To those who sold doves he said, "Get these out of here! Stop turning my Father's house into a market!"* (John 2:13-16, NIV).

Anger's effect is not only the visible characteristics we see, such as facial expression, but also includes increased heart rate, high blood pressure, and increased levels of adrenaline (a hormone secreted by the adrenal glands, especially in conditions of stress, increasing rates of blood circulation, breathing, and carbohydrate metabolism and preparing muscles for exertion), and noradrenaline (a neurotransmitter and a hormone that plays an important role in your body's "fight-or-flight" response (fight or flight response is an automatic physiological reaction to an event that is perceived as stressful or fearful).

When anger takes over your being, it turns into rage or wrath, and may temporarily suspend your good reasoning or judgment, and this can lead you to bad decisions and actions.

Anger, just like any emotional state, is temporary, and if you can only hold on for a moment, your emotions and judgment will be clarified and wisdom will lead you to the right decision, and course of action you should take.

> *"Anger, just like any emotional state, is temporary, and if you can only hold on for a moment, your emotions and judgment will be clarified and wisdom will lead you to the right decision."*

Uncontrolled anger or rage is suicidal or self-destructive. Your bad actions instigated by anger will not only affect the person who provoked you, but you as well. When you destroy something, hurt or kill someone in anger, it is much more like you being on the same bridge with someone and cutting the ropes or pillars of the bridge. Or you being on the same ship with someone and blowing up the ship. You will go down with the person. So what is the benefit? Why would you punish yourself for someone or because someone else provoked you? The results of actions taken in anger have never been the right ones, or the expected end of the offended, and it always results in regrets.

The Wise man King Solomon admonishes, *"Do not be quickly provoked in your spirit, for anger resides in the lap of fools."* (Ecclesiastes 7:9, NIV).

The Dangers of Fabricated Happiness

The Bible encourages us to count our trials as joy. (James 1:2-8). And not worry about our needs because our Heavenly Father will take care of them. (Matthew 6:25-26). However, this is not an encouragement to fabricate our joy, and we cannot fabricate joy. Fabricating joy or happiness is like putting water in a pot on fire and expecting it to become cold water.

This is not an advocacy for complaining or murmuring and being grumpy all the time. You can keep your composure while not trying to impress anyone. Keep in mind that you don't owe anyone a demonstration of happiness, and don't have to impress anyone even when things are bad or not going well. Don't force yourself, situations, or things to look glamorous while they are not, especially when you have to do it by disobeying God. Obviously, truth is so powerful to the extent that sooner or later it will come out or be revealed. While you don't have to share your private challenges with everybody, remember also that you don't owe anyone proof of happiness, so don't waste your time, energy, money, or resources just to show people how happy you are; even if you think so, just don't do too much.

Yes, you should not let your current negative situations control your joy; but when you start getting delusional and suppressing pain with a fabricated joy that doesn't exist or is not a reality, one way or the other, sooner or later it can become a bigger spiritual, physical and psychological problem for you. Sometimes, it is just a good thing or blessing to stay objective or, what some people will call low-key.

One of the most dangerous facts in our world today, is the tools or ways to be able to filter or makeup, which is actually a cover-up, and social media is one of them. Our world is increasingly filled with platforms to make it easier for people to be able to hide real pain, failure, and danger in their lives. And you as an individual have to be careful and not to be caught up in these fake identity and situation makeups. These platforms, tools, or features are very tempting, so you have to restrict yourself and be your own control agent. As humans, we are all tempted to make things look more than what they are, but it's a temptation you have to personally fight and overcome; or you will fall into other dangerous traps sooner or later that can lead to your destruction.

Be content, happy, positive, and hopeful, and don't let circumstances kill your joy, but avoid fabricating peace and happiness to impress people. There is nothing wrong with letting people know you are not well.

> *"Avoid fabricating peace and happiness to impress people."*

The Drunkenness of Excitement

Happiness, joy, "enjoyment" or whatever you call it, we all long for it. But just as you should learn how to manage your sadness, frustration, stress, and anger, you must learn how to graciously manage your excitement. Among many unpleasant consequences, excitement can make you say and do things you are not supposed to. Do not be too excited and make promises you cannot fulfill, share information you are not supposed to share, or do what you are not supposed to do before the due time or at all.

> *"Among many unpleasant*

> *consequences, excitement can make you say and do things you are not supposed to."*

One of the most troubling stories I have ever learned is that of Chrysippus and many others who died of medical conditions caused by laughter over the years. Chrysippus, also referred to as "the man who died from laughing at his joke," was a prominent Greek philosopher who died of laughter after seeing a donkey eat his figs, and he asked a servant to give the donkey an undiluted wine to pair or accompany it. Then, he laughed till he died.

It is said, "Laughter is medicine." That's true, but too much laughter can cause other medical conditions, including Asphyxiation, which can lead the body to shut down from the lack of oxygen.

Excitement is good, but too much excitement can result in saying or doing too much. Watch out for what you are saying and doing when you are excited otherwise, you will regret it sooner or later.

The Temptation of Food

I won't say a lot here – because you already know it. But let me remind you.

"Delicious," we say when it tastes really good. But maybe eating that food all the time and for a very long time, and too much might not be good. We all know we can't live in our physical body without food. We are attracted to what smells, looks, feels, and sounds good, including food.

I have learned and I'm convinced that if we can eat food as medicine and the right energy source, then it can benefit us, rather than becoming a bad source of consumption. Think about this, and look at it in a figurative manner, the fruit (food) became death or destruction to Adam and Eve in the Garden of Eden when they ate the fruit God had forbidden them to eat (Genesis Chapters 2 and 3). And in the book of Revelation, the Bible confirms that in the coming New Jerusalem, there will be a "tree of life", and we read, ***"In the midst of the street of it, and on either side of the river, was there the tree of life, which bare twelve manner of fruits, and yielded her fruit every month: and the leaves of the tree were for the healing of the nations."*** (Revelation 22: 2-3, KJV). This reveals that there is either life and healing or death and sickness in the very foods that we eat. So, we have to be mindful of what we are eating and drinking.

Food is the fuel of the body because it produces energy, but then it could be the healer, medicine, and recoverer of the body if we eat the right things; and trouble to the body if we eat the wrong things and also at the wrong times. Foods contain a lot of accumulated chemical energy. When we eat, our body breaks down the foods into smaller elements and absorbs them to use as fuel. This energy is produced from the three main nutrients known as carbohydrates, protein, and fats, among which carbohydrates are the most important energy source.

In short, we either eat to build or destroy, heal, or sicken our bodies. God is the giver of longevity, but we also have a responsibility to eat the right things that can keep our physical bodies healthy. Unfortunately, sometimes we behave just like the joke a man of God who likes making people laugh told, and I paraphrase, "Let me have more cheese please; and when I die, I will die smiling." Sometimes, we know the right food to eat, but we just don't care enough to discipline ourselves in order to stay away from the wrong ones.

If we can understand and look at it seriously that every meal or drink we put in our mouth is either adding or subtracting from the days of our lives in this physical world, then it may help us do better with our eating habits. Remember that not everything that looks, smells, tastes, and feels good, is actually good or healthy for our body.

While we understand that some diseases are hereditary, many discoveries have confirmed that many of these diseases can also be prevented by just changing our diet or eating habits. Be wise with your diet.

Medications and Medical Procedures

I thank God for medicine and medical technology advancement. I hold the medical domain in high esteem. I highly respect their efforts to keep humanity safe, healthy, and sane. I pray God continues to bless them and give them more ability and capacity to discover and do more to help humanity.

This is not a medical advice. Please, always consult with your physician or professional healthcare provider for medical advice and decisions. However, as a reminder, any human invention, make, or creation is not perfect or fully safe. Medications and medical procedures have their side effects, and sometimes serious deterioration effects on the human body. This calls for personal alertness and wisdom about the use of some medications and medical procedures. The doctors are just doing their best job to save lives; but remember it's your body and your life, so be vigilant about medications and medical procedures, including even some supplements. Surely, your doctor or physician will prescribe them to you because he believes you need them. Use them when needed, but be careful and watch out for the side effects so you can notice the dangers before they kill or destroy your body or sanity one way or the other. Listen to the doctors, but listen to your body and God as well so that a medication or medical procedure that is supposed to make you feel better will not rather make you feel or end worse or dead.

The Temptation and Abuse of Sex

Sex is a creation of God, and He is not against you experiencing it. However, like any good thing, the abuse does cause spiritual, physical, and psychological destruction to the human spirit, soul, and body.

No matter how you deny this, it has been proven scientifically that sexual activities consume your energy. And when it comes to anything that consumes your energy, the abuse of it can be detrimental to your body in one way or another. The fact that your energy nurtures and powers your body's internal functions like fuel, anything that drains it constantly and quickly must be controlled, or your body will quickly age and be out of order sooner. Keep in mind that your energy also repairs, builds, and maintains cells and body tissues, and supports your physical or visible activities.

While you hear about all the benefits and reasons why it's good to have sex, experience and enjoy it, what you often don't hear are the side effects or consequences of an immoral and abusive sexual life.

Enjoy it with care – or it can kill you. There are many

stories of people who died either during or after sexual activities. And I have been close to some of these incidents. I remember how a prostitute or young lady was found dead, literally a few hours after sexual activities with men at a hotel where I stayed. It was a very sad incident.

The pleasurable and all-wanted sexual acts can also be dangerous if abused. Like anything else, too much sex does have a negative effect on the body. Sexual activity can be physically demanding and exhausting. Due to the release of certain endorphins that can have sedative effects during sexual acts, there may be drowsiness, dizziness, and confusion, problems with memory, depression, and anxiety, impaired attention and judgment.

While naturally it's believed that the increased level of your heart and respiratory rate, and blood pressure are slight and remain safe during sexual activities, these tensions on the body continuously in an abusive manner can become destructive and unhealthy even for a healthy person–not only for people with heart or Cardiovascular disease. The bottom line is, that sexual activities take a lot from your body and you should do your best to keep the balance or not abuse it. Even some experts have revealed that too much sex is not good for the body.

Ironically, people tend to believe that sexual acts are compared to physical exercise to some degree, doing it too much will not cause any harm to their body, which is a deep misunderstanding. How could you replace your physical exercise or the gym with your sexual activities?
Excessive sexual acts negatively affect your physical body. Too many sexual acts can drain your body and speed up your aging.

While it's believed that the aging process is impacted by

your diet or food, sensory perception, or the ability to understand and interact with the environment using your senses of sight, smell, hearing, taste, and touch, signals from the reproductive system or sex can also contribute to either longevity or termination.

In effect, scientists have confirmed that signals from sex organs can affect the aging rate of the body. Research by one of the trusted Universities in the United States revealed that excessive sex can influence the aging of your body badly. In other words, a balanced, or normal sexual life can increase your lifespan, while excessive or abusive sexual life can quicken the aging of your body.

Sex Is Not a Commodity

Sex is given to you by God to enjoy, but at the same time, it is sacred, and whether you believe it or not, anything sacred that you turn into profanity and use immorally becomes not only an offensive or disgusting practice, or lifestyle, but also a damnation.

Sex is also spiritual, and not only physical. When you turn sex into a commodity, product, or service, you are not only destroying your body, health, or physically, but psychologically and spiritually as well with the distress, depression, and demonic effects that follow as the consequences of misusing the gift of God to you that you should experience with morality.

> *"Sex is also spiritual, and not only physical. When you turn sex into a commodity, product, or service, you are not only destroying your body."*

Unfortunately, people in the sex industry keep lying to themselves and others that it's a safe and good practice to be sexually abusive and immoral.

If you take two cars, one is constantly being driven every day, all day, and against the recommendations of the manufacturer, and the other one is driven at a normal and recommended usage, which one will technically and logically have problems the most and ultimately be broken down sooner than later? Common sense would tell you and I that "the one being driven constantly without observing the manufacturer's recommendations will be out of order sooner."

The human body is an organism, skillfully and deliberately designed, arranged, and connected by God. When one organ is abused or misused, it affects all the other organs.
Many of the girls or individuals who end up in the sex industry are from poor families, or families who don't have a whole lot. Yes, there are, and maybe individuals from well-to-do families who can be sexually perverted, but they usually don't end up as pornographic individuals or pornstars as some may call it. Many of the girls or individuals who end up in that industry are after making themselves relevant, money, or getting rich. And obviously, that is what their recruiters tell them, "You will be famous and rich." "And have fun."

In effect, these girls put their lives into these immoral lifestyles hopping they will be famous and become rich, all while having fun. And of course, sex can be addictive, so they become addicted to sex as well. But the truth is, they realize they are destroying themselves at some point but cannot get out of it. They become slaves to their recruiters and the sex addicts. They honestly feel and look for a way out to live a normal life but feel it's impossible. They can't survive without it, but deep down in their souls, they cry out.

Poverty, needs, and desperation can pressure you to make the wrong decisions and take risks that will sooner or later destroy your life physically or spiritually. Remember, I mentioned earlier that many people are physically alive, but internally or spiritually, in their souls, and hearts, they are in deep pain, unrest, and peace is unreachable to them.

I remember the interview of a journalist who was doing a documentary with a young lady who was in the so-called "adult movie industry" on a national TV network. The journalist asked her, "So, how do you feel being in this industry?" Sadly, she replied, "I love sex, and I get paid to do what I love." The truth is, what she was completely ignoring was the spiritual, physical, and mental consequences of that lifestyle. When you get addicted to something, you want more of it, and the thought of getting it even in a dangerous and immoral way to feel better becomes a trap. The fact that you feel good and better temporarily while abusing something does not make it safe for you. You are actually destroying yourself morally, physically, psychologically, and spiritually. That is the reason you constantly feel like it is the only thing that can give you happiness, and always want more of it at any cost. The Bible says, **"People are slaves to whatever has mastered them."** (2 Peter 2:19, NKJV).

Everything that masters your life consequently controls your life, and everything that controls your life controls your happiness, and everything that controls your happiness holds your death and life because it has power over you.

Even if you deny the spiritual reality about sexual activities, science proves that during sexual acts, a stream of a hormone called oxytocin is released. This hormone is also released during and after childbirth, and plays a bonding role, which means it bonds the mother and the child. Now, just understanding the function and capacity of this hormone, proves that whoever you are having sexual activities with is being bonded or attached to you at some invisible level, which is spiritual and psychological. Imagine walking around all your life with the attachments of all the people you have sex with. It sounds unreal, but that's the truth, and is that you cannot be at peace with all those attachments. Think about the depression, mental, and emotional instability you may be experiencing, which are actually drawing you to do more of the same things that are leaving your body, mind, and soul broken, thinking they are healing and making you whole. No, instead, you are just digging yourself into the deep pit of unfulfillment; it will not stop until you identify or recognize that the main reason for your unfulfillment is because your soul and spirit are broken, and nothing physical, sex, food, money, material, and fabricated joy can heal that.

I don't mean to offend you, but I'm trying to help you understand some truths people will never tell to help you be free and have a purposeful and fulfilled life in this world. If all you can achieve as a woman in this world with your beauty is to sleep with multiple men, either for pleasure, money, position, job, degree, or access to something, you are wasting your life. And if you are a man, and all you can do is lure and sleep with as many women as you can, then you are useless.

Don't let your makeup lie to you. You may be dressed up nicely, but under that makeup is living a broken body, mind, heart, and soul because God never created you to sell your body as a product or service.

The passion for physical things does fade. Cars, clothing, homes, beauty, or appearance will fade away sooner or later. It may look like all eyes are on you now. But sooner or later, many or nobody will even have the pleasure to look at you twice. Your fulfillment is in fulfilling your purpose.

> *"Your fulfillment is in fulfilling your purpose."*

Money Is Not Everything

There is nothing wrong with having money, even in excess. We all get that good feeling when we know our bank account has enough to pay our bills or cover our needs, and when it is enough to spend and still have more left. But it does not include everything that can make you happy. Look around, and you may notice that some of the most miserable people in the world have a lot of money and materials.

Money is power, but just to some extent, it's not all-powerful. Money is power when it can buy things that can be bought. Money is something, but just to some extent, and it's only the things you can exchange it with or things it can be used for. In other words, there are things in life that money can never buy, or be replaced with. You may ask, "Aren't people who have money able to do and get everything they want?" The answer is no. If people who have a lot of money can get everything they want, then they will live forever, always be the happiest, and never get sick; and if they do, they can pay for all the cure at any cost. However, you may agree that some of the richest people in the world still don't have happiness. In fact, some of them are the most miserable people in the world because they don't have peace. And when they get sick, they can only buy medication for curable diseases.

Yes, money is good, and everybody should have some to be able to afford what they need and experience the relief and comfort it provides – but it's not everything. And if the only reason you want to be successful in life is to be a millionaire or billionaire and buy all that you want to satisfy your lust, greed, and ego, then you will regret it sooner or later. If the only reason you want to get rich is to be able to buy and get everything you want, then you will be miserable soon after. When you are chasing money, remember that it cannot replace your sanity, peace, lasting happiness, health, and spiritual state.

Make money genuinely, but keep the balance; do not chase money and forget about your humanity, health, peace of mind, and genuine happiness. The happiness the things you can buy can offer you is temporary, but genuine happiness comes from a peaceful soul, and a peaceful soul is the one connected to God, the God of peace, his creator, who is the source of life. The Bible says, *"What will it profit a man if he gains the whole world, yet forfeits his soul? Or what can a man give in exchange for his soul?"* (Matthew 16:26, BSB).

> *"Money is good — but it's not everything."*

Smiles and laughter are not always proof of happiness and may come from any source, including illegal drugs, hypocrisy, and personal denials or delusions. Real happiness comes from peace.

I understand all the motivation, psychology, and faith behind the saying, "Wear your smile." But it's also important that you understand the consequences of hiding all your pains behind fake happiness and smile, even to your loved ones -- it's spiritual or physical death.

Beware of Positional and Personal Powers, and Authoritarianism

You may have heard it several times, that someone is so powerful because of his position, wealth, talent, or social status. Even though there is a certain power that comes with holding a position of leadership or social class, you have to be careful and keep the balance because you will never be in that position forever, especially if it was given to you by men or you ascended there by force. Positional power is the kind of power you have when you have a specific position, class, or title in a community, country, world, or even an organization. This power comes with approved actions, behaviors, and rewards that you have to carefully watch out for.

Personal power can be the kind of power you have based on your natural and spiritual gifts, and these could be your skills, abilities, and anointing. This power is influential, attractive, and directional. It can impact others' beliefs, change their mind, and develop them into your image or being like you.

There is nothing wrong with positional and personal

power if they are used in a Godly and morally sound way. However, when they are misused, they become a weapon and dangerous not only to the people around you, but to yourself. Remember, while these powers come with good rewards, they also test your character, morality, and relationship with God.

> *"There is nothing wrong with positional and personal power — However, when they are misused, they become a weapon and — they also test your character."*

You surely know or heard of people who were so much respected and feared, but after some time, they lose that status because of their foolishness. Remember that the people you don't respect today can become just like you and be in your current position, and if you don't treat them well today, tomorrow they will not only disrespect you but not treat you also well. Remember that your class or position can change at any time, especially if you just use it for evil deeds, and someone else can also have your title sooner or later. Do not let positional and personal powers turn you into a monster against others because God can turn the table at any time.

    I remember a few years ago, there was a picture of a former African president who was driven out of his country by his own people who didn't like how he ascended to the presidency and the economic situation of the country eating at what looked like a roadside eatery in another country. It was sad to behold. I thought if anyone had told this man a few years earlier that he would find himself in a situation like that he would not have believed it.

The danger of personal and positional powers is that they can easily become authoritarianism, which is a lack of concern for the wishes or opinions of others. This simply leads to the disrespect and mistreatment of others from a place or position of power. Do not abuse your power by disrespecting and mistreating people under you in society, on your job, business, organization, family, or government. If you do, it will only backfire sooner or later by making a fool out of you. Remember, nothing is permanent in this life; things do change, including positions and conditions.

Authoritarianism is defined as "the enforcement or advocacy of strict obedience to authority at the expense of personal freedom." While this is only occasionally noticeable on a government level, it runs in individuals throughout our societies.

Do not disrespect people or be bossy because they need you now. It may be your turn one day to need their service or help one way or another – believe it or not, God is good at that.

While we all have to be mindful and respect people for their services and positions wherever we go, sometimes I go to places or travel and meet people in many places, including workplaces and services, who would be so much powered up by their position and be rude, talk and instruct you like you are a nobody, or you have to obey them or else you can't get what you want. Most of the time, I ignore these behaviors and gracefully manage the situations to diffuse their ego. However, sometimes, I do rebuke them when needed. And one of these situations was at a time when I arrived at a train station and had to add money to the transit card to exit. I went to talk to the man I assumed was the station's manager at the time, to go to the other side and add money to my card. This man started instructing me to do it the other way around, which was a waste of time. At least, I have been riding the train for a while to know how it should be done. So, I brought it to his attention that the procedure he was suggesting was the other way around. Then, he said in a stiff voice and raising his hands, "I can't help you if you don't want to listen to me." "Ok, tell me what to do," I said. And he made me go through a process that I could have simply done at one machine. In effect, when I finished and came back to swipe my card to pay for the exit, I was honest with him and said, "Sir, that was just a waste of time. I could have done everything from one machine." Then he replied in a disagreement manner, "That's a compliment, and we do take all compliments here." At that point, I firmly said back to him, "Sir, that was a waste of time," and walked away.

That incident brought to my memory many times I found myself in places, including even churches, where people would mistake and mistreat you because of their position. I do believe in respecting authorities and people in positions who are doing their job everywhere in societies or the world, just like the Bible admonishes us, "Everyone must submit to governing authorities." (Romans 13:1, NLT). However, if you are also the one in power or position, use it to serve people humbly, properly, and respectfully.

When you get positional or personal power, do not use it to satisfy your ego, oppress, or mistreat others; rather, use it to positively influence, love, develop, and be a blessing to others.

Beware of the Praises of Men

"The same people who said, "Hosanna" earlier, may later say "Crucify him." I would usually hear older Christians say this for one reason or the other.

Then I later understood it was actually indirectly taken from the Bible; specifically, referring to the fact that the same people who hailed the Lord Jesus as the King during His triumphant entry to Jerusalem from the Mount of Olives (Matthew 21:1-11), and shouted, "Hosanna to the Son of David!" "Blessed is He who comes in the name of the Lord!" "Hosanna in the highest!" (Matthew 16:26); are the same people who "cried, saying, Crucify him, crucify him" to Pilate. (Matthew 27:23).

I heard Evangelist Reinhard Bonnke say a few times, "I'm not impressed by the praises of men, just as I'm not worried about their criticism." In other words, you owe people an explanation for everything if you ride their praises, and you are at peace when they criticize you while you do not feed on their praises either.

It is a good thing for people to have a good report about you or your character, appreciate your contributions to their lives, and be grateful for your help, and the impact your natural, and spiritual gifts had on them. In effect, when it starts going beyond some limits, be the first to advise to stop the praise. After all, the glory belongs to God, the Lord of all. Throughout human and Biblical history, the praises of men and pride have been some of the primary causes of downfall for many leaders, men and women alike. The praise of men also contributed to the ungodliness of many, who never repented because they felt that the majority of the people supported their sinful behaviors or lifestyles.

Be careful, the praise of men can pollute and cloud your mind about truth and the will and plan of God. And also remember that the same people who are cheering you on today because you are feeding their emotions, telling them what they want to hear, and showing them what they want to see, may become the same people who will curse you later if all of the above cease. Many people will praise you for profit and curse you for loss. In effect, you have to mature to live and operate above the praises of men. In other words, do not let the praises of men cloud your understanding to get away from truth, honesty, humility, and godliness. If the whole world agrees with and praises you, but God hates you, you are in trouble, with an eternal rebuke and damnation, and will be miserable sooner or later, even in this world. But if the whole world hates you, but God loves you because you keep His precepts, then you are one of the blessed with an eternal reward.

> *"People will praise you for profits and curse you for losses."*

True leaders are humble. And as I mentioned earlier, there is a difference between leadership and administration. Even according to the Oxford Languages Dictionary, leadership is "the action of leading a group of people or an organization." And administration is "the process or activity of running a business, organization... Etc." There are people who are born and raised to be leaders and can also run the administration, but then there are people who cannot be and do both because they are only good at either one of them and not both. Both abilities can be learned, but I personally do believe that some people are naturally born leaders or administrators. When you are not both, but you try to take on both responsibilities, the family, business, organization, or government will collapse. Unnecessary problems arise when you are in a position that you do not belong to. True leaders who understand why they are in their position are humble, and crooks are not.

> *"True leaders who understand why they are in their position are humble, and crooks are not."*

Helping or Pleasing People

There is a difference between helping and pleasing people. While helping people may become pleasing to them, pleasing people may never become helping them. Helping people is meeting their needs, delivering them from their problems, and ultimately changing their lives for the better. Pleasing people may just be making them happy by giving them whatever they want, either out of lust, selfishness, greed, or bad judgment, but it is not needed or essential. Remember, there is also a difference between a need and a want.

> *"There is a difference between helping and pleasing people."*

When you are just trying to please people, it may turn into a problem and increase their appetite for what is not essential. It will drain, and destroy both the provider and receiver in the end.

Spirituality

There is no spirituality without God, and living in this world without understanding the spiritual world is a misery. Everything you see in the physical world is influenced, controlled, and manipulated by the spiritual world. And not every spiritual practice or religion will connect you to God. In fact, some will only connect you to demons who will later torment and destroy you and your descendants.
Life here on earth is spiritual, and only those who understand this reality can survive, thrive, and fulfill their purpose and destiny.

> *"Not every spiritual practice or religion will connect you to God."*

There are two forces or powers that influence the spiritual world: God and the devil. Unfortunately, with the lack of this understanding, people believe anything spiritual is connected to God. No, it's God and the angels at His service, or the devil and the demons at his service. Ultimately, God is the Almighty, Sovereign, and Lord of all. (Genesis 35:11; 2 Samuel 7:22). The devil only has a moment to try to take as many people as he can with him to hell, which is his final destination and dwelling place for disobeying God. (Revelation 20:10). And one of his strategies is to make you believe all things spiritual are connected to God, and every way leads to God. The Bible is clear on the way that leads to God, and you have to be careful, or else you would be fooled by the devil and his demons to believe all sort of spiritual practices lead to God.

May I remind you again that the spiritual world is divided into two, and not everything spiritual is connected to God. Note that the only harm-free or nonnegative consequential way to have access to God's spiritual world is through the Holy Spirit, who is the Spirit and power of God. Every other way you try to reach God spiritually apart from the Holy Spirit will result in serious bad consequences for you and your descendants. Why? Because the devil never fellowship with you for good reasons, and he does not give you anything without you not paying for it with your peace, blood, or life. That's why the Lord Jesus warned humanity by saying, ***"The thief (the devil) comes only to steal and kill and destroy; I have come that they may have life, and have it to the full."*** (John 10:10, NKJV).

The only way you can be introduced to the Holy Spirit is through Christ Jesus. Through the Lord Jesus, you have a connection to God through the Holy Spirit. The Lord declared, ***"I am the way, and the truth, and the life. No one comes to the Father except through me."*** (John 14:6, NLV). God has made Christ Jesus Lord of all, and the Way to connect to Him through the Holy Spirit. (Acts 10:36; Romans 10:12).

Beware. Note that there are many spiritual practices or things that one may do that open the door to demons or evil spirits to enter your life to oppress and possess you and your descendants. When you compromise the state of your humanity with the consultation of demons knowingly and unknowingly, magic, and witchcraft… Etc., it will lead you into spiritual bondage; in other words, you become a slave to the devil and his demons.

If you want peace, advice, and power, turn to Christ Jesus, and connect to God through the Holy Spirit. For the Bible says, *"The government will be on his shoulders. And he will be called Wonderful Counselor, Mighty God, Everlasting Father, Prince of Peace."* (Isaiah 9:6, NIVUK). If you want to be successful, turn to God through Christ Jesus, He made Joseph successful. The Bible says, *"The Lord was with Joseph and gave him success in whatever he did."* (Genesis 39:23, NKJV).

All you need to do or prioritize in your life is submission or obedience to God, and He will lead and provide you with all you need and make you who He created you to be, and what he sent you here in this world to do. The Bible says, *"Be strong and very courageous. Be careful to obey all the law my servant Moses gave you; do not turn from it to the right or to the left, that you may be successful wherever you go."* (Joshua 1:7, NIV).

Fasting and Prayer

This is not an advocacy for spiritual laziness. However, even as a Christian, you surely need to do your best to keep the balance with the practices the Bible recommends for your spiritual growth, and power or authority. For instance, when you are fasting, be careful to observe common sense measures before, during, and after the fast. Short-term fast does not necessarily need preparation, but when you want to fast for a long time, you must prepare that. For example, finding or staying in a clean place, gradually adjusting your food to vegetables and light foods, drinking much water, and if you are taking a supplement vitamin, or medication for health reasons, you have to think about how to deal with that as well during the fast. This is not a lack of faith, but if you have that type of faith, do so accordingly. In short, you have to prepare yourself and your body for the long-term fast. And what you eat to break or after your fast is also important for your health.

Fasting is important for your spiritual growth or maturity and is a must if you really want to subdue or discipline your flesh to be a prayerful and spiritual person. However, do not fast like a fool. Unless it's a direct order from the Lord to you, make sure that you are fasting at a location where help can get to you as soon as possible if something goes wrong with you. Growing up as a young Christian, it was wonderful for me to go to the bush or isolated places to pray or fast, and I liked that. But I have also learned that even if you want to isolate yourself to pray and fast, it's wise to go to secure or danger-free places unless the Lord specifically asks you to go or come to a specific location, as He told Moses. (Exodus 24:12-15).

Ensure that you break your fast with the right foods. I know and have learned of people who ended up with ulcers or other stomach diseases because they were not breaking their fast with the proper foods. I have also learned about a brother who broke his seven (7) days and nights fast with bread and had to be rushed to the hospital, where he was put on IV fluids or specially formulated liquids that were injected into his vein to prevent or treat dehydration.
There were people who went to the mountains or remote locations such as forests, and some things happened to them that could have been prevented if they were in places where help could have gotten to them quickly or as soon as possible. We may say, surely they went to be with the Lord, but would it not be a good thing if they were still in this world to do more for the Lord over here? Even if you plan

to go to remote places to fast, you have to plan and equip yourself very well with anything you think you will need. Nevertheless, do not be lazy in fasting because you need it to discipline or subdue your flesh and grow spiritually. There are even physical benefits in fasting that I may not be able to elaborate here. But the Bible says if you fast the right way, *"You will call, and the Lord will answer; you will cry for help, and he will say: Here am I."* (Isaiah 58:9, NIV). Fast, but fast wisely.

Work and Life

Working is good and should be commended. The Bible requests that everybody should work. However, work wisely to avoid killing yourself gradually.

You cannot be lazy and expect a good and successful life. The Bible says, *"The one who is unwilling to work shall not eat."* (2 Thessalonians 3:10, NIV).

A healthy or non-disabled human being who does not work, is not respecting and honoring himself. This will lead you to dishonesty, cheating, and stealing, which will destroy your life sooner or later. We live in a world today where people want to be successful, but they do not want to work, they do not want to pay the price for success. However, working also does not mean you have to overwork and oppress your body and destroy your health. Take good care of yourself while you work. Take breaks and rest well. Keep the balance in your workforce and schedule. You have to be in good health to appreciate and enjoy the results of your hard work, anything you do for a living, or building something, whether it's a dream, project, business, organization, or ministry. So be mindful of your health, family, and relationships or people you love while working to fulfill your purpose and destiny.

> ## *"We live in a world today where people want to be successful, but they do not want to work, they do not want to pay the price for success."*

The Bible says, *"So on the seventh day he (God) rested from all his work."* (Genesis 2:2). Later, the Lord enforced this principle to the children of Israel, not only for its spiritual meaning, but for their physical rest as well. We read, *"Remember the Sabbath day by keeping it holy."* (Exodus 20:8-11, NIVUK). Sabbath simply means a day of observance and abstinence from work. Keep the balance in your workforce, and make sure you get a break otherwise, you will break your health.

When the Lord was on earth in the flesh, His lifestyle reflected how we are supposed to live in this world, and one of the things He taught us was to rest. He was also subject to tiredness as the Bible noted, *"Jacob's well was there, and Jesus, tired as he was from the journey, sat down by the well. It was about noon."* (John 4: 6, NIV). And on another occasion, the Bible mentioned that He was sleeping, and we read, *"Jesus was inside the boat, sleeping with his head on a pillow…"* (Mark 4: 38, ERV). The lesson here is that we have to observe moments of work abstinence and get some rest.

Sometimes, you may be carried away by the demands and excitements emanating from your career, business, or ministry. And you have to use wisdom to keep the balance, not to be lazy, but to get some rest. In the past and present, even several ministers or pastors have succumbed to unrest, which at some point starts to take a toll on them and eventually breaks their health. Even as a minister, you have to learn and practice rest. God wants you to have longevity here on earth to do more for the kingdom of God on earth. Take care of yourself through good rest, diet, and exercise.

> *"You have to use wisdom to keep the balance, not to be lazy, but to get some rest."*

The Good and Bad Stress

Too much of any stress is not good for a human being. However, wisdom requires that you wisely choose good stress, the balanced stress that can occur when you are doing the right thing. When you're working on a good project, building a family, career, or business, doing God's will, helping people, and making the world a better place. All this can cause you a level of stress, but you have to do your best to keep the balance and avoid that stress becoming destructive to your mental stability and overall health.

Bad stress is the stress that you unwisely undergo because of your unwise choices or decisions. And this could be avoided by just saying "no" to some things or people. You would rather say "no" sooner, but if you missed the point or mark in the beginning but later realized that it was not a wise decision, you would rather change your "yes" to "no" as soon as possible; Godly, respectfully, peacefully, and graciously than letting it kill you spiritually, mentally or physically sooner or later.

Unnecessary Changes

This is not to say you should not work or strive for better conditions or things in your life, or not to get out of perilous situations. But one of the truths about life in this realm is that you will always want "another one," "the new one," and "more." You may either get used, bored, or unsatisfied with what you already have because of "the other one." But keep in mind that the urge to want "another one," "the new one," or "more" does not go away as long as you live in this world, and you have to control it at some point. Remember, sooner or later, you will surely be used, bored, and unsatisfied with whatever you feel and call the "new one" and that you want to get at all costs right now.

Understand that one of the laws of the physical world you live in is that "the new" will become "the old" sooner or later. The new clothes, shoes, car, phone, house, woman (wife), and man (husband) will become "the old" sooner or later. So, you must learn how to consider, create/make, appreciate, and keep what you have now as "the new" continuously. The temptation to be attracted to the look or beauty of another woman, man, cloth, shoe, bag, car, house, or even devices and appliances, will be there, but remember that sooner or later, they will all become "the old one (s)" as well. In effect, avoid changing your mind and heart for unnecessary reasons, temporary gratifications, and ungodly things that do not possess substance.

> *"One of the laws of the physical world you live in is that "the new" will become "the old" sooner or later."*

Before you change your mind, heart, or decision about something, make sure it's either in obedience to God, or God told you to do so, your safety or security, peace, health, purpose, and destiny. If you change your mind, or decision just because of the look/beauty, money, or materials, you will regret it sooner or later.

While there are things you may change in your life for convenience, there are also things you cannot change because you don't feel like keeping them anymore. Some of these people or things are may be your God-ordained secret weapons, spiritually and physically, that you are not even aware of. So, your survival depends on them one way or another, whether you realize it or not, and these may include your wife, husband, friend, or business or work partner.

One of the mistakes you can make in life is thinking that just because you have something someone else does not have means they are the only ones who need you, and you do not need them, so they are replaceable. Think again, you are lying to yourself. Even the most common or lowest person in this world can be a part of your life's puzzle, whether rich or poor, intelligent or not intelligent, gifted or not gifted like you, or with the same gifts. Everybody in this world is divinely gifted in one thing or the other. And God brings them in your life to be part of the puzzle. So, do not replace them unless you are sure they are a problem and not a solution to your purpose and destiny.

> *"While there are things you may change in your life for convenience, there are also things you cannot."*

Sometimes, you may just be trying to replace people in your life because of your selfishness, or something that only satisfies or benefits you, so think twice, be honest with yourself, or be realistic about your decisions of replacing people and things.

The old saying stands, "If it's not broken, don't fix it." But also, what you think is broken might not really be broken, but it's not just what you are feeling. Just because you feel like something is broken or not the way you want it does not mean it's broken, it might even be working at its best at that very moment. For instance, just because you feel like a car or TV is not working might not necessarily be that it's not working, but maybe you are using it the wrong way. So make sure your decision comes from good reasoning or judgment and confirmation, and not just your feelings.

One of the reasons even married people get to some point in their marriage and feel like they need someone new, their first love or feelings have disappeared is because there is no purpose in the marriage. Everything you do and have in this world that has no purpose in it will devalue in your heart, and mind, and will get to your feelings. But if there is purpose in your marriage, then you understand that it's not all about your feelings and the pleasures that you can get out of the marriage; but there is a higher cause that brought you both together. Believe it or not, even if you leave to marry someone else, that time will catch up with you again. After some time, the good feelings about that next person will soon also run out.

Even if you are all by yourself, there are times you will wake up and not feel and want to talk. Do you separate or divorce yourself from "yourself'? No. You take coffee, a good shower, do some physical exercise, or do whatever you think can give you that "wing" or motivation as we say. However, when that odd feeling is about your loved ones, wife, husband, children, relatives, or other people, you immediately think is because you do not love them anymore. Really?

Listen, no matter how deeply you love someone, there will be moments when you will not have any feelings for them. You will wake up and feel like everything around you is an object – no feelings. It's human and natural. It will be like, "Do I know you somewhere?"

You cannot separate love from morality, right or wrong. And whenever you try that, the result will be regretted. God created love and sex and gave us moral laws to guide them or make them safe, so if you ignore the moral laws, they will destroy you.

The Wrong People at the Right Places

Your life is an entity with many positions. And until you understand that God granted you the grace or ability to run your life by the guidance of His precepts, and Spirit, and you must place the right people at the right places in your life, you will keep blaming people for doing you wrong and walking down the road of deep pain with regrets in your soul.

This is not to say that people don't mistreat you, but one of the reasons some people are able to wrong you is that you put them in the wrong places or positions in your life and misplaced your trust and expectations. In other words, you have given them the opportunity to wrong you – and sadly, maybe repeatedly.

> *"The reasons some people are able to wrong you is that you put them in the wrong places or positions in your life and misplaced your trust and expectations."*

Love all people, but mature and know where to place who in your life. Do not even successful business and leadership rules teach us to put the right employees in the right positions? God might not be responsible for many of your pains, but you with the wrong choices or decisions.

There are people in your life that God doesn't give you the opportunity to choose, such as your biological parents and relatives. But He does give you the choice of people such as your husband or wife, friends, business partners, neighbors, and so forth. It's your responsibility to choose the right people who can contribute the best to your life one way or the other. The accomplishment of the purpose and destiny God has ordained you for is ultimately influenced by the people you allow into the circle of your life.

You will cross paths with many people in life. Some of them are to be your acquaintances, friends, partners in business, teammates, co-workers, bosses, supporters, customers, or ministry partners. In effect, understand that someone who is ordained by God to be any of the above in your life cannot be your husband or wife, and vice versa. For instance, someone who is to be your husband or wife cannot remain your friend; or someone who is to be your friend by God's plan, cannot become your husband or wife because that relationship will not work. It's vital to pray and be sober and disciplined so that you will not misplace any of them, otherwise, it will cause disruptions, troubles, or bad redirections in your life and toward your purpose and destiny. Make sure you do not misplace them in the various places or areas in your life.

Failed Expectations

Do not force things when they do not happen the way you expected. Fight for the best and what you deserve the best way you can. However, keep in mind that forcing what is not supposed to be can only destroy you sooner or later. Many times, God protects you from things that you don't know and will not know until several days, weeks, months, or years later before you may find out or know. Sometimes, things will run differently than you have imagined, planned, and expected. The truth about life in this world is that not everything you want, in a certain manner, time, and place will come true. God's will and plan will surely override yours; especially if you desire to obey and serve Him, and fulfill your purpose and destiny. You must understand that many times, even though you might not realize it immediately, your failed expectations are actually your blessings because they could deprive you of real happiness, peace, and ultimately, the fulfillment of your God-given purpose and destiny.

The One-Way Pilots

Throughout your life, some of the many people you will cross paths with are one-way pilots — and if you are not careful, their evil and selfish hearts can cause serious damage to your purpose, destiny, peace, happiness, security, stability, and longevity.

So, how do you recognize the one-way pilots in your life?

September 11, 2001, or Nine Eleven (9/11) as we know it, is one of the worst days in American history when 2,977 precious people lost their lives to a senseless attack. Many analysts compared the dark day to December 7th, 1941, when Imperial Japan launched an aerial attack against the US Pacific fleet at Pearl Harbor in Hawaii. This ultimately led the United States into World War II.

The concurrence of the two events is based on two realities as noted, the historical similarity, and figurative effect. But can we also learn some lessons that we can apply to our personal lives?

According to Special Reports about the tragedy released publicly by authorities, the flight school that one of the attackers was attending reported to authorities that, and I quote, "They considered it odd that (he) said that all he wanted to learn was how to take off and land."

In effect, there was this guy in a flight school, and all he ever wanted to learn was "how to take off and land." He literally didn't have any interest in learning anything else between takeoff and landing. This really describes and reveals his intentions materialized on the day of the attack — he actually didn't have any interest in landing either, all he wanted to know was how to take off and run the aircraft into a building.

To minimize being fooled, when people cross paths with you in life, pay attention to their speech and actions, as well as the words they use when you talk to them – do they talk about the future? Or can you see them in your future? This is very important, and if you mislead yourself about these signs, you will be surprised that they never planned to have a lasting friendship, romantic, business, successful relationship, or a legacy or accomplish any good thing with you. How can you detect this kind of people? First, check their interest. What are they interested in knowing the most, even about you, what you have, and what you are doing? Do they care about what happens in between? Are they concerned about the risks, challenges, and most importantly, the consequences of the failure of things, or going in the wrong direction? "One-way pilot" people never care about the process of things, and the consequences of their bad decisions, unsuccessful operations, or whatever. They care less about you, how you feel, your purpose and destiny, but their own interest and gratifications.

The Dangers of Nature

God has given us nature to enjoy, including forests, mountains, rivers, oceans, and animals. However, we should also note that nature is a force to be recognized and keep a balance with, otherwise, you will be hurt senselessly by it. And unless for well-planned and organized research or scientific purposes, stay away from the dangerous forests, mountains, rivers, oceans, and animals.

We are not in the Garden of Eden or Paradise right now, where and when animals, including the dangerous ones, lived with men (Adam and Eve). (Genesis chapters 1-3). So, until the New Jerusalem described in the book of Revelation chapter twenty (21), where things will return to the original plan of God, stay away from dangerous animals, and do not keep them in your dwelling place as pets. As beautiful as they may seem, remember they are animals, and sooner or later, they may act just as what they are and can harm you.

Some people would say that as long as you treat and handle them well, they will not harm you. But the truth is, many professionals and experienced nature and animal handlers have been hurt because no matter how you know the tricks to handle them, a time will come when you will ignore or forget about these tricks and it will result in your injury.

Amusement and Entertainment

Doing or experiencing something fun, and entertaining is good for your well-being, but when the means of amusement, and entertainment are not safe, that's foolishness. Honestly, I do not think the only way you can create, have fun, and be entertained is by doing it dangerously. You can ride your boat in safe waters, you don't have to take your boat to the deepest oceans for fun or fishing; fishing ships are meant for that. You can still fish in safe waters. You don't have to ride or take your children to ride some dangerous systems, machines, or devices, carnival rides in an amusement park somewhere in the pursuit of happiness and making memories.

> *"When the means of amusement, and entertainment are not safe, that's foolishness."*

While accidents can happen with and in anything, even the safest, it's not wise to take too much risk in the pursuit of amusement and entertainment. Your life in this world is already exposed to too many dangers. Why should you take risks even in amusement or entertainment? These mechanical apparatuses are dangerous no matter what safety measures are set in place. I wonder why parents can take their children to some of these parks to ride these dangerous machines to have fun. Are there any other ways to create fun and entertaining memories with your children other than riding dangerous machines? Some parents may say it teaches the children courage. That's foolishness. Do you want your child to die before becoming courageous? There are too many better ways to teach your child courage or boldness.

Listen, Watch, Evaluate, and Be Honest With Yourself

Sometimes, it's difficult to know when you are out of balance, so it will take other people and circumstances to remind you of how out of balance you are at a certain point. In effect, it's advisable to keep your ears, eyes, and understanding open in order to listen, evaluate, and be honest with yourself to avoid your complete destruction.

Moses was out of balance and nearly killed himself by doing too much, but God never directly told him or sent an angel to tell him until he listened to his father-in-law. The Bible says, "Jethro saw Moses judging the people. He asked, "Why are you doing this? Why are you the only judge? And why do people come to you all day?"

Then Moses said to his father-in-law, "The people come to me and ask me to ask for God's decision for their problem. If people have an argument, they come to me, and I decide which person is right. In this way, I teach the people

God's laws and teachings."

But Moses' father-in-law said to him, "This isn't the right way to do this. It is too much work for you to do alone. You cannot do this job by yourself. It wears you out. And it makes the people tired too. Now, listen to me. Let me give you some advice. And I pray God will be with you. You should continue listening to the problems of the people. And you should continue to speak to God about these things. You should explain God's laws and teachings to the people. Warn them not to break the laws. Tell them the right way to live and what they should do. But you should also choose some of the people to be judges and leaders.

"Choose good men you can trust—men who respect God. Choose men who will not change their decisions for money. Make these men rulers over the people. There should be rulers over 1000 people, 100 people, 50 people, and even over ten people. Let these rulers judge the people. If there is a very important case, then they can come to you and let you decide what to do. But they can decide the other cases themselves. In this way these men will share your work with you, and it will be easier for you to lead the people. If you do this as God directs you, then you will be able to do your job without tiring yourself out. And the people can still have all their problems solved before they return home."

So Moses did what Jethro told him. Moses chose good men from among the Israelites. He made them leaders over the people. There were rulers over 1000 people, 100 people, 50 people, and ten people. These rulers were judges for the people. The people could always bring their arguments to these rulers, and Moses had to decide only the most important cases." (Exodus 18:14-24, ERV).

As mentioned earlier, you may not always get it right, or make the right decisions and do the right things all the time as a human. Things can go wrong, but if you are willing, can listen, pay attention, and seriously evaluate your steps, you may correct things before they get worse.

Love, Dating, Relationship, and Marriage

Let me start by saying that too much weight on any side of a ship can cause it to sink. This is also true for relationships, when you focus too much on one thing while going into a relationship, it will sink. And if you do not focus on anything at all, that also will sink it. So what do you do? Keep the balance.

The trap in relationships for men is beauty or physical appearance, and for women, is money and material things. You don't need the best or perfect woman or man, and will not find one – that person does not exist. The person you need is a woman or man who is willing and doing the best possible and whom you can support to become his/her best version spiritually, purposefully, physically, financially, and materially. Remember, whatever you invest in one way or another naturally becomes one of the most precious things in your life. However, it's important that both of you have a similar understanding of God, moral values, and purpose, or the things that matter in life.

> *"The trap in relationships for men is beauty or physical appearance, and for women, is money and material things."*

It's dangerous to undertake a relationship established on conditional love and selfish interest – the moment the condition is no longer met or the interest ceases, the relationship dies.

For instance, if you can only love someone when they lose weight, then what happens when they gain the weight back? This is not an endorsement for obesity. However, when someone's love for you is only established on provisional things, it will not last. And if you are the one interested, and you know that your love for the person is only rooted in temporary things, then do not engage in that relationship because appearance and the human body will surely change.

Stop losing weight for someone to fall in love with you and start losing weight to stay healthy. I'm dismayed to see women at the gym just trying to lose weight because they want their husbands or boyfriends to fall in love with them. I believe in staying healthy, whereby you may not even need healing; part of it is to eat and live right, including physical exercise and sleep. But if your goal is to lose weight for a man to fall in love with you – and in most cases, even a man who will not spend the rest of his life with you, then you are a prisoner or slave to an idea that is not true. If a man cannot love you, thin or big, then it's dangerous for you as a woman to try to lose weight for him to love you. Think about what will happen when you start getting older and cannot lift or do all the things you can do now in the gym. Do your best to stay healthy, including exercising. But stop doing it with the idea that you must do it for a man to love you. You are more than just a body – your power as a woman also resides in your heart for God, purpose, intelligence, knowledge, wisdom, ability, capacity, and kindness in various ways. Many of these guys wanting ladies to kill themselves in the gym to have the so-called sexy body for them are walking around themselves with big bellies.

> *"It's dangerous to undertake a relationship established on conditional love and selfish interest – the moment the condition is no longer met or the interest ceases, the relationship dies."*

The idea that even God-fearing people nowadays have adapted to the vain games of before and during romantic relationships is really unbelievable, and we can see the negative results all over. The world's views and understanding of relationships are based on want, need, lust, gain – just selfishness. And whether you believe it or not, everything humans do that is mainly focused on gain as the primary goal is destructive.

When you are entering into a relationship or want to be with someone, and the main focus is all about what you will gain from it, not purpose and substance, you are setting yourself up for destruction and unhappiness. Why? Because nothing in this world is permanent, things do change, and even if it lasts for over a hundred (100) years, it's still temporary. And if the only things drawing your attention towards someone are beauty (physical appearance), money, materials, and position, you are setting yourself up for heartbreak, disrespect, misery, unhappiness, and dishonor.

> *"The world's views and understanding of relationships are based on want, need, lust, gain – just selfishness."*

Ungodly people know exactly what a woman or man wants to see, hear, and know to say "yes" to a relationship, a man or woman. So they will do everything to present themselves to you as the man or woman you are looking for, or as it goes, "The catch." I wonder how many times you have already caught bad fish thinking they were "The catch"? Funny, but not funny, right?

We usually equate some of life's essentials to the ocean, but what we forget is that the ocean not only has good things, but terrifying things or beings that can horrify you, and make your breath stop. There are beings in the oceans that will make you repeatedly ask, "What's that?"

"There are plenty of fish in the ocean," you say when it comes to finding a spouse. But let me remind you, not all of them are good fish. In fact, some of them are monster fishes. Did you read that? Yes, not only are they bad fish, but monster fish. So be careful while you are out there trying to find your wife or husband.

> *"Ungodly people know exactly what a woman or man wants to see, hear, and know to say "yes" to a relationship, a man or woman."*

Some men are out there only looking for another woman to add to their list of women they were able to sleep with. Then, after they get you, sleep with you, and use you as much as they can and are satisfied, they will throw you away and move on to the next woman because they have nothing to lose anyway. Therefore, as an unwise woman, you literally become a sex object for some men.

It amazes me how many women keep making the same mistake of falling for the tricks of men who are just out there to fool and sleep with them and throw them away as disposable items. I say jokingly, yet seriously that "These men just read books like 'How to Easily Get Any Woman You Want'" and use these tactics to play mind games with vulnerable and weak women, or the women who just want to have any type of man in their lives or pursue men for money and materials.

A lady once said, "I don't know why I only attract and end up with the wrong men?" The answer is simple: You have a choice, and you are the one choosing the wrong men for the wrong reasons, just like men who also chose the wrong women for the wrong reasons. When you are a woman, and all you are looking for in a man are money, materials, sex, and someone you can just call "a man" in your life, you will be vulnerable and fall prey to ungodly and immoral men.

> *"It amazes me how many women keep making the same mistake of falling for the tricks of men who are just out there to fool and sleep with them and throw them away as disposable items."*

A lady once posted on her social media page that she doesn't date "men who can't provide." That sounds like a smart statement, but honestly, there is a difference between a man who can't provide for a woman and a man who doesn't want to provide for a woman. What am I trying to say? We are in a world where people, including men and women, are valued, accepted, and respected based on what they look like, have, and can provide, more than their character. Rarely would you hear a woman or man mention good character and morals as the attributes they would like to see or know their spouse to have. No wonder the majority of relationships are broken.

One time on a TV show, I heard someone say, "I tell my daughter not to date a man with a job, but a man with a career." This advice sounds smart to the ordinary person. But in truth, a father advising his daughter like this may be setting her up for a lifetime of misery, believe it or not. I'm not saying as a father, you should not wish your daughter the best, but our world is fast-tracking towards fame, money, and materials more than peace, real happiness, purpose and destiny, and healthy relationships. Money and materials are good, but when you start placing them above everything else, you will never experience true happiness and peace.

I'm not saying you should marry someone who doesn't want to do anything meaningful in life. In fact, you should want to marry someone who understands and has a good vision for life, someone who wants to be fruitful and fulfill purpose and destiny, someone who wants to achieve good things for his wife and children or family and be successful. However, understand that money, materials, and social status do not necessarily indicate success in life. What you want to focus on among others like the person's relationship with God, family, and other people is the character, the desire, and vision to work and accomplish that vision, purpose, and destiny, and surely, money and materials will indispensably come or follow sooner or later.

Seldom will you see someone with a vision in life, but who doesn't have enough in the present and will not have it in the future as long as God permits and grants him longevity and strength. The poor man or woman today can become rich tomorrow. The one who doesn't have enough today can have more than enough tomorrow as long as the latter has a vision and the desire to pursue and work to bring it to fruition.

Don't marry someone for money or material things and end up unpeaceful and unhappy.

Marriage or romantic relationships are not supposed to be your primary way out or source of physical, financial, and material needs. These may become an add-on to your relationship, but they should not be the main reason you want to be in a relationship or marry someone. And if you do, you will regret that. If you can have everything in a relationship, but peace, you will be miserable, and your life will be a pit of flowers with sorrow. You will not be happy.

There is a difference between a broke person who doesn't have money, vision, and the desire to work and accomplish his dreams and goals of prosperity, and someone who does. And I encourage you to choose a Godly person with good character and morals who has a vision for life and the desire to work and fulfill it over someone who has money, but with a bad character and morals. A good person with a vision for life will one day realize it and become the person of your dreams or expectations. Money, materials, and position don't necessarily make someone a good or the right person in your life, and this is true even when it comes to the person you want to marry or spend the rest of your life with.

> *"A good person with a vision for life will one day realize it and become the person of your dreams or expectations."*

Some women are also out there looking for a man who will take them on a vacation, and buy them the next thing they desire. Unfortunately, both sides are caught up in a foolery circle playing with each other, not knowing that the other person also has an agenda.

Obviously, some women also don't want to build the life they want with a man who has vision and is in the process of building and owning it with him; rather, they want a man who has it all together, and all they will do is enjoy it. This idea is poisonous for so many reasons I can't elaborate on all of them here.

I remark and advise women on this now and then: Realistic and successful men usually are not interested in marrying beautiful women with no substance or competence, but they do fool with them as a side benefit and throw them away. Most successful men only marry women with substance and purpose, then fool with the beautiful ones who think their beauty is everything to attract and keep a man, but don't have any substance. So, if you are a woman, watch out for the type of men you desire because some of them never plan to marry you. They want to marry a woman who has the ability and capacity to help them maintain and continue to grow their hard-earned riches. And if you are their side benefit or girl, they don't mind buying you a few bags, and shoes, and maybe taking you on a vacation, but marriage will never be one of the things to expect from them.

> *"Realistic and successful men usually are not interested in marrying beautiful women with no substance or competence, but they do fool with them as a side benefit and throw them away."*

We should also understand that there is a difference between someone who has a relationship with God, and an individual who has a relationship with a church, ministry, or organization. The person who has a personal relationship with God tries to develop and exercise Godly values and morals in everything he does, including relations, and notably, in his romantic relationship as well. However, a person who just has a relationship with a church or organization may pay tithes, support church and missions projects, pray, and fast like anyone else, but may develop and have a bad character, even in a romantic relationship, and that's why even marrying a preacher or pastor is not a guarantee for a successful marriage. Always look for character, character, and character as well.

It becomes concerning when one side is serious and looking for a real-life partner, and this may be the man or woman. And if you are that serious man or woman, you have to be wise to avoid being fooled.

The Difference Between What You Need and Want

FOOLISHNESS | Keeping the Balance

Understand this, when you get all that you want, including your preferences, but what you need is missing, you can never be fulfilled and happy. However, when you get what you need, but what you want and prefer is missing, you can do well without it, have peace, and be happy. This is true with all the important or necessary things in life, including your career, relationship, or marriage.

Do not let your preferences override what is right for you. Sometimes what is your preference might not be what you need or is right for you. And things that are not the right ones for you can lead your life into pain, and unrest.

Don't let your beauty or handsomeness take the best from you. What your body looks like right now will not be in the next five or ten years. So if you are a woman or man, it's wise to accept a good spouse when he comes around because the same person may look at you a few years down the road and may not even be interested in you anymore. You may not look like that attractive lady or man a few years back.

Sometimes, God will give you a package fully loaded with everything you need spiritually, physically, psychologically, financially, and materially, including everything you want. But sometimes, He can also give you a package with only what you need (This is not just physical things) because He knows what you really need, and knows you better than yourself. And sometimes, you will find yourself between a package that has only what you need, and another package that has what you want, and you can only choose one. In this case, choose wisely the package that has what you need, and let go of the one that has what you want. Why? Because the package that has what you need will meet your needs at every level sooner or later. But the package with only what you want may not meet your needs no matter how you tweak or manipulate it and wish it changes for the better.

> *"Do not let your preferences override what is right for you."*

Keep the balance when looking for a spouse, or even when you are already married. Remember that everything that glitters is not gold. Thank God if your potential spouse is everything you ever needed and wanted. However, if the person is who you need spiritually, emotionally, and morally, or at every necessary level, choose that one over who you want just to satisfy your physical lust or fantasy, but doesn't have the true substance you need to be fruitful, and happy in life. Money and beauty are not everything; only God is, so choose God and character over money and beauty if you do not find all of them in someone. And guess what? It's difficult or rare to find all of them at once in a person.

    Look at it this way, no matter what the person looks like, has, or can do, you will only experience that in a short time, even if it's for a hundred (100) years. For example, if the person can just give you what you want and when you want it, including sex, money, or even show off talents, pray, preach, or sing, it's always for a short time. But you will live and experience the person's character more often, all day, week, month, year, and lifetime. So what is it good for?

    Don't be caught up in the image of what you're looking for to the extent that you miss the essence or substance of what you need. It's easy to miss what you need by focusing too much on what you think it should look and feel like. Not everything that you need and are looking for will look like it. Sometimes, what you need and are looking for can be right in front of you, and you will miss it because it doesn't look like it.

God designed and created our senses so that we could enjoy life with them even here on earth morally. However, the devil tries to use them to his advantage by seducing us into dangerous desires and lifestyles that can destroy our lives and render us miserable in the process.

I should also remind you that if you do not like what you are hearing, seeing, and experiencing while getting to know someone as a potential spouse, do not sign up for it expecting the person will change. Expecting people to change is a wish or hope that may never come true. This is a dream that may never come to pass. Generally, people do get better, but not completely changed. It takes a miracle working of God for a person to completely change from a bad character, behavior, and lifestyle to the right or good one. So don't bet on a wish or hope that someone's character and morals will change unless you know you are strongly convinced otherwise.

The Pursuit and Playing Hard to Get

While both things, principles and tricks cannot elude improvement, one always has a short-term or life cycle, and that is the trick. Tricks are built or constructed out of thoughts, and do not produce lasting results. Principles are revealed or found, and do not lose their effectiveness after years, even though they can be improved. And one of the reasons you must choose to accomplish things with or by principles instead of tricks is that a trick, cunning, or deceitful way of doing things does not build lasting foundations — it fades away. But principles, which are fundamental truths that serve as the foundation for a system of belief, behavior, and a connected series of thinking about something in a logical way or reasoning just get better, and better over time.

> *"Tricks are built or constructed out of thoughts, and do not produce lasting results."*

If someone is pursuing you so hard, inviting you to date, buying you flowers, and gifting you materials and money regularly, and you think these are signs that the person is a great person and really loves and wants you, excuse me to say, you are delusional. Note that there is nothing wrong with showing love with flowers and materials, but if that's all you see and know as a confirmation or sign that someone really loves you, then you need to do more homework.

Ladies, note, there is a difference between someone who wants you for a given time to fool with your body and someone who wants to spend the rest of his life with you, love, honor, and cherish you. Ungodly men know exactly what women want to hear, see, and feel in order to lay down their guards and surrender to them. A man pursuing you does not necessarily mean he really loves you and wants to spend the rest of his life with you. He may just want to get you to prove to you that you are not beyond his reach just like the other women he already fooled with and walked away satisfied.

Remember this, every man or woman you get by psychology "mind and behavior games," will leave you sooner or later the same way.

> *"Every man or woman you get by psychology "mind and behavior games," will leave you sooner or later the same way."*

Knowing whether someone is the right person for you takes serious communication, questions and answers, observation, and time, not "measuring interest with pursuit" and "playing hard to get."

Why are you convinced he's the right person just because he's pursuing you? Anyone can really be interested in you, but does that mean they really want to be with you? You think the only way to know if a man really loves you is how hard he pursues you? No. It is time for you to wake up, ladies, and throw away those psychological and manipulative relationship books. Listen, as a man and a minister, I have observed and witnessed the beginning and the end of so many relationships. I have also listened to so many men and women, including the ones who do not really live or have devoted their lives to honor God in many ways, I mean worldly men. I can tell you with certitude that men do not pursue a woman necessarily because they want to spend the rest of their lives with her but to prove to the latter that she is not beyond their reach, and will end up discarding her just like he does to any woman he was able to pursue and sleep with.

Ungodly men know exactly what women want to see and hear in order to give themselves to them. They know women want to hear things like, "You are so gorgeous," "I want to marry you," "I can't wait to put a ring on it," and all the fine lines there are. Ladies, look for the real signs of a real man, a lover, leader, visionary, provider, protector, keeper, and someone who wants to cherish, honor, and respect you, and spend the rest of his life with you. Do not be fooled.

Do not let the pursuit of men be your measure of their interest, character, and what you need in a relationship. Keep the balance, and if you notice and can confirm that the man is a good man by virtue or character, do not waste time playing "hard to get." Show your interest as well to start the process of communicating, and getting to know each other better and see how far it can go.

> *"Do not let the pursuit of men be your measure of their interest, character, and what you need in a relationship."*

A brother liked a sister and was talking to her in order to get to know her. The sister was playing "hard to get," and the brother, out of frustration and as a gentleman, decided to stop advancing the sister and went his way. Later, the sister revealed to the brother how she was also in love with him, but it was too late for the brother to get back to her. If you can perceive that the person is a good man or woman, and are also interested, show it and start the process of getting to know each other to confirm whether it's true or not. I'm not saying you should not respect yourself as a lady, but there are limits to that. Keep the balance.

Remember this and watch out: Some men or women were never coming into your life to stay. You think the relationship did not work out, but he knew right from the beginning he would not keep you anyway. He only wanted to sleep with you. So, instead of saying the relationship didn't work out, just know you were fooled one more time.

> *"Some men or women were never coming into your life to stay."*

And if you are a man, do not let the world tell you what confidence, bravery, smartness, and moral standards are because the world itself does not know what these virtues are. Living soundly, holding up your moral standards for God's sake and your life toward women, and courting or dating a lady respectfully and honorably is not a weakness. The confident man is not the one who pursues a woman without not respecting, honoring, communicating, and knowing anything about her. Your confidence and respect as a man are not shown in pursuing a woman and sleeping with her without wanting to marry her or in a proper way, but in respecting ladies, even if you have the power, materials, and money to get them.

To both men and women, you are not winning just because you are tolerating someone's foolishness. When a man or woman doesn't show commitment to marry you, it could be that the person needs some time to get to know you better. But when you know the person has been fooling around with other people, including sleeping or having sex with them, then you have to wake up and draw the line. Keep in mind that accepting someone's continuous immoral lifestyle just because you need a spouse is not also wise. Some people were able to leave that person because they were wise and bold enough to refuse their continuous immorality and foolishness. It may be the only reason the person keeps playing with you, and you think you are the one winning, but it is because he knows you are the only fool he can be with, and you are the only one who can accept all the lies, manipulations and threats on their terms. This is not to say that you should not be patient and give people time to make up their minds and make the right choices for themselves, but giving people time to make up their minds is different than giving people time to continue their foolishness. Be patient, but when you are convinced that they are playing with you, stop it, and get out of that relationship before it's too late and the worst happens to you and before you start counting all your wasted time.

As a man, I understand very well that responsible men usually do not feel ready to get married when they are not financially stable or ready, but with an understanding woman, this should not be a problem. With a woman who comes into your life as a partner or teammate, she knows she's coming into your life as a "helpmate" to build together. This will also lead us to talk about women who want an already-built empire as a man's life so they can just come and enjoy. Listen, ladies, it's easier for a man to kick you out of his life when he already built everything before you came into it. This is not to say that there are not also wicked men who can discard the woman who suffered with them to build a life. But notice I said "easier", meaning the probability of a man who built with you to kick you out of his life is lower than a man who already got it together before you marry him.

I don't understand why a woman who is giving a man sex without marriage will be wondering why he's not ready to marry her. A woman who is giving a man sex without marriage is encouraging that man not to marry her.

Believe it or not. You may argue that not all men are like that, but most men are the same. A man you are giving sex and any other marriage benefits without marriage will not feel the need to marry or settle with you. Men are often bold enough to tell women if they don't give them sex, they will leave them because sex is important to men. On the other hand, women tend to give away what is important to them, which is commitment, marriage and support, without any conditions. Do not wonder why your potential husband is not ready to marry you while you are giving him sex and all the marriage benefits without a marriage.

> *"Men are often bold enough to tell women if they don't give them sex, they will leave them because sex is important to men. On the other hand, women tend to give away what is important to them, which is commitment, marriage and support, without any conditions."*

Money, Materials, and Moral

We live in a world where everything is about money and materials, and if something is not monetary or material, it is not valued or worth our love, time, attention, and work. And the results in our societies are people who are still alive but have dead consciousness and souls. Even within family members, relatives, and friends, some can easily betray the other for money, materials, and position.

One of the reasons our world is full of drunks, drug addicts, and sexual perverts is that we have a world that is full of people who are continuously violating their own conscience and moral standards while violating others. So, the result is to drink, take drugs, and have disorderly sex to pacify and momentarily forget their guilt, which is hunting them every second of their lives. The Bible says, *"What will it profit a man if he gains the whole world, yet forfeits his soul? Or what can a man give in exchange for his soul?"* (Matthew 16:26, BSB).

Making decisions under the influence of alcohol or any substance can result in dangerous events for you and others. Many people are aware of the driving laws concerning "Driving under the influence." But how about making decisions under the influence of anything else? Yes, don't make serious decisions while you are under the influence of alcohol or any substance. The Bad thing about making decisions under the influence of any substance is that you are not truly aware of what you are doing at that moment, not even the decision that you are making.

Nevertheless, you can also make the wrong decisions under the influence of people, money, and material things. Every decision you make under the influence of anything other than a clear or good judgment and the leading of the Spirit of God will result in unexpected surprises and bad experiences.

> *"You can also make the wrong decisions under the influence of people, money, and material things."*

Sometimes, what you need for circumstances to change for the better is not money or material, it is just the wisdom to make the right choices or decisions. Unfortunately, the common comment you may hear here and there from some people is, "What am I supposed to do with this or that"? Why? Because money or material gains are not attached to it.

We forget that wise, good decisions or choices of morals, work ethics, vision, and good planning can give us, in a very peaceful way, the happiness, prosperity, and secure life we are longing for sooner or later.

Life is a give-and-receive sequence – whether you realize it or not, you are always giving or receiving something – good or bad. Sincerely, nothing is free in life, you always pay for everything with something knowingly or unknowingly. The question is, what and how do you want to give to receive what you want or need to avoid causing distress, destruction, and regrets to yourself and others?

The word of God says, ***"Get wisdom, get understanding; do not — turn from them."*** (Proverb 4:5, NIV).

Chapter 7
Measuring Against Time

"What has been will be again, what has been done will be done again; there is nothing new under the sun."
Ecclesiastes 1:9

ONE OF THE THINGS we hate the most as human beings is time, especially when it's working against us. When what we are doing, feeling, seeing, and hearing feels good, and we like it, we do not want the clock to tick – we want the planet to stop rotating. However, if we do not like it, we want to reinvent how time is calculated – we want the clock to magically change to what we want or in our favor.

God put us in time to save us from ourselves (Internal dangers) and other people (External dangers). Whether you realize it or not, time has saved you from yourself, other people, and many hazards that could ruin your life. And it's a blessing that our memories, feelings, and desires are somehow integrated into time – the longer it takes or has been, the less effect they may have.

Everything in our lives is, in one way or another, controlled by time. Except you are just a ghost; you came into this world on time. Your mother carried you for nine (9) months and birthed you into this realm. Even if you were prematurely birthed, you still were birthed into this world on and in time. You started drinking and eating specific drinks and food at particular times. You began creeping, crawling, stepping, pulling up, and cruising before walking in distinct times.

> **"Everything in our lives is, in one way or another, controlled by time."**

Everything in this realm of life is timed – your activities throughout every day are measured or limited in terms of duration by yourself or someone else, directly or indirectly. And if you do not understand how to arrange and restrict yourself from abusing the beginning and the end of things anyhow, you will make a fool of yourself – you have to know when to start and stop. Have you ever seen someone who keeps dancing even when the music is no longer playing? No matter how hard he tries to dance to the beat, it does not collaborate because the music has stopped.

The fact that we have twenty-four (24) regions or locations and Time Zones worldwide means everybody and everything has its time – there is a time for every human being and entity's existence. And while some things can be outdated, some do not. Therefore, it's up to you to know and gracefully handle it as such.

"This fragrance smells great on my wife." Said a man. Another lady confirms, "I have been wearing this perfume for 20 years." Another woman commented, "I like wearing this perfume; it smells great, but some people tell me it's old-time. But I get a lot of compliments when I wear it – it smells heavenly."

One of the benefits of being a minister and operating multiple businesses simultaneously is the lessons I often learn during my interactions with customers and strangers trying to buy products or use services. I'm privileged to talk to people from different backgrounds, faiths, opinions, or ideologies. And even though I may disagree with them on many things, first as a Christian and second as a thinker, there is always a takeaway at the end of each interaction.

My takeaway from these women's feedback was, "Do not change or replace the good with the new just because it's old. It may be old, but good or better. Why replace it?" Even if the new one looks nicer in appearance, the matter of quality is essential. One of humanity's problems is that we always want something new, even if the old one is good and better. You want every new version of your phone, appliances, kitchenware, and car – even if the old one is good or better than the new one. So, at some point, we are no more about quality but newness. You even want to replace your wife or husband because of the new person you have just met and do not even know yet.

Perfection Versus Value

Perfection does not exist in this world, and you will not find anything perfect, including people. But you can find value, so look for the value. Search for value in everything you are doing instead of perfection. If you can find your values in it, then it's worth it. But if you cannot find your values in it, then it's not worth it. Do not place your values on money but on Godliness, morality, and character because these are the elements that surely guide people's judgment and decisions when it comes to money, materials, position, and status, and they should guide yours as well when you are choosing them.

> *"Perfection does not exist in this world, and you will not find anything perfect, including people."*

When a person is deciding about you or what to do with you, they are guided by their values. Therefore, remember, when you are also deciding on a person you will deal with in any area of your life, whether as a friend, husband or wife, employer or employee, business partner, ministry partner, leader, or manager, you are explicitly choosing what will happen to you in the next few days, months, years or your entire life in this world.

Additionally, it is not what matters to God that matters to us generally as human beings. But what we must keep in mind is that what matters to God is what matters to Him. And He measures our accomplishments, and success in this world based on what matters to Him, and not what matters to people and even us.

There is no perfection without perspective. By looking at the same thing from different angles and views, you may spot what needs to be adjusted to become good or better. It seems God wanted to see humans from every perspective. So, He led humanity through seven (7) distinctive presentations, arrangements, or periods in history, which are called dispensations in theology. This forms the framework through which God relates to mankind.

"There is no perfection without perspective."

Quality or Newness

Another example that comes to my mind is the pot, the potter, and the pottery wheel. The potter's wheel not only helps him to easily mold the clay into a specific design or layout but also gives him a good perspective of the art he's working on. Each time a side of the pot comes into the potter's view, he corrects something that does not look the way it should or looks. Sometimes, all you need is to correct or re-arrange something about what you already have and make the best use of it instead of completely replacing or rejecting it.

Some time ago, I was trying to help a couple (husband and wife) select a fragrance for the husband. I was on the other side of the set, so when I noticed the couple was struggling with which perfume to choose for the husband, I moved closer to them and suggested one of the favorite perfumes in my own collection of scents that I like so much and wear more than any other scents. I said, "Here, smell this. You will love it." The husband took it from my hand, smelled the sample, then put it down. I thought something must have been wrong with his nose, so I gave it to the wife and said, "Here, smell it. It's a great scent!" The wife smelled it and also put it down, smiling and shaking her head in a sign of rejection. "What, you don't like it?" I said. Both of them smiled and shook their heads. There, I was standing in amazement with my eyes wide open as I looked at them like something was seriously wrong with them. In my mind, I thought something must be wrong with these people – maybe they came from another planet, or they were aliens. "Who would not like this scent?" I thought.

Then came another surprise: They picked up one of the perfumes I absolutely do not like, smelled it, and were happy with it. I asked them, "Do you like that one?" They smiled and said, "Yes." Out of confusion, I felt sad and angry at the same time. But a few minutes later, I started reasoning with myself, "What's my part in their decision? They don't like what I like. What's the problem?" My savvy soul, who believes he knows the best perfumes that everybody should like and wear, was still unhappy that they chose a perfume I hate instead of what I suggested to them. After all, I have tested and tried many fragrances and know better than them because I sell them anyway.

With time, that day, I forgot about the couple until I got back home in the evening, and then their matter came back to my mind. I walked to my closet, picked up that same perfume I suggested to them out of my collection, sprayed it, and smelled it again. Then, I said to myself, "I can't believe why in the world someone would not like this perfume." Then came the moment of truth: It came to my mind, "That's how the world is; what you like might not be what everybody likes." That's correct, and as long as they are not disobeying God, let them like what they like. Otherwise, you will be turned into a fool.

Show me the beauty, and I will show you the flaws, and show me the flaws, and I will show you the beauty — there is no perfection in this world. This is one of the absolute truths about life I have observed on this side of the universe or realm – everything is flawed. However, how you handle or manage the good and bad determines the results or consequences. Your flaws, which invoke mistakes, can cause you all the misfortunes in the world and prevent you from reaching your full potential in every area of your life until you honestly recognize and deal with them.

> *"Show me the beauty, and I will show you the flaws, and show me the flaws, and I will show you the beauty ."*

Unfortunately, the fool thinks he's a perfect human being — and everything he says or does is perfect. He owes no one an explanation and apologies. The truth is that there are flaws in every beautiful thing in this world, including beautiful human beings, machines, buildings, and even nature's most beautiful elements. However, your flaws become painless to others when they are admitted, handled, improved, or tried to improve on with accountability and responsibility — this does not make you weak, but a human being, morally sound, and honorable. On the contrary, your flaws become a pain and unbearable to others when you arrogantly, pridefully, stubbornly, or unquestionably do not even admit you have them and do nothing to improve your character to become a better version of yourself but blame everyone else for all the misfortunes you create for them and yourself.

Everyone has flaws, and you do have flaws that you don't even know or forget sometimes that you have. Many of us know and admit we do have flaws. But it's also important to understand that there are flaws in our lives that we don't even know exist, or don't recognize as one, and only close people around us can see, experience, and complain about them. That's why it's vital to listen to people, even children. This doesn't mean you have to believe and do everything people, even your closest friends, tell you. But you must be open to listening to them and evaluate what they are telling you to confirm whether it's true or false.

"Your flaws become a pain and unbearable to others when you arrogantly, pridefully, stubbornly, or unquestionably do not even admit you have them and do nothing to improve your character."

Dangers of Growing Flaws

Flaws can be remediated, but when they keep growing, they will affect everybody because everyone will get tired and start reacting to them directly or indirectly, while the originator cares less about their pain or suffering due to the flaws. When people do not realize, admit, and work on their flaws, they can become dangerous to themselves and all the people related to them who deal with the latter on various levels. Imperfection in itself is not perilous. However, it becomes treacherous when the individual is not sincerely working on it and balancing it – it becomes a serious deficiency that can lead to unexpected situations.

Wisdom suggests that you love but stay away from people who do not know they have flaws because they become serious problems that can create crazy problems, which can drive you crazy in return for doing crazy things you never thought you would have ever done in your life. This is not an advocacy for bad reactions and violence, but some people are in jail now because someone else's flaws drove them crazy to do something crazy that landed them in prison for life. Some people committed murder and various crimes because they felt betrayed by someone. Other people's destructive behaviors can lead you to commit ungodly acts, so if you know someone is not working on their flaws and you cannot handle that, just stay away to save yourself from doing something crazy.

> *"Other people's destructive behaviors can lead you to commit ungodly acts."*

Trying Versus Faking

There is a difference between trying and faking it. The person who is trying may be honest and exercise all he can to become what is good despite multiple failures. But the person faking it, is dangerous because his intentions are never pure, and may never become or produce a good result.

When the Old Is Out of Order

All the same, it's important to know when something or someone has to be replaced. There are times in life when the old must necessarily be replaced and not fixed; otherwise, more damages may occur. There are things that can be fixed, and some that, even if you fix them, will never work again as they were. In effect, wisdom would suggest replacing it instead of fixing it unless the probability of the replacement is highly low or impossible.

   My experience with cars started with owning a brand of car I won't mention due to the bad publicity it may bring to them. When I got the car as a second-hand or used car, I really liked it. It was driving smoothly, and when I took it on a long trip, it felt hefty and powerful on the road, which made me like that brand, and I decided that even my next car would be it. Little did I know that the brand has flaws despite the power of the engine and its weight, which helps it stay strong and stable on the road during high speed.

A couple of years later, the car started having electrical problems. I have done my best to find the right mechanics to fix the problems. Surprisingly, when I fix one thing, another issue would arise. I was determined to keep fixing the car's electrical problems until one of my friends said, "Honestly, I owned this brand of car before, and that's what happens after you use them for a few years – they start having electrical problems." Then he added, "It will continue like that." I only listened to him with one ear, I didn't care about what he said. After spending more money to keep fixing the car, I started realizing that he was right because the electrical problems of the car were not going away, but coming one after the other. To shorten a long story, regrettably, I finally decided and bought another car.

While it's possible to fix old things if they are good and better in quality, sometimes it's just good or better to let go of things that are out of order and replace them, especially if it's morally sound and Godly.

There are things you cannot test before having or allowing them into your life, yet there are things you can fully test before accepting them into any area of your life. And to prevent damages and regrets, ensure you always allow that testing time to confirm or validate the authenticity, and probable problems it can cause in your life, family, business, or ministry before you allow it.

For example, some people got married a few weeks, or months after they met and have been happy ever since. However, it's also to be noted that some people regret it for the rest of their lives. Take time to know the person you want to marry or who wants to marry you before you approve of that. It's vital that you allow testing (not in an immoral way as some people do), or if I may say trial time to get to know people before allowing them in your close circle. Remember, dealing with difficult people from a distance is better than closer. This may sound canal, but I can assure you that when you have problematic people in your inner circle, you cannot even function effectively spiritually. Even if you are strong-willed and have mastered the art of ignoring disturbances and distractions, some will catch up to you and demand your attention, and you will have to address them or the matters, or else they will constitute an absolute obstacle to whatever you are doing, including your spiritual exercises and endeavors. These traps are more dangerous when the toxic person is in your inner circle, or close to you, or someone you have to deal with daily such as your wife, relative, employee, staff member, business or ministry partner. Anyone whose behavior or character carries negativity and distress to your life can be an obstacle and in the worst scenario, a destroyer of every good thing you work and stand for, have accomplished, and are in the process of building.

> *"When you have problematic people in your inner circle, you cannot even function effectively spiritually."*

There is a difference between a problematic person and a

flawed person. A flawed person is one who makes honest mistakes and tries to amend them and get better. The problematic person is the one who does not even know and admits that he has flaws and is not doing anything about it. In fact, problematic people think everybody else is the cause of their problems. They will exhaust you and destroy every good thing you try to build. You may work with a flawed person as long as you know where to place them in your life, but problematic people are dangerous to deal with because they may even destroy you on their way to self-destruction or while destroying themselves.

> *"In fact, problematic people think everybody else is the cause of their problems."*

The Power of Time

One of the forces that reveal genuineness is time. Give it some time. Whatever you are feeling, seeing, smelling, touching, or experiencing, give it time – time will reveal its genuineness. Fake people understand this natural law, so they tend to rush you to action or acceptance either by force or trick before time reveals the truth. Whenever possible, especially if it's not an emergency situation, always allow time to do its work. It will save you from many troubles.

All the same, appreciate genuineness, honesty, and integrity — do not mock genuineness. It's evident that human beings tend to like fakeness and lies — it's in nature. People cheating and hurting others to make it happen quickly in life are respected and praised more than the genuine ones trying to make it with fairness, honesty and integrity while they struggle. Remember, they will eventually make it with God on their side — and their success will last.

> *"One of the forces that reveal genuineness is time."*

Proceed Carefully With Testimonies

Testimonies do not guarantee an expected end or results. Testimonies are good and a glimpse of what people and things can actually be, but should not be accepted and acted on without precautions. It's also important to know things and people for yourself.

According to the Oxford Languages Dictionary, a testimony is "a formal written or spoken statement, especially one given in a court of law." And here is the part of the definition that commands attention, an "evidence or proof provided by the existence or appearance of something."

Now, the word "appearance" is essential to be noted here. Appearance is "the way that someone or something looks," according to the dictionary. You would agree that just because something appears to be, or is like, doesn't mean it's exactly what it appears to be.

The justice system repeatedly taught us that even in a court of law, testimonies, whether written or oral under oath or affirmation under penalty of perjury as evidence obtained from a witness who makes a solemn statement or declaration of fact, have not always been true. The testimony of a plaintiff, defendant, or even a witness crying tears has not always been true.

Just because someone tells you this or that about a person or something doesn't mean it is guaranteed to be exactly that. You should only take testimonies as a starting or preliminary asset or information. You have to know it for yourself, so proceed carefully.

Keep in mind that in an attempt to protect their relatives, friends, employees, neighbors, leaders, countries, and companies, they can give you false testimonies. So it's up to you to do your best to authenticate any information you are provided as a testimony to prevent you from falling like a fool and regretting it.

Everything Is Mutable In Humanity

Nothing in humanity is immutable — they will all naturally change sooner or later, even if they are not forced to change. As I mentioned earlier, the new, will surely become the old.

> *"Nothing in humanity is immutable — they will all naturally change sooner or later."*

Whether you like or accept it or not, the new will surely become the old. And as I mentioned in a preceding chapter, the word of God makes it clear that everything in this world will pass away or change, except God's word and Himself. The Lord stated, *"Heaven and earth will pass away, but My words will never pass away."* (Matthew 24: 35, NIV). In effect, no matter who you are, and what your beauty, finances, position, social status, and how much political, corporate, and even ecclesiastical power you have, they will all pass away – it's just a matter of time.

One of the worst things you could do to disgrace yourself is to be fighting against the "potential incoming" instead of thinking about how better you can do to improve what you have to offer the world. You should care about the history or story you are writing knowingly and unknowingly about your life, character, and legacy more than someone or an entity who wants to be like you or do something you have done. This behavior will always leave you looking like a fool and disgrace, and destroy your legacy in a particular area of your life, career, business, or ministry. Therefore, instead of fighting the right incoming leader, person, entity, and achievement, support and celebrate them.

If you remember the story of King Saul and David, who later became the King of Israel, you know how disgraceful King Saul's ending was. Nothing in this world lasts forever; respect and do yourself a favor to understand this and behave appropriately. (1 Samuel 13: 1-30; 2 Samuel 5).

As the saying goes, "A success without a successor, is a failure." How true is this? It's entirely true, and I believe that we should think about this not only concerning prominent leaders, but also in every aspect of life, including homes, families, communities, and generally in our societies. Unfortunately, the world is in a chokehold of leaders, and in many cases, bad leaders who do not want to leave their positions and fight tooth and nail to stay in a position the people sincerely want them to vacate for another person also to give it a try.

Power Without Respect

Do not lose respect for power because power without respect is vanity. How foolish does it look when a leader is no longer respected by the people he's leading by force? For instance, imagine you are dressed in a nice suit, shirt, tie, and shoes, but you stink. This is the same sense people have about you when you are holding onto power without respect. Any position you hold without respect from the said people makes you look like a caricature. The worst is when everybody pretends to respect you, but they honestly do not. So, what's the point? The Bible says, ***"Do nothing out of selfish ambition or vain conceit. Rather, in humility, value others–"*** (Philippians 2:3, NIV).

> *"Do not lose respect for power because power without respect is vanity."*

One misinterpreted thing I have observed is people's definition of success. Keep this in mind, regardless of your interpretation of success, remember success is never a success until you fulfill your purpose and destiny. You can become rich, have, and do all you want, but if you do not fulfill your purpose, it's vanity. Many want to be successful only to be able to live a lavish life, not necessarily to fulfill their purpose and destiny.

One of your greatest dreams and desires should be how to live to be a respectable young man with vigor and an old, decent, respectable, and honorable person with gray hair. As we discussed earlier, there is a difference between respect and honor. You are respected for your character, and honored by your age, status, position, office, and accomplishments.

People See You in the Mirror of Who They Are

While people's opinion of you may be valid, sometimes it could also be a reflection of who they are themselves. Pay attention to who people believe you are because it may as well be an image of who they are.

As you know, generally, a mirror is an object that reflects an image or a reflective surface. When you stand in front of a mirror, what you see, is what you look like. In other words, people often see you through their heart or spirit, just as they are – good or bad. A hater will see you as a hater. A criminal will think of, and see you as a criminal. Likewise, if you are a good person, you can mistakenly believe everybody is as good or has a good heart as you. And this may be one of the biggest mistakes you make now and then in life. Understand that every person is an individual; therefore, you must get to know them individually or for who they are. And until you know someone, do yourself the favor of understanding that you do not know them.

> *"A criminal will think of, and see you as a criminal. Likewise, if you are a good person, you can mistakenly believe everybody is as good or has a good heart as you."*

Sometimes, because you can never do something – a bad thing or behavior, you would believe no one can do it either. No, you are lying to yourself. What seems abnormal and seriously immoral to you, may just be the pleasure of someone else – you wouldn't even know it. So, you must guide yourself against that belief, especially if you haven't spent a long time with some people. Understand that you only know people based on the amount of time you have spent with them, and in a particular area or matter in life. For example, you may only know your co-worker, just as a co-worker, and everything else about that person may be a mystery, or you don't know. People tend to present you with the image they want you to see about them, and you can only know them based on who they are or how they relate to you. You would not know how your co-worker treats the spouse at home until you are the spouse. Even though genuine people treat everybody genuinely, people can have hidden characters you can only know about if you deal with them in that capacity. Some people can be the most congenial co-workers, managers, and leaders – but the bad husbands or wives at home and in their own families. Therefore, before concluding, be cautious in observing someone's performance in a setting or area of life and think or make decisions based on that. Ensure you know the person's conduct in other areas of life before deciding. And let the most important things be your guide to avoid making everybody a hero based on a single thing you know about them.

> *"Avoid making everybody a hero based on a single thing you know about them."*

At the same time, don't be surprised when someone becomes so suspicious of you. They may just be thinking you are just like them. A thief always thinks everybody is a thief, so he would seriously protect his belongings when you are around. Why? Because he knows what he does to other people. A cheater will always think everybody is a cheater and will make sure no one cheats him. That's why sometimes you will meet people who will be behaving funny, and you wonder why. And you will only discover in the end that they were fighting their own phantom or enigmatic personality.

A woman said, "I like shooting straight, but I don't like people shooting straight at me." And I thought, "How do you like shooting straight at people, meaning you say it as is, but you don't like people telling it to you as is?" This woman was not the only one to be like that. Many people hate you doing to them what they actually like to do to others.

Faith Is Not the Absence of Wisdom

I mentioned this earlier. When it comes to human relations, you must look at things as they are, except God directly and explicitly tells you differently. Even if you choose to love according to God's commandments, you must take the necessary measures to protect yourself and others. Faith, just as love, is not the exclusion of wisdom. In fact, where there is faith, there is wisdom. You cannot separate divine wisdom from God because He is wisdom. The reason you believe in God and believe He can do what He says He can do is because of Godly wisdom, and Godly wisdom is God Himself. There are high risks that you should only take or act on faith when God specifically tells you so, or gives you a Rhema. For example, until Peter heard the Lord say, "Come", he never stepped out of the boat. And of course, stepping out of the boat itself was faith. (Matthew 14: 22-33).

Pay Attention to the Dreams You Have About People and Things

While many dreams may just be an extension of your thoughts, stress, or fear, and not from God or a revelation, it's important to understand that some dreams you may have are direct messages from God to you about things and even people. You should take them seriously before it's too late. These dreams may be about past, present, or future events that will occur with things or people. Therefore, ignoring them could be dangerous for your well-being physically and spiritually.

God knows hidden things that you don't know, and He knows hidden things about people you don't know. Considering that, He may show you some things in your dreams to guide and protect you against dangerous decisions, things, and people. This is not to say that everything you see about people in dreams may be true. Some of them could just be an extension of your thoughts. However, properly analyze your dreams and pray about them to confirm whether is God talking to you or it's just your thoughts. We read again, *"For God does speak—now one way, now another—though no one perceives it. In a dream, in a vision of the night, when deep sleep falls on people as they slumber in their beds, he may speak in their ears and terrify them with warnings."* (Job 33:14-16, NKJV).

> *"God knows hidden things that you don't know, and He knows hidden things about people you don't know."*

Personally, it's so evident that God sometimes would show

me specific things in dreams years before they even occur. Sometimes, I just watch things God has shown me in dreams years back happening and literally playing in front of me like a movie. And it's amazing how powerful the Spirit of God is in the manner He recalls these dreams to my remembrance while they are happening. In the beginning, I would have dreams that I even forgot about till they were occurring right in front of my eyes. In effect, I started getting serious about them. There were people that I had seen in my dreams, days, months, or years before meeting and knowing them physically. There were events that God warned me days, months, and in some cases several years in advance before they even happened in my personal life, business, and ministry, and I would be shaking my head in amazement that they were happening a long time after God had shown these things to me and I have forgotten. Why does God do that? Because He loves us, and wants to help us make the right decisions, knowing that each one of the decisions we think are insignificant or not a big deal contributes to the bigger occurrences that will shape the rest of our entire lives.

Divine Warnings

If you remember, to save baby Jesus, God sent an angel that appeared to Joseph in a dream. The angel told Joseph in a dream, "Get up now and flee to Egypt. Take Mary and the little child and stay there until I tell you to leave, for Herod intends to search for the child to kill him." And the Bible says, *"So that very night he got up and took Jesus and his mother and made their escape to Egypt and remained there till Herod died."* (Matthew 2: 13-23).

In the same way, God used a dream to warn Joseph about what was about to happen and help them escape the evil plan of Herod. God also talks and warns you in dreams, so you must pay attention to your dreams to understand and use them to guide your decisions. However, I should also warn you that the misinterpretation of your dreams is something you must be careful about. Be careful not to think God is telling you one thing in a dream while he's saying something else. The correct interpretation of your dreams is vital when God gives them to you.

> *"God also talks and warns you in dreams, so you must pay attention to your dreams to understand and use them to guide your decisions."*

Everybody Loves God Until It's Time to Do His Will

Don't be fooled. When people say, they love God, it does not necessarily mean they fear God. Loving God should equal fearing God. Unfortunately, it's not in the lives of everybody. I have witnessed the behavior of people who claim they are in love with God, yet their character is not in line with the commandments or precepts of God. I have known people who can preach or do ministry, and donate significant sums of money and materials to the work of God, but do not fear God. People can use the name of God to get closer to you, only to hurt you one way or the other. Therefore, you must be careful, and until the fruits of their character confirm their profession, do not trust them with your life and important things related to your well-being.

It's concerning when you see people live as they can define who God should be and what He can do or not. You cannot define God; God gives you the definition of Himself, and that's the ultimate order you have to accept. Everything else is just a lie you are telling yourself. You must live according to God's precepts, not how you think it should be.

Chapter 8
Thought Drills

"Meditate on it day and night, so that you may be careful to do everything written in it. Then you will be prosperous and successful."
Joshua 1:8

"FOR AS HE THINKS IN HIS HEART, so is he" (Proverbs 23: 7, NIV) is one of the most known, memorable Bible quotations, and it is quoted regularly. We often quote this when we talk about prosperity, success, or well-being. However, there is an additional understanding in this portion of the scriptures that I would like us to dissect.

Meditation influences your decisions. And there is a stage or level of meditation that I refer to as "Thought Drills." That's where deep thoughts come from or happen. During these times, you have sincere conversations with yourself – you ask yourself pertinent questions and answer them, and if you do not find immediate answers, it leads you to a quest to find answers or solutions. In most of these times of deep search within your soul, the distant yet close world or environment, God's word, and Spirit, you can find hidden answers to thoughts, breakthrough ideas, problems, creativity, innovation, or inventions.

> *"Meditation influences your decisions."*

Thought drills are the cradle for receiving deep insight or revelations from God through the Holy Spirit, clarity, good judgment or understanding about your purpose and destiny, and preparation for anything that is up next in your life – these are times when you do some deep thinking. Above all, it's also a time when, knowingly and unknowingly, you build or establish the foundations of your moral values, which influence your judgment or decision-making.

To many, meditation just sounds like a quiet time of prayer or communication with God. For others, it involves breathing in and out and focusing on an object, thought, or activity. While prayer is part of meditation, it's also a time of Thought Drills.

> *"During these times, you have sincere conversations with yourself – you ask yourself pertinent questions and answer them."*

Drills are mandatory in many working, school, residential, and community settings to train or prepare you to properly respond and handle what could be a possible accident of fire, natural disaster, and nowadays an active shooter. During these drills, you may or may not receive a notification from an electronic device, machine, or verbally from someone about what is happening and what to do. However, in some cases, you are on your own to use your understanding or judgment to save yourself from danger.

Many people hate drills and don't want to spend time doing them until there is an incident that threatens to take their lives. However, the good thing about drills is that they prepare your mind about what to do in dangerous situations and help prevent confusion that can worsen a dangerous event. In other words, they keep you grounded or settled in your decision-making about dangerous situations.

Safety experts took time to study many past catastrophic events, or incidents that caused great damage or suffering to formulate procedures, and prepare you for the possible next one. And during these drills, the procedures that have been proven to be successful and saved lives in the past are taught, so if you properly follow or use them, they may save your life and others as well.

It's imperative to understand that in some cases, you must follow your good judgment because there may be something different about that particular situation. Therefore, a good instructor or coach would always tell you to remember everything he's teaching you, but always rapidly evaluate the situation and exercise what you believe is the right thing to do according to what you have learned and how you have been trained, in conjunction with your judgment.

The drills also provide some level of awareness of what could happen if you do something wrong in a particular setting, so providing a certain level of sobriety and discipline because you don't want to be hurt or die.

Fundamental Thoughts

Fundamental thoughts are your power thoughts, and they may be dynamic because they can evolve or change over time according to your understanding. And you must ensure that they change for the better in a Godly way or grounded in the undiluted word of God. Our understanding as humans can deepen or grow over time through the word of God, the Holy Spirit, and the knowledge He impacts to our spirit, the learnings or educations we open ourselves to, and things we have experienced. Therefore, being careful about the teaching or education you are opening yourself to is vital. Not all education is good, especially if it destroys your morals and Godly understanding.

> *"Fundamental thoughts are your power thoughts, and they may be dynamic because they can evolve or change over time according to your understanding."*

Fundamental thoughts are very important because if you would understand, they are the power or energy behind every decision you make in life. They are fundamental or the foundation of your everyday decision-making measures. They constitute your belief, the very cornerstone of your decision-making process. They come from your longtime premeditated, settled, and accepted truth and facts.

Whether you have recognized it or not, your fundamental thoughts are a force behind your major decision-making process. Every major decision you make in life at a certain time or moment was made a long time before then. Even though the events surrounding the decisions might not be the same, in your thoughts of the past, you have thought and processed directly or indirectly these types of situations and settled on how you will react or respond to them, and the decision you will make in case of such events. If you are a child, this may not be true or collateral, but the older you get, the more thoughts you process about real-life situations or occasions. After all, these premeditated and processed thoughts become the mindset that governs your heart in your decision-making processes.

"They are fundamental — They constitute your belief — They come from your longtime premeditated, settled, and accepted truth and facts."

The Power of Thought Drills

Meditation has been considered just as a religious practice. In fact, every religion on Earth believes in meditation or something similar. Even though the practices or ways are not identical, many believe there is something spiritual to it. In other words, it's good for the soul to contemplate, reflect, or think, train attention and awareness, and attain a pure and clear mind, and emotional stability.

The truth is, meditation doesn't only yield those good results; it goes beyond that to grant us as human beings a better understanding, judgment, or interpretation of things and situations. And when you have a proper understanding of something or a situation, you can easily make the right decision. From my understanding, following up with the lives of many successful leaders and prophets in the Bible, they were men of prayer and meditators: Abraham, Isaac, Jacob, Joseph, Moses, and Joshua – Talking about Isaac, the Bible says, *"He went out to the field one evening to meditate."* (Genesis 24:63, NIV). This must not be the only time Isaac practiced meditation. And he must have learned it from his father, Abraham who was a man of prayer. (Genesis 20:17). You can't separate prayer from meditation, and meditation from prayer. There are times when you get to a meditation stage in prayers without even knowing. These are times when all you are doing is contemplating the magnitude of God, His ultimate power, and His creation or the universe. And it's in moments like these that God grants you revelations, answers or solutions, ideas, plans, and strategies.

When God gave His commandments to the children of Israel, He told them to meditate on them. He would command Joshua by saying, *"Keep this Book of the Law always on your lips; meditate on it day and night, so that you may be careful to do everything written in it. Then you will be prosperous and successful."* (Joshua 1:8, NIV).

Meditation is not something you only do in quiet times; you can meditate everywhere, knowingly and unknowingly. There are times when I find myself in deep thought, even in public, on a plane, train, bus, and sitting at restaurants eating. And surely in your private times and places, such as the bedroom, bathroom, and kitchen.

Adam's Weakness

Obviously, I have come to the understanding that I have to talk honorably and respectfully about Adam and Eve just as I would about my grandparents – don't you think so? We often talk as if we were in the Garden of Eden; we would have done better. However, looking at our current lives and behaviors, even thousands of years later, we might have done worse than Adam and Eve. The truth is, we are not doing any better than Adam and Eve when it comes to following God's instructions. However, we must learn from their mistakes and do our best to do better.

I wonder if Adam was spending his meditation time doing the wrong things, which led to his failure to clearly think or have a good understanding or judgment to know that the devil or the serpent was duping him through the wife.

The Bible reveals that *"The man and his wife heard the sound of the LORD God as he was walking in the garden in the cool of the day, and they hid from the LORD God among the trees of the garden. But the LORD God called to the man, "Where are you?" He answered, "I heard you in the garden, and I was afraid because I was naked; so I hid."* (Genesis 3:8, NKJV). Perhaps if Adam was spending that cool of the day doing some thought drills, we wouldn't be where we are today with a world full of problems. You cannot compare the Garden of Eden or Paradise with this world or life outside of it. I have concluded that one of the ways for me to avoid losing in life is to be a man of prayer and meditation because it gives me deep insight or revelations from God through the Holy Spirit, clarity, sound judgment or understanding about my purpose and destiny, creativity, breakthrough ideas, and preparation for anything that is up next in my life.

What we generally don't realize is that even if we don't select a particular time that we knowingly meditate, we do continuously or now and then think about things that we have experienced, or want to experience, and believe were, are, and will be a part of our lives, education, career, business, relationships, marriage, children, travel, pleasure, ministry, success, failure, profit, and loss of any kind. These random thoughts and processes end up building our decision-making power unknowingly. And when the time comes to decide, we tend to quickly lean into that direction and conclusion we have made in our mind several days, months, or years before – generally, this is controlled by our present beliefs, morals, and understanding built on the past thought drills that we knowingly and unknowingly had.

Additionally, the ability to quickly reference not only to your past decisions, but others' as well and their consequences can help you make the right decisions in the present and future. Sometimes, something that you have already thought about or analyzed while you were not even dealing with it at that moment prepares you for a better decision-making in case it comes or crosses your way.

Just as you train yourself to be apt in various things in life, you must also train yourself for better decision-making.

I suggest that you write down your random thought drills. This will make it possible and easy for you to remember, read, and enforce them in your decision-making processes. They become your way of life and a support system for your decision-making.

Thinking Up Before Going Up

It's dangerous not to take some time to meditate on crucial matters before deciding. Some people will go to career, business, and some life-changing meetings without not even taking a few minutes to meditate on, and think through these meetings, and the possible things they will have to say, do, and decisions they will make, which eventually will seal their wishes in what will be a lifetime, long or short-term experience of any kind. The first thing people think of is money, the good present feeling or pleasure, fame, and show; and never take the time to think about the possible consequences of all those things that sound like benefits. And in many cases, they are not even benefits because you will never experience them, or they will never be what you thought, they will steal away your peace of mind and true happiness. They look or sound like, but they might not be what they look or sound like. Remember, experiences are not pleasant all the time. In fact, the experience of money, materials, position, fame, or even sex in the middle of frustration, disrespect, dishonor, or slavery of any kind will never make you happy. And where happiness does not exist, peace doesn't either.

You will be surprised that ninety-nine percent of the things that draw your attention at first sight, feeling, hearing, and touching, will turn into things that are not exactly like that. So, taking the time to think up, and meditating about it before deciding will save your life, time, energy, peace, health, and long-term happiness.

Start by asking yourself pertinent questions about the reality of the matter, person, or thing. Don't play yourself.

Be honest as much as you can be with yourself. And as I mentioned earlier, never let your current needs and wants to be the primary baseline for your decision-making measure. Otherwise, you will regret it sooner or later. Remember that what can be your needs and wants right now, may not be in the next few minutes, hours, days, months, or years. So, if you make a decision that will have a lifetime effect based on that, you will regret it.

> *"Experiences are not pleasant all the time. In fact, the experience of money, materials, position, fame, or even sex in the middle of frustration, disrespect, dishonor, or slavery of any kind will never make you happy."*

Esau was hungry when he returned from the fields. He saw Jacob cooking and asked him for some food. Jacob told him the only way he could give him some of the food was by selling his birthright to him. Now, birthright at the time and even today have a special significance and privilege – it's a lifetime privilege of ranking, inheritance, power, and even spiritual access. But without thinking up, he said, "Look, I am about to die," "What good is the birthright to me." (Genesis 25: 32, NIV). Whatever it is that is forcing you to make a wrong decision, in most cases, is just temporary discomfort, pain, or situations. They will surely pass away if you can only hold on for a moment. Otherwise, you will exchange a temporary pleasure, relief, or satisfaction with a lifetime problem, unhappiness, pain, or misery that you will never recover from for the rest of your life. Esau definitively regretted his decision and never recovered from it, not even his descendants. (Genesis chapter 25).

The story of Joseph and his brothers is rich in life lessons that we all need, especially during the famine and their trip to Egypt to buy food for the family. This period reveals how reasonable, intelligent, and wise the entire Jacobs family was, including their father, Jacob. However, one of the most intriguing elements in the matter of Joseph and his family's reunion is how he played his brothers to detain his younger brother. And how Judah rushed to bind himself with his own words.

"Start by asking yourself pertinent questions about the reality of the matter, person, or thing. Don't play yourself."

Avoid Binding Yourself with Your Words

Always patiently do your homework, get the facts, ask, and confirm before responding or reacting to things, accusations, criticism, and questions whenever necessary. Without doing his homework, Judah rushed to literally swear that, "If any of your servants is found to have it, he will die; and the rest of us will become my lord's slaves." (Genesis 44:6, NKJV).

The Bible says, Joseph recognized his brothers immediately when he saw them but did not reveal himself to them at that moment. (Genesis 42:7).

Then in Genesis 42:12-18, Joseph plays a trick on his brothers to force them to leave Simeon behind in Egypt as a guarantor that they are not spies, it was not anything about spying, but a way to keep contact with his family that he has lost for years.

We read from the Bible: "Joseph said to them, "It is just as I told you: You are spies! And this is how you will be tested: As surely as Pharaoh lives, you will not leave this place unless your youngest brother comes here. Send one of your number to get your brother; the rest of you will be kept in prison, so that your words may be tested to see if you are telling the truth. If you are not, then as surely as Pharaoh lives, you are spies!" And he put them all in custody for three days.

> *"Whatever it is that is forcing you to make a wrong decision, in most cases, is just temporary discomfort, pain, or situation."*

On the third day, Joseph said to them, "Do this and you will live, for I fear God: If you are honest men, let one of your brothers stay here in prison, while the rest of you go and take grain back for your starving households. But you must bring your youngest brother to me, so that your words may be verified and that you may not die." This they proceeded to do."

Following that, in Genesis 44:1-33, Joseph played another trick on his brothers in order to force them to leave Benjamin with him, and we read:

"Now Joseph gave these instructions to the steward of his house: "Fill the men's sacks with as much food as they can carry, and put each man's silver in the mouth of his sack. Then put my cup, the silver one, in the mouth of the youngest one's sack, along with the silver for his grain." And he did as Joseph said.

As morning dawned, the men were sent on their way with their donkeys. They had not gone far from the city when Joseph said to his steward, "Go after those men at once, and when you catch up with them, say to them, 'Why have you repaid good with evil? Isn't this the cup my master drinks from and also uses for divination? This is a wicked thing you have done."

When he caught up with them, he repeated these words to them. But they said to him, "Why does my lord say such things? Far be it from your servants to do anything like that! We even brought back to you from the land of Canaan the silver we found inside the mouths of our sacks. So why would we steal silver or gold from your master's house? If any of your servants is found to have it, he will die; and the rest of us will become my lord's slaves."

"Very well, then," he said, "let it be as you say. Whoever is found to have it will become my slave; the rest of you will be free from blame."

Each of them quickly lowered his sack to the ground and opened it. Then the steward proceeded to search, beginning with the oldest and ending with the youngest. And the cup was found in Benjamin's sack. At this, they tore their clothes. Then they all loaded their donkeys and returned to the city.

Joseph was still in the house when Judah and his brothers came in, and they threw themselves to the ground before him. Joseph said to them, "What is this you have done? Don't you know that a man like me can find things out by divination?"

"What can we say to my lord?" Judah replied. "What can we say? How can we prove our innocence? God has uncovered your servants' guilt. We are now my lord's slaves—we ourselves and the one who was found to have the cup."

But Joseph said, "Far be it from me to do such a thing! Only the man who was found to have the cup will become my slave. The rest of you, go back to your father in peace."

Then Judah went up to him and said: "Pardon your servant, my lord, let me speak a word to my lord. Do not be angry with your servant, though you are equal to Pharaoh himself. My lord asked his servants, 'Do you have a father or a brother?' And we answered, 'We have an aged father, and there is a young son born to him in his old age. His brother is dead, and he is the only one of his mother's sons left, and his father loves him.'

"Then you said to your servants, 'Bring him down to me so I can see him for myself.' And we said to my lord, 'The boy cannot leave his father; if he leaves him, his father will die.' But you told your servants, 'Unless your youngest brother comes down with you, you will not see my face again.' When we went back to your servant my father, we told him what my lord had said.

"Then our father said, 'Go back and buy a little more food.' But we said, 'We cannot go down. Only if our youngest brother is with us will we go. We cannot see the man's face unless our youngest brother is with us.'

"Your servant my father said to us, 'You know that my wife bore me two sons. One of them went away from me, and I said, "He has surely been torn to pieces." And I have not seen him since. If you take this one from me too and harm comes to him, you will bring my gray head down to the grave in misery.'

"So now, if the boy is not with us when I go back to your servant my father, and if my father, whose life is closely bound up with the boy's life, sees that the boy isn't there, he will die. Your servants will bring the gray head of our father down to the grave in sorrow. Your servant guaranteed the boy's safety to my father. I said, 'If I do not bring him back to you, I will bear the blame before you, my father, all my life!'

"Now then, please let your servant remain here as my lord's slave in place of the boy, and let the boy return with his brothers. How can I go back to my father if the boy is not with me? No! Do not let me see the misery that would come on my father."

"When he caught up with them, he repeated these words to them. But they said to him, "Why does my lord say such things? Far be it from your servants to do anything like that! We even brought back to you from the land of Canaan the silver we found inside the mouths of our sacks. So why would we steal silver or gold from your master's house? If any of your servants is found to have it, he will die; and the rest of us will become my lord's slaves." (Genesis 44:6).

As you know, to shorten the story, the cup was found in Benjamin's sack, and according to Judah's words, Benjamin was supposed to be killed, and all the other brothers must become slaves. The main lessons in the story are, always think up before going up, and do your homework before swearing to avoid binding yourself with your own words.

The Traps of Pleasure and Satisfaction

Another interesting thing we must look at during Joseph's encounter with his brothers, is how much they told Joseph about their family because of food, and during their mealtime with him. One may ask if the meal also contributed to his brothers telling him too much about their family. Obviously, their father remarked this and asked them, "Why are you making my life so difficult! Why did you ever tell the man you had another brother?" (Genesis 43:6, MSG).

They presented their case to their father saying, "The man pressed us hard, asking pointed questions about our family: 'Is your father alive? Do you have another brother?' So, we answered his questions. How did we know that he'd say, 'Bring your brother here'?" (Genesis 43:7, MSG).

After all, sitting and eating at the house and table of the prime minister (Joseph) of the whole of Egypt could be impressive and influential enough for Joseph's brothers to talk too much. Be careful what you say during your pleasure and satisfaction moments. You may easily lose guard and talk too much about things you are not supposed to say. Remember, Samson let out his secret while on the lap of Delilah. (Judges 16:16-17).

I watched a video of a police interview and laughed throughout the video. The officer was interviewing the robber, who was eating a nice burger that I believed was offered to him by the Police Station. Apparently, he was telling the officer everything about the robbery while savoring the juicy burger. This is just to say that when we are enjoying some things in life, we can easily lay down our guard. And while it might be safe with good or trusted and Godly people, it could be dangerous when that happens with ill-intentioned individuals.

Correcting Your Statements or Words

The Bible says, *"Do you see someone who speaks in haste?*

There is more hope for a fool than for them." (Proverbs 29:20, NIV). Speaking in haste or too quickly before it's needed can cause you a multitude of problems, including violating yourself. When you talk or say some things too early before you give it a thought, you might regret it later. But what do you do after you say something too early before thinking? Information is not retractable once you give it out. However, you may cancel or retract some things as soon as possible. The earlier you cancel, retract, or correct a hastily signed agreement, statement, permission, or decision, the better. The longer you let your mistakenly spoken words, agreement, and permission last, the harder they will become to cancel, retract, or redo.

Enforcing Your Decision-Making Golden Rules

It's important to find creative ways to enforce your decision-making golden rules or principles to yourself so you can easily remember them even when under pressure. Remember God told Moses, Joshua, and the children of Israel several times to write things down to remember and to be careful to observe them. (Joshua 1:8). And one of the ways to enforce your decision-making golden rules to yourself, is to write them down and remind yourself. Second, talk and have conversations with yourself. Third, judge yourself. If you do not learn how to graciously judge yourself and make corrections before it's too late, you will misbehave, and someone else will judge and punish you for them. This is not about beating up yourself with negative thoughts, but rather with good thoughts and enforcing good behavior to yourself.

Personal Thought Drills

If you properly maintain your thought drills, in time and essence, they will become your lifeboat, and quotations to reinforce good morals and behaviors to yourself. In other words, your thought drills will stimulate your mind, boost your energy, grant you clarity, and inspire you to behave well.

In the following paragraphs, I will share some of my personal thought drills that I have written down when I talk and have conversations with myself. It may seem insane, but it's a reality of life in this world that you have to learn how to talk and have conversations with yourself before anyone else. Many of my sermons, teachings, and even books originated from me talking, rebuking, or conversing with myself.

"Essentials for life:

8 - Use What You Have Now

God asked Moses, "What do you have in your hand"? (Exodus 4: 2) Later, the rod of Moses would be what God used to perform signs and wonders to free the children of Israel. No matter how small and insignificant what you currently have is, use it with the help and wisdom of God to get what you need and get to where you have to be — Don't wait for bigger things and opportunities to come before doing your best — Start now. (Exodus 4: 2, Zachariah 4: 10).

7 - Obey The Holy Spirit

Especially in these perilous times in which we are, allow the Holy Spirit to override your plans, will, and decisions – Move, when he says move. Stop, when he says stop. Don't go, when he says don't go. Cancel it, when he says cancel it. A few minutes, hours, days, weeks, months, or years later, you will know why.

The Holy Spirit is not only a Supernatural Force, Power and Authority. Over the years, through personal experiences, I have learned, and sometimes the hard way, that He's also a Master Conductor. He knows best how to handle everything concerning you, including some of the least things in your personal life, business, and ministry. He might not talk to you the same way He talks to others, but when you master how He talks to you personally, and learn how to obey His guidance, He will save you from dangers. He knows how to guide you to succeed in all your endeavors. (John 10:27).

6 - Have No Enemies

Have no enemies but the devil and his demons. Only the Divine or Holy Trinity (the Father, Son, and Holy Spirit) have a permanent agreement and the same understanding related to spiritual and physical matters, or realities, occurrences and processes without variations. Learn how to disagree with people without not considering them your enemies. Keep your values and believes, stand your ground, but love unconditionally. (I Corinthians 13:4-5).

5 - Seek Understanding

Avoid rushing to conclusions and judgments before understanding. A wise person tries to get the facts by listening and getting knowledge of all sides of a thing or a matter before drawing conclusions, judgments, and decisions — One of the devil's tools to prevent you from making the right decisions in your life is misunderstanding and lack of knowledge about a thing or matter. (Proverbs 4:5).

4 - Avoid Mistakes

You might make mistakes. But try your best to avoid any spiritual, physical, financial, medical/health, business, and relationship mistakes. Be analytical. The devil uses mistakes to delay and sometimes terminate your progress and accomplishments, whether big or small. Learn how to pause, review, and see through situations in order to detect the end target of the devil. He always uses one thing to get to the other, or someone to provoke your unwise reaction or decision, which leads to his expected end or results, and sometimes, they are humanly irreparable. (Proverbs 19:8).

3 - Be Grateful

Be grateful for where you are and what you have now in life – Someone doesn't even have that. There are things God has ordained for someone to have earlier or sooner and the other to have later in life. All you need is to be faithful and obedient to God, do your best, and stay the course. Your time and turn will surely come. Don't force it. (1 Thessalonians 5:16-18, Ecclesiastes 3:1).

2 - Avoid Competitions

Compete with yourself to complete yourself or get better – it always leads you to self-discovery and God. And self-discovery and God lead you to purpose, talents, ideas, works, ethics, integrity and a changed or blessed life. Avoid useless competitions – they will only twist your purpose and destiny, and push your life into destruction. (Ecclesiastes 4:4-6).

1 - Seek God's Presence

If there is anything you should have confirmed, it's that God swore He will never leave nor forsake you – there is not an exception -- He is, and will always be there for you. (Hebrews 13:5)."

"Honesty and loyalty formulate the currency of trust, love, forgiveness, and peace."

"Now, what or who determines your future – Whatever you are doing right now will decide what you will get, who will trust you, be in your life, and where you will be. So do it well with God-fearing, humility, honesty, integrity, and moral standards."

"Beauty or handsomeness will attract men or women to you, but your character will make you a wife or husband. Your talent and charm will attract friends to you, but your character will keep them. Branding will attract customers to your business, but your character will keep them. Anointing will attract people to your ministry, but your character will keep them."

"Life can get tough and tiring sometimes. But if you understand your purpose, it all makes sense – tired, not feeling like it, or failure cannot stop you – Soldier, get up!"

"The moment you outgrow truth, correction, listening, judgment, and learning, it's at that very moment that your wisdom dies."

"When there is no way, remember, the only one you have is the one between you and God – and if you can walk that one in prayer, you will surely get to where you are going or you are supposed to be."

"When you choose or decide before consulting Him (God), you will be responsible for the outcome. But if you consult Him before choosing or deciding and doing what He prompted you to do, He will be responsible for the outcome."

"You never know how good God is until you know how evil the devil is – it's all good, whatever God allows."

"Greater victories and accomplishments require greater battles. Are you wondering why your battles and tests are bigger than others? It's because of your purpose and destiny. Be brave."

"Life will always not be fair, but God will always be Good – see the good in it."

"Build your life by spiritual and practical calculus that will guarantee a lasting success and a Godly legacy, not a temporary solution."

"Personal change and deliverance start from telling yourself the truth. Until you start being honest with yourself, you won't be delivered from your personal issues. And until you are delivered from your issues, you won't be happy."

"When you are hungry, you may eat anything – be careful of accepting anything when you are hopeless; you may regret it."

"The biggest questions are not if you can be saved, but if

you can stay saved. It is not if you can be married, but if you can stay married. It is not if you can be successful, but if you can maintain success. It is not if you can get a job, but if you can keep a job. It is not if you can go to school, but how you use your education or knowledge."

"Many have walked the earth, but a few have left their footprints. Would you?"

"Those who live up to their purpose and destiny always leave a legacy in this world. But those who live for themselves, ignoring that they are on a mission and must positively impact the world, leave it without a real legacy. Are you living up to your purpose and destiny? No time to waste."

"The sister of impatience is a mistake, and mistake produces problems. You can undo some problems, but you cannot undo others. In effect, double-pray and think before you do or say what you feel like doing or saying. Just a little patience may save, protect, and defend you against evil."

"Beware of quick fixes – they may create future long-term problems and misery. While we want temporary solutions, God wants us permanent solutions."

"Panic is what the devil uses to displace our faith in God's promises. Emotional stability and prayer are needed to diffuse the devil's attack against our blessings."

"When it seems all doors are closed – there is no way, don't panic because one is opened somewhere, which you can't see. Only patience, faith, hope, and search can help you find it."

"The unknown is what surprises me. Nothing is a surprise to God--He knows all (Omniscient). There are good surprises and bad surprises. Let God surprise me with good surprises."

"As hidden as the solution to your problem could be, patience, resistance, endurance, action, and prayer can bring it forth. Don't give up now. Someone is praying for you somewhere now."

"The greatest harm you can do to yourself is to do what is not the will of God. You may not see the consequences today, but surely, sooner or later, you will find out. Don't be fooled!"

"Reflection before acting always protects and saves one from mistakes and gives better ways of doing or dealing with daily positive and negative situations. Before acting, pause and think."

"You may fail, but don't fall.
You may be hurt, but don't make it a harbor.
You may cry, but don't crack and let evil in your heart.
You may be curved in life, but don't curse God.
You may be discouraged, but don't be disconnected from God.
You may lack some things, but don't lack the Word of God.
You may be tired, but don't try your ways; they lead to dangers.
You may pray, but pray according to His will to get results."

"There is still time to win. The end of the day, week, month, or even year is not the end of your winning time."

"If I would ask God only one thing – Himself. If I have Him, I have everything."

"When everybody likes you, but God is against you, you are in trouble. However, when God is with you, but everybody dislikes you, you will emerge victorious. Popularity is not a sign or measure of success, but righteousness is."

"If you made it through yesterday, you would make it through today."

"Thank God for problems – they are chasing/pushing you to where God wants you to be and forcing you to obey God and do what you would have never done without them."

"There are no unfinished businesses in God's book. It might take years, but He will surely settle it."

"God trusts us with situations we think we might be unable to handle and overcome. Situations bring the best out of us – intelligence, knowledge, wisdom, talents, and natural and spiritual gifts we didn't even know we possessed. Let God use your current situation to help you achieve the positive unimaginable."

"Focus. Ignore the enemy. The end results matter."

"When purpose and destiny are taken from life, the remaining equals nothingness. Have you worked on something part of your purpose and destiny today?"

"Sometimes when it seems like you are losing, you are not losing anything – you are just getting loosed from something bad, the enemy's traps and craftiness. God never let you lose something, except it's beneficial for you not to have that."

"Don't let fear prevent you from experiencing possible plans and work of God. Just because an angel is not sent to tell you doesn't mean it might not be God at work. Sometimes, God's will is revealed in the process of time. Pray. Try it. But be careful. Tune in for God's voice and guidance as you boldly advance. Stop or move forward at His commands."

"The benefit of integrity is trust. When you learn and practice integrity--obeying God by observing His moral laws, God trusts you; so do people."

"Do not be over-minded of your individual purpose and destiny to the extent that you ignore a collective purpose and destiny. Be also involved in your family, group, church, organization, and country's collective purpose and destiny to make it come through. Every individual has a purpose and destiny, and so does every entity."

"We earn people's trust when we do things the way they want and expect. Likewise, we earn the trust of God by obeying His word and with our behavior in difficult times."
"Your talents or gifts are summed in one thing — duty. They are not for you to glorify yourself, but God and serve humanity (People)."

"Be so mindful of where you're going in life than worried about where you're now."

"Success is for people who are not ashamed and afraid of failure."

"Stop wasting your time to prove to people who you are. Use the time to prove instead to improve your life, goals, purpose, and destiny – they will not understand until the results prove it."

"Real men and women don't waste their time gossiping and mocking people, but support or help them."

"You can never know yourself or who you are until you know God. And it's unlikely to know God and not know yourself because He becomes the measure of your life."

"Know God and know yourself – Stop trying to find yourself without God before you become ridiculous. The only way to know yourself is by knowing and understanding God. When you discover God and understand that you came from Him, then you know that whoever you are, you are amazing, despite your flaws, and can do amazing things."

"While you are here on earth, let the world see how much of God you have – love and morals. How many lives has your life changed for the better? How many problems have you solved and not created? And how helpful your wisdom, knowledge, and gifts or talents have been to your family, society, nation, and the world."

"Real happiness is hidden in a soul who is connected to God and fulfilling his purpose and destiny regardless of circumstances."

"Humility is a beautiful thing and is never weakness. One can still be intelligent, strong, or powerful, yet humble."

"Good ideas might not necessarily be Godly ideas. Regarding real-life matters, you must choose whether you want to practice the Bible. Or, practice people's ideas or ungodly psychology which you read in books or listen to, and mostly not Biblical principles."

"Don't worry about losing a car than the maker or manufacturer, especially if it's bad. It's better to lose a car and keep the maker because he can make and give you another one -- even better. Why do you worry about bad or negative people trying to leave your life than God? God created people. He can bring better ones into your life."

"If your dreams, visions, aspirations, and efforts only benefit you, they are not of God. Carefully re-evaluate them."

"Your mind is the steering wheel of your whole life – it takes you where you want to be. Ensure you don't drive your life into the jungles or seas of impossibilities and bitterness. You can get better! Trust God. Make wise decisions or choices."

"Your name is a child of God. Any other names the devil calls you are not you. You're not looser, nothingness, broke, ugly, poor, fat, stupid. When you're walking down the street, and someone calls Mr./Mrs. Jones, do you answer? So why are you answering the names the devil is calling you? Keep moving – it's just not you."

"You don't have to be and have the best to make someone feel and be better. Try to make a little difference in people's lives, one person at a time."

"God always talks in many different ways when we are on the wrong route anywhere in life. We either ignore or misinterpret it, or think we have already gone too far to return until the worst happens. Return before the worst happens."

"After all, Christ is the easiest and safest way to have an already paid-for and deepest relationship with an infinite and powerful God. You don't need other ways to God."

"The only thing holding the human race, including you and I, from destruction is God's love. God loves you! And that's the only thing you could blame him for."

"Learn to be happy regardless of the results of your prayers and expectations - God knows better."

"You're never empty, feeling meaningless or insignificant, if you know, and are fulfilling your purpose, what you're created to be and do. As little as it could be, this keeps you happy and fulfilled. Are you doing what you are created to do?"

"The Holy Spirit is irreplaceable! Life is heavy and difficult without Him. He's better than alcohol, cigars, drugs, and sexual immorality. I can't imagine a life without Him!"

"The biggest problem is having problems and not knowing that you have them."

"You're not cheap. You were bought with the blood of the most high. When you forget your identity according to God's word, people can define or tell you who you are by their actions or behaviors. But when you know who you are, you don't let people define your value."

"Time is one of the most powerful revelation and confirmation tools God has given his children on earth. Don't just rush into things because someone or you have a 'revelation' or 'feeling' about it. Let God confirm it through time. Things and people can hide their real identities from you, but not from God and time."

"While praying for a spouse, stay away from a man or woman who does not have an agape love, or unconditional love, God's love. You can see this in the way the person treats or deals with other people, relatives, friends, co-workers – If your husband or wife's love is only based or associated with sexual feelings, or Eros, erotic love, the marriage will come to an end when that feeling comes to an end."

"Change for God, not for people. When you change for God, you will eventually become a good person in attitude and behavior – according to his Word. When you change for someone, your change is surely not real because it's a change with benefit intentions."

"Trust God. There's nothing he didn't help you get or execute your prayer about that you will ever regret or cry over tomorrow or later."

"This life is too short to stumble multiple times, even if you can get up that many times. Try to respectfully and lovely avoid people and things that can make you stumble too many times."

"Life is more than just being born, married, having a

name, title, fame, degrees, good paying job or profitable business, wealth, all the pleasures which can be found in this world and flesh. Life is bigger than oneself. Life is only worthy and noble when it adds, makes a difference, or changes other lives for the better spiritually and physically."

"Life is too fragile to live without a real Savior, Protector, Defender, Provider, Healer, Comforter, and Helper, and his name is Jesus. Let Him be all the above in your life now and forever."

"Be in charge of your situations. Don't let your situations be in charge of you or influence your behavior negatively."

"To every problem, there is a solution. The challenge is how to find it. Most likely the problem contains its own solution. So don't panic; trust God, pray, be patient, wait, and don't rush to fix the problem to create other problems. Review the problem several times as you think about the best way to solve it."

"Don't try to avoid the least pain to cause someone else a worse pain. If you're not ready for the least, why should someone else suffer the worst?"

"Let what matters to God matters to you. Five to ten years from now, you will look back and regret it because you fought for some temporary things. And perhaps will look so stupid to yourself."

"Three things will be remembered: Your love for God, the difference you make in your family and the world, or people's lives."

"One day, you will thank God for allowing people who made mistakes that you thought hurt you because you will understand that without those matters, you won't be where God wanted you to be."

"God doesn't operate in your life having only you in mind; he always considers people related to you and your descendants."

"Your real happiness is not in having or doing the next big thing, but in making peace with God."

"Sometimes, all God can do is to be silent and let time speak – only time can tell."

"Face your fear. Wisely and prayerfully deal with it. Sometimes you never know what good or bad is hidden in the things you fear. Don't let fear prevent you from getting the good things God wants for you. Let it be that at least you have tried."

"God does not need your help to be God, but you need Him to be you."

"When God delays it, he's either preparing you, making it better or bigger. Stay obedient, calm, and hopeful. Don't force it."

"Respect people regardless of where they are and what they are going through. The value of a human being is not determined by his circumstances, but instead by the value God has placed on him -- and if you want to know that, it equals the sacrifice of the only begotten son of God."

"You cannot reach some levels of your purpose and destiny when you think and act like you're smarter than God and everybody else."

"Being active and working towards your purpose and destiny cost you just something, but laziness and indifference will cost you everything sooner or later. Get to work."

"Popularity or fame is not a good personality and success measure. Even Barabbas was popular in the days of Jesus."

"Patient will save you the best – time, energy, money,

and prayer that you can use on other important things."

"There are some moments the devil likes in your life because he scores very well in those moments – when you're in need, tired of waiting, hungry for something, angry, offended, God doesn't act when you wanted or expected it."

"Let God become the center of your prayers instead of your needs – when God becomes the center of your life and prayers, everything will be normalized or changed by His presence."

"Always remember that before all the spiritual and natural gifts God deposited in you, you are a Christian – like Christ."

"Have a good attitude, it will bless you in return. It will connect you to the right people, spouse, job, and position – There is nothing like being filled with the Holy Spirit or God, but having questionable attitudes. It puts good people away from you."

"God does – the issue is not if God does talk to us. But if He speaks, do we pay attention, consider, and obey?"

"Use what you already have wisely, intelligently, and godly, and what you need next will come your way. God has already given you all you need to succeed. Don't wait for the big things to start. God uses what you already have to give you what you need and want."

"Greatness is in being who God created you to be, and doing what He created you to do. This is more than titles and positions."

"You are great because your heavenly Father, God, is the Greatest."

"Seek for long-term solutions through obedience to the commandments of God -- at all cost, avoid violating moral laws for short-term solutions."

"God will not sit you down in a classroom to teach you life and spiritual lessons. The challenges He let you face are His classrooms for lessons."

"Don't get trapped in people's opinions; find God's opinion and be freed from humans' selfishness and slavery."

"Be considerate in your dealings with people – especially the good people. They are not disposable. And you might need them again one way or the other somewhere in your life."

"God uses people to contribute to your life, your purpose, and destiny in various ways – with their prayers, finances, times, talents, advice, or love. You don't always and only need money to reach your purpose and destiny."

"Awareness. It's so vital that we talk about it in all areas of life. But the most important awareness we lack is spiritual awareness – Be aware of the spiritual world and always be alerted to foresee the enemy's attacks."

"When you discover your purpose and destiny – you know who you are; and when you know who you are, you fight till you become. "

"God uses the process to reveal things in you, and around you, good or bad to prepare you to effectively handle His blessings, your purpose, and destiny in life. Don't force or breach the fulfillment process in your life otherwise, you will pay for it sooner or later with troubles."

"There are seven indispensable ingredients to an authentic success: Understanding, preparation, work or investment, sacrifice, time, and integrity. If you violate any of them, your progress or whatever you call "success" will become an ocean of spiritual and physical troubles that will engulf you sooner or later. Avoid hazardous shortcuts or easy ways to succeed. I am not suggesting that you accept a miserable, mundane, or tedious life, but watch out for the so-called "Easy Life" or "Easy Success" Gospel. Every authentic success has a price. You will pay with time, hard and intelligent work, service, exercise, and learning -- success is progressive."

"You are unique with unique purpose and destiny, talents, and anointing. You can only train and develop what you already have in you, or what God has deposited in you, and get better at it. Train and develop every good thing God has granted you."

"Don't compromise with the devil in any way — it will only leave you broken, hurt, disappointed, and lost sooner or later."

"The only thing that can motivate you every second of your life to live up to the ordinances of God is the understanding that everything in this world is fadable, perishable, and temporary."

"God can turn what you already have into what you need and want. Think again; maybe there is a way to turn something you already have into what you want or need instead of abandoning it."

"The difference between winners and losers is that winners see the victory – its importance and benefit, and fight tirelessly until it comes to pass. Losers do the opposite, and trade in their victory for easiness and comfort."

"Never do life without Christ Jesus otherwise, life will do you."

"Another best is not coming – if you keep destroying the best God has been giving you with a bad character or behaviors. Do what you have to do to keep the best."

"Part of maturity and leadership is the growth and discipline to not respond to everything."

"Slavery is more than just one man enslaving another – it's also voluntary subjection to devilish conditions and activities in every area of life."

"The only spirit God wants to abide with you, guide, and enlighten you is the Holy Spirit – any other one holding your life is an intruder."

"When you understand the mission of Christ that He came to set you free, there should be a holy revolution in your inner being to deny the devil any opportunity to oppress or possess you."

"You don't know someone when he's happy – wait till he's angry, doesn't get what he wants, or has his way to discover his real identity."

"Obedience to God comes with peace."

"Use the time to prove and impress others to improve yourself instead. You have too much to accomplish in life. Don't be caught up in activities intended to impress people."

"Don't run your life on emotions, otherwise it will be filled with regrets sooner or later. Look for Godliness and value or substance."

"Find God, and you will find the right people and things in life to have lasting peace and happiness."

"Be careful, God is not under obligation to change your mess into a blessing, especially if you keep creating them willingly."

"One of the ways for you to know if you are making the right decision is to evaluate your motives."

"Aligning with falsehoods and lies, bad or wrong, will not change it to truth or right."

"It's within you – everything you ever needed to change

your life and the world, God has put it in you. Use it."

"Don't be greedy to eat what you can eat forever at once."

"You are not lucky – it's God in action in your life. Don't mess it up."

"What did you do with the last blessing of God? Learn to properly and Godly manage the blessings of God."

"The Holy Spirit is also your spiritual and emotional Helper."

"Make God your first partner in everything you do."

"As open-minded as I can be, to learn and discover new things I don't know, I don't think it's ever OK for a woman to propose to a man and put a ring on his finger – Ladies, it's the other way around. And there is nothing cute or aww about this."

"Life is a mission. Maximize your time, resources, energy, talents, spiritual and natural gifts. Live so that one day you can favorably, graciously, and thankfully say, "Mission Accomplished.""

"Make someone feel better today. It starts with a servant's heart anywhere with the little things."

"Sometimes, the best gift God can give you, is not allowing you to have something you want — it's for your own good."

"What's your value? I have learned over the years that the real value of people is not in how much money, material, position, and privilege they have, but in their character, attitude, wisdom, morals, and relationship with God."

"Be careful – the voices or people you're listening to shape your life – Demons do talk via people."

"If you want it to last, build it on God, morals, and character."

"Have a good reason that you're living for – When the reason for living is just about you, you lose passion for living and working because you're just one reason. But when your life and work are also about others' needs and wellbeing, you have many reasons to live for."

"See the champion in others as well and support it. Real champions are humble and selfless."

"Preparation is vital for the extraordinary. God is preparing you, and preparation time is not a delay."

"Do not create your own pain or misery. Sometimes, we create our misery out of pride, greed, selfish desires, sin, and disobeying God."

"The will and plan of God do not exclude obstacles, challenges, and fights."

"It's a divine crime to take God's glory – always know that you couldn't without Him, and give Him the glory."

"Never forget why you are here in this world. It will be a blueprint/ benchmark for everything you do and how you live your life."

"It's easy to set boundaries for people. But how about you? Setting boundaries for yourself will save your life and time."

"Challenges will force you into the right direction to find the right things God has ordained you for."

"It will always make sense to you later – Keep following God's directions even when you're disappointed and don't understand. It will all make sense to you when He finishes what He's doing."

"Everything in life has a price – you will either pay with your time, energy, or money. Wisely choose what you pay for. Pay for what it worthy, lasting, morally sound, and Godly — Pay for what is in your purpose and destiny."

"Purpose and destiny survive till their divine or God-given time-out. You can't kill or destroy purpose and destiny – they survive the unimaginable."

"Your first people are the Father, Son, and Holy Spirit. They are the first of your family, board, office, or team members in every area of your life. Talk and discuss everything in your life with them first for guidance."

"The Holy Spirit is your best antidepressant. Fellowship with Him and His communion will create joy unspeakable within you."

"There is nothing wrong with having what you want, but how ugly and far can you go to have it? If trying to have what you want will not honor God and change or make others' lives bitter, then decide only to have what you need. There is a difference between what you want and what you need."

"Never put the wrong person in the driver's seat of your purpose and destiny if you really want to reach and maximize them. Do your best to avoid having the wrong leader or leadership, partner, teammate, husband or wife."

"Don't spend your entire life in endless searching. Sometimes what or who you need can only come from what or who you already have – all you must do is consider and work on it to become what or who you need."

"When what is important and priority in life to God becomes important and priority to you, you will break into your well of real and lasting peace, happiness, security, and stability."

"Until you start seeking and serving God not for what you want from him, but for who he is, you will not experience His fullness."

"The unknown or unseen can be either a surprise blessing or regret. Be brave, yet insightful and cautious."

"Real life is leaving a good footprint or legacy in the world – It's more than drinks, foods, cars, homes, and gold chains."

"Distraction is an enemy of your purpose and accomplishments. You can't be unnecessarily everywhere and doing everything and be able to fulfill your purpose and destiny. Discern your cause, and focus on it from all angles or avenues to fulfill it."

"God uses the right people, husband, wife, relatives, friends, and strangers to build and change your life for the better. All the same, the devil uses the wrong people to destroy your life, purpose, and destiny. Ming your relationships and associations."

"Rush or hurry does not guarantee success or good results; neither does slowness, but can cause errors. And man's precision is not perfection either — just try to get it close to the perfect will of God as much as you can and be worry-free."

"Some things will never change in your life until some things change within you – your relationship with God, priorities, vision, purpose, character, desires, planning, time usage, laziness, spending, budgeting, people you hang around with, and expectations."

"Purpose, destiny, and kindness are attractive – Knowing and exercising the main reason you are here in this world is beautiful."

"Already-made is great, but self-made is even greater. When you are looking for something you can't find, create one with God's help – God the Father is a Creator, and He created you in His image. You're a creator as well. Create peace, joy, jobs, and happy relationships."

"Whenever it seems God made a mistake, it's either you made it, and He's fixing it, or He's redirecting you to His master plan and will for your life, which is better than yours – just trust Him."

"No substance or pleasure can replace God in your life."

"Take a break, vacation, rest – But never be overjoyed about little progress and forget to reach the main goals or accomplish bigger things. Be grateful for the little progress and treats, but don't let the devil fool you to stop praying, working, and fighting smart until full victory is fulfilled."

"He will help, but not do it for you – There are things God will help you with, but will not do it for you, including making the right decisions, discipline, maturing, using your intelligence, knowledge, and wisdom."

"Pleasure or purpose? Any pleasure that will cost you your purpose and destiny, gradually or instantly, is not only immoral but dangerous to your sanity, happiness, health, and relationship with God — Don't make a fool out of yourself."

"Low self-esteem or inferiority complex can rob you of many blessings, opportunities, and God's divine plan for your life. Keep your head up high. Be bold/courageous, yet humble. Nobody is bigger or smaller than you. See yourself as God sees you."

"Don't Chase good life. Build or create your good life."

"Smart people are humble. Their intelligence, knowledge, and wisdom increase with time as they humbly yet purposefully, knowingly, and unknowingly learn, collect, or draw from everyone else. But the proud and arrogant remain unknowingly stupid and stagnant."

"Be humble enough to do whatever Godly and morally sound that you don't have the desire to do, to establish whatever you desire to be doing forever — is the way."

"Propositions or resolutions? The end or beginning of the year should not be the only time you want to get things right in your life, business, or ministry. Make up your mind to be productive to God, your family, and the world in every second of your life."

"You are an agent of amendment – You can't change the past, but you can amend it. The Bible starts with, 'In the beginning,' – Meaning the past or history will always be recalled. But, you can amend it. No matter what your past has been, with God, you can amend it and make it be its best."

"The big deal is, you haven't arrived until God arrives – even though He doesn't need you, you need him. Make God happy, and you will be happy."

"Are you running or ruining it? Success starts with doing things right."

"Some people are only gifted to successfully start, create or setup things, and some people are only gifted to successfully run what others have started, created or setup, and others are meant to do both. Know your gifts or talents and what you are meant to do. You don't necessarily have to run everything you started, created or setup otherwise you will ruin it."

"Your purpose is not a proposal – the calling of God about your life is not a proposal, something to be discussed or considered whether you want to do it or not. It's an order, the very force behind your existence in this world. Fulfill it to be at peace and happy. Or, do what you want and stay miserable now and hereafter."

"Be more concerned about who you are than what you have because who you are can produce what you will have."

"You don't need to have everything you like and want – control your heart and mind. Wanting to have everything you like will always keep you on an unending and insatiable quest, which will rob you of peace and happiness."

"Achievement is a friend of happiness – Part of the things that can make you fulfilled and happy is the good accomplishment of your purposeful goals, dreams, and visions. That's why it's important to accomplish some things on your own or as a team and not always expect already-made things in life."

"Resolutions and wishes are empty if you don't act. What have you done today towards your dreams and visions?"

"Catch the light – Each time God wants to bless you or change your life for the better, He will bring a light on your way, either in form of an information, idea, opportunity, or a good person. This could be a momentum for your purpose and destiny to change for the better forever. Sometimes it may not look like it at beginning, so open your eyes and spiritual understanding to catch the light and walk in by faith."

"When your intentions and desires are not Godly or genuine, you may attract the wrong people and things."

"Inconsistency is the parking of your success – Follow up."

Thanksgiving:

On behalf of Team Quatro, I would like to thank you for taking the time to read or listen to this book. Now let's go get some good scores for our decisions/choices to make our lives better and the world a better place to live.

"Get wisdom, get understanding; do not forget my words or turn from them."

Proverb 4: 5, NIV

"The fear of the LORD is the beginning of knowledge, but fools despise wisdom and instruction."

Proverb 1:7, NIV

"The fear of the Lord is the beginning of wisdom, and knowledge of the Holy One is understanding."

Proverb 9:10, NIV

Historical References:

Plutarch, *Life of Titus Flamininus*
Plutarch, *Life of Julius Caesar*
Aulus Gellius, *Attic Nights book 7 chapter 17*

Bobrick, Benson, *Fearful Majesty,* G.P. Putnam's Sons
Hosking, Geoffrey, *Russia, and the Russians*, Harvard University

Guy, John, *My Heart is My Own: The Life of Mary Queen of Scots,* Harper Perennial
Guy, John, *Queen of Scots: The True Life of Mary Stuart,* Mariner Books
Calendar of State Papers, Scotland: Volume 2

Twitchett, Denis, *The Cambridge History of China: Volume 9, The Ch'ing Dynasty to 1800, Part 2,* Cambridge University
Dennerline, Jerry, *The Shun-chih Reign,* Cambridge University

Messenger, R. James, *Of Time, Tombs and Treasures,* documentary
Baker, Charles F., F. Rosalie, *Ancient Egyptians: People of the Pyramids,* Oxford Profiles

Fuller, J.F.C., *The Generalship of Alexander the Great*
Waldemar, Heckel, *The Conquests of Alexander the Great,* Canto Classics, Cambridge University

Ambroise, *The History of the Holy War,* Boydell Press
Edbury, Peter W., *The Conquest of Jerusalem and the Third Crusade,* Ashgate

Terrell, Katherine H., *Richard Coeur de Lion,* Broadview Press
Nicholson, Helen J., *The Chronicle of the Third Crusade,* Routledge

Willie Yeboah is an evangelist, author, poet, songwriter, and entrepreneur. He's the founder and president of Action Jesus Christ International, an interdenominational global evangelism ministry, and Churches Adoption International, a global ministry focused on supporting and empowering local churches in third-world countries to reach their people with the Gospel.

www.ingramcontent.com/pod-product-compliance
Lightning Source LLC
Chambersburg PA
CBHW060447030426
42337CB00015B/1513